Wonderful. I use it more often than Xerox's own manual!
— *Jennifer Grant, Shelburne, VT*

A **super** book!
— *M.T. Parker, Denver, CO*

Very useful!
— *Elinor C. Cruze, Redwood City, CA*

An excellent reference source.
— *Michele L. Spencer, Raleigh, NC*

I loved your *Ventura Tips and Tricks*!
— *Thomas F. Collura, Chagrin Falls, OH*

Very informative and helpful.
— *Susan Pratt, Leesburg, VA*

Enjoyed your book very much.
— *Guy Temieux, Montreal, Canada*

Your book has been **invaluable** to me.
— *John G. Conway, Burwood, Victoria, Australia*

I have found this book to be **of considerable value** to me in working with Ventura Publisher.
— *R. Carl Stoufer, Gainesville, FL*

Your book is great. **The most understandable text on Ventura I've found.**
— *Barbara Peterson, Windermere, FL*

Very interesting and informative
— *Timothy J. Ambroshe, Clearwater, FL*

Real helpful!
— *Jeannette Roerig, Des Moines, IA*

A great help!
— *Paul Weiss, Santa Barbara, CA*
— *Guido M. Haas, Amsterdam, The Netherlands*

Outstanding!
— *Dennis C. Kelly, Searcy, AR*

Thank you for publishing a book of this caliber.
— *Lawrence J. Kolbrak, Chippewa Falls, WI*

Am impressed with the quality of information in your book. It's **easily read and there's a ton of tips.**
— *Bill Fales, Nappanee, IN*

We have been having quite a time mastering Ventura, and **this book has helped greatly.**
— *Marlin G. Waechter, Stanton, NE*

As one who has struggled with the Xerox documentation, your book was really a fresh wind. **A fantastic book.**
— *Earl Selby, Carmel Valley, CA*

Ventura Tips and Tricks is **the most up-to-date reference** yet published not only on Ventura Publisher but on the whole desktop publishing industry.
— *Jan Reid, Santa Cruz, CA*

This is the first book that's **really made sense** out of Ventura style sheets.
— *Gary Tarbet, Washington, DC*

Ventura Tips and Tricks is a drop of dew! **Everything so clear!** I was so

grateful to see a few words about Ventura's voodoo.
— *Davina Baker, Aptos, CA*

I just purchased *Ventura Tips and Tricks* and **don't know how I've made it without it.** Don't change a thing.
— *Paula V. Green, Colorado Springs, CO*

I have gotten **a tremendous value** from your *Ventura Tips and Tricks,* especially the chapters on managing files and Lotus worksheets.
— *Chuck Fairchild, Washington, DC*

Your book is **fantastic.** It's been an incredible help in teaching Ventura.
— *Victoria Rose, Shelburne, VT*

Your book **helped clear up a lot of the little problems** I've had with Ventura.
— *Ken Rubman, Westbury, NY*

Your book is **by far the best supplemental publication** on Ventura.
— *Tedd Powell, Pittsburgh, PA*

I found your book to be **one of the best (if not the best) third-party book on Ventura.** The information is excellent. Keep up the outstanding work!
— *Eric N. Foster, Pittsburgh, PA*

I really was impressed with your book. I've been using Ventura since Day One. It was nice to pick up something I can throw in front of a student.
— *Lorian Lipton, Winsor, CT*

Thank you for a **fine book**!
— *Larry Marshall, Los Angeles, CA*

I have found the book **invaluable** in my business.
— *Hilda Farley, Bucks, England*

A super book!
— *Cris Sandifer, Key Largo, FL*

We love your book!
— *Chuck Gittelson, San Francisco, CA*

A very good book. I was impressed by it.
— *Kevin Dean, Charlottesville, VA*

Your book is excellent. I'm recommending it highly.
— *Nina Johnson, Novato, CA* Good information!

Well written and very useful.
— *Patrick Gaffney, Chicago, IL*

I have really gotten a lot from your book.
— *Gale Noble, San Diego, CA*

I am a very satisfied user of *Ventura Tips and Tricks*.
— *Chris Cowdrey, Modesto, CA*

First rate! Just what I needed!
— *John S. Taylor, Arnold, MD*

Truly helpful!
— *Michael J. Stubler, Phoenix, AZ*

Very helpful!
— *Bob Stoulill, Albany, OR*
— *Pam Granquist, Phoenix, AZ*

- *Paul Glick, Skokie, IL*
- *Debbie Crane, Washington, DC*
- *Nancy Anderson, Colorado Springs, CO*
- *Richard Niefield, Houston, TX*
- *John Conway, Victoria, Australia*
- *Robbin C. Lynch, Vero Beach, FL*
- *Robert F. Dugan, Woodinville, WA*
- *Fred W. Hays, Kettering, OH*
- *Frank R. Eichenlaub, Seattle, WA*
- *Brian Nunes, Los Angeles, CA*

Very good!
- *Gary Minniss, Scottsdale, AZ*
- *Marc Gander, Hampstead, England*

Very informative!
- *Rick Fenstermaker, St. Paul, MI*

Very useful!
- *Peter Johnson, Los Altos, CA*
- *Ralph F. Rumpf, Stevensville, MI*
- *Robert A. Walker, Falls Church, VA*
- *George Fleming, Westbrook, CT*

Excellent!
- *Robert U. Guthrie, Omaha, NE*
- *Jean Lhoirh, Brussels, Belgium*
- *R. Carl Stoufer, Gainesville, FL*
- *Timothy J. Ambroshe, Clearwater, FL*
- *Philip H. Dossick, Forest Hills, NY*
- *Robert Dufon, East Chicago, IN*

Extremely useful!
- *Bette A. Grunkemeyer, Dublin, OH*

Invaluable!
- *Sue Horton, London, England*

Outstanding!
- *Kurt Kiesow III, Los Gatos, CA*

Great!
- *Jerome Wahlert, Mundelein, IL*
- *Gale Noble, San Diego, CA*
- *Peter Schneider, Philadelphia, PA*
- *Evelyn O'Donnell, Sunnyvale, CA*
- *Lee Jones, Hiroshima, Japan*
- *Stefanie Korner, Munich, West Germany*
- *Juli Perry, Orlando, FL*

Wonderful!
- *Rita Schultz, Minneapolis, MN*
- *John F. DePaola, Capitol Heights, MD*
- *Robert Watkins, New York, NY*

Ventura Tips & Tricks

3RD EDITION

Ted Nace
with Daniel Will-Harris

PEACHPIT PRESS

VENTURA TIPS AND TRICKS, 3RD EDITION
Ted Nace
with Daniel Will-Harris

Peachpit Press, Inc.
1085 Keith Ave.
Berkeley, CA 94708
415/527-8555 (phone)
415/524-9775 (fax)

Portions of this book originally appeared in *PC World*, *Publish*, *Personal Publishing*, *Desktop Communications*, *Ventura Professional!*, and *Computer Currents* magazines.

Many of the designations used by manufacturers and sellers to distinguish their products are claimed as trademarks. Where those designations appear in this book, and Peachpit Press was aware of a trademark claim, the designations have been printed in initial caps or all caps.

Library of Congress Cataloging-in-Publication Data
Nace, Ted.
    Ventura tips and tricks. / Ted Nace, Daniel Will-Harris. — 3rd ed.
        p.   cm.
    Includes index.
    ISBN 0-938151-20-7 : $27.95
    1. Desktop publishing.   2. Ventura publisher (Computer program)
I. Will-Harris, Daniel.   II. Title.   III. Title: Ventura tips and tricks
Z286.D47N33   1991
652.5′536—dc20   91-48732
                                                              CIP

0 9 8 7 6 5 4 3 2
Printed and bound in the United States of America
ISBN 0-938151-20-7

This book is dedicated to the memory of
Benjamin Linder.

Thanks

This book would be far less complete without the contributions of Daniel Will-Harris, who wrote most of the profiles of software and hardware products that work in conjunction with Ventura. It's been written that "nobody knows more about desktop publishing with PCs than Daniel Will-Harris." Actually, nobody knows *anywhere near* as much, except maybe God and Toni Will-Harris. My sincere appreciation also to Lindsay Mugglestone, who did the research for bringing the "Resources" section up to date and who also checked the manuscript for accuracy. (Of course, after Lindsay was finished I went through and added a whole new set of mistakes.) Thanks to Cathy Cockrell and Kimn Neilson for proofreading the book and to Dennis McLeod for designing the cover.

Thanks to the many people who shared their favorite tips and tricks. Among the tipsters: Rick Altman, Janet Bein, Andrew Buc, Don Heiskell, Dee Knight, Lee Lorenzen, John Meyer, Randall Newton, Sally Robinson, Douglas Smith, Jim Smith, and Mary Westheimer. For smoking out inaccuracies in the previous two editions, thanks to Peter Donnelly, Neil Sandow, Peter Hardy, Craig Seligman, Luther Sperberg, and Will Tait.

Thanks to Larry Gerhard and the folks at Ventura Software and Hill & Knowlton (Ventura's PR agency), for their continued support of this book. Special thanks to Andy Miller, who not only works 9 to 5 as Ventura Software's shepherd to third-party developers, but also genuinely cares about the future of Ventura Publisher. While the administration running the marketing of Ventura Publisher has changed several times since the first release of the program, one person who has been consistently helpful over the years is Cheryl Downing. Thanks, Cheryl!

Additional thanks to others who provided software and hardware, including LaserMaster Corporation, which loaned a LaserMaster LM1000 Plain Paper Typesetter and a GlassPage monitor; Radius, which loaned a TPD/21 monitor; Hewlett-Packard, which loaned a LaserJet III printer; Adobe Systems and Bitstream, which loaned fonts; Anderson Consulting & Software, which loaned the Tiffany Plus utility used for Windows screen snapshots; and Symsoft, which loaned the HotShot Graphics program used for DOS/ GEM screen snapshots.

Other colleagues who gave inspiration and encouragement include Rick Altman, Jesse Berst, Michael Copeland, Bob Cowart, Steve Cummings, Mike Cuthbertson, Louise Domenitz, Susie Hammond, Richard Jantz, Bob Moody, Bill Neuenschwander, Jay Nitschke, Katherine Pfeiffer, Ernest Priestly, David Ranson, Gene Rodrigues, Steve Roth, Sally Skanderup, Lynn Walterick, Bob Weibel, Tony Webster, Jim Welch, Toni Will-Harris, and Joe and Elizabeth Woodman.

When I had almost given up the hope of ever finishing this book at my own busy office, a compassionate Kit Duane offered to let me use her house as a secret work hideaway. I never actually schlepped all my stuff down to the Duane's, but just knowing I *could* go there was a great feeling.

I can't imagine a better group of people to work with than my compañeros at Peachpit Press. Hearty applause and forearm bashes to Carl Bruce, Gregor Clark, Keasley Jones, Gaen Murphree, Dawn Stevens, and Elizabeth Weiss.

Finally, thanks to my wife, Helen, for being incredibly nice to me and bringing me all kinds of plants and candy. Thanks to Jasper and Emma for working and playing with me. Now we get to do all those things we said we would do after the book got done!

Production Note

Most of this book was written using WordPerfect and Microsoft Word, though a significant portion was typed directly into Ventura. The computer system consisted of a PC's Limited 386 from Dell Computer, a Relisys VGA monitor, and a LaserMaster Glass-Page monitor. DOS/GEM screen snapshots were made and cropped using Hotshot Graphics from Symsoft; Windows Ventura screen snapshots were made with Tiffany Plus from Anderson Consulting & Software. Other illustrations were assembled from a variety of sources. Some were loaded into frames with Ventura; others were photostatted to size, and taped or pasted in place.

Aside from the figures that were manually pasted in, the book (including tables, figures, index, and table of contents), was formatted with the DOS/GEM version running under Windows 3.0. Master pages were printed on a LaserMaster 1000 Plain Paper Typesetter. Principal fonts were Adobe's Garamond and Avant Garde.

At the printer during creation of negatives, the 8.5- by 11-inch master pages created by the LaserMaster 1000 were photographically reduced by 18 percent, resulting in the final 7- by 9-inch trim size. The cover was designed and produced by Dennis McLeod using a combination of Macintosh typesetting and traditional graphic arts methods. The book was printed on a web press. I'm ashamed to admit that the paper is *not* recycled, but we're working on it and hopefully will switch over sometime soon.

Table of Contents

SECTION I — ORIENTATION

SECTION II — HARDWARE

3. Configuring Your System 41

4. Printers 49

SECTION III — USING VENTURA

SECTION IV — GRAPHICS

SECTION V — FONTS

SECTION VI — SPECIAL TOPICS

Introduction

I first saw Xerox Ventura Publisher in the spring of 1986, when Ventura Software president John Meyer and head programmer Don Heiskell visited the *PC World* offices in San Francisco to show off a fledgling version of the program. At that time the agreement between Ventura Software and Xerox Corporation to market Ventura Publisher did not yet exist. Ventura Software was still just an unknown startup with a whistle and a song, one of a crowd of small companies claiming to do something new and different with words, pictures, and laser printers.

As Meyer and Heiskell set up their XT-compatible computer in *PC World's* glass-walled demonstration room, I reflected on the irony that two years earlier this same room had been rigged up with peek-proof curtains to sequester a prototype of the Macintosh computer while a small team of *PC World* staffers worked in secret to create the first issue of *Macworld* magazine. For the first year of its existence, the Macintosh had been widely ridiculed as a $2500 Etch-A-Sketch, a fun machine to play around with but hopelessly devoid of any useful software.

Now that little machine was showing it could throw fast balls too. With the introduction of its LaserWriter printer and the advent of a new generation of slick page makeup software, Apple was opening up a vast new market, dubbed desktop publishing by its enthusiasts, or CAP (computer-aided publishing) by the more acronymically minded. As yet, nothing existed on the PC-compatible side of the industry to rival the Macintosh/LaserWriter combination, a situation that was causing no small degree of consternation in places like *PC World.*

With various editors and production managers clustered around a long table in *PC World's* demonstration room, Meyer started up Ventura and immediately went into a blistering tour. While the staff looked on, increasingly absorbed, he set up a document in multiple columns, added pictures, and demonstrated the use of Ventura's style sheet method of formatting.

I wasn't sure which was more astonishing, the speed of the program or the number of features that Meyer was showing. Compared to other PC programs then on the market that purported to provide desktop publishing capabilities…well, there just was no comparison.

Expressing the general sentiment in the room, someone jested, "You got a Macintosh hidden in that computer?" Meyer only smiled, but the response was implied: That's obviously not possible — this program's way too fast.

But it wasn't a comparison against the Macintosh that Meyer seemed to be interested in stressing, it was between two levels of PCs. "I want to emphasize," he said, "that the speed you're seeing isn't the result of us using a souped-up computer. We're purposely showing the program on an XT-compatible rather than an AT-compatible."

Abruptly, the demonstration halted with an unexpected program crash. For a moment, even the garrulous Meyer seemed at a loss for words, but Heiskell actually seemed to take a sort of perverse satisfaction in the blowout. He flashed a laid-back smile, leaned forward, and jotted a few notes on a legal pad. "That's the one I was trying to get on Sunday," he remarked, grinning.

At the time of the Ventura demonstration, I had just finished typesetting the book *LaserJet Unlimited* the old-fashioned way, that is, using Microsoft Word. With the version of Word that existed at that time, you could easily incorporate various laser printer fonts in a document and format the appearance of text using flexible style sheets. However, when it came to adding illustrations to a document, you had no alternative to the light table and the X-ACTO knife. Facing the prospect of repeating the manual pasteup ordeal with my next book, I couldn't wait to get my hands on Ventura.

❖ So What's It For?

To make a long story short, I did get my hands on Ventura, I experimented with it, and I confirmed that it was indeed as good a tool as I had hoped. The book you're holding is physical evidence that Ventura is ideally suited for long documents such as books, and also manuals, long reports, and other hefty publications.

But what about shorter documents like newsletters? Again, I can only refer to my own personal experience, which is that the longer I've used Ventura, the more I've found myself leaning on it for all kinds of jobs: designing flyers, running off each week's invoice forms, typesetting poetry, designing business cards, making phone logs — you name it.

❖ About This Book

Now in its third edition, this book is a product of discoveries made by myself and others during our explorations into Ventura.

If you're new to Ventura, my advice is to first install the program on your computer and then read Chapter 2, "How Ventura Works," which explains the basic concepts behind Ventura. If you're already experienced with Ventura, you can simply browse through the book, exploring those topics that interest you most.

The book is organized into seven parts. Section I, "Orientation," covers the features of Ventura and also explains the basic concepts underlying the program.

Section II, "Hardware," discusses the three main elements that make up a publishing system: computer, printer, and monitor, plus an increasingly popular fourth element, the digital scanner.

Section III, "Using Ventura," begins with the critical topic of managing files on your hard disk, then explains the various stages of assembling and formatting a Ventura document.

Section IV, "Graphics" examines some of the important new graphics tools that can be used in conjunction with Ventura, explains Ventura's own graphics features, and covers several special topics: clip art, Encapsulated PostScript, and screen snapshots.

Section V, "Fonts," tells how to install new fonts into Ventura and provides background information on a variety of useful third-party tools that enable you to generate, enhance, and edit your screen and printer fonts.

Section VI, "Special Topics," is a miscellany of information that hopefully will be of use as you attempt to "push the envelope" with Ventura: speeding up your work, enhancing your printer output, overcoming memory limitations, evaluating third-party utilities, printing envelopes and label sheets, using Ventura without a mouse, and overcoming some of Ventura's glitches and rough spots.

Finally, the book contains three appendices. The first is an extensive survey of the variety of third-party resources that have gravitated around Ventura as it has risen to become the leading publishing program available today. Second is a listing of graphics software compatible with Ventura. Third is a glossary of typographic terms and Ventura jargon.

As you make your own Ventura discoveries, I hope you'll take the time to share them with me and/or with the Ventura Publisher User's Group, whose phone number is provided below. Please let me know what you think ought to be added to the book, where the explanations went astray, entries that should have been included in the index — whatever. The more detailed, the more downright picky your critiques, the better!

Also, if you have bought this book from a bookstore or a dealer rather than directly from Peachpit Press, take a moment to send us your name and address so we can drop you a line when the next edition comes out. Dealers of Ventura Publisher and Ventura trainers are especially encouraged to contact Peachpit Press about promotions and quantity discounts.

◆ Getting Help

If you have complaints about Ventura Publisher, the person to send them to is Larry Gerhard, President, Ventura Software Inc., 15175 Innovation Drive, San Diego, California 92128. Although Ventura Software is a subsidiary of Xerox, it has a good deal of autonomy which allows it to be more responsive to user needs. The phone number of Larry and crew at Ventura Software is 619/673-0172. To get technical assistance from Ventura, you have several options. First, anyone who upgrades to version 3.0 can have 60 days of free support from the time they receive their upgrade. A second option is to pay $150 for an annual support contract, which gives you unlimited calling privileges to an 800 number, a subscription to *Ventura Professional!* magazine, a $50 discount coupon for training classes, and a 10 percent discount on your next upgrade. A third option is a corporate group support plan, which provides a variety of benefits and costs $1,000 per year. Finally, if you'd rather pay by the call, you can dial 900/896-8880, and pay $15 for a support call of any length. For more information on Ventura's support plans, call 800/822-8221 in the U.S. or 800/228-8579 in Canada.

Other sources of help are your local user group (see Appendix A for listings) and *Ventura Professional!* magazine (408/227-5030).

Good luck!

Ted Nace
Berkeley, California

Orientation

1

Which Ventura Is Right for You?

Make new friends but keep the old,
One is silver and the other gold.

Greetings, fellow monitor lizards! Ventura Publisher, which began strictly as a DOS program, is now running on four platforms: DOS, Windows, OS/2, and Macintosh. This book covers Ventura Publisher Gold Series: DOS/GEM Edition and Windows Edition. Users of the OS/2 and Macintosh versions of the program may also find the book helpful, but those editions are not explicitly discussed.

For both new and experienced Ventura users, the two questions most frequently asked are (1) What's new about the Gold Series? and (2) Should I use the DOS/GEM version or the Windows version? The purpose of this chapter is to answer those two questions.

❖   What's New About the Gold Series?

Basically, the Gold Series offers the same features as Ventura 2.0, which was introduced in 1988. Yes, there are some minor improvements (see below), but in general, instead of adding new features, the programming team put their energy into creating Windows and OS/2 versions of the program that matched the existing DOS/GEM version. Meanwhile, a separate programming team prepared the Macintosh version.

Although Ventura's decision to move the program to new platforms rather than upgrade was probably logical, it doesn't do much for the people who have been using version 2.0 and have been wishing for some new capabilities. So, to make the product more attractive, Ventura Software decided to include the Professional Extension and the Network Server modules in the regular package at no extra cost.

That's a pretty good deal, because the Professional Extension has five powerful features: table generation, equation generation, cross-referencing, vertical justification, and EMS support. The EMS support is a great boon, because being able to work with EMS solves many of the crashes and tight memory problems that used to plague Ventura. The table generation feature is also fantastic — basically the equivalent of a separate forms generation package.

◆ Minor Improvements

As for improvements in the DOS/GEM version of the program, these are all fairly minor. Numerous bugs have reportedly been fixed, though no list of such fixes has been released. Other improvements include support for longer footnotes that can flow from page to page, improvement in the HPGL graphics import capability (note: HPGL stands for Hewlett-Packard Graphics Language, a format used by AutoCAD and other CAD programs), better importing of Mac Pict II graphics and Microsoft Word 5.0 text files, and support for LaserJet IID duplex printing.

◆ Conclusion

If you already had the Ventura 2.0 (base version), upgrading to the Gold Series is definitely worthwhile because of all the new Professional Extension features you'll now be able to use. If you were already using the Professional Extension, the upgrade is of minor benefit but probably worth doing anyway, if only for the bug fixes.

❖ Should I Buy the DOS/GEM Version or the Windows Version?

This is the most commonly asked question. Windows 3 has achieved instant popularity for good reason: in addition to offering an attractive, Mac-like user interface, it also makes switching back and forth between different programs as easy as pressing Alt-Tab. For the latter reason alone, it would at first glance seem obvious that you would be better off switching to the Windows version of Ventura. Actually, however, the decision is somewhat complicated because the Windows and DOS/GEM versions both have certain advantages and disadvantages.

◆ Features Comparison

For the most part, the Windows version provides the same features as the DOS/GEM version. In a few areas, however, there are differences:

- **Keyboard Shortcuts.** In keeping with the standard protocol for Windows applications, menus can be accessed by pressing the Alt key, which takes you to the menu line, and then pressing one or more keystrokes. This gives you an alternative to using the mouse, but whether it is faster or slower depends on your style of working.

- **Macro Recorder.** One of the accessories that comes with Windows 3 is the Macro Recorder. You can use this utility to save sequences of keystrokes, allowing you to access frequently used commands more quickly.

- **Help Screens.** In the DOS/GEM version, you can get a brief explanation of any dialog box by pressing the small question mark box in the upper right corner of the dialog box. In the Windows version, the help facility is a good deal more detailed and complete, but it is also somewhat more difficult to access.

- **Ruling Lines.** In the Windows version, Ventura provides a number of pre-cooked options for ruling lines. In the DOS/GEM version, you can create the same sorts of ruling lines, but it takes a bit more work.

- **Tagging.** Here's one of the nicest features of the Windows version. You can assign any tag to any paragraph right from text editing mode — no need to switch to tagging mode first. In the DOS/GEM version, you can also assign tags from text editing mode, but only for the ten tags that you have previously assigned to function keys.

- **Cutting and Pasting Tags.** With the Windows version, you can copy a tag from one style sheet and paste it into a different style sheet. This is only possible in the DOS/GEM version if you buy a third-party utility such as VPToolbox.

◆ Monitors

By now, most vendors of large-screen monitors have made drivers available for Windows 3. In some cases, however, a driver doesn't exist and may never be written. If you have such a monitor, you may be prevented from using Windows altogether or else may have to use Windows with the monitor running in EGA or VGA emulation mode. Check with your monitor vendor before switching to Windows Ventura.

◆ Printing

Some of the Windows 3 printing drivers are still painfully slow, especially the PostScript driver. The problem is compounded by the fact that if you use one of your old width tables from the DOS/GEM version, Ventura assumes that any fonts you use in a chapter must be downloaded each time, and you can't selectively turn font downloading on and off for particular fonts. There are third-party printing utilities that provide better performance than the Windows driver, of course, and eventually Microsoft and/or the printer vendors can be expected to correct the problem. Until then, however, printing from the Windows version will be slower than with the DOS/GEM version.

◆ Scalable Screen Fonts

Here's an area where the Windows version of Ventura has an advantage over the DOS/GEM version. As described in Chapter 22, "Font Tools," several utilities are now available for Windows, including ATM from Adobe and FaceLift from Bitstream, that can create screen fonts at any size on the fly from your PostScript or Bitstream printer font outlines. This brings Ventura much closer to the ideal of What You See Is What You Get and also removes the need to store large numbers of space-gobbling bitmapped screen fonts on your hard disk. With the DOS/GEM version, scalable screen fonts are only available for the LaserMaster GlassPage monitor.

◆ Organization of Commands

Although anyone who has used the DOS/GEM version for awhile can usually find any menu selection without breaking stride, there's no denying that the organization of the menus is slightly idiosyncratic. For instance, why is Remove Text/File found under the Edit menu rather than under the File menu? Why is Set Printer Info (which lets you choose your printer and width table) located under the Options menu rather than next to the Print command under the File menu?

In the Windows version, the organization of the menus is more logical. Also, the lists of files and tags are contained in small windows that you can drag to a convenient location on the screen and adjust to any size you want. That's a more flexible setup than the one used by the DOS/GEM version. Whether it provides a significant speed advantage, however, is doubtful. But for beginners, the Windows version should be a bit less confusing.

◆ Importing Text

One of the best things about Ventura has always been that it could import text and graphics from virtually any program. Currently, however, the Windows version does not provide an import filter for any Windows-based word processing program. To get around this limitation, you'll have to remember to save your Word for Windows text files in a format such as ASCII or DOS Word.

◆ No Undo

Standard in almost every Windows application is an Undo command. Unfortunately, it's not present in Windows Ventura — a serious omission that will hopefully be corrected soon.

◆ Multiple Clipboards

In the DOS/GEM version, there are actually three clipboards, one for frames, one for box text, and one for regular text. This means that you can save a block of text and also a frame containing a graphic from one chapter, then open up another chapter and paste in both the block of text and the frame. In the Windows version there is only a single clipboard. This makes the Windows version slightly less convenient from a cut-and-paste perspective. But as noted above, the Windows version has a very useful cut-and-paste feature not found in the DOS/GEM version: being able to cut and paste tags from one style sheet to another.

◆ Working with Multiple Chapters

The Windows version would have a great advantage over the DOS/GEM version if you could have two chapters open at the same time in adjacent windows. That would allow easy cutting and pasting of text, frames, box text, and tags. Unfortunately, you can only have one chapter open at a time with the Windows version, and you cannot run multiple sessions of the program itself concurrently. (You can, however, run Windows Ventura and DOS/GEM Ventura concurrently and switch back and forth with Alt-Tab, though doing so is of limited value.)

◆ Speed

Provided you use a disk caching utility (see Chapter 23 for details), the DOS/GEM version is faster than the Windows version. But the speed of Ventura itself isn't the real issue: what you need to consider is the overall speed of your computer work. If you work exclusively with Ventura and not with any other programs, the DOS/GEM version may be a better choice from a speed perspective. But if you frequently go in and out of Ventura to use your word processor, to perform tasks in DOS, to log onto CompuServe or MCI Mail, or to use other programs, you may really fall in love with the ability of Windows to let you jump from one program to another with a simple Alt-Tab.

One way to get the best of both worlds — the speed of the DOS/GEM version and the convenient task switching of Windows 3 — is to run the DOS/GEM version of Ventura from within Windows. That's what I currently do, and that's what I plan on doing at least until a new version of Windows Ventura is released with fewer bugs.

◆ PostScript Printing

For those with PostScript printers, the availability of scalable screen fonts via Adobe's ATM for Windows is a powerful inducement to use the Windows version. However, for printing to PostScript, the Windows version has two drawbacks. One is that the driver is ridiculously slow. The other is that the PostScript preamble (PS2.PRE), which many Ventura users have edited to create special effects such as rotated and outline type, is replaced by the Windows PostScript driver, which is not easy to access.

◆ Buginess

Because it's been in existence in almost exactly the same form for over two years, the GEM/DOS version has had time to be thoroughly debugged. It's still possible to make the program crash, but it's not easy.

Like any new program, the first release of the Windows version still has some bugs, many of which are probably caused by Windows itself. By the time you read this, most of those initial bugs will hopefully be fixed, so check with your dealer or Ventura Software to see if the version you are considering has a number later than 3.0. Generally, a number such as 3.01 or 3.02 will indicate a bug-fix release. In fact, as this book was going to press, the first free fix-it patch was already being released. To receive your copy of the latest patch, call Ventura Software customer support at 800/822-8221 and ask for "the latest Ventura Windows patch." Or you can download the patch from the Ventura bulletin board on CompuServe.

◆ Computer

Although more and more people are migrating to 80386 computers, one of the nicest things about the DOS/GEM version of Ventura has always been that it didn't require an expensive computer. Any XT (8086 chip) or AT (80286 chip) with 640K and a hard disk will work fine. Although Microsoft says that Windows 3 will run on an AT computer, you really do need an 80386 with at least 2MB and preferably more RAM to get decent performance. So if you're one of the millions of people using an XT or AT, you'll definitely want to stick with the DOS/GEM version.

◆ Running the DOS/GEM Version from Windows

For those with 80386 computers, Windows 3 is an irresistable piece of software. Once you've installed it on your computer, you can continue to run your familiar DOS programs like WordPerfect, Word, dBASE, and Lotus, while selectively sampling some of the new generation of Windows software such as Corel Draw, Excel, Amí, and Persuasion. As for Ventura, my advice is to stay with the DOS/GEM version but to run it from Windows. That way you can have the best of both worlds. Eventually, when the Windows version is sufficiently debugged and has all the necessary drivers in place, you can switch to that version.

Here's how to set up the DOS/GEM version to run from Windows:

- If you haven't installed Ventura to run from DOS, do so.
- If you haven't installed Windows 3, do so.
- Copy the VENTURA.PIF file from the utility disk to the Ventura directory.
- (Optional) If you don't already have a program group called Non-Windows Applications or DOS Programs, create one by selecting New from the File menu.
- Open the window for the program group in which you want the icon for DOS/GEM Ventura to appear. Select new from the File menu then select Program Item.
- In the Description box, type DOS Ventura (or whatever you want to call it).
- Select Browse.
- In the Browse dialog box, change the extension in the Filename from *.exe to *.pif.
- From the Directory List, select the drive containing Ventura. Usually this will be C.
- VP.PIF or VPPROF.PIF should now appear in the File List. Select the one you want to use.
- Select OK or press Enter.

Now you can run Ventura directly from the Program Manager.

2

How Ventura Works

"Everything should be made as simple as possible, but no simpler."

So said Albert Einstein in reference to physics, but the observation applies equally well to software. While learning Ventura does take effort, there's no getting around the fact that preparing documents is an inherently complex task.

Mastering Ventura requires hands-on practice creating documents; however, it may also help to review some of the concepts that the program is based on.

Mode Icons, also called function boxes. From left to right they are Framing, Tagging, Text Editing, Graphic Drawing, and Table Editing.

Path and name of the current chapter (selected from the File menu).

Full Box. It makes the screen full size again after you shrink it with the resize box; not used unless you accidentally shrink the screen.

Style Sheet currently loaded (selected from the File menu).

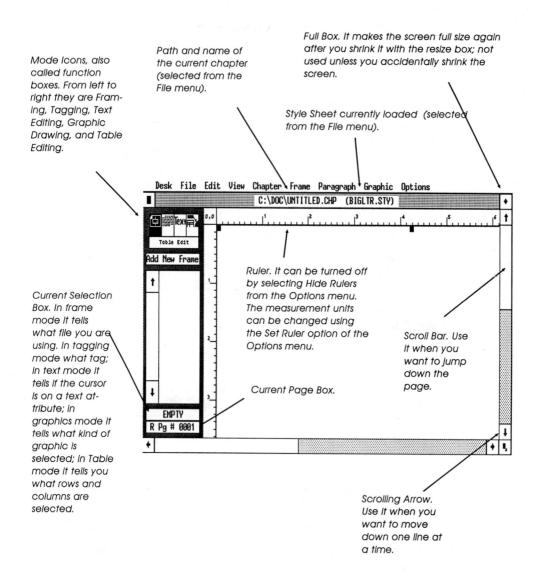

Current Selection Box. In frame mode it tells what file you are using. In tagging mode what tag; in text mode it tells if the cursor is on a text attribute; in graphics mode it tells what kind of graphic is selected; in Table mode it tells you what rows and columns are selected.

Ruler. It can be turned off by selecting Hide Rulers from the Options menu. The measurement units can be changed using the Set Ruler option of the Options menu.

Current Page Box.

Scroll Bar. Use it when you want to jump down the page.

Scrolling Arrow. Use it when you want to move down one line at a time.

Figure 2-1a: *The parts of the Ventura screen (DOS/GEM version).*

Addition Button. In frame or graphics mode it must be selected before you draw a new frame. In tagging mode it must be selected to create a new tag. In text mode it reads Set Font and must be selected to change the attributes of a single letter, word, or phrase. In table mode it must be selected before you add a new table.

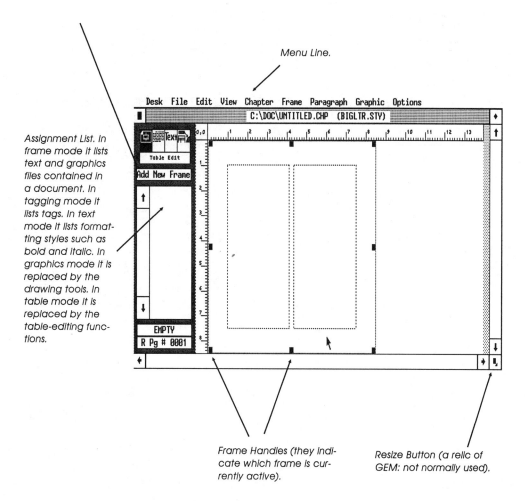

Menu Line.

Assignment List. In frame mode it lists text and graphics files contained in a document. In tagging mode it lists tags. In text mode it lists formatting styles such as bold and italic. In graphics mode it is replaced by the drawing tools. In table mode it is replaced by the table-editing functions.

Frame Handles (they indicate which frame is currently active).

Resize Button (a relic of GEM: not normally used).

Figure 2-1b: *The parts of the Ventura screen (DOS/GEM version).*

Control Menu Box. It lets you change the size of Ventura's window, close Ventura (same as selecting Exit from the File menu), or switch to the Windows Task List.

Title Bar. It tells the name and path of the current chapter and style sheet.

Style sheet currently loaded (selected from the File menu).

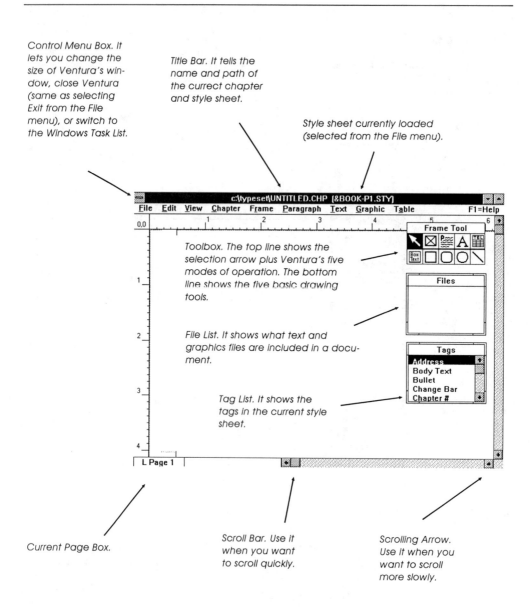

Toolbox. The top line shows the selection arrow plus Ventura's five modes of operation. The bottom line shows the five basic drawing tools.

File List. It shows what text and graphics files are included in a document.

Tag List. It shows the tags in the current style sheet.

Current Page Box.

Scroll Bar. Use it when you want to scroll quickly.

Scrolling Arrow. Use it when you want to scroll more slowly.

Figure 2-1c: *The parts of the Ventura screen (Windows version).*

Menu Line. You can access
each set of commands either
by clicking on them with the
mouse or by press Alt and
then the first letter of the
menu name.

Minimize and maximize buttons enlarge
Ventura to fill the whole display or else
shrink it down into an icon.

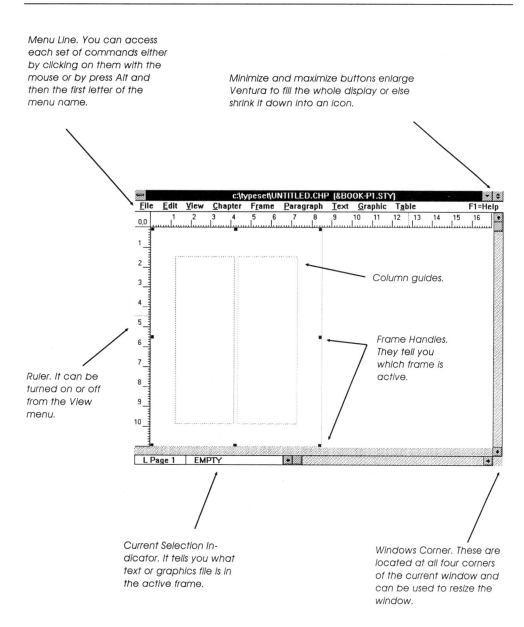

Column guides.

Frame Handles.
They tell you
which frame is
active.

Ruler. It can be
turned on or off
from the View
menu.

Current Selection In-
dicator. It tells you what
text or graphics file is in
the active frame.

Windows Corner. These are
located at all four corners
of the current window and
can be used to resize the
window.

Figure 2-1d: *The parts of the Ventura screen (Windows version).*

❖ What Can Ventura Do?

Before we get into exploring the workings of Ventura, let's take a brief inventory of what the program actually lets you accomplish.

- It lets you merge text and graphics files created by other programs into a single document. Graphics can be scaled and stretched. Text blocks automatically reformat to flow around inserted graphics.

- It gives you full typographic control over the appearance of text, including hyphenation, kerning, tracking, spaceband control (i.e., spacing between words), letter spacing (spacing within words), and leading (spacing between lines). It also provides a variety of controls over boxes and ruling lines.

- It provides batch pagination features such as automatic page, figure, and section numbering, index and table of contents generation, and chaining of multiple chapters at print time.

- It provides a simple text editor that allows insertion and deletion as well as block moves. Any changes you make in text are reflected back to the original files.

- It provides an internal graphics program that allows you to generate lines and arrows, empty or shaded rectangles, and empty or shaded ellipses.

- Results of formatting, including actual typefaces and line breaks, are shown on the screen. Most monitors that work with the IBM PC are supported by the program, including large-screen, high-resolution displays.

- Output options include dot matrix and color inkjet printers, laser printers, and PostScript-compatible typesetters.

❖ Some History

So far so good. We've noted what Ventura can do. But we still haven't established just what Ventura is. According to which magazine article you read, it has been variously described as a "super word processor," a "WYSIWYG batch-pagination program," and as a "page makeup" or "page layout" program. All these terms are more or less accurate, but they also apply to any number of other programs on the market. So why is Ventura, among all these other products, a runaway bestseller?

To really understand the significance of Ventura, we need to look at the history of computer-based publishing. From the first use of computers for creating documents, a gap existed between two types of systems. One type was systems that provided a what-you-see-is-what-you-get (WYSIWYG) view of the final page and allowed you to "paste up" text and graphics on-screen. This approach, which might best be described by the term "page makeup" (since the user created a document one page at a time), had its roots in the computer-aided design (CAD) and computer graphics technology that moved from experimental to commercial during the 1960's. It came into use in the publishing industry in the 1970's, when it was adapted for onscreen layouts of display advertisements.

Meanwhile, other systems were being developed that used a non-WYSIWYG, code-based approach. With these programs, documents were created in two stages. First, the user embedded typographic and pagination codes (and macros representing sets of codes) in the text of a document. Then the program processed the codes all at once, automatically generating pages with the proper headers, footers, page numbers, and so forth. The advantage of this approach was that the user didn't have to create pages one at a time; the disadvantage was that these systems didn't provide the interactive visual feedback provided by page makeup programs. Only when the document was printed could the final result be proofed.

Before Ventura, many experts assumed that the page makeup and the batch approaches were irreconcilable. And indeed, as publishing systems were introduced for personal computers, they typically fell into one or the other camp. Some of the early Macintosh

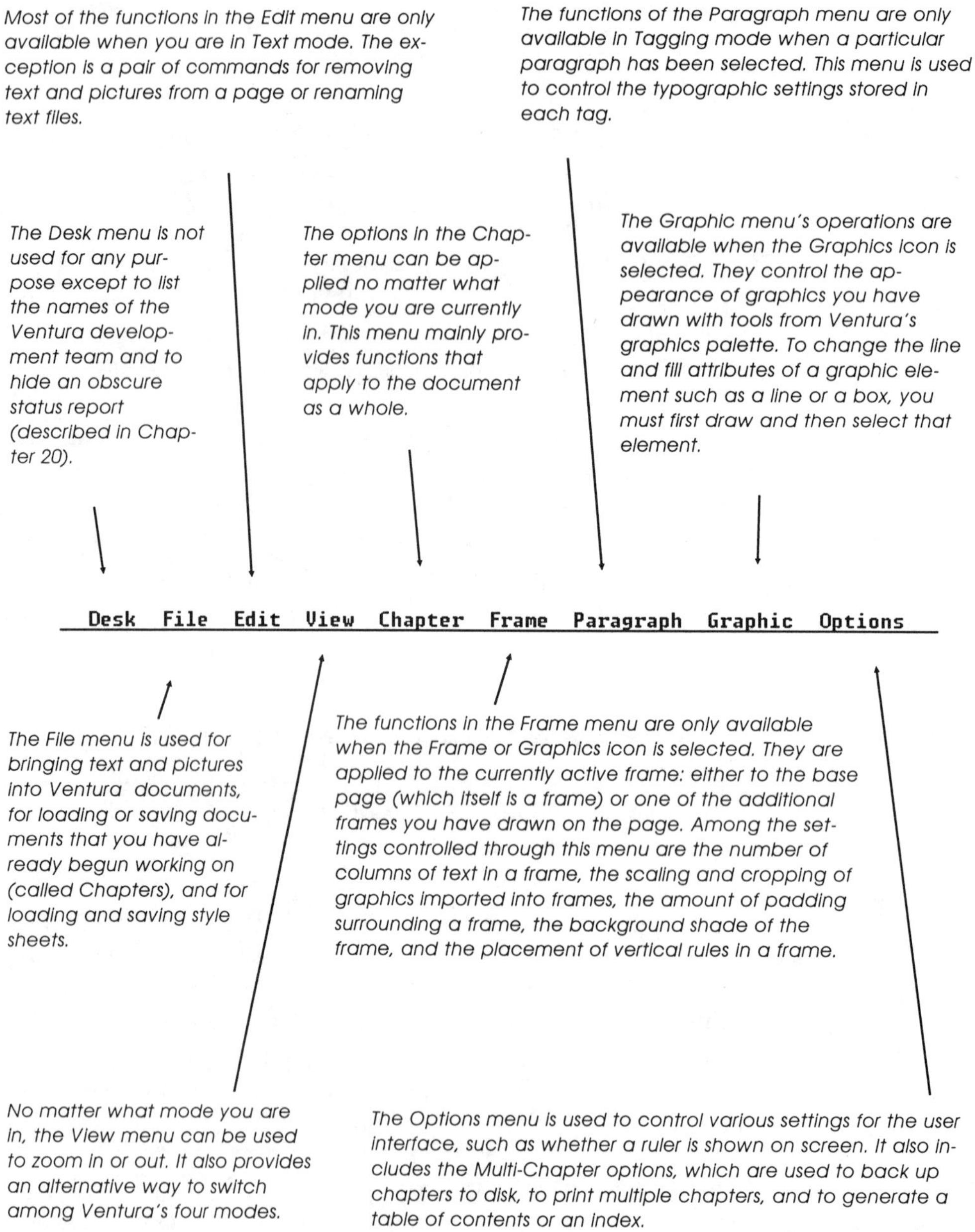

Most of the functions in the Edit menu are only available when you are in Text mode. The exception is a pair of commands for removing text and pictures from a page or renaming text files.

The functions of the Paragraph menu are only available in Tagging mode when a particular paragraph has been selected. This menu is used to control the typographic settings stored in each tag.

The Desk menu is not used for any purpose except to list the names of the Ventura development team and to hide an obscure status report (described in Chapter 20).

The options in the Chapter menu can be applied no matter what mode you are currently in. This menu mainly provides functions that apply to the document as a whole.

The Graphic menu's operations are available when the Graphics icon is selected. They control the appearance of graphics you have drawn with tools from Ventura's graphics palette. To change the line and fill attributes of a graphic element such as a line or a box, you must first draw and then select that element.

```
 Desk  File  Edit  View  Chapter  Frame  Paragraph  Graphic  Options
```

The File menu is used for bringing text and pictures into Ventura documents, for loading or saving documents that you have already begun working on (called Chapters), and for loading and saving style sheets.

The functions in the Frame menu are only available when the Frame or Graphics icon is selected. They are applied to the currently active frame: either to the base page (which itself is a frame) or one of the additional frames you have drawn on the page. Among the settings controlled through this menu are the number of columns of text in a frame, the scaling and cropping of graphics imported into frames, the amount of padding surrounding a frame, the background shade of the frame, and the placement of vertical rules in a frame.

No matter what mode you are in, the View menu can be used to zoom in or out. It also provides an alternative way to switch among Ventura's four modes.

The Options menu is used to control various settings for the user interface, such as whether a ruler is shown on screen. It also includes the Multi-Chapter options, which are used to back up chapters to disk, to print multiple chapters, and to generate a table of contents or an index.

Figure 2-2a: Notes on the Menu Line (DOS/GEM version).

The Edit menu provides basic cut, copy, and paste for both text and graphics. In addition, it contains commands for updating anchors (pictures connected to text) and automatically generated numbers. Finally, this menu contains the Set Preferences dialog box.

The functions in the Frame menu are applied to the currently active frame: either to the base page (which itself is a frame) or one of the additional frames you have drawn on the page. Among the settings controlled through this menu are the number of columns of text in a frame, the scaling and cropping of graphics imported into frames, the amount of padding surrounding a frame, the background shade of the frame, and the placement of vertical rules in a frame. In addition, you use this menu to remove or rename files.

No matter what mode you are in, the View menu can be used to zoom in or out. It also lets you customize the appearance of the screen with options to hide or show windows, rules, column guides, etc.

The Graphic menu's operations are available when the Graphics icon is selected. They control the appearance of graphics you have drawn with tools from Ventura's graphics palette. To change the line and fill attributes of a graphic element such as a line or a box, you must first draw and then select that element.

The Table menu lets you insert a table between two paragraphs and then set and alter the structure and appearance of the table.

File   Edit   View   Chapter   Frame   Paragraph   Text   Graphic   Table   F1=Help

The File menu is used for bringing text and pictures into Ventura documents, for loading or saving documents that you have already begun working on (called chapters), for loading and saving style sheets, and for printing. The Manage Publication dialog box controls document backups and multi-chapter operations.

The functions of the Paragraph menu are only available when a particular paragraph has been selected. This menu is used to change the typographic settings for tags.

The Help menu lets you get quick information without resorting to the manual. In addition, selecting Help with the mouse (not with the F1 key) provides you with a report on Ventura's memory allocation for frames and tags and for paragraphs and text. You can change the allocation if necessary.

The Chapter menu controls headers, footers, footnotes, paper size and orientation, inserting pages, and jumping backward and forward to a different page.

The Text menu lets you override the character formatting of a tag to change the appearance of a single letter, word, or longer passage. You can apply italics, underlining, etc. In addition, this menu lets you insert "special items" such as hollow boxes and equations.

Figure 2-2b: Notes on the Menu Line (Windows version).

hits, such as PageMaker and ReadySetGo!, were strongly rooted in the page makeup tradition. Other Macintosh programs, such as JustText, and programs for the PC such as ScenicWriter, TeX, and MagnaType, followed the batch approach.

What sets Ventura apart is that it merges some aspects of both approaches. Just as in the typical page makeup system, you can work interactively with each individual page, watching the results of your formatting decisions on the screen. On the other hand, the program provides the speed of a batch program by automatically setting up as many pages as are required to compose your documents. In a real sense, with Ventura you get the best of both worlds.

❖ A Scenario

Let's bring the discussion down to earth by describing a typical scenario. Caroline is a freelance technical writer who writes and produces manuals for several companies. The manuals combine text, scanned images, and simple diagrams.

To create her text, Caroline types it into WordPerfect. She scans images using an HP ScanJet Plus scanner, editing the pictures using Picture Publisher and saving them in Tagged Image File Format (TIFF).

Once she has created the text and graphics files for a chapter of the manual, Caroline loads Ventura Publisher (DOS/GEM version) and then loads a style sheet, using the operations in the File menu. While the screen is still blank, she uses the operations in the Chapter menu to select the dimensions of the paper she intends to print on. She then uses the Options menu to turn the column guides on. Next, she switches to frame mode (by clicking on the frame icon) and uses the operations in the Frame menu to adjust the margins of the base page. By viewing the column guides, she checks that the margins are satisfactory.

With the page size and margins set, Caroline loads text from her WordPerfect files onto the page. She then switches to tagging mode and begins "tagging" her document. Each of the tags contained in her style sheet contains the formatting information appropriate to a particular type of paragraph. Tags have names like "Headline," "Subhead," and "Body Text" and are listed on the left side of the screen. To tag a paragraph, she merely clicks her mouse once on the paragraph and then once on the name of a tag in the list of tags.

If no tag is available for a given purpose, Caroline creates a new one, using the Add New Tag option. She names the new tag and then uses the options in the Paragraph menu to specify such elements as font, first line indent, left and right spacing, spacing between lines and paragraphs, ruling lines, and special features such as bullets.

The work of tagging goes fairly fast. Most text doesn't need to be tagged at all, since Ventura automatically assigns the Body Text tag to any untagged text.

Once the text is completely tagged, Caroline switches to text mode and uses Ventura's built-in word processor to make minor insertions and deletions to accommodate last-minute changes in her text.

Having finished using Ventura's word processor, she switches to frame mode again, clicks on Add New Frame, and draws several frames to accommodate pictures. She then uses the File menu to load scanned images into these frames. Next, she uses the Margins and Columns option of the Frame menu to place margins between the pictures and the frames, and uses the Sizing & Scaling option of the Frame menu to adjust the scaling and cropping of the pictures. Then she uses the Anchors & Captions option of the Frame menu to add captions to the pictures.

Caroline now switches to Ventura's internal graphics mode and uses the line drawing and box text tools to label her pictures.

Then she switches briefly back into text mode to add some text to the boxes and then switches to tagging mode to format the text.

Having formatted the text and graphics on each page of the manual, she now uses the Chapter menu again to add Headers and Footers to her pages. Finally, she uses the File menu to give her document a chapter name, save it, and print it out.

❖ Modes: Five Programs in One

As the above scenario illustrates, the process of creating a document with Ventura involves continually moving in and out of the five modes provided by the program and using the commands that are available in each. Once you have become experienced with Ventura, you'll find yourself choosing the right mode and looking into the right menu more or less automatically, and you'll find that the various modes work together quite seamlessly. However, in first attempting to grasp the way the program works, it's useful to recognize that the five modes actually represent five different programs merged into one.

The first two programs are a page layout program and a pagination program (some functions of each are assigned to the frame drawing and tagging modes). The third program is a simple word processor (text editing mode), and the fourth is a simple drawing program (graphics mode). The fifth is a forms-generation program (table editing mode). When you're in a given mode, some of the items in the pull-down menus are shown in black and can be selected, while others are shown in gray and cannot be selected. This is Ventura's way of allowing the five programs to share the same set of menus.

In addition to the commands available in the various modes, there are also some commands that can be used no matter which mode you happen to be in. These include commands for loading text or graphics into Ventura, printing documents, and customizing the program's user interface.

❖ Analyzing the Operations

Clearly, it's important to know the purposes served by each of Ventura's five modes. But to grasp the program we need to take a slightly different tack. Let's now look at Ventura's operations not in terms of what mode they are assigned to but in terms of what they let you accomplish. If you analyze Ventura's structure from that perspective, you'll see that the operations available to you fall into four categories:

- Operations for importing and exporting various items such as text, graphics, and style sheets
- Operations for customizing the Ventura interface
- Text and graphics processing operations
- Formatting operations

❖ Category 1: Bridges to the Outside World

Before you can format a document you have to pull text and graphics into Ventura, and after you format the document you have to either print it or store it on disk. In addition, with any program there are various housekeeping chores that need to be attended to, such as saving style sheets and documents to use later.

This is where Ventura's "bridging" operations come into play. Most of these reside in the File menu, including commands for loading text or pictures into Ventura, saving documents that have been formatted, printing, and using DOS to create new subdirectories to hold documents. In the DOS/GEM version, a few bridging commands, particularly those for removing text or pictures or text from a document, reside in the Edit menu rather than the File menu. Finally, in the DOS/GEM version, the Options menu includes a selection, Add/Remove Fonts, for increasing or reducing the number of fonts available for use in documents.

Most of your bridging work will typically occur when you are first beginning to create a document and when you are ending your work. At the beginning, you load the appropriate files and style sheets; at the end you print the document and save the completed (or partially completed) chapter.

❖ Category 2: Customizing the Interface

No user interface is perfect for every type of user and every type of document. For that reason, Ventura provides an extensive range of operations for customizing the appearance of Ventura's main screen as well as for controlling the type of feedback provided about the status of a document. In the DOS/GEM version, these customizing controls are mainly located in the Options menu; in the Windows version, they are found in the View and Edit menus. These controls let you hide or show elements such as rulers, column guides, and pictures; flag loose lines; turn column snap and line snap on and off; use pull-down or drop-down menus; adjust the double-click speed of the mouse (DOS/GEM only—in the Windows version, you do this via the Windows Control Panel); and view on-screen kerning.

Another location of such operations is the View menu, which lets you specify the degree of magnification of the screen. Finally, the scroll bars on the right side and bottom of the screen let you control the portion of the page you are currently viewing.

❖ Category 3: Text and Graphics Operations

Ventura's internal word processor and graphics generator are useful for making last-minute changes and for enhancing pictures generated by scanners, CAD programs, drawing programs, and business graphics programs.

The word processor is activated when you select the Text icon. Its commands are located in the Edit menu and in the sidebar (DOS/GEM version) or the Text menu (Windows version).

The graphics generator is activated when you select the Graphics icon (DOS/GEM version) or one of the Graphics tools (Windows version). Additional graphic controls are found in the Graphics menu.

❖ Category 4: Formatting

While the operations we've discussed so far are certainly important, formatting is at the center of what Ventura is all about. It is also the most complex of the capabilities provided by the program, with commands scattered in various menus. In the remainder of this chapter we'll go through the various tools provided by Ventura for formatting various levels of the document.

◆ Style Sheets and Tags: Formatting at the Paragraph Level

A style sheet might be thought of as a cookbook, a compilation of recipes (called "tags") for how individual paragraphs are to be formatted. For example, a tag called Subhead might specify that a given paragraph is to be centered in the column and set in 18-point Palatino Bold type, with 3 picas (half an inch) of leading (vertical space) separating it from the previous paragraph and 1 pica separating it from the following paragraph. Every time you attach this tag to a paragraph of plain text, it will assume all the attributes stored in the tag.

Much of the work of formatting a document in Ventura involves setting up the specifications for the various tags and then attaching these tags as needed throughout the document.

Sounds simple enough. Unfortunately, the style sheet alone doesn't provide quite enough information to completely set up a document. What do you do when a single letter or word within a paragraph is formatted differently from the rest of the paragraph? And what about formatting directions that transcend the individual paragraph, such as the margins for the entire page or the numbering scheme for the entire document?

To take care of the issues of document formatting that extend above and below the level of the individual paragraph, Ventura provides a number of tools. None of these tools works quite as simply as the style sheet concept, and the way the tools are organized within menus is at times confusing. Although it's not possible within this chapter to explain completely the relationship between these various tools, the following is a simplified synopsis of four levels of formatting control that Ventura provides, for the document as a whole, for frames on pages, for words and phrases within paragraphs, and for graphics.

◆ Document Specifications

Operations that affect the entire document are mainly located in the Chapter menu. These include the size of paper being used and whether the document is to be in portrait (vertical) or landscape (horizontal) orientation; the numbering of chapters, pages, and subheads; and the contents of headers and footers.

Generally, when you lay out a document, the first menu to pull down is the Chapter menu.

◆ Frame Specifications

Frames are one of the most confusing concepts in Ventura, since they serve so many different purposes. When you start any document from scratch, Ventura automatically creates a frame that coincides with the dimensions of the paper and hence is called the "base page" frame.

Specifications that are set for the base page frame, such as margins and background shading, apply to the entire document. On the other hand, you can create smaller frames on individual pages to hold text or pictures. These frames must each be given individual settings for such things as margins and columns, and unlike the settings for the base page frames, the specifications you enter for a smaller frame on the page apply to that frame only.

While the difference between the base page frame and additional frames tends to cause confusion, so does the fact that the scaling of graphics is handled in the same dialog box (the Sizing & Scaling option of the Frame menu) as the size specifications for frames themselves.

◆ Sub-Paragraph Specifications

For altering the specifications of a letter, word, or phrase within a tagged paragraph, Ventura provides two methods of control. One is a list of attributes that appears on the left side of the screen when you are in text editing mode. To apply these, you hold down the mouse button while dragging the icon across a portion of text, then click on the name of the desired attribute.

A second method of controlling text formats is the Set Font button. This works in a similar fashion: highlight a passage of text, click on Set Font, then use the dialog box that appears to specify the desired font formats.

◆ Graphic Specifications

Ventura allows you both to import graphics and to generate graphics within the program. Generating internal graphics is done using the tools that appear on the left side of the screen when the Graphics icon is selected. Once graphics are drawn, the options in the Graphics menu can be used to alter them: for instance, to change the thickness of a line or the background shade of an ellipse.

It is somewhat confusing that there is no menu specifically devoted to sizing and positioning graphics imported into Ventura from other programs. Some of the commands for doing that are accessed via the Sizing & Scaling option of the Frame menu (scaling and cropping the picture), others via the Margins and Columns option of the Frame menu (margins around the picture).

❖ A Final Concept: Ventura As a Software Hub

One of the insights designed into Ventura is the recognition that publishing is a modular effort; that is, it comprises distinct series of stages such as writing, editing, proofing, layout, and preparation of graphics. In our scenario above, Caroline was doing all the work herself. Typically, however, publishing is a group effort, in which various specialists merge their respective crafts towards a common end.

Translated into the computer world, publishing's modular and sequential nature means different people using different software tools. Ventura's design allows it to be a useful adjunct to almost any of the most popular computer applications, including word processing, database, graphics, spreadsheet, and CAD programs.

Most people are already comfortable with a particular word processing program and don't care to change. Ditto with respect to graphics programs. For instance, the preparation of the typical manual may involve one writer using WordPerfect, another using XyWrite, and an illustrator using AutoCAD, Publisher's Paintbrush, and perhaps other graphics programs as well. Not only does Ventura allow importing a diverse array of file formats, but it does so smoothly and easily.

◆ A Bi-directional Exchange

If Ventura only allowed files to be imported, you'd be faced with a difficult situation when it came time to update and revise a major document. Fortunately, the exchange is potentially bi-directional. If a document needs to be reworked, you can use Ventura's editing tools to make changes, and those alterations will be reflected back in the original files.

The method chosen by Ventura's designers to implement the open systems concept is worth noting. For each document you generate with the program, Ventura creates a unique file with the extension CHP. This chapter file contains pointers to all the other files that together make up a document, including associated files generated by Ventura and the original word processing and graphics files. Because of this scheme, Ventura does not need to generate an immense file containing the entire document, which helps the speed of the program while minimizing the demands it places on your system's storage. Other files that Ventura uses are the INF file, which stores various settings in between your sessions with the program, and GEN files that Ventura creates to contain text it automatically generates such as tables of contents and indexes. These files are discussed in greater detail in Chapter 7, "Managing Files."

◆ Benefits of the Open System Approach

The open system approach used by Ventura has two additional benefits. As noted, it allows easy revision of documents, such as manuals and parts catalogs, that move through multiple generations. With Ventura, a document can be dynamic: revised and rewritten with each printing.

The second benefit of the open system approach is that it allows those using Ventura to stay with the various personal computer programs they are already comfortable with. This is convenient, of course, but also has the enormous practical benefit for organizations of minimizing the amount of retraining that needs to take place.

◆ A Drawback of the Open System Approach

The drawback of the open system approach is that it leads to a proliferation of files for every document. While Ventura provides some techniques for managing these files and moving them about, the work of avoiding confusion on your hard disk requires a great deal of attention to detail and time-consuming file management. Special utility programs, such as VPToolbox (discussed in Chapter 7, "Files") have even been introduced for the specific purpose of managing the multiple files that make up a Ventura document.

❖ Putting It All Together

Hopefully, this chapter has persuaded you that despite the seeming complexity of Ventura's structure, there's method in the madness. Once you get used to the quirks of how operations are organized in menus, you'll find that formatting documents with Ventura is a speedy, natural process. In the end, you'll appreciate Ventura's power when you see the results on paper. In other words: the proof is in the printing.

Hardware

3

Configuring
Your System

Using Ventura as the software hub, you can build a wide variety of publishing systems, depending on your budget and your needs. One of the beauties of the program is that it can run on a relatively cheap hardware system. According to Xerox, the minimum configuration for the DOS/GEM version is a PC XT with 640K of memory, a mouse (of virtually any variety), a graphics monitor (of virtually any variety), and one to three megabytes of extra hard disk memory. By today's standards that's a modest, inexpensive system, one that can be had for around a thousand dollars, which makes Ventura one of the real bargains among the current crop of desktop publishing programs.

❖ Choosing a Computer

Of course, you should always be a bit skeptical when people talk about a "minimum configuration." What exactly do they mean? As I'm sure you're aware, simply being able to run a program on a machine is not enough; it must run fast enough to make work go forward without too much finger tapping.

I've used Ventura on a number of machines: a 1983-vintage IBM PC with a CGA monitor, a 10MB hard disk and 576K of memory; a Compaq DeskPro, an Everex AT clone (10MHz, 1 wait state), a Hewlett-Packard Vectra AT compatible, an AST Premium 286 AT compatible (10 MHz, no wait states), and a PC's Limited 386 computer (16 MHz). The table on the following page shows the results of speed tests on several of these. The figures, however, don't convey anything about the feel of the program, the subjective difference in performance from one machine environment to another.

I found even the plain IBM PC to give adequate performance, provided the document I was working on didn't include any graphics. Because that computer lacked much memory, it would resort to disk swapping to handle pictures, and the result was a tremendous wait. Working with text was no problem. Also, the Color Graphics Adapter proved not to be the hindrance I'd expected. Despite its meager resolution, I found it easy to do fairly exacting work (by zooming in closer when necessary). The only real drawback with the CGA was not being able to read most text in Normal view.

On the Compaq DeskPro, which uses the 8088 chip, Ventura zipped along quite nicely, and in fact the performance seemed just as good as on the HP Vectra, which uses the 80286 chip. Of course, on the 10 MHz machines the performance was yet another notch higher, but the striking similarity between using Ventura on the DeskPro and the Vectra proved to my satisfaction that it isn't the microprocessor that counts so much as the speed of your hard disk. At the time I did the comparison my Vectra hard disk had

Table 3-1
Speed Tests on Different Computers

	(A)	(B)	(C)	(D)	(E)	(F)	(G)
1. Load Ventura	39	24	19	9	4	8	3
2. Load 3-pg chapter	19	13	10	5	3	4	3
3. Load bit-mapped image	10	8	5	3	2	2	2
4. Load object graphic	11	6	5	3	2	1	1
5. Move bit-mapped image	3	2	2	2	1	1	1
7. Jump to end of 25-pg doc	N/A	7	5	4	4	3	3

All times apply to the DOS/GEM version and are recorded in seconds. The computers were **(A)** *an IBM PC with a 10 Mb hard disk;* **(B)** *a 640K Compaq DeskPro with a 20 Mb hard disk;* **(C)** *a 640K Hewlett-Packard Vectra with a 20 Mb hard disk;* **(D)** *a 640K Everex AT clone with a 40 Mb hard disk;* **(E)** *Everex AT using the Flash disk caching program;* **(F)** *a PC's Limited 386 computer (16 MHz); and* **(G)** *a PC's Limited 386 computer (16 MHz) using the Vcache disk caching program.*

become badly fragmented over time and had definitely become somewhat sluggish. The moral: Go ahead and use Ventura on an XT-class machine, and if considering the options for upgrading such a machine for better performance, invest in a faster hard disk.

Of course, you can get better performance from systems that have more memory, larger hard disks, faster microprocessors, higher-resolution monitors, and special RAM-disk and disk caching utilities. By the time I was laying out the first edition of this book, I had graduated to a fast AT clone with a Viking I 19-inch monitor — and I definitely appreciated the increased speed and the convenience of working on the full-page monitor. For the second edition, I used a 16-MHz PC's Limited 386 computer made by Dell

Computer Corporation with an Amdek 1280 high-resolution monitor. Moving from a 286 computer to a 386 computer definitely changed the feel of the program. For the first time, I could set my own pace in formatting a document, not have the pace dictated by the computer. Consequently, the work seemed that much smoother.

My own experience is that Ventura is flexible enough to adapt to your hardware resources. Assuming your budget has some limits, the question is: what sort of hardware investments will yield the most bang for the buck? In this chapter we'll start by looking at some hypothetical configurations. In the following chapters we'll look at each particular type of hardware in detail: laser printers, monitors, and scanners.

❖ Five Configurations

As the following brief case studies show, prices for a publishing system built around Ventura can range from $900 for a minimal system to $62,000 for a full-blown, multi-workstation system, including a Linotronic imagesetter.

◆ A Low-End System

System A is used by a graduate student who plans to typeset her 240-page thesis with Ventura, as well as to create the questionnaires and other materials. Since her budget is quite limited, she makes use of the laser printers at the local desktop publishing service bureau, which provides laser printers and computers on an hourly rental basis. Her computer is an XT clone with a 20-MB hard disk and a Hercules clone graphics card. She uses Ventura's optional keyboard controls but plans to add a mouse as soon as she can afford one. For output she uses an Epson dot matrix printer. Although the quality of Ventura's output on the Epson isn't good enough for master copies, it is sufficient for creating proofing copies. For final copies, the student rents time on an Apple LaserWriter, or possibly on a Linotronic 200, to produce the final version of her thesis. The price breakdown of her system is as follows:

System A		
20MB XT clone	$	600
dot matrix printer		300
Total	$	900

◆ An Inexpensive Laser Printer System

System B is used by a business consultant who frequently designs forms for clients and prints reports containing business graphics and tables. He does not have the funds for options such as a full-page monitor or a high-end laser printer. His system is the least expensive laser printer system:

System B		
20MB AT clone	$	900
LaserJet IIP		900
Total	$	1,800

◆ A Medium-Priced System (Speed Oriented)

System C is used by a freelance technical writer who prepares manuals for small software companies. Her priority is speed, not output quality, so she has chosen to spend most of her budget on a fast computer and a high-resolution monitor, and to save money by buying an inexpensive laser printer. She uses an IBM AT clone computer with a 40MB hard disk and a mouse, and a Wyse 700 monitor. Because she can get by with the standard Swiss, Dutch, Courier, and Symbol typefaces provided with Ventura, she opted not to buy a PostScript printer, and instead bought a used HP LaserJet printer and retrofitted it with a LaserMaster LC2 printer accelerator. This controller resides on a board installed in the computer and connected with an ultra-high-speed cable directly to the video interface of the printer, a scheme that allows extremely fast printing. The cost of her system:

System C

40MB AT clone	$ 1,000
Wyse 700 monitor	900
HP LaserJet (used)	1,200
LaserMaster LC2 controller	1,800
Total	$ 4,900

◆ A Medium-Priced System (Type-Oriented)

System D is used by the proprietor of a walk-in desktop publishing shop that produces a wide range of materials: books, business reports, résumés, newsletters, forms, and manuals. Customers are generally businesses that provide him with files in WordStar, WordPerfect, MultiMate, or Microsoft Word format. The shop does not have a scanner. When images need to be merged into documents he advises clients to have halftones made at a graphic arts shop and then to paste them onto boxes that he creates with Ventura. Because of the variety of typefaces needed by customers, he uses a QMS-PS 810 PostScript laser printer, which includes about a dozen built-in scalable typefaces. Because his budget is limited, he uses a Hercules clone board with an AT clone computer, but plans to purchase a higher-resolution monitor as his next investment. His system:

System D

40MB AT clone	$ 1,000
QMS PS 810	3,000
Total	$ 4,000

◆ A High-Priced System

System E was assembled by the manager of a department that produces all the manuals for a small but well-heeled engineering company. The company decided to pull out all the stops in setting up a desktop publishing system — well, almost all the stops: they balked at her request for a Linotronic imagesetter. The system includes an IBM PS/2 Model 80 computer with 80 MB of storage, a QMS-PS 810 printer, a LaserMaster LC2, a Viking 2 full-page display, and a Microtek scanner. The price of the system is as follows:

System E	
IBM PS/2 Model 80 Computer	$ 4,500
QMS PS-810	3,000
LaserMaster LC/2	1,800
Microtek scanner	2,000
Viking 2 display	2,000
Total	$ 13,300

◆ Full-Blown Publishing

System F is used by a task force that is developing prototype systems, procedures, and training materials for a Fortune 1000 company. The company intends eventually to invest in Ventura-based systems for its offices in numerous different locations in the United States and overseas. The system includes six 386 clone workstations — three attached to PostScript printers, the other three to LaserJet III printers. The group shares a single scanner and a Linotronic imagesetter. The entire system is as follows:

System F	
Six 80MB 386 clones	$ 12,000
Three QMS-PS 810 printers	9,000
Three LaserJet III printers	5,100
Six Wyse 700 displays	4,200
One Microtek scanner	2,000
One Linotronic 200 Imagesetter	30,000
Total	$ 62,300
Price per workstation	$ 10,383

❖ Conclusion

Some interesting conclusions can be drawn from these scenarios. The first is that publishing systems based around Ventura start at around $1,800 (assuming the system includes a laser printer), but that a bare-bones configuration can cost as little as $900, provided you are willing to put up with the inconvenience of proofing on a dot-matrix printer. On the other hand, if you decide to set up a no-holds-barred workstation with all the fixin's and buy the latest IBM-brand computers, your bill can run upwards of $13,000. With careful selection of computers, however, and sharing of typesetting equipment by a workgroup, you can have an even better system (since it includes a typesetter) for under $11,000 per workstation. Note that such a system is vastly superior to the traditional multiterminal typesetting systems of yore, since each "terminal" is actually a powerful personal computer rather than a dumb terminal serving the typesetting machine.

Printers

In the fall of 1983, an announcement was made at the immense Comdex Computer Show in Las Vegas that drew little notice at the time, but that in retrospect marked the firing shot of the technological revolution we now call desktop publishing. That announcement was by Canon Corporation, a Japanese manufacturer better known for its cameras than for its computer equipment. At Comdex, Canon offered to provide other companies with laser printer engines for a price, when purchased in quantity, of under $1000.

❖ Laser Printer Engines

Unlike a car engine, a laser printer engine includes all the mechanical parts of the printer and usually the chassis as well — everything but the microelectronics controlling the machine. Previously, a price of under $1,000 for a laser printer engine would have been laughable. However, Canon had found ways of adapting the design of its low-cost office copiers, and was planning to push laser printers into the realm of mass production economies.

Among the first to take Canon up on the offer was Hewlett-Packard, which designed its own controller to add to the Canon engine, called it the LaserJet, and started selling the fast, quiet little printers to businesses for $3,500 each. Eventually, several scores of companies were to do likewise, customizing their own particular laser printers around the Canon engine.

To this day, laser printer manufacturers have continued to follow the pattern set by Canon and HP. A relatively small number of Japanese firms create the laser printer engines. Canon and Ricoh are the leaders; others include Kyocera, NEC, and Epson. American and Japanese companies then enhance these engines with their own controller designs — companies such as Apple Computer, QMS, and Hewlett-Packard.

The engine is the physical mechanism of the printer, determining such factors as print quality, durability, paper handling, and cost of toner and other replaceables. The controller is the brain of the printer, determining such factors as availability of fonts and graphics capabilities. In general, most of the important matters to be concerned about are the controller's domain, since most of the printer engines (with some notable exceptions) are capable of competent printing and paper handling.

A number of criteria set them apart, including print quality (crispness of characters, quality of gray shades, blackness of blacks), paper handling, speed, availability of fonts, graphics capabilities, compatibility with typesetting machines, and quality of graphics.

Among laser printer engines, the most basic difference is whether the printer uses write-black technology or write-white. In a write-black engine, the portions of the drum marked by the laser are identical to the areas of black produced on the page. In a write-white engine, a reverse-imaging technique is used in which the portions of the drum marked by the laser are identical to the areas of white produced on the page. Write-black engines produce round pixels and are better at printing fine lines and serifs. Write-white engines produce scalloped pixels and have trouble with fine lines and serifs. From a print quality standpoint, it appears that write-black engines are clearly superior, and most of the popular laser printers being sold these days, including those from Hewlett-Packard and Apple, use write-black technology.

◆ Canon Engines

The first wave of laser printers, including the LaserJet, LaserJet Plus, LaserWriter, and QMS KISS, were based on the Canon LBP-CX. The LBP-CX was reliable and capable of crisp, clean output. The engine had some annoying drawbacks, notably small input and output paper trays and blacks that weren't quite black.

The Canon LBP-SX was a major redesign of the LBP-CX. Like the LBP-CX, the LBP-SX has excellent print quality, and like the CX has all its replaceable supplies, including toner, in a single convenient cartridge. The cartridge lasts for 4000 copies, compared to the 3000 copies of the CX cartridge. Print quality is improved over the LBP-CX: the new engine retains the former one's crisp handling of serifs and fine lines, but now prints blacks that are truly black. An important feature is a toner intensity control, which lets you adjust the darkness of type to your liking. At about 50 pounds, the LBP-SX is 30 percent lighter than the LBP-CX. However, paper trays are larger and paper emerges in the correct order (i.e., face down). Most of the leading printers today, including those from Hewlett-Packard, Apple, and QMS, use this engine or the LBP-LX, a slower engine featured in the LaserJet IIP and other compact printers.

Tip 4-1

The Importance of Intensity Control

Advertisement after advertisement emphasizes the ability of this printer or that one to print "blacker blacks." As is well known, solid areas printed by the first low-cost laser engine, the Canon LBP-CX, were too light for most people's liking, and subsequent laser printer designs have all compensated for the problem.

However, perhaps more important than whether a printer can print true black is whether the printer provides a way of controlling the print intensity. This turns out to be extremely important if you are producing master copies on your laser printer that will be reproduced on a photocopying machine or at a print shop. As a general rule, master copies should be as light as possible without beginning to fade. That's because all reproduction methods tend to darken type. Type that looks acceptable on the master tends to become excessively dark after reproduction.

The moral: When you buy a laser printer, check to see that it has an intensity control.

❖ Higher-Resolution and Enhanced Resolution Printers

While 300 dpi has become the de facto standard for laser printers, there is no reason that desktop laser printers should not graduate toward better quality. The resolution of most laser printers is 300 dots per inch, which is too coarse for replacing actual typeset output in most situations. On the other hand, printing at 1200 dpi, the low end of phototypesetting, is far more expensive. Some sort of technology is needed to bridge the gap between 300-dpi laser printing and 1200-dpi phototypesetting. That technology is now appearing in commercial products.

The techniques vary. Some printers, such as the Printware 720 IQ

Professional Laser Imager, sport a higher number of dots per inch. On the other hand, the Hewlett-Packard LaserJet III provides higher quality without increasing the dots per inch by means of a technology known as Resolution Enhancement. Finally, some printers, including the LaserMaster LM1000, combine increased resolution with some sort of enhancement technology.

Of course, there's only one sure-fire way to judge the effectiveness of one approach versus another: ask for sample pages and compare them under a magnifying glass.

❖ Page Description Languages

The laser printer controller is the "brains" of the printer, the part that endows the printer with its ability to generate graphics and characters. It is also known as the raster image processor (RIP). In most cases, the RIP is located inside the printer itself. The AST Turbolaser, the IBM Personal Pageprinter, the LaserMaster LC2, the QMS JetScript, and some others locate their RIPs on circuit boards within the computer.

The capabilities of printer RIPs vary widely. As a result, some laser printers are capable of printing only one or two mono-spaced fonts and have no graphics capabilities, while others can print fonts of virtually any style or size as well as graphics of any sort. The difference is in the software used by the RIP, which is referred to as the page description language (PDL).

Ventura works with virtually all the page description languages on the market, including Adobe's PostScript and HP's Printer Command Language or PCL. However, the capabilities of Ventura will vary, depending on which page description language your printer is running. Let's now look at these two page description languages in turn.

◆ PostScript

PostScript is by far the most important page description language. It was developed by Adobe Systems, which in turn sells other companies the rights to incorporate PostScript into their laser printers and typesetters. So far, the list of PostScript printers includes the Apple LaserWriter IINT and IINTX, the QMS PS 810, the QMS PS Jet printer retrofit kit, the QMS JetScript retrofit kit, the IBM Personal Pageprinter, the TI OmniLaser, the Compugraphic CG 400-PS laser printer, the 1690-dpi Linotronic 200 phototypesetter, the 2540-dpi Linotronic 300 typesetter, and many others.

The first notable feature of PostScript is that it allows device independence; that is, files created for any one of the printers listed above can be printed on any other (with certain exceptions related to differences in the amount of RAM built into the printers).

The second notable feature of PostScript is that it uses fonts generated from outlines. This method is vastly superior to the alternative, which is to store the actual pattern of dots in each font as a bit map. With PostScript's outline method, fonts of any size can be generated from a single outline, and only one master outline file needs to be stored for each typeface. The Adobe collection of fonts includes scores of commercial typefaces licensed from the ITC, Mergenthaler, Stempel, and Haas type collections.

PostScript makes it possible to apply various graphic effects to type, including rotation, stretching, filling with patterns, and distorting. However, Ventura does not provide commands to exploit these talents. Similarly, PostScript's extraordinary abilities with graphics are not fully tapped by Ventura. The one exception is the Encapsulated PostScript option, which allows special effects written in PostScript to be incorporated into documents. For more information on this format, see Chapter 18, "Encapsulated PostScript."

◆ PCL Level 4 and LaserJet Clones

PCL, or Printer Command Language, is Hewlett-Packard's designation for the set of internal commands used by the LaserJet printer family. The LaserJet Plus, LaserJet II, LaserJet IIP, all feature PCL Level 4, and this version of PCL Level 4 is also built into the LaserJet clones sold by virtually every printer manufacturer.

Compared with PostScript, PCL Level 4 has fairly rudimentary capabilities. Whereas PostScript printers use master font outlines that can be automatically scaled to any size, PCL Level 4 printers must work with fonts at fixed sizes. Despite the fact that there are now software programs such as Glyphix that can automatically create fonts at different sizes for the printer, the absence of font scaling remains a major drawback of PCL Level 4 printers.

PCL Level 4 printers also lack the sophisticated graphics capabilities of PostScript printers, but from a practical standpoint this problem does not actually prove to be much of a hindrance. Most of the graphic effects generated by Ventura as well as by drawing programs like Corel Draw can be printed on a standard PCL Level 4 printer.

When you install Ventura for any PCL Level 4 printer, you should select both the 300-dpi and the 150-dpi LaserJet Plus drivers. Select the 300-dpi driver first so that it is the default driver. (The 150-dpi driver need only be used if you are printing a page with lots of graphics and your printer is short on memory.)

Because there is no formal certification process for PCL printers, some differences between the LaserJet clones and the real LaserJet tend to crop up from time to time. Generally speaking, the clones have no problem in handling fonts in HP format, including the fonts supplied with Ventura. As long as your documents are text-only, using a LaserJet Plus clone is a safe bet.

With graphics, clones sometimes show subtle differences from the LaserJet Plus and LaserJet II. Problems include streaking in scanned graphics or clip art, anomalous vertical lines, difficulty producing all eight shades of gray, and trouble producing graphics in landscape orientation (i.e., across the length of the paper).

Tip 4-2

Testing a LaserJet Clone

If you're shopping for a printer and aren't sure whether it provides a good emulation of the LaserJet Plus, ask the salesperson to print out a copy of SCOOP.CHP, the sample newsletter that is provided with Ventura in the \TYPESET directory. If the clone can handle that newsletter, the emulation is up to snuff.

◆ PCL Level 5

The LaserJet III and IIID feature the newest, highest stage of HP's Printer Command Language, PCL Level 5. The most important new element of Level 5 is the ability to scale fonts within the printer. If you are using the Windows version of Ventura, you can have direct access to these scalable fonts. The DOS/GEM version, however, does not provide a LaserJet III driver, but such drivers are available from VPUG (Ventura Professional Users Group) and from SWFTE International. For access information, see Appendix A, "Resources."

❖ Printing Speed

Speed is a major issue when using a program like Ventura. You want to be working on your document, not sipping coffee while the printer takes its time printing a page. The time it takes to print a document can vary tremendously from printer to printer. A page that requires 4 minutes on one printer may take 20 seconds on another. Two factors determine the speed of a printer.

A big factor affecting the speed of printing is the transmission channel between computer and printer. Many printers, in particular the Apple LaserWriter family, do not have a parallel port and hence must be connected to the computer via a serial cable operating at 9600 baud or via an AppleTalk cable. Neither the serial option nor the AppleTalk option is well suited for PC users: the former is slow, and the latter requires you to buy a special AppleTalk board. Much better is a parallel channel, and as a rule of thumb you should avoid any printer that doesn't provide one.

There's one way of linking a computer to a printer that is even faster than a parallel interface. This is the direct link to the I/O port used by accelerator boards such as the LaserMaster LX series.

The second factor affecting printer speed is the efficiency of the printer's controller and the type of page description language used by the printer. PostScript printers tend to be somewhat slower than other laser printers; PostScript typesetting machines are infamous for their sluggishness. The situation for PostScript is gradually improving, however, as Adobe Systems improves its PostScript controllers. In addition, some of the PostScript clone printers on the market are significantly faster than Adobe Post-Script printers. In addition, it should be noted that Ventura's own PostScript driver has been souped up since the initial release of the program and is now rated at 30 percent faster than before.

If you've already settled on your hardware, you can't do much about the speed of the transmission channel or the speed of the printer itself. However, there are a variety of other techniques that you can apply to speed up the printing process, including downloading fonts ahead of time and using a print cache. These are detailed in Chapter 25, "Printing Tips."

❖ The Printer Capabilities Page

Laser printers differ in their capabilities, and these differences are summarized in a printer capabilities test that is automatically installed on your hard disk when you install Ventura. To use the test, load CAPABILI.CHP from the \TYPESET subdirectory. Printing out this page on your printer gives you the following information:

- What the boundaries of the imaging area are. With most printers, the black border will extend to within about ¼-inch of the edge. The white margin shows the unprintable portion of the page.

- What sizes of fonts are currently available. With printers that use bitmapped fonts, such as the LaserJet II and IIP, you're generally limited to fonts of about 24 or 30 points, though on-the-fly font generators such as Glyphix, FaceLift (for Windows), and Adobe Type Manager (also for Windows) are able to overcome that ceiling. With PostScript printers, the limit is 240 points. With LaserMaster controllers and printers there is no limit.

- Whether your printer can handle transparent and opaque graphics. The LaserJet can print transparent graphics but not opaque; PostScript can print opaque but not transparent.

- Whether your printer can print reversed (white on black) type. PostScript and LaserMaster printers can. LaserJet III printers can as well, though only with a LaserJet III driver. PCL Level 4 printers cannot unless you are using a specially generated white-on-black font.

- Whether your printer can print opaque shaded graphics on top of ruling lines. With the LaserJet, the ruling lines show through.

- Whether your printer can print text at various rotations. PCL Level 4: no. PostScript, LaserMaster, and PCL Level 5: yes.

- Whether the fonts supplied with Ventura for your printer include kerning information. In Ventura 3.0, the answer is yes for both PostScript and LaserJet printers.

- Whether the printer can render type formatted for various colors as different shades of gray.

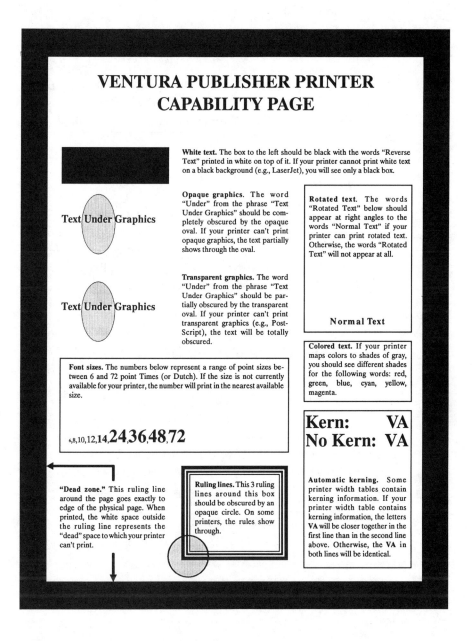

Figure 4-1: *The printer capabilities page produced by an HP LaserJet II printer with 512K of memory.*

Tip 4-3

Parallel Versus Serial

When setting up a LaserJet printer, make sure you select a parallel interface rather than a serial one. That's because serial transmission makes downloading of fonts and graphics is considerably slower.

◆ LaserJet Fonts

Besides the Bitstream-designed Dutch (Times Roman) and Swiss (Helvetica) fonts provided by Ventura for the LaserJet, hundreds of other fonts are available from third-party vendors. For details, see Chapter 21, "Adding New Fonts." For a full-scale treatment of the subject, see Peachpit Press's *The LaserJet Font Book*.

Tip 4-4

How Much LaserJet Memory?

The LaserJet IIP comes with 512K of RAM; the LaserJet III comes with 1MB. As long as you stick to using three or four fonts at a time, don't print any bitmapped graphics larger than about a quarter of a page, and don't use any fonts larger than 30 points, this built-in memory should suffice. If your needs go further than that, you can buy upgrade board from HP or from third-party suppliers such as Pacific Data Products. If you're someone with a big appetite for graphics and large fonts, get 2MB. The 4MB upgrade is only necessary if the printer is used on a network and several people all want to download their own fonts into the printer.

❖ Printer Upgrades

There are several reasons why you might want to upgrade a standard LaserJet or other laser printer: to add PostScript, to speed up printing, or to increase the size and number of fonts available for printing. Fortunately, a number of upgrade options are readily available. These include the LaserMaster LX6, which is a pair of boards that are inserted into the printer and into your computer. More convenient to install are the new PostScript cartridges that install into one of the slots on the front of the LaserJet II, IIP, or III. For details on these cartridges, see Appendix A, "Resources."

When using an external printer controller, such as the LaserMaster LX upgrades, you remove two screws and slip a card in, just like you do in a computer. These cards use the I/O slot to bypass the normal printer controller of the printer, so that the computer sends the image directly to the printer, rather than sending data which the printer must construct into an image.

Image doesn't always mean a painting or drawing. Each letter of a bitmapped font is actually made up of pixels, or dots, to form an image, just like a paint-type graphic. These pictures of letters are combined with other graphics into the image of a single page, which the printer then prints.

Transmission speeds through the I/O slot are much faster than through a parallel cable, and this is one of the speed advantages of cards like the LaserMaster and JLaser.

Tip 4-5

The Missing I/O Slot

Despite the tremendous value of the optional I/O slot, not all SX engines have it. The QMS-PS 810 and the HP LaserJet IIP don't. So before you rush out to buy a Canon-based printer, look in the back for the little I/O slot, gateway to a world of wonder — or at least speed.

Profile—————————————————————————————

LaserMaster

Considering what they offer — speed and higher resolution at an affordable price — it's not hard to see why LaserMaster's various printer controllers amnd plain-paper typesetters have taken the desktop publishing market by storm. At the low end is the LX series of controllers, which are upgrade boards that you install in your computer and connect with a special cable to the back of your LaserJet (except the IIP), Canon LBP, or IBM laser printer. At the high end is the LM1000 Plain Paper Typesetter, which comes complete with board and printer. The LX controllers increase the resolution of the printer to anywhere from 400 by 400 TurboRes to 800 by 800 TurboRes, depending on the model. The LM1000 Plain Paper Typesetter offers 1000 by 1000 TurboRes quality.

Note that LaserMaster avoids rating its controllers in terms of dots per inch and instead uses the term TurboRes. That's because, strictly speaking, 800 by 800 TurboRes only means 800 dots per inch in the horizontal direction. In the vertical direction, the actual resolution is 300 dpi, which LaserMaster enhances using a patented method of controlling the size and placement of laser printer dots. The enhancement is real, but whether 800 by 800 TurboRes is really just as good as 800 by 800 dots per inch is debatable. To really judge the quality of LaserMaster output, have your dealer print out a sample for you and compare it to actual imagesetter output. This book, by the way, was printed on a LaserMaster 1000 using converted Adobe Type 1 fonts, and then photographically reduced at the printer by 18 percent.

Besides the higher quality of type from TurboRes technology, the LX controllers are also extremely fast. The only time I've seen my unit slow down is when it's attempting to deal with pages containing TIF graphics or large numbers of   fonts.

The LX controllers vary in price from around $1,500 to $5,000, depending on whether you opt for the 400 by 400 model with 35 fonts or the 800 by 800 model with 135 fonts. The LM-1000 costs about $7,500 (including the printer itself, software, and fonts), and the LM-1200 (see below) weighs in at $16,000 (including printer, software, and fonts — plus $2,500 a year for a service contract, a standard requirement on all large format, high-res printers). Compared to the costs of other high-resolution printers and imagesetters, such as Linotronics starting at around $25,000 and other high-resolution lasers priced at over $10,000, these are a great value.

◆ Tabloid News

The latest thing from LM is the new 11- by 17-inch printer, 1200 dpi "TurboRes" printer, which can crank out *twenty-five* 8- by 11-inch pages or *fourteen* tabloid-size pages per minute. It comes standard with 16 megabytes of memory (expandable to 32) and can handle up to 25,000 pages a month.

The speed and high duty-rating make this a great "on-demand" printer for churning out impressively high-quality originals. This printer is great not only for printing tabloid size pages, but its extra size makes it easy to print camera ready 8- x 11-inch pages with bleeds, something you can't do on an 8- x 11-inch printer. And the high-resolution means you can print impressive photos at up to 133 lines per inch.

Compared head to head with other high-end lasers in terms of resolution, speed, and cost, the LM-1200 is in a class by itself.

◆ Fonts-a-plenty

All these systems come with 135 typefaces. That's right, not 35, but 135. The faces include the standard 35 that are resident in most PostScript printers, plus 100 others for your dining and dancing pleasure. As a font critic myself, I have to say that these faces are currently not as good as Bitstream or Adobe's offerings, although LaserMaster's new font division, "Digital Type Corporation," is working to improve them. The faces are acceptable, and type *is* a subjective matter, but if you're a type connoisseur you may prefer Bitstream or Adobe renditions of classic faces.

That poses no problem, however, as all LaserMaster systems can use fonts in both the Adobe PostScript Type 1 format and the Bitstream Fontware format *complete with hints,* so there are literally thousands of typefaces to choose from. You simply run your Bitstream or Adobe fonts through LaserMaster's font conversion utility and store them on your hard disk in LaserMaster's own scalable LXO format. Plus, if you work with a LaserMaster DPS-1 for your display, the same printer font files do double duty as onscreen scalable fonts.

By the way, the core 35 fonts that come with all the LaserMaster controllers are PostScript width compatible, and because of this you can proof pages on the LaserMaster and then send them to a Linotronic for final printing while still retaining perfect character and line spacing.

◆ Special Font Effects

Besides speed and smooth, crisp type, LaserMaster has a few more neat little tricks up its board. A drop-down menu in Ventura allows you to access a score of special effects. You can rotate fonts in 1 degree increments, rather than the standard 90 degrees available in Ventura. You can create outline type, or fill type with gray. You can also break Ventura's 256 point font-size limit. And one especially useful and wonderful effect allows you to create "either/or" type. If the background is white, the type prints black, if the background is black, the type prints white. Most interestingly, even if the background changes right in the middle of a character, the type is always the opposite of the background.

◆ Printing Complex Pages

Printing complex pages can be a problem for other printers. LaserJets are limited in the number of typefaces that can reside in the printer at once. PostScript printers without hard disks can run out of memory when you try to use too many faces on a page.

But in all the time I've used a LaserMaster, I've *never* had a page refuse to print for any reason. In my latest book I created a complex table that helps you see which typefaces work well together. The table displays the typeface names in their actual typefaces, so there are 61 different typefaces on a single page, with type in three orientations at once. If that weren't enough, the page also contained ruling lines and gray backgrounds. Printing this page (in a single pass) would be out and out impossible on most other printers, but the LM-1000 printed it in a mere 30 seconds.

◆ What About PostScript Graphics?

The only drawback to the LX controllers is that they're not Post-Script compatible. This limitation means that these boards are much faster, but it also means that Encapsulated PostScript files won't print.

The EPS matter is a problem *only* if your EPS files contain fountain fills, dotted lines or other special PostScript effects. If they don't, you can easily export the graphics in your drawing program to GEM or CGM and have them output as smoothly as they would from EPS. Unfortunately, neither CGM or GEM support fountain fills (or dotted lines from Corel), so if you need them, you need EPS. Since TrueImage is PostScript compatible, EPS files (and TrueType) will be supported when TrueImage is implemented.

Another downside is that the LaserMaster printers don't work with all software. Ventura, WordPerfect, Word, and anything that runs under Microsoft Windows will print. Nothing else will. You can still use your LaserJet like a LaserJet, without having to switch cables or change anything, but it will just be a LaserJet with other programs, and the speed and quality of the LaserMaster will soon spoil you for anything else.

5

Monitors

As ecumenical with monitors as it is with laser printers, Ventura gives you options ranging from the 80- by 35-dpi resolution of the IBM Color Graphics Adapter (CGA) standard up to the 150- by 150-dpi resolution of the most expensive full-page monitors. Prices also vary widely, from a mere $200 or so for a Hercules-clone graphics board and an accompanying amber monitor, to $2,000 or more for some 21-inch dual-page models. At the low end, some standards exist that make it simple to mix and match equipment. At the high end, shopping and installation is complicated due to the absence of standards and the fact that such monitors tend to push personal computers to the limits of their performance.

In addition to the general information here on monitors, you can find information on specific monitors in Appendix A, "Resources."

❖ Monitor Lingo and Standards

Every monitor comes in two parts: the monitor itself and the adapter (also called the controller), a board in the computer that is connected via cable to the monitor. Monitors are generally classified according to their resolution, which is measured in horizontal pixels by vertical pixels.

Virtually every kind of monitor used with the IBM PC can be used with Ventura, except the Monochrome Display Adapter (MDA), the text-only "green screen" commonly used for word processing. The lowest resolution is provided by the Color Graphics Adapter (CGA). Its resolution is 640 by 240 pixels, or about 80 by 35 pixels per square inch.

Surprisingly, the resolution of Ventura on a CGA, though somewhat coarse, is still adequate for some types of work. I used Ventura on a CGA for several months and found the resolution acceptable even for creating complex layouts such as forms and brochures. The big drawback of using Ventura in CGA mode is that you can't read most text in Normal view, which is possible in EGA and HGC (Hercules Graphics Card). Another annoying problem with the CGA is that when you attempt to select and move a small frame or a small box text graphic, you may inadvertently change its size. Otherwise, the CGA works well: when you need to read text, you merely switch into Expanded view.

One step above the CGA on the scale of resolution are the Enhanced Graphics Adapter (EGA) and the Hercules Graphics Card (HGC). The EGA provides 640 by 350 pixels, or about 80 by 51 pixels per square inch. The resolution of the Hercules Graphics Card is slightly better: 720 by 348 pixels, or about 90 by 51 pixels per square inch.

Using Ventura with an EGA or a HGC board is much more comfortable than using it with a CGA board. With the EGA or the HGC, most text is readable in Normal view, ruling lines and frame boundaries are crisper, and it's much easier to move or stretch frames and boxes.

The advantage of the Hercules card over the EGA is that it can be used with a standard IBM Monochrome Monitor or an inexpensive monochrome monitor such as a Samsung, priced at around $100. In addition, many makers of IBM XT or AT clones provide a Hercules clone board as standard equipment on their machines.

With a Video Graphics Adapter (VGA), resolution is somewhat better than either the EGA or the Hercules at 640 by 480 pixels, or about 80 by 70 pixels per inch. Another advantage of the VGA is that each pixel can display various intensities of gray, allowing an amazing realism in gray-scaled images.

Tip 5-1

Hercules Clones

The most economical monitor/adapter combination is a Hercules adapter with any monochrome monitor. Hercules clones are much cheaper than the real thing and usually just as good.

Profile

Soft Kicker
(the $99 Full-Page Monitor)

Attention EGA or VGA graphics owners: if you don't use the Soft Kicker from Aristocad, you should have your head examined. I don't say things like that very often, but for only $99 ($139 for the Windows version) you could have all the advantages of a full-page monitor and make the time you spend with Ventura much more productive. If you've never heard of the Soft Kicker before, you're excused, but if you read this profile and still don't want one, well...

What the Soft Kicker does is make Ventura think you're using a full-page 1024- by 1024-pixel monitor. Ventura creates a full-page work area (or virtual page) and stores it in the memory of your

EGA or VGA card. Your screen then becomes a window on this full page.

But unlike normal Ventura, where you have to use the scroll bars and wait while the screen redraws, the Soft Kicker pans around this big screen any time the mouse nears the edge of the screen. The entire page scrolls, allowing you access to any part of the page without having to use the scroll bars. You're working at full-size, but you still can move smoothly, easily, and instantly to any part of the page, without even having to wait for Ventura to redraw.

◆ ZAP Mode

On a VGA monitor, Soft Kicker also allows you to see the entire page on-screen at once, using something akin to a super-enhanced "reduced" mode. On an EGA, this same capability gives you three-quarters of the page. Press the second mouse button and you are instantly in "ZAP" mode. In this mode not only is the text more readable than in the normal reduced mode, but Soft Kicker adds a small magnification window to the sidebar on the left side of the screen. As you move the mouse around the reduced screen, this window simultaneously shows a full-size picture of where you are on the screen. This means you can do detail work, even in reduced mode, while seeing the entire page on-screen. Going from normal view to ZAP reduced view (with the magnification window) is virtually instant — Ventura doesn't have to redraw the screen between normal and ZAP mode.

This may not sound like much at first, but think about these common scenarios:

- You're trying to mark some text. You start the mouse at the top of the screen and then — oh no — all the text doesn't fit in one screen. You could go into reduced view, but then the text is either greeked or impossibly tiny. With the Kicker, the screen automatically scrolls when the mouse nears the edge, so this is no problem at all.

- Suppose you have many graphics on a page and Ventura is taking a while to redraw the screen. Sure, you could turn some of the pictures off, but you really need to see how they all look together, and you're getting bored with waiting for Ventura to redraw the screen each time you move or go into reduced view. With the Soft Kicker this is no problem because Ventura only draws the screen once. You move around without redraw, and even go into full-page ZAP view without redrawing. Seeing the Soft Kicker in action is worth the price of admission. The bottom line is: you save a lot of time.

◆ Software Compatibility

Because the Soft Kicker is software, it doesn't affect how your EGA or VGA works with the rest of your software. You can still do everything you could before, only now it's like you have a full-screen monitor as well. The same Kicker screen drivers you use with Ventura also work perfectly with all GEM applications, such as Artline. Installation is fast and easy and mimics Ventura's own installation, so it seems familiar right off the bat. It's even considerate enough not to change or overwrite the original VP.BAT or VPPROF.BAT files you've used to start the program. After installation you type SK or SKPROF to start Ventura using the Soft Kicker. Of course, once you've used Ventura with the Kicker I don't see any reason why you'd want to use Ventura without it.

The optional Soft Kicker Plus package allows you to have kicker power with any programs that run under Microsoft Windows, such as Corel Draw or Micrografx Designer. Soft Kicker Plus does everything for Windows that it does for Ventura, with the exception of the Zap mode.

The Soft Kicker isn't a luxury — it's an absolute essential for anyone with EGA or VGA; if I were shopping for Ventura utilities, it would be at the top of my list.

❖ Large-Screen Monitors

The big drawback of using standard monitors with Ventura is that you have only a fraction of your page on the screen at once. As a result, when you're working on a page, you suffer the annoyance of making lots of mouse trips over to the scroll bar to move the page up and down. Ironically, as explained below, large-screen monitors won't necessarily free you entirely of those trips to the scroll bar. But the ability to work with larger portions of the page at once and to read very small type is definitely a boon to productivity.

Large-screen monitors divide into two strata. The lower tier, which includes the Wyse and the Genius, are priced as low as $700. These monitors arc smaller and do not let you see the full page in Normal view, so you still do quite a bit of scrolling. The higher tier monitors cost in excess of $2000. Many of these monitors use the 16½ inches wide by 12½ inches wide, easily large enough to let you see (and read) two full pages in Facing Pages view.

Tip 5-2

Measuring Large-Screen Monitors

Monitors are typically referred to by the diagonal measurement of the screen. Thus, monitors measuring 15 inches by 12 inches are often referred to as "19-inch" monitors and monitors measuring 16½ inches wide by 12½ inches wide are referred to as "21-inch" monitors.

My bottom-line opinion on large-screen monitors is that despite the high prices, they are a tremendous value because of how much faster you can work and how much less tired you are at the end of a work session. At the same time, because of the various issues described below (especially speed and quality of screen fonts), you should never buy one of these products until you have a chance to really try it out under realistic conditions (i.e. with a document that you typically work with). For specific product information on large-screen monitors, refer to Appendix A, "Resources." The following are some general factors that you should consider as you check out systems.

◆ Screen Fonts

It's essential that your monitor have screen fonts in the standard sizes you use for type, such as 10 and 12 points. Without screen fonts, Ventura has to draw each character individually. Not only does this result in type that is difficult to read, but more seriously it drags down the speed of the display dramatically. Don't get involved with any monitor that doesn't have a full set of screen fonts.

◆ Aspect Ratio of Pixels

Some monitors have square pixels, others rectangular ones. For desktop publishing, square pixels are definitely preferable, since laser printers and typesetting machines universally use square pixels. If your monitor doesn't have square pixels, your image of the final page will be distorted — either stretched vertically or horizontally.

Tip 5-3 ─────────────────────

Not-So-WYSIWYG

The Wyse WY-700, perhaps the most popular high-resolution monitor in use, has pixels that are taller than they are wide. As a result, pages appear to be narrower on the screen than when printed.

◆ Size of Display

The reason large-screen monitors are known as "full-page displays" is that all of them can display an entire page of text — 66 lines — when used with a word processing program. The benefit here is obvious: if you can work with an entire page at a time, you don't have to scroll up and down the page. Most of the "full-page" monitors don't actually let you see an entire page when used in Ventura's Normal view. For example, the Xerox monitor cuts off about an inch on the side of the page; the Wyse cuts off about an inch at the bottom of the page.

◆ Flicker

Large-screen monitors have to display an immense number of pixels; to do so, some use a technique called "interlacing," which means that every other scan line is refreshed during each cycle. Interlacing is apt to produce annoying flicker, though noninterlaced displays may also produce flicker if they don't refresh the screen often enough.

◆ Heat and Power

Large-screen monitors and the boards that drive them draw lots of power and tend to produce lots of heat. If your computer is already running a bit on the hot side, you may need to install a larger power supply to handle the new monitor.

◆ Software Compatibility

Some monitors have been around long enough so that drivers now exist for many popular programs. With monitors that have been introduced more recently, you may find it difficult to use your favorite graphics program. Note that it's not enough to verify that your software will work with the monitor. You'll also need to find out whether the quality of the display is adequate. For example, when some monitors are emulating the CGA or EGA standards, they squeeze the display area into the upper left portion of the screen, making text excessively small. Make sure that you're buying something you can use with your software.

Tip 5-4

There's Still Hope

Ventura Publisher 2.0 and 3.0 both allow drivers to be installed for peripheral devices that were not supported in the program. Even if a particular large-screen monitor does not appear on the list of supported devices, you'll still be able to use it with Ventura if the manufacturer provides you with a driver.

◆ Primary versus Secondary Display

Some full-page monitors are designed to be used as the only monitor with your system. These are called "primary displays." Other monitors, called "secondary displays," can only be used if a standard graphics board (usually an EGA board) is installed in your computer as well. Make sure you know what kind of monitor you are getting.

◆ Ease of Installation

Some monitors require a substantial level of technical expertise to install and operate effectively. For example, if you have EMS memory and are installing the Viking 2, you may have to adjust the hexadecimal codes of the EMS memory addresses to avoid a conflict between that memory and the Viking 2 controller. While the installation manuals for some monitors are quite good, most are poorly written and excessively technical.

◆ Contrast

Some monitors allow contrast to be adjusted, a desirable feature in dealing with various lighting conditions.

◆ Cabling

Surprisingly, some large-screen monitors come with relatively short cords, a real drawback if you want to use the monitor for teaching purposes or move it aside so that you can run another monitor.

◆ Computer Compatibility

If you are using an IBM compatible or clone, you can generally expect to run into some compatibility difficulties when you attempt to install a full-page monitor. Make sure the vendor has tested the monitor with the type of computer you intend to use it with.

◆ Edge Effects

Some monitors, such as the Genius, run the image right up to the edge of the screen, which can cause some distortion at corners and edges and make it difficult to work on those parts of a page. Other monitors, such as the Viking 2, leave a roomy margin surrounding the active area of the screen and hence avoid such distortion.

◆ Orientation

For creating documents, it makes sense to have a monitor that is taller than it is wide (since that's the shape of the page itself). Some monitors, including the Xerox and the Genius, are of the tall variety but may be slightly too thin, since they cut off some of the right edge of the page in Normal view.

Tip 5-5

Portrait and Landscape

"Portrait" refers to monitors that are taller than they are wide. "Landscape" refers to monitors that are wider than they are tall. The terms derive from the characteristic shapes of portrait and landscape paintings.

◆ Graphics Coprocessors

Although a large-screen monitor is supposed to make you more productive, some put such a large computational burden on the computer's CPU that they slow down Ventura's operations to an unacceptable degree. The answer is a new generation of graphics coprocessor chips, introduced by Intel, Texas Instruments, Hitachi, and others. Whatever you do, don't burden a normal XT with a large-screen monitor that lacks a coprocessor.

◆ Use with a Mouse

Some monitors provide drivers for a variety of mice; others support only one mouse, a factor that can be a major nuisance if you don't happen to have that mouse.

◆ Health Effects

Yes, Virginia, computers do produce electromagnetic radiation, and the sort of radiation they produce has been tied to biological effects in animals such as chickens and miniature swine. The main culprit appears to be ELF (extremely low frequency) radiation, which is produced by the flyback transformer at the rear of the monitor. Over the past few years, a growing number of researchers have concluded that low-intensity ELF radiation may pose a health risk. Why? One theory proposes that since the body itself uses ELF fields to govern inter-cellular processes, external ELF fields have the potential to interrupt those processes, affecting the body's hormonal and immune systems.

Of course, it isn't just computer monitors that produce electromagnetic radiation. So do high voltage electrical transmission lines, electrical substations, and even local transformers — those cylindrical objects attached to power poles in streets and alleys. Household appliances also produce electromagnetic radiation. The difference is that you don't sit within a foot or two of an operating Cuisinart for hours at a time, the way you sit in front of your monitor. Note: besides monitors, the other household appliance that has caused concern is the common electric blanket.

Naturally, large corporate organizations such as the Electric Power Research Institute (EPRI) have tended to pooh-pooh such concerns. In at least one instance they have even suppressed discoveries by their own researchers of biological effects caused in animals by ELF radiation. (See Paul Brodeur's account in *Currents of Death* of the suppression of the results of animal studies conducted by EPRI.) So don't hold your breath waiting for the computer industry or the government to do anything about the problem.

Here are some practical things you can do now:

- **Stay in front!** This is the most important piece of advice, especially for people who work in a room with several monitors. Measurements show that the ELF fields are much stronger on either side and possibly in back of a monitor than in front of the monitor.

- **Keep your distance!** ELF radiation decreases rapidly as you move away from the source. An easy rule to remember is the "Hitler salute." If you're a full arms-length away from your monitor, you're probably OK.

- **Consider black-and-white over color!** Color monitors emit far more radiation than monochrome monitors.

- **Spread the word!** There have been a number of excellent articles recently. See *PC Magazine*, "Lab Notes," December 12, 1989; *Macworld*, "Commentary," July 1990; and *Currents of Death* (1990) by Paul Brodeur, published by Simon and Schuster. Brodeur's book is derived from a ground-breaking three-part series of articles he wrote for *The New Yorker* in the spring of 1989.

- **Agitate!** It's not hard to design and build monitors that produce less radiation. The standards in European countries are stricter than in the U.S., and computer companies readily comply over there. If even one percent of the people who use PCs raised a stink and demanded stricter radiation standards for monitors, I think the standards would be put into effect.

Wyse WY-700

This monitor has extensive software support, due to the fact that they have been on the market longer than most other large-screen displays. With its combination of low price and high resolution, these are probably the best values on the market.

Unlike the other monitors described here, the WY-700 is not a true "full-page" monitor. The screen is slightly larger than a standard display: 10 inches wide by 7.5 inches tall. Resolution is 126 pixels per inch horizontally by 105 pixels per inch vertically, a density somewhat higher than that of most high-resolution monitors, and more than four and a half times that of the EGA. In Ventura's Normal view you can see about 60 percent of the length of the page and 95 percent of its width.

Unfortunately, the WY-700 does not have square pixels. The aspect ratio of pixels is 1.2, which means they are slightly taller than they are wide. Hence, the proportions of a document on the screen are different than on the printed page.

Besides working with Ventura, the WY-700 works with GEM, Windows, PC Paintbrush, HALO, AutoCAD, Lotus 1-2-3, Symphony, and most other graphics and CAD packages. If software doesn't specifically support the WY-700's high-res mode, the monitor is compatible with CGA. While CGA still has low resolution, it *looks* better on the WY-700 than on regular CGA monitors. Any text-based program (including word processing programs) will work fine, with the characters being exceptionally large and sharp. Text programs display as white characters on a black background, not black characters on a white background.

The WY-700 is able to clearly display 8-point type in Ventura, but it is *not* a full-page screen. It will display considerably more of a page than a Hercules monitor, but less than the Genius or Laser-View. In Facing Pages view, it shows two full pages side by side at about two-thirds of actual size. While the clarity of this monitor makes even reduced pages readable, it may not suit you if you need to see an entire page, actual size. Although it's comfortable to work with, mine occasionally develops an annoying flicker, and some shades of gray in Ventura appear as striped, instead of as solid, even grays.

If you work with Ventura day in and day out, you'll probably find that the WY-700 is a bit too small for comfortable use. I used this monitor to lay out the second edition of this book, and I must say that the strain of trying to read text on the screen eventually caused me to switch back to using a regular VGA monitor with SoftKicker.

Profile ———————————————————————————————

Radius TPD

Radius made its name developing large-screen monitors for the Macintosh. Its monitors for the PC, the 19-inch Radius TPD/19 and the 21-inch Radius TPD/21, feature the same elegant hardware engineering as its Mac monitors. The TPD mounts on a swivel stand that is easy to adjust, and both the power and the contrast/brightness controls are right up front for easy access.

A notable feature of the TPD is its ability to display shades of gray. However, the monitor does have several drawbacks. With the model I tested, the menus for Ventura, both in the Windows and the DOS/GEM version, were too high on the screen and in fact were partially hidden. With the driver for the DOS/GEM version, the monitor occasionally showed annoying interference patterns in the form of stray pixels shadowing text. Of course, such adjustment problems can affect any monitor as large as the Radius TPD, so when you buy such a monitor, make sure that a service technician is easily accessible.

LaserMaster GlassPage 1280 and DPS-1 Graphics Card

While WYSIWYG has long been the buzzword of desktop publishing, sometimes the reality has been more like WYSIPMWYG (What-you-see-is-pretty-much-what-you-get). That's all changed, thanks to LaserMaster, a company known for its fast printer controller boards.

While LaserMaster's previous boards scaled fonts "on-the-fly" for the printer, the company's newest creations, the DPS-1 and the GlassPage do the same thing on your monitor. Since the screen fonts are scaled from the same Bitstream outlines as the printer fonts, what you see is really and truly what you get. No matter what size font you request, from 3 point to 250, the on-screen font is as sharp as the monitor can produce. No more "close-enough"—everything is letter perfect.

The GlassPage 1280 includes a controller board and a large-screen monitor. The DPS-1 is a controller board that takes a standard multiscan monitor, boosts resolution to 800 by 555 (800 by 600 tends to flicker on multiscan monitors), and gives it a "virtual area" of 1024 by 1024 (the size of a big-screen monitor). When the mouse touches the edges of the on-screen area, everything scrolls automatically (a feature which should have been included with Ventura), allowing you access to the rest of the page. You have complete access to the entire page, even when highlighting long blocks of text, or tagging paragraphs. While it doesn't have all the advantages of a big-screen monitor, it's very fast and works with a relatively inexpensive multi-scanning monitor.

Scanners

The purpose of a scanner is to convert two-dimensional or three-dimensional images into a digital form that can be processed by computer software and printed. Scanners can be classified into two varieties, optical and video, depending on the method they use to convert a continuous image into a digital form.

◆ Optical Scanners

In the optical method, a bright light is scanned back and forth across a page, recording the intensity of the image at each point in a fine grid. The advantage of these scanners is that they are faster and more precise than video scanners. Optical scanners are the most widely used type. They come in a variety of forms:

- flat-bed scanners, which resemble small copy machines
- sheet-fed scanners

- hand-held scanners that you move across the image
- print-head scanners that attach to the head of a dot-matrix printer and scan an image line-by-line as it moves through the printer

◆ Video Scanners

Video scanners are less common than optical scanners. As the name implies, they work in conjunction with a video camera, processing the video signal into a digital one. The advantage of video scanners is that they can be used to process three-dimensional images.

❖   Scanning Software

Most scanners are sold along with a software program that is used to set the parameters for the scanning process and also provide some editing capabilities. In addition, some graphics programs such as PC Paintbrush IV Plus, Publisher's Paintbrush, and Halo DPE can be used to control the scanner. For example, to scan an image from PC Paintbrush Plus, you select the Scan option from the Page menu. This brings up a dialog box that lets you specify brightness, contrast, scanning mode, type of dithering, and resolution. Once you have selected the options you wish to use, you select OK. The scanner then scans the picture and loads it automatically into PC Paintbrush IV Plus. With either of these programs there is an option on the menu that allows you to select the area of the page you want scanned. This pre-cropping is extremely useful, since it allows you to save storage space on your hard disk by scanning less than the full 8.5- by 11-inch area. You also can specify whether you are scanning line art or images, and select a dithering pattern.

After you have used Paintbrush to scan the image, you can use Paintbrush's graphics tools to clean up stray pixels or otherwise alter the image. Then you can save it as a PCX file, a format recognized by Ventura. Other formats that can be used to store scanned images are GEM IMG, EPS, and TIFF.

❖ Black-and-White versus Grayscale Scanners

Lately, the scanner world has begun dividing up into two camps. In one camp are scanners that save an image as an array of 0's and 1's, with 0's representing white and 1's representing black. Technically, this is known as saving an image in a single "bit plane," since each pixel in the image is recorded with a single digital bit, either 0 or 1.

The alternative is to record each pixel in the image as a number between 0 and 256, where 0 stands for white, 256 for black, and the numbers in between for shades of gray (some scanners set the range from 0 to 16, others from 0 to 64, but the principle remains the same). The most commonly used file formats for storing images, PCX (PC Paintbrush) and IMG (GEM Paint), can't handle this sort of grayscale information. But a new format has been developed for grayscale images, called TIFF (Tagged Image File Format), and Ventura 2.0 can handle images in that format.

◆ Displaying TIFF

One of the delights of TIFF images, provided you have a gray-scale monitor such as a VGA (not an EGA or Hercules), is that they are displayed with almost photographic realism. The irony, which is explained later in this chapter, is that the image won't look anywhere near as good when printed on a regular 300-dpi laser printer. To get decent output of a TIFF image, you need to move up to the resolution of a phototypesetter, preferably a 2540-dpi Linotronic 300 rather than a 1690-dpi Linotronic 200.

An alternative output option is a board from Intel Corporation called the Visual Edge. This board works with the HP LaserJet II and requires that you have at least 2MB of EMS memory in your computer. With the Visual Edge, you can print grayscaled images of approximately newspaper quality: 80 dots per inch and 64 levels of gray. A Ventura driver and a PC Paintbrush driver are provided with the board.

◆ Memory Demands

The lack of any cheap output devices is one factor that currently limits the popularity of grayscaled images. Another is the enormous memory and storage demands that such images make on the computer. For example, a 4-inch by 4-inch photograph sampled by the scanner at 300 dpi with 256 levels of gray takes up 1.5MB of memory or storage. Fortunately, data compression techniques are available that can reduce the amount of storage by as much as 85 percent. Still, if you're serious about scanning, you'll need a big hard disk and a good method of archiving your pictures.

Tip 6-1

What to Look for in a Scanning Program

Here are some features that you should look for when buying scanning software:

- *What formats can it save in? In a grayscale scanner, TIFF is mandatory; in a black-and-white scanner, you'll definitely want PCX.*

- *Does it offer data compression?*

- *If it's a grayscale scanner, can it save 256 levels of gray? That's how many you'll need to print the full range of grays available on a PostScript typesetter.*

- *If it's a grayscale scanner, does it let you manipulate the gray scales? Specifically, can you change the gray-value curve to improve the appearance of a particular picture?*

- *Does it let you print a quick-and-dirty proof of the scanned image? This is a critical time-saving feature.*

Does it let you easily draw a box on your screen around the part of the image you want to save? Manually typing in margins is the awkward alternative.

Tip 6-2

What's the Best Grayscale Editing Program?

The consensus favorite for grayscale editing programs is Xerox's Gray/FX. Not only is it powerful, but it's easy to use. For access information and a brief profile, see the "Graphics Software" section of Appendix A, "Resources."

❖ The Problem with Laser Printers

Because laser printers do such a nice job of imitating typeset text, you'd expect that they could also print photographs that look at least as good as, say, a newspaper. After all, as anyone who has looked at them closely knows, a photograph in a newspaper (and in any other sort of publication as well) is actually just a matrix of dots, right? The problem is that those dots in the newspaper photo are of varying sizes. Television uses this same effect, varying the intensity of each pixel to create various shades of gray. So does a grayscale monitor such as a VGA.

Unfortunately, there isn't yet a laser printer on the market that can vary the size of its pixels (though that may change soon, with reports appearing about new circuit boards that can tweak the electronics of the laser printer and cause it to print pixels of different sizes).

To get around this limitation, laser printers resort to two techniques, "synthetic halftones" and "dithering." In a synthetic halftone, pixels are clumped together to create the appearance of dots of varying size. In dithering, dots are printed in semi-random patterns that are denser in darker areas of the picture, less dense in lighter areas.

Neither technique produces very good results. In a synthetic halftone, the printer has to clump anywhere from 1 to about 36 pixels together to form each dot, and therefore can't print 300 dots per inch any more. With dithering, the random patterns give the picture a computer-made appearance.

The inevitable conclusion is that you should avoid scanning photographs and printing them on a laser printer, unless you're willing to settle for mediocre-quality images in your publication. Instead, it's best to simply create a block marking where the image is to be placed, take the photograph to a graphic arts shop, and have a halftone made.

However, if you're printing your publications on a PostScript imagesetter (preferably a Linotronic 300), you'll get great results. The resolution of these machines is high enough that you can create a 160 dot-per-inch halftone with 256 levels of gray. While a resolution of 160 dpi may seem low, it's actually quite satisfactory for almost any sort of publication, since halftones produced using traditional methods range from around 75 to 150 dpi.

❖ Scanning Line Art

Although laser printers can't handle shades of gray, they do a fine job with black-and-white images. In the graphic arts, such pictures are called "line art." (Unfortunately, this term is used in a different sense in Ventura. In the Load Text/Picture menu, "line art" refers to object-oriented graphics formats such as CGM and HPGL.) Scanners are great tools for digitizing any sort of line art such as a logo or a piece of clip art. Simply save it in PCX or IMG format, touch it up with PC Paintbrush IV Plus or some other program, and load it into Ventura as an "image" file. (For more on this, see Chapter 15, "Using Graphics.")

Tip 6-3

Scanning Hardcopy Clip Art

Although this won't be news to graphic artists, others may be surprised to learn that you can buy collections of professionally-drawn images, called clip art, in graphic arts stores and reproduce them to your heart's content in your publications. Why doesn't this violate copyright laws? Because the clip art companies obtain art from old books whose copyrights have expired, or else they create it themselves and grant purchasers the right to reproduce it.

Profile

Hewlett-Packard ScanJet Plus

The Hewlett-Packard's ScanJet Plus uses the same sheet-fed Canon engine as several other scanners, including Canon's own model. But the ScanJet Plus has several distinguishing features. First, the ScanJet is easy to install — no need to change any dip switches. Second, the ScanJet can save 16 levels of gray, as opposed to just black and white for many other scanners. Third, the ScanJet can actually scan up to 600 dots per inch. Fourth, the software program provided for driving the ScanJet, called Scanning Gallery, is well implemented and packed with convenient features. You can print either the whole image or a portion to determine where to crop, then you can save in PCX or IMG format. IMG format can be imported directly into Ventura. Pictures in PCX format can also be imported by Ventura, but in doing so Ventura must first generate a matching IMG file, which eats up space on your hard disk. For grayscaled images, Scanning Gallery can save in TIFF format, which can also be imported into Ventura.

Using Ventura

7

Managing Files

If you're like most people, your first exposure to personal computing was through word processing. When you use a word processing program, keeping track of files is simple, since each document you create is stored in exactly one file. When you need to send a document in the mail or over a modem, you merely transfer that file onto a floppy disk using the DOS COPY command.

With Ventura, file management is no longer so simple. Any document you create will comprise at least several files, and in many cases a dozen or more. Some of these are the text and graphics files you created with other programs and now are merging together with Ventura. Others are files generated by Ventura itself.

Text Files	Bitmapped Graphics Files
MultiMate or MS Word (DOC) WordStar (WS) ASCII or XyWrite(TXT) Xerox Writer (XWP) WordPerfect (WP) DisplayWrite and Samna (DCA)	PC Paintbrush (PCX) GEM Paint and Halo DPE (GEM) MacPaint (PNT) Tagged Image File Format (TIF)

Chapter File (CHP)

Contains pointers to text, graphics,
and internally generated files.

Object Graphics Files	Files Generated By Ventura
Lotus and VideoShow (PIC) CGM (CGM) MacDraw (PCT) AutoCAD Slide (SLD) Encapsulated PostScript (EPS) Hewlett-Packard Graphics Language (HPG) GEM Draw (GEM) Mentor Graphics (P__) Windows (WMF)	Style Sheets (STY) Captions and Box Text (CAP) Program Status (INF) Publications (PUB) Backups ($__) Indexes and Tables of Contents (GEN) Print to Disk Files (C00) Internal Graphics (VGR)

Figure 7-1: *This schematic shows how the chapter file knits together other types of files, including text files, graphics files, and files generated by Ventura itself.*

❖ Why Pay Attention to Files?

It's easy — too easy, perhaps — to generate one document after another and never pay any particular attention to the various seemingly obscure files that Ventura generates as you go about your work. Eventually, however, you will have to learn what those files are and deal with them directly. Here are two examples of when that might be necessary:

- If storage becomes tight on your hard disk, you'll need to start removing some of the documents stored there, which means removing the family of files associated with that document. One of the notable oversights in Ventura's design is that the program provides no easy way to delete a chapter and all its files. You'll have to do it using DOS commands.

- If you begin working with long documents or documents that include multiple graphics, you'll probably run into difficulty at some point getting a chapter to load. In that situation, a potential solution (described in detail in the tips at the end of this chapter) is to rename or move certain files associated with the chapter.

❖ Underlying Concepts

The key concept underlying Ventura's design is that a desktop publishing program should act as a hub for other programs, rather than being an all-powerful megaprogram. Hence Ventura does not replace existing tools such as word processors and graphic programs; instead, it provides avenues for you to import existing text files and pictures into the program. This "don't reinvent the wheel" philosophy is key to understanding the function of Ventura's chapter and style sheet files.

◆ Every Document is a Family of Files

Like Ventura, other desktop publishing programs merge graphics and text, but typically they merge the various files into one immense document file. Ventura's approach (and one of the keys to its remarkable speed) is to keep all the files separate, but to manage them as a coordinated group. Thus every document is a family of files. At the head of the family is the chapter file (CHP), which contains pointers to the location and contents of the other files. The categories and extensions of the other files shepherded by the chapter file is shown in Figure 7-1.

❖ The Chapter File

The job of the chapter file is to act as master of ceremonies for the document. It contains pointers that keep track of the following:

- The text and graphics files that make up the contents of a document.

- The style sheet file, in which Ventura stores the names of all the tags and the formatting information associated with each tag.

- The files generated by Ventura itself to store the contents of captions and headers, internally generated graphics, and other internal information.

Because Ventura's chapter file merely contains pointers to other files, rather than absorbing them into one enormous master program, you can continue to edit and change those files even after you have merged them to create a Ventura document. No matter how much you scale or distort a graphic within the Ventura document, the graphics file itself remains completely unaltered. Text files are altered somewhat, in that Ventura inserts the names of tags as well as codes for character attributes such as boldface. Generally speaking, the changes Ventura makes in original text files do not get in the way of reusing the same files when you have to revise the document — a real boon if you are creating manuals that need to be periodically updated.

Another real benefit of Ventura's use of the chapter file as the hub is that the text, graphics, and style sheet files used for a document need not all be located in a single directory on the hard disk. The chapter file keeps track of the other files not only by name but by location. Thus, you might use one picture for several different documents, or apply the same style sheet to two different chapters.

❖ The Style Sheet File

Style sheet files, identifiable by their STY extension, are devoted mainly to storing the attributes of tags. In addition to storing tag specifications, the style sheet file contains the page size and orientation, widow and orphan settings, autonumbering settings, footnote settings, and margin and column settings for the underlying page.

Each chapter uses one style sheet — you can't have more than one style sheet attached to a single chapter at a time, even if the chapter comprises several text files. On the other hand, you can switch style sheets after you have formatted a chapter.

❖ INF Files

While the chapter and style sheet files are the two main files created by Ventura when you lay out a document, a third set of files should also be noted. These files include VP.INF or VP-WIN.INF (depending on whether you are using the DOS/GEM or Windows version), EGAFSTR.INF or VGAFSTR.INF (depending on whether you are using EGA or VGA screen fonts), and EGAFHDR.INF or VGAFHDR.INF (also depending on the type of screen fonts). All INF files are stored in the \VENTURA directory.

Have you noticed that Ventura always remembers what preferences you have for whether a ruler is shown on the screen, what directory you last looked into to find a graphics file, or whether pictures are shown or hidden? Even if you quit the program, load it again, and choose a different chapter to work on, those settings will remain in force. Keeping track of the myriad of user-selectable options is the job of the INF files.

While the VP.INF or VPWIN.INF file contains most of the information on user-selectable defaults, EGAFSTR.INF and VGAFHDR.INF contain information about screen fonts.

The main reason to know about the INF files is that deleting VP.INF, VPWIN.INF, or EGAFSTR.INF can "cure" certain maladies that occasionally can strike your chapters. These problems and their cures are described in Chapter 30, "Voodoo Tricks."

Tip 7-1

Loading Troublesome Chapters by Deleting the VP.INF or VPWIN.INF File

Sometimes the data in a chapter will become contaminated, causing it to repeatedly crash or fail to load. When this happens, try deleting the VP.INF, VPPROF.INF, or VPWIN.INF file from your Ventura directory. Although this will have the effect of deleting your preferences for onscreen ruler, current printer, etc., it will probably solve the problem you are having with your chapter. (For more details on dealing with chapters that crash or fail to load, see Chapter 30, "Voodoo Tricks.")

Tip 7-2

Recovering Large Screen Fonts by Deleting EGAFSTR.INF

On occasion Ventura appears to lose your large screen fonts. When this happens, the type in large titles will be displayed by smaller fonts. The reason for the problem is that Ventura did not have enough memory available for its screen font buffer, perhaps because too much memory was being taken up by a very large chapter or by a memory-resident utility. The problem is most likely to occur if you are using VGA screen fonts, since these take up more memory than EGA screen fonts. The solution is to delete the EGAFSTR.INF or VGAFSTR.INF file from your Ventura directory. After you have done that, your large screen fonts will work again. (For more details on recovered large screen fonts, see Chapter 30, "Voodoo Tricks.")

Tip 7-3

Saving Multiple Default Configurations (DOS/GEM version)

Let's say that two people are sharing Ventura on one computer, and each has a different set of defaults that he or she wants to use. Or suppose that sometimes you want one set of fonts, and sometimes you want another.

In the DOS/GEM version, the way to maintain two or more default configurations is to use your word processor to add the following switch at the end of the VP.BAT file: /I=DIRECTORY, where DIRECTORY stands for any subdirectory you care to name. You then give this edited batch file a new name, like VP1.BAT or JANE.BAT and use the command VP1 or JANE to start Ventura whenever you want to use the alternate configuration. For example, Jane's batch file, JANE.BAT might look like this:

```
CD C:\VENTURA
DRVRMRGR VP %1 /S=SD_WY705.EGA/M-23/I=C:\DEFAULTS
```

For more details on editing the VP.BAT file, see Appendix A of the Ventura manual.

Tip 7-4

Saving Multiple Default Configurations (Windows version)

Let's say that two people are sharing Ventura on one computer, and each has a different set of defaults that he or she wants to use. Or suppose that sometimes you want one set of fonts, and sometimes you want another.

In the Windows version, you'll need to use the Windows Program Manager to modify the Ventura startup command. Within Windows, switch to the Program Manager (by pressing Alt-Esc) and open up the group that contains the Ventura icon. Usually it is the Applications group. Click once on the Ventura icon, then select Properties from the File menu. Next to Description, it should read

VPWIN

Next to Command Line, it should read

`C:\VENTURA\VPWIN.EXE.`

Change this line so that it reads

`C:\VENTURA\VPWIN.EXE /I=directory`

where **directory** *stands for the subdirectory where you want to save the VPWIN.INF file.*

❖ The PUB File

Most documents consist of a single chapter. At times, however, you may want to group chapters together to take advantage of Ventura's multichapter capabilities (sequential numbering, indexing, automatic table of contents). In that case, you'll work with the Multichapter selection of the Options menu to create a publication (PUB) file. Note that you don't have to create a publication file every time you generate a document with more than one chapter. You can simply print one chapter at a time. As long as you're not interested in automatic number, indexing, and table of contents generation, you'll have no need to create a publication file.

❖ Other Files

Here are some of the other files that Ventura automatically generates as it formats a document:

- Caption files (CAP extension). These store not only text entered into captions, but also headers, footers, empty frames, and text boxes.

- Backup files ($** extension). These files are automatically created by Ventura as you work on a chapter. They are useful for reconstructing your document if the system locks up or crashes.

- Generated files (GEN extension). These are text files created by Ventura when you use the program's capability to generate an index or a caption.

- Print files (C00 extension). This type of file is created on your hard disk when you direct Ventura to print to a file rather than sending information directly to the printer. It allows you to create documents on a computer that lacks an attached printer. Later, you can print the file by typing

COPY *filename*.C00 LPT1:

- Ventura Graphics files (VGR extension). These store graphics that you create using Ventura's graphics tools.

Tip 7-5

Renaming Backup Files

Using a backup file is easy. Just rename it so that the $ is replaced by the appropriate letter. For example, $AP files become CAP files, $IF files become CIF files, and $GR files become VGR files.

Tip 7-6

Controlling the Size of Print Files

If C00 files include downloaded fonts, they may well exceed the size of even a 1.2MB floppy disk. To keep them at a manageable size, avoid including downloaded fonts. Using Add/Remove Fonts from the Options menu, make sure that all the fonts in your document are designated as Resident. When you go to the typesetting service bureau with your print file, inform them that they will have to download these fonts.

❖ Pros and Cons

At this point it may already seem to you that Ventura's way of splitting documents up into numerous files is needlessly complicated. The obvious question is: Why not simply have all the parts of a document combined into one single document file?

As noted above, that is the method used by PageMaker and many other desktop publishing programs. From the standpoint of easily keeping track of things the method clearly has its merits. Ventura's scheme, however, has these advantages:

- It is one of the major factors accounting for the program's unrivaled speed.

- It allows files to be modified after they have been merged together in a document. Since text and graphics files remain separate and remain in their original formats, you can make a small change in a drawing or a chart at the eleventh hour, or continually update a manual even after you've laid it out.

But while Ventura's family-style way of dealing with files has its distinct benefits, it also places a burden on you to organize your hard disk in such a way that all those files don't lead to utter chaos. We'll now turn, therefore, to a review of the tools at your disposal for handling files, and to some suggestions regarding an architecture for organizing those files on your hard disk.

❖ Refresher on DOS

If you've avoided until now the chore of learning how directories, paths, extensions, and filters work, you'll need to acquaint yourself with these terms as well as several DOS commands.

The DOS operating system provides a simple method for organizing computer files. At the highest level of organization are the floppy and hard disk drives used by your system, which are assigned letters, followed by a colon. Normally drives A and B are floppy disk drives. Drive C is normally a hard disk drive. Since DOS cannot handle drives larger than 32MB, a 40MB hard disk is typically partitioned into drive C and drive D. In addition, a block of RAM can be set up to appear to the system as a very fast drive; this is normally drive E.

Each drive, such as C or D, may contain files and directories. Each directory may in turn contain additional subdirectories or files. Any file can be described in terms of the directory and subdirectories in which it is located, and this is known as the path to the file. Files are further identified by their names (up to eight characters) and an extension of three characters, which typically describes the type of program that created the file.

◆ Creating Directories

To create a new directory on drive C, let's say NEWDOCS, you type the following from the DOS prompt:

MD C:\NEWDOCS

You can also do this within Ventura (DOS/GEM version) via the DOS File Ops option in the Files menu. To create the NEWDOCS file from Ventura, execute the following steps:

- From the File menu, select the DOS File Ops option.
- Backspace across the existing File Spec and type
  C:\NEWDOCS
- Select MAKE DIRECTORY.

In the Windows version, you have two options for creating new directories. One is to switch to the Main Menu of the Program Manager by pressing Alt-Esc, and then clicking twice on the DOS icon or the File Manager icon. If you decide to go the File Manager route, you can create directories from the File menu.

In both versions of Ventura, removing directories is similar to creating directories. Remember, though, that before you can delete a directory you must first delete all the files in the directory.

Once you have created a directory, you can create a subdirectory within that directory. To create the subdirectory C:\NEWDOCS \MARCH from the DOS prompt, you type

MD C:\NEWDOCS\MARCH

Alternatively, you can use Ventura's DOS File Ops or the Windows File Manager. Remember that you can't create the subdirectory C:\NEWDOCS\MARCH until you have created the directory C:\NEWDOCS.

◆ Paths, Filters, and Wildcards

No matter which version of Ventura you use, it's useful to understand the concepts of paths, filters, and wildcards. In DOS, a path is simply a sequence of directory names, separated by a backslash (\). It's purpose is to indicate the location of a file. For example, consider the following:

C:\NEWDOCS\MARCH\LETTER1.DOC

In this expression, C:\NEWDOCS\MARCH is the path. The expression means that on the C drive there is a directory called \NEWDOCS, within which there is a directory called \MARCH, within which there is a file called LETTER1.DOC.

If you wanted to know the names of all the DOC files in the MARCH directory, you could use the asterisk wildcard as follows:

DIR C:\NEWDOCS\MARCH*.DOC

If you wanted to know the names of all the DOC files in the MARCH directory that ended with the extension DOC or TOC, you could type

DIR C:\NEWDOCS\MARCH*.?OC

Notice the use of the question mark as a wildcard. Whereas the asterisk can stand for any number of characters, the question mark substitutes for a single character. Thus, it provide a more precise way of locating files.

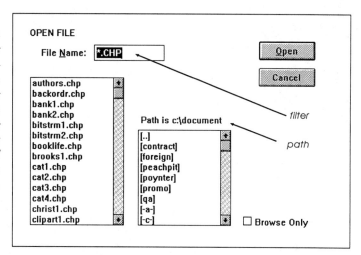

*Figure 7-2: In Windows version's dialog boxes, directories are listed on the right and files in the current path are listed on the left. The **filter** is shown on top and the **path** is shown on the right.*

Any expression that uses wildcards to limit the number of files being show is called a filter. For example, when you select Open Chapter from Ventura's File menu, Ventura automatically uses the filter *.CHP, so that only chapter files will be listed. In the Windows Ventura dialog box shown in Figure 7-2, the path (c:\document) is shown above the list on right. That list tells you all the directories that are contained within c:\document as well as containing [..], [a], and [c]. If you select [..], Ventura will take you one level higher on the path, in other words, to the root directory of the C drive. Alternatively, you can click directly on [a] or [c] to go directly to the root directories of those drives.

Unlike the Windows version, the DOS/GEM version doesn't provide separate lists of directories and files within the current path. Instead, it shows both directories and files in one list. You can tell the two apart because Ventura puts a diamond (◆) in front of directory names (see Figure 7-3). In addition, file names usually, though not always, have an extension, while directory names usually do not.

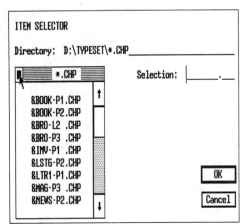

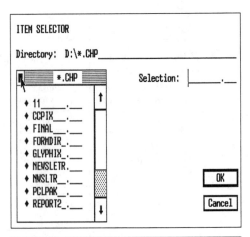

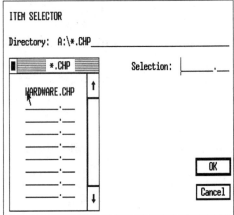

Figure 7-3: *This sequence shows the use of the Backup Button (■) to change directories and select a file. Once the correct file is shown on the Selection line, you can select it by clicking on OK or pressing Enter.*

❖ The Backup Button (DOS/GEM Version)

Many DOS operations, especially searches for files using filters, can actually be conducted from within Ventura. Whenever you load a text file, a chapter, a style sheet, or an illustration, you can save a great deal of time if you learn to use Ventura's easy "step-ladder" method of climbing up and down directory hierarchies. The method, which can be used in any dialog box that contains a Directory line on top and a Selection line on the right, is shown in Figure 7-3.

Let's say you're looking for a chapter file (one with the CHP extension) but aren't sure where it is located on the hard disk. Do the following steps:

- From the File menu, select Open Chapter. Notice that Ventura automatically displays the *.CHP filter on the Directory line.

- Place the cursor on the small black square, known as the Backup Button, in the corner of the scrolling list. As shown in Figure 7-3, each time you click on the Backup Button, you move one rung up the ladder; i.e., one level upward in the hierarchy of directories. After you click on it once or twice, the scrolling box will list the drives on your system — A, B, C, etc.

The diamond in front of the A, B, and C indicates that these are directories, not files. Now you can climb back down the directory hierarchy and see the contents of a particular drive.

- Select the drive on which you installed Ventura. In most cases that will be drive C.

- The scrolling box will now list all the directories in the C drive, as well as all the files in the root directory of the C drive that have the CHP extension.

- Select the TYPESET directory. The scroll bar now displays the list of chapter files in that directory.

- You can now select a chapter from that list. The name will appear in the Selection line at the right. You can now choose that file by pressing Enter or selecting OK.

❖ Hands Off \TYPESET

When you install Ventura, two directories are automatically created on your hard disk: \VENTURA and \TYPESET. The former contains all the program files and fonts, the latter the sample chapter files and style sheets.

You'll find yourself frequently using the style sheets provided with the program, since it's generally easier to modify an existing style sheet than to create one from scratch for the specific sorts of documents you are formatting. Be careful, however, to always save a modified style sheet under a new name. Also, it's highly recommended that you save the modified style sheet in a directory other than \TYPESET, as described below.

By renaming style sheets before you save them, you'll preserve the original style sheets for future use. If, however, you have already modified one of those style sheets and wish to restore the original version to the \TYPESET directory, you can copy it from the Examples disk.

❖ Two Organization Strategies

As I mentioned above, it's not a wise idea over the long run to save the chapters and style sheets you create in the TYPESET directory. Doing so will very quickly cause the number of files in that directory to grow to an unmanageable size and cause real problems later when you have to move files off your hard disk. Therefore, you need to develop an effective structure for files on your hard disk so that you can easily locate the family of files that makes up each chapter. Of course, no single method of organizing a hard disk is appropriate for every type of work. I'll suggest two here; you may find others that work better for your needs. The point is to have a deliberate system.

❖ Plan I: A File Strategy for Short Documents

Perhaps the simplest way of avoiding confusion on your hard disk is by means of the following method:

- Create a directory on your hard disk to contain all your Ventura documents;
- Within that directory, create a unique subdirectory to hold all the files associated with a particular chapter.

This method is good for fairly short documents — i.e., those consisting of a single chapter. This applies to forms, business reports, short technical manuals, and newsletters. Later in this chapter, we'll cover a different method that is suitable for longer documents, such as books and technical manuals.

Figure 7-4 illustrates the first method. On the hard disk, the directory that holds all the Ventura documents is \VPDOCS. Within that directory, a subdirectory is created to hold each new chapter. These subdirectories are given names that identify the type of document within. For example: \FORM1, \FORM2, \BK1, \BK2, \BK3, \BK8, etc. If necessary, you might set up even more levels.

Within each subdirectory are all the files associated with a given chapter: document files, a chapter file, caption files, a style sheet file, image files, etc.

One big benefit of isolating all the files associated with a document is that it automatically provides protection for the style used with that document. Otherwise, if you alter a tag within one publication, perhaps to make the text fit the needs of that document's pagination, you will also affect any other publications you have saved that share the same style sheet.

Another benefit of the one-chapter-per-subdirectory principle is that it allows you to easily move documents from one system to another or to take documents off the hard disk for floppy disk archiving when more room needs to be created on the hard disk.

Here are the specific steps to implement the system I've described above:

- From the DOS prompt, create a directory for all your Ventura documents. Type
  MD \VPDOCS

- Before beginning work on a document with Ventura, create a new directory to hold the document. For example, if the document is a report, type
  MD \VPDOCS\REPORT1
  Copy all text and graphics files into the document directory.

- After you enter Ventura, load the master style you want to use from the \TYPESET directory by selecting Load Diff.

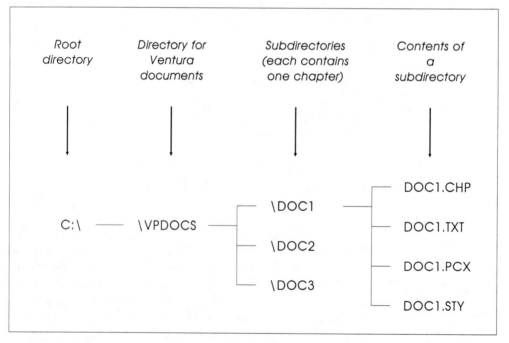

Figure 7-4: A suggested directory structure for single-chapter documents such as newsletters, forms, and directories.

Style from the File menu. Place the cursor on the Directory line, press Escape to remove the entry that is already there, and type

C:\TYPESET\ *.STY

to see the list of styles. Select the style you want to use as the master template for this document. With that style showing on the Selection line, select OK or press Enter.

- Select Save As New Style from the File menu. Place the cursor on the Directory line, press Escape to clear the line, and type

C:\VPDOCS\REPORT1

Then on the Selection line type

REPORT1.STY

and select OK.

- From the File menu, select Save As. Enter

C:\VPDOCS\REPORT1

on the Directory line. On the Selection line type

REPORT1.CHP

and select OK.

If you follow the above steps, each chapter you create will have its own unique directory, containing all the text and graphics files associated with that chapter, along with all the files generated by Ventura itself.

❖ Plan II: A File Strategy for Long Documents

Now let's consider a different procedure that is more appropriate for long documents containing many chapters. It is illustrated in Figure 7-5. In this method you still create a new directory for each document, but not for each chapter of that document. Instead, within the document directory you create a subdirectory for all text files, a subdirectory for all graphics files, and a subdirectory for all style sheets and chapter files. Other files generated by Ventura will automatically be stored with the chapter files.

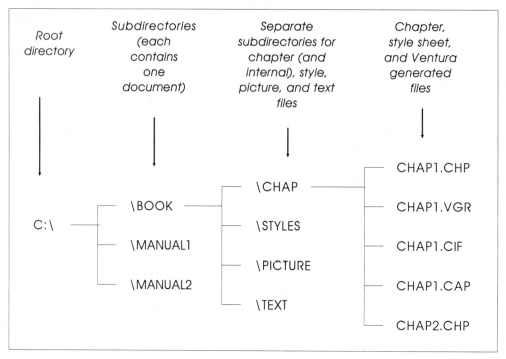

Figure 7-5: A suggested directory structure for mulitple-chapter documents such as books and technical manuals.

❖ Archiving and Transferring Documents

Often it is necessary to transfer all the files associated with a document from one computer system to another. This might be necessary, for example, if the computer used to create the document is not hooked up to a laser printer. Another task that is frequently necessary is to archive all the files associated with a document onto a floppy disk to clear some room on the hard disk.

If you have stored all the files associated with a document in a single directory unique to that document, it is a relatively simple matter to use the DOS Copy command to transfer all the files from that directory onto a formatted blank disk. But watch out: when you later recopy these files onto another computer or back onto the same computer, they must be placed back into a directory with the identical name. For example, if they were originally in C:\VPDOCS\BOOK5 on computer A, they will have to be copied into directory C:\VPDOCS\BOOK5 on computer B.

Why is it necessary to replace them in an identical directory when you use the DOS Copy command to move them? The reason is that Ventura's master file, the .CHP file, keeps track of all the files that make up a document both by name and by directory. If one of the text files that makes up a document is moved to another directory, the program will not be able to find it.

There's another way to transfer documents, which has the advantage of not requiring you to have the same subdirectories on both the source and the destination computer. It is to use Multi-Chapter option (DOS/GEM version) or the Manage Publication option (Windows version).

❖ Using Multi-Chapter or Manage Publication for Backups

In general, moving the files for a chapter onto a floppy and then back onto a hard disk is best done with the Multi-Chapter selection in the Options menu (DOS/GEM version) or the Manage Publication selection in the File menu (Windows version). Despite its name, Multi-Chapter or Manage Publication can and should be used even for backing up a single chapter. Its usefulness is that it automatically finds all the files associated with a given chapter, transfers them to the new location, and alters the pointers in the CHP file to reflect that new location.

You should use the Multi-Chapter or Manage Publication selection no matter which direction you're going: both when you copy a document from a hard disk onto a floppy disk, and when you copy a document from a floppy disk onto a hard disk. Also, you can use it to copy a document into a new directory if you reorganize your hard disk and find this necessary.

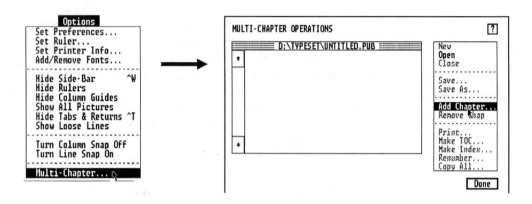

***Figure* 7-6:** *In the DOS/GEM version, use the Multi-Chapter option for backups.*

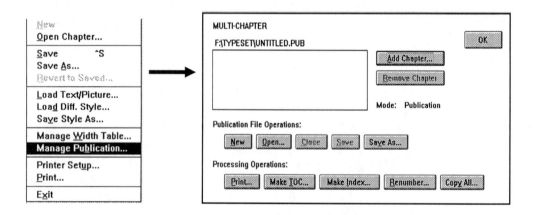

***Figure* 7-7:** *In the Windows version, use the Manage Publication option for backups.*

Here are the steps to follow to copy all the files associated with a chapter onto a floppy:

- **DOS/GEM:** From the Options menu, select Multi-Chapter (Figure 7-6). **Windows:** From the File menu, select Manage Publication (Figure 7-7).

- Select Add Chapter in the dialog box (Figure 7-6 or 7-7). Note: From here on out, we'll just be showing the dialog box for the DOS/GEM version. If you're using the Windows version, don't worry — it looks different, but everything works exactly the same.

- Select the appropriate Chapter file and press OK (Figure 7-8).

- The screen will now show the name of the Chapter file you have selected, as shown in Figure 7-9. In the DOS/GEM version, you now have to click on the Chapter name. If you do not confirm your selection by clicking on the Chapter name, you will not be able to access the Copy All feature.

- Select Copy All (Figure 7-10).

- The screen should list as Source the letter of your hard disk, the directory that your chapter file is in, and the name of

Figure 7-8

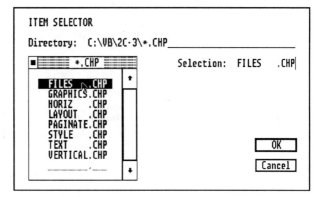

Figure 7-9

Figure 7-10

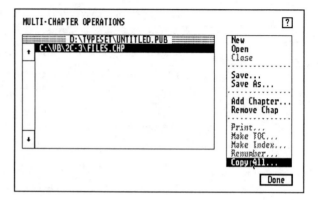

Figure 7-11

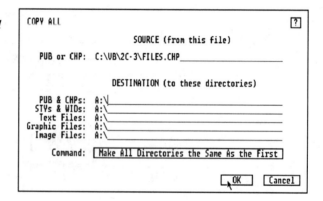

your chapter file, as shown in Figure 7-11. Change the first destination point to A:\. You can save time by selecting the option to Make All Directories the Same. Select OK. Then sit back and relax while Ventura copies your files.

❖ Restoring a Chapter from a Floppy to a Hard Disk

Restoring a chapter back onto a hard disk is similar to the above operation, but it is a little more complicated. The steps are as follows:

- **DOS/GEM:** From the Options menu, select Multi-Chapter. **Windows:** From the File menu, select Manage Publication.

- Select Add Chapter. The dialog box will display the drive letter of the hard disk together with a directory name. Select drive A.

- Ventura will now display a list of the chapter files on the floppy. Select the one you wish to copy and select OK. Now that chapter will appear in the list. In the DOS/GEM version, you now have to click on the chapter name to make Copy All light up.

- Select Copy All.

- A dialog box will appear indicating a source and a destination. The source should be the name of your chapter file in drive A. Type the desired location in the first line and then select Make All Directories the Same As the First. Select OK.

Tip 7-7
File Search Utilities (DOS/GEM)

Because the various files that make up a document can be stored in different subdirectories, you may at times find it difficult to locate a particular file. Two handy utilities for such circumstances are WHEREIS.COM and WHIZ.EXE. Both are available from most public domain software collections, and they're both quite easy to use. WHIZ is reportedly much faster than WHEREIS.

Tip 7-8
The File Search Utility (Windows)

The Windows File Manager includes a handy utility for locating any file on your hard disk. Select Search from the File menu in File Manager. Then type the name of the file you're looking for, using the asterisk and question mark wildcards if necessary.

Tip 7-9

When to Use DOS Copy Rather Than the Multi-Chapter or Manage Publication Option

You can save time by using the DOS Copy command to move a chapter from one computer to another under the following conditions:

- *If all the files used for the chapter are located in a single directory.*

- *If that directory is the same on computers A and B.*

If both conditions are met, you can simply use the command COPY *.* to copy the contents of the directory onto a floppy disk, and then use COPY *.* again to copy them from the floppy onto the second computer.

Tip 7-10

Directory Limits

Having too many files stored in a single directory can slow your system down dramatically. The number varies according to how many buffers you have specified in your CONFIG.SYS file and also depends on whether you are using a disk caching program (the latter will tend to mitigate the problem). As a rule of thumb, however, you should avoid having more than 200 files in any directory.

The place where you will run up against this limit most quickly is in the directory that stores your chapter files. For example, let's say you have created a manual that contains 35 chapters. To store each chapter, Ventura creates a CHP file, a CIF file, and a CAP file. It may also store one or more GEN and VGR files. On average, you can count on there being about 5 files for each chapter, which means that your 35 chapters actually amount to 175 files in the chapter directory. And remember: that's not counting text files, graphics files, and style sheet files, just files generated by Ventura and automatically saved to the same directory as the CHP file.

The best way to avoid ending up with a directory that is too clogged is simply to keep an eye on the number of files, and set up a new directory when the number gets past 150 or so.

❖ File Management Utilities

If you use Ventura often, you'll soon find that its way of handling files can lead to confusion. And for those working in a publication group, with text files and even entire chapters circulating from one computer to another, the confusion is compounded many times over. Fortunately, three utilities, VP Manager, VP Mover, and VPToolbox, can ride herd over your files.

VP Manager is aimed at workgroups. It is a memory-resident program that pops up from within Ventura and provides various ways of categorizing and tracking a document as it moves through successive stages of editing and formatting. The program is described in detail in Chapter 27, "Utilities."

VP Mover makes it easier to transfer your chapters, along with all associated files, from one directory to another. For details, see Chapter 27, "Utilities."

VPToolbox, keeps track of which files are associated with which other files, deleting files that are no longer needed, and identifying files by date, time, and contents. The program is discussed at length in Chapter 9, "Working with Style Sheets." The following are some of the most important file management capabilities of VPToolbox:

- Lists all the files associated with a chapter, tells where they are located, tells how big they are, and tells how many words are in text files;

- Lets you delete, move, or copy a chapter, including all the text and graphics files associated with that chapter;

- Allows you to add comments to chapters, making it easier to identify them at a later date without going into Ventura;
- Prints out a list of the files associated with a particular chapter.

8

Preparing, Loading, and Editing Text

While graphics are certainly a big part of Ventura, text is the meat and potatoes of publishing. This chapter covers the basics of preparing text with a word processor, importing it into Ventura, and editing it within Ventura.

❖ Creating Text

To create text, you can use any of the most popular word processing programs. In addition, you can use Ventura's native text editor to type text directly into a document. As of Version 3.0, the list of word processor file formats that can be imported includes WordPerfect 4.2, WordPerfect 5.0 and 5.1, WordStar, WordStar UK, Microsoft Word, MultiMate, Xerox Writer III, and XyWrite. In addi-

Text Preparation Guidelines

Text Attributes

Text Attributes That Carry over into Ventura

* *boldface, superscript, subscript, strikethrough, underline, discretionary hyphen, and nonbreaking space.*

Attributes That Ventura Ignores

* *justification, margins, centering, headers, and fonts.*

Tabs

* *Tab characters are carried over, but positions set for tabs in the word processor are not.*

Line Endings

ASCII Text

* *Separate paragraphs with two carriage returns.*

* *Import into Ventura as an ASCII file.*

Word Processed Text

* *Separate paragraphs with one carriage return;*
  or
  Separate paragraphs with two carriage returns and include @PARAFILTR ON = as the first line of the file before importing.

* *Import into Ventura under the appropriate word processor format.*

Table 8-1: *The main rules of thumb for preparing text prior to importing it into Ventura.*

tion, files in DCA (Document Content Architecture) version 2.0 can also be imported. Word processors that can produce text in DCA format include Displaywrite III and IV, Volkswriter 3, Office Writer, WordStar 2000, Samna Word, and Lotus Manuscript.

Unfortunately, the Windows version cannot import text directly from Word for Windows. You have to save your Word for Windows files in ASCII or DOS Word format before importing them.

Text Limitations

Size of Imported Files	4MB	*2MB without EMS. If the size of the file exceeds available memory, it will be spilled out to the hard disk (or to a RAM disk). When this happens, you'll notice a definite reduction in performance even if the file is smaller than 2MB.*
Number of Paragraphs Per Chapter	1,000 per 16K of memory	*This is an approximate figure that depends on how much memory is taken for other uses such as graphics.*
Number of Tags Per Chapter	128	*The number of tags that can be included in a style sheet is 128. This includes tags you have created and tags generated by Ventura. In addition, if the text you are importing includes tags that are not included in the current style sheet, they too will be counted. If the total is more than 128, the file will not be loaded.*

Table 8-2: Limitations for imported files, paragraphs per chapter, and tags per chapter.

In addition to regular word processed files, Ventura also has the capability to load spreadsheet print files (PRN extension) directly into tables. This feature is discussed in Chapter 11, "Tables."

Finally, Ventura can load plain ASCII text, which means that you can format Sidekick note files, Lotus 1-2-3 spreadsheets, dBASE files, and files created by other spreadsheet and database programs. Generally, converting the output of such programs into ASCII format is done by creating a print file, that is, by specifying a file on your hard disk rather than the printer itself as the printing destination. For example, in Lotus 1-2-3, the command sequence to create a print file is /Print File. When you create a print file, make sure you first set your margins to zero.

Tip 8-1

Importing Troublesome ASCII Files

Ventura refuses to import some ASCII files and instead responds with the error message "You're trying to load a file containing a paragraph that is larger than 8000 characters. This has corrupted memory, so quit as soon as possible." The reason for this error message is that Ventura expects to see a single hard return at the end of each line of an ASCII file and a double hard return separating paragraph. But some ASCII files don't have a hard return at the end of each line and only have a single hard return at the end of each paragraph, leading Ventura to think that the whole file is a single enormous paragraph. The solution is to tell Ventura that the file is a WordStar file.

In the case of dBASE III Plus, the way to create text for import is to use the TO FILE option with either the REPORT command or the LABEL command.

❖ Attributes: Converted and Ignored

In preparing text that will later be imported into Ventura, the following attributes in the word processed file will be automatically carried over when that file is loaded into Ventura: boldface, superscript, subscript, strikethrough, underline, discretionary hyphen, and nonbreaking space. Discretionary hyphens are hyphens that will only be printed if they occur at a line break. Nonbreaking spaces are spaces that will not be broken by automatic word wrap; they are used if you want to keep a particular combination of words all on the same line.

Other formatting done using your word processing program will not carry over once you have loaded a text file into Ventura. And when you save the chapter containing that file, the formatting will be lost in the original file. This implies that when you prepare text for Ventura you shouldn't waste time setting margins, centering headlines, and the like.

On the other hand, it is possible to embed a variety of special formatting codes in text files, a procedure known as "preformatting." Preformatting may be appropriate in work environments where writers and editors need to specify certain formatting information to the production staff. By embedding the appropriate codes in your text files, you can specify words to be printed in boldface, for example, or lines to be bulleted. The topic of embedded codes is covered below. First, however, we need to mention a couple of peculiarities in how Ventura handles line endings and tabs.

Tip 8-2 ————————————————————————————

Avoid Double Spaces

If you ever took a typing course, you were probably taught to type two spaces after every sentence. When preparing text for Ventura, you should avoid doing so or else do a search and replace to get rid of double spaces. The reason is that Ventura converts the first space into a normal space but converts the second space into a non-breaking space.

❖ Line Endings

In standard ASCII format, line endings are indicated with a carriage return, the same character used by Ventura to denote the end of a paragraph. Obviously, it wouldn't make sense for Ventura to make each line of the ASCII text file a separate paragraph, so Ventura simply ignores any isolated carriage returns it encounters. When the program encounters two carriage returns in a row, however, it substitutes a paragraph break. Thus, when creating an ASCII file, press Enter twice to separate your paragraphs.

With spreadsheets, you do want every line of information to constitute a separate paragraph once the file is imported into Ventura; otherwise, separate lines would run together and wrap around continuously rather than breaking. The solution here, after creating a print file from Lotus, is to load the file into Ventura as a WordStar file.

Unlike ASCII, most word processor formats do not use a carriage return to indicate a new line. Like Ventura itself, they reserve the carriage return command to indicate new paragraphs. Thus, Ventura doesn't have to filter out solitary carriage returns from such files. With ASCII files, it was recommended above that you press Enter twice between each paragraph. With files in word processor formats, that's not necessary; in fact, if your files do have two carriage returns between every paragraph those carriage returns will result in an extraneous blank paragraph once the file has been imported.

Many people, of course, are in the habit of pressing Enter twice between paragraphs in order to make the text more readable. You can continue to do that if you embed the following command on the first line of your text file:
@PARAFILTR ON =
with spaces both before and after the equal sign. When it en-

counters this command, Ventura will automatically replace double carriage returns with paragraph breaks.

❖ Beware of Tabs

Ventura does allow you to include tabs in your word processed document. However, as discussed in Chapter 10, "Formatting Text," tabs are handled differently by Ventura than by word processing programs. For example, a tab placed in justified text will be ignored. And a tab placed in unjustified text will prevent that text from wrapping onto a second line. So, unless you need to use them for a table or for some other special purpose, avoid including tabs in the files you import. In particular, do not use a tab to indent the first line of a paragraph. Instead, use the In/Out-dent setting from the Alignment dialog box (in the Paragraph menu) to set your indents.

Tip 8-3

Embedding Tabs in Text Files with <9>

If the regular tabs that you're placing in your text files don't seem to be importing properly into Ventura, try embedding Ventura's tab code <9> in the text files instead. If your word processor uses five spaces for tabs, do a search and replace for each occurrence of five spaces and replace the spaces with <9>. If the tabs still don't work, make sure that the paragraph you're trying to place a tab in is not justified and make sure each of the tabs is turned on in the Tab Setting menu.

❖ Dashes and Quotation Marks

Remember high school typing class, when they taught you to type an Em dash as two hyphens? The reason was that the standard typewriter keyboard did not include a true Em dash mark (—).

That deficiency has carried over to the standard computer keyboard, which also lacks an Em dash. Similarly, the keyboard lacks true open-and-closed quotation marks.

Within Ventura's text editor, you can enter an Em dash by holding down the Alt key while typing 197 on the numeric keypad. Alternatively, if you include the number 197 in angle brackets (like this: <197>) when you originally create the document, Ventura will automatically replace the <197> with a dash. An even simpler way to include an Em dash in a document is simply to type two hyphens in the original document. Then load the document. If you have selected "Auto-Adjustments: " and - - " (or Both) under Set Preferences in the Options (DOS/GEM version) or Edit (Windows version) menu, all double hyphens will be converted to Em dashes, and all paired quotation marks will be converted to true quotation marks. Ventura uses a special algorithm to determine whether to convert quotation marks. Obviously, it doesn't make any sense to convert every instance of " to true quotation marks, since this piece of punctuation by itself is used to indicate seconds and double primes.

According to some typographers, there should be no space on either side of an em dash—like this. Other typographers prefer that there be a thin space on either side — like this. If you prefer the latter, you can use search-and-replace to embed the code for a thin space in your document. The code is < | >, or you can insert the thin spaces in Ventura with Ctrl-Shift-T.

Tip 8-4

Makeshift Quotation Marks

Some fonts, including those that use the unextended ASCII character set and those that use Hewlett-Packard's Roman-8 character set, lack true open-and-closed quotation marks. In many cases, the following is an easy solution. For left quotation marks, type the grave accent, located in the upper left corner of your keyboard under the tilde (~), twice; for right quotation marks,

Figure 8-1:
Codes embedded
in text files can
contain a variety
of information. In
this example from
Microsoft Word,
code **A** *causes*
Ventura to ignore
any double
carriage returns it
finds in the
document; **B** *is*
an embedded tag
name; and **C** *is*
the code for an
open quotation
mark. Note at **D**
that no embedded
tag is necessary
for Body Text.

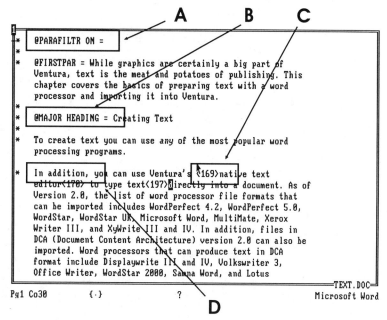

type the apostrophe twice. Whether this works or not depends on
the typeface. In some typefaces the grave accent does not match
the apostrophe, while in others it does.

❖ Embedding Formatting Information

Embedded formatting is a topic that you don't need to concern yourself with while you are learning Ventura. At first, you can simply create your text with your word processing program and do all the formatting within Ventura. However, after you become proficient at formatting within Ventura, you may decide to explore the possibilities for embedding special formatting codes in your original text files. There are two possible reasons for using embedded formats:

- In organizations where one work group prepares text and a different work group lays it out with Ventura, embedded

Embedded Codes

Breaks and Spaces

Line Break .... <R>
Discretionary Hyphen .... <->
Non-Breaking Space .... <N>
Thin Space .... <|>
Figure Space .... <+>
En Space .... <~>
Em Space .... <_>
Tab .... <9>

Character Attributes

Boldface .... <B>
Italics .... <I>
Medium Weight .... <M>
Light Weight .... <L>
Small .... <S>
Underline .... <U>
Double Underline .... <=>
Overscore .... <O>
Superscript .... <^>
Subscript .... <v>
Color Index (where 0 is white, 1 black, 2 red,
3 green, 4 blue, 5 cyan, 6 yellow, 7 magenta) .... <Cn>
Reset to Original Color .... <C255>
Turn Off Special Attributes .... <D>
Typeface (where n is the typeface ID number)...................... <Fn>
Reset to Original Typeface .... <F255>
Baseline Jump .... <Jn>
Kerning/Tracking .... <B%n>
End Kerning .... <D%n>
Point Size .... <Pn>
Return to Original Point Size .... <P255>

Table 8-3: *These codes can be used to format text with a word processor prior to importing.*

Special Codes

Footnote ....<$F*text of footnote*>
Picture Anchor (same page) ....<$&*anchor name*>
Picture Anchor (below) ....<$&*anchor name*[v]>
Picture Anchor (above) ....<$&*anchor name*[^]>
Picture Anchor (automatic)...............................<$&*anchor name*[-]>
Hidden Text ....<$!*text*>
Hollow Box ....<$B0>
Filled Box ....<$B1>
Current Chapter Number....................................... <$R[C#]>
Current Page Number ....<$R[P#]>
Fraction .... <$E*numerator/denominator*>
Fraction .... <$E*numerator* over *denominator*>
Index ....<$Primary[Primary sort];Secondary[Secondary sort]>

Table 8-3 *(continued)*

formatting may provide a way of giving the first work group a larger role in formatting text.

• Embedding codes, especially with the aid of a keyboard macro program, is frequently faster than doing the formatting within Ventura.

◆ Tags

To apply a tag to a paragraph, type the @ sign, then the name of the tag, then a space, then the = sign, then another space. Note: the @ sign must be in the first line and column of the paragraph. Figure 8-1 shows an example of a text file with embedded tags.

◆ Breaks and Spaces

To force a line break, insert <R> at the point where you want the line break to occur. To insert a discretionary hyphen, insert <->. For other codes, see Table 8-3.

◆ Character Attributes

Character attributes include bold, italic, medium, small, super-script, subscript, underline, double underline, strikethrough, and overscore. The codes for such attributes are shown in Table 8-3. Note that any time you want to return to the default character attributes, you embed the code <D>. For example, if you have formatted a word in bold with <B>, you end the bold passage with the code <D>, not with a second <B>.

◆ Special Codes

You can embed formatting information for footnotes, anchors, hidden text, boxes, and other special features. See Table 8-3.

◆ Nonkeyboard Characters

Only those characters in the ASCII range below 127 are displayed on the keyboard, yet Ventura's International character set, which is the character set used by the fonts provided with Ventura as well as by many other fonts, includes characters numbered from 128 to 255. These include symbols needed by European alphabets, graphics symbols, typographic symbols, and special symbols. To embed a nonkeyboard character in text, insert its ASCII code within angle brackets. For example, to insert the © sign, insert <189> at the appropriate place in your text. A list of codes is provided in Table 8-4.

If you want to use symbols from the Symbol font or ITC Zapf Dingbats, you'll also have to embed a code that causes Ventura to switch to that font (<F128> for the Symbol font, <F129> for ITC Zapf Dingbats), then embed the code for the character you want (see Tables 8-5 and 8-6), then the code to return Ventura to the default font (<F255>).

For example, the code to embed the character ♣, which is character number 135 in the Symbol font, is <F128><135><F255>.

Ventura International Character Set

128	Ç	153	Ö	178	Ø	203	Ë
129	ü	154	Ü	179	ø	204	Ì
130	é	155	¢	180	œ	205	Í
131	â	156	£	181	Œ	206	Î
132	ä	157	¥	182	À	207	Ï
133	à	158	¤	183	Ã	208	Ò
134	å	159	ƒ	184	Õ	209	Ó
135	ç	160	á	185	§	210	Ô
136	ê	161	í	186	‡	211	Š
137	ë	162	ó	187	†	212	š
138	è	163	ú	188	¶	213	Ù
139	ï	164	ñ	189	©	214	Ú
140	î	165	Ñ	190	®	215	Û
141	ì	166	ª	191	™	216	Ÿ
142	Ä	167	º	192	„	217	ß
143	Å	168	¿	193	…	218	-
144	É	169	"	194	‰		
145	œ	170	"	195	•		
146	Æ	171	‹	196	–		
147	ô	172	›	197	—		
148	ö	173	¡	198	°		
149	ò	174	«	199	Á		
150	û	175	»	200	Â		
151	ù	176	ã	201	È		
152	ÿ	177	õ	202	Ê		

Table 8-4: *The code assignments for the nonkeyboard characters of Ventura's International character set. To embed these characters in a file prior to importing the file into Ventura, type the code number in angle brackets. For example, to insert ‡ in text, type <186>. Once the file is loaded into Ventura, you can embed a nonkeyboard character into text by holding down the Alt key while typing the code on the numeric keypad. For example, to insert ‡ from within Ventura, type Alt-186.*

Symbol Font Character Set

33	!	60	<	87	Ω	114	ρ
34	⊃	61	=	88	Ξ	115	σ
35	#	62	>	89	Ψ	116	τ
36	∃	63	?	90	Z	117	υ
37	%	64	≅	91	[	118	ϖ
38	&	65	A	92	∴	119	ω
39	∋	66	B	93	]	120	ξ
40	(	67	X	94	⊥	121	ψ
41	)	68	Δ	95	_	122	ζ
42	*	69	E	96	‾	123	{
43	+	70	Φ	97	α	124	|
44	,	71	Γ	98	β	125	}
45	–	72	H	99	χ	126	~
46	.	73	I	100	δ	127	
47	/	74	ϑ	101	ε	128	
48	0	75	K	102	φ	129	ϒ
49	1	76	Λ	103	γ	130	′
50	2	77	M	104	η	131	≤
51	3	78	N	105	ι	132	/
52	4	79	O	106	φ	133	∞
53	5	80	Π	107	κ	134	*f*
54	6	81	Θ	108	λ	135	♣
55	7	82	P	109	μ	136	♦
56	8	83	Σ	110	ν	137	♥
57	9	84	T	111	o	138	♠
58	:	85	Y	112	π	139	↔
59	;	86	ς	113	θ	140	←

Table 8-5: *The Symbol font character set. Note that there are no symbols associated with ASCII 127 or 128. Also, some PostScript printers cannot print character 208.*

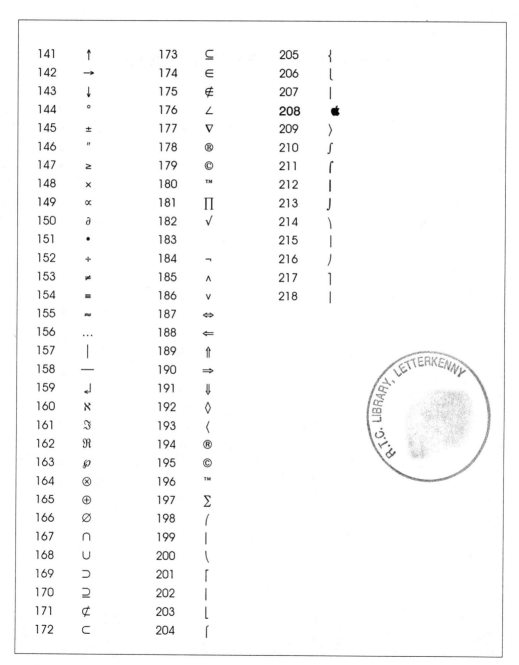

141	↑	173	⊆	205	{
142	→	174	∈	206	⎩
143	↓	175	∉	207	⎪
144	°	176	∠	**208**	
145	±	177	∇	209	⎭
146	″	178	®	210	∫
147	≥	179	©	211	⎧
148	×	180	™	212	⎪
149	∝	181	∏	213	⎩
150	∂	182	√	214	⎞
151	•	183		215	⎟
152	÷	184	¬	216	⎠
153	≠	185	∧	217	⎤
154	≡	186	∨	218	⎥
155	≈	187	⇔		
156	…	188	⇐		
157	∣	189	⇑		
158	—	190	⇒		
159	↵	191	⇓		
160	ℵ	192	◊		
161	ℑ	193	⟨		
162	ℜ	194	®		
163	℘	195	©		
164	⊗	196	™		
165	⊕	197	∑		
166	∅	198	⎛		
167	∩	199	⎜		
168	∪	200	⎝		
169	⊃	201	⎡		
170	⊇	202	⎢		
171	⊄	203	⎣		
172	⊂	204	⎡		

Table 8-5 *(continued)*

ITC Zapf Dingbats Font Character Set

33	✂	60	♣	87	✳	114	❐
34	✐	61	†	88	✳	115	▲
35	✁	62	☥	89	✳	116	▼
36	✂	63	✝	90	✺	117	◆
37	☎	64	✠	91	✷	118	❖
38	✆	65	✡	92	✳	119	◗
39	✇	66	✢	93	✳	120	❘
40	✈	67	✣	94	❀	121	❙
41	✉	68	✤	95	✿	122	❚
42	☛	69	✥	96	❁	123	❛
43	☞	70	◆	97	❂	124	❜
44	✌	71	✧	98	❂	125	❝
45	✍	72	★	99	✹	126	❞
46	✎	73	☆	100	✺	127	
47	✏	74	✪	101	✼	128	
48	✐	75	✫	102	❃	129	❡
49	✑	76	✬	103	✳	130	❢
50	✒	77	★	104	✳	131	❣
51	✓	78	✭	105	✳	132	❤
52	✔	79	✮	106	✳	133	❥
53	✕	80	✰	107	✳	134	❦
54	✖	81	✱	108	●	135	❧
55	✗	82	✲	109	○	136	♣
56	✘	83	✳	110	■	137	◆
57	✙	84	✴	111	❏	138	♥
58	✚	85	✵	112	❐	139	♠
59	✛	86	✶	113	❑	140	①

Table 8-6: *The ITC Zapf Dingbats Character Set. To use this character set, you need a PostScript printer or a LaserMaster enhancement board for the HP LaserJet. Note that there are no symbols associated with ASCII 127, 128, and 208.*

141	②	172	❸	203	⇦
142	③	173	❹	204	⇦
143	④	174	❺	205	⇨
144	⑤	175	❻	206	⇨
145	⑥	176	❼	207	⇨
146	⑦	177	❽	208	
147	⑧	178	❾	209	⇨
148	⑨	179	❿	210	⊃
149	⑩	180	→	211	➤+
150	❶	181	→	212	↘
151	❷	182	↔	213	➤+
152	❸	183	↕	214	↗
153	❹	184	↘	215	↘
154	❺	185	→	216	➤+
155	❻	186	↗	217	↗
156	❼	187	→		
157	❽	188	→		
158	❾	189	→		
159	❿	190	→		
160	①	191	➠		
161	②	192	➠		
162	③	193	➡		
163	④	194	➢		
164	⑤	195	➢		
165	⑥	196	➤		
166	⑦	197	➥		
167	⑧	198	➡		
168	⑨	199	▶		
169	⑩	200	➡		
170	❶	201	⇨		
171	❷	202	⇨		

Table 8-6 *(continued)*

Tip 8-5

An Easy Way to Figure out Embedded Codes

If you want to embed formatting codes in your text with your word processor, but aren't sure how to set up the codes, format some text in Ventura and save it, then load the file back into your word processor. Make a note of the codes or save them as word processor macros.

Tip 8-6

Rules about Embedded Codes

Here are four rules to guide you in using embedded codes:

1. Two codes can be combined. For example, <F135><M> can be compressed to <F135M>.

2. Any new text attribute series cancels out all previous attributes.

3. The code <D> returns the text to the default attributes.

4. All attributes return to the defaults at the end of a paragraph, even without <D>.

❖ Loading Text

Once you have created a text file using your word processor (or by generating a report file or print file with your database program or spreadsheet), you can load the file into Ventura. The procedure for loading text files into Ventura is as follows:

- Select frame mode.
- Create a frame on a Ventura page, or select the base page.
- Select Load Text/Picture from the File menu.
- Select the appropriate file type in the Load Text/Picture dialog box.

- Select List of Files as the destination.

- Using the Item Selector, select the text file. For a detailed explanation of the Item Selector, see Chapter 7, "Managing Files."

- The text file will now be listed in the list of files. To load it into the base page or into a frame, click on the page or the frame, then select the name of the file from the Assignment List.

If the file is not immediately loaded onto the page, select frame mode, select the frame you wish to load it into and again select the name of the file.

❖ Text Destinations

You can specify three different locations into which to load text. Normally, you'll select List of Files, which places the text file in the Assignment List, ready for loading onto the page.

◆ Text Clipboard

If you select Text Clipboard, the file will be loaded into the same location in memory that Ventura uses to store text after you use the Copy Text and Cut Text options in the Edit menu, or after you press the Del key. Once it is in the Text Clipboard, the text can be inserted at the text cursor position by pressing Ins or by selecting Paste Text from the Edit menu.

◆ Text Cursor

The third destination, Text Cursor, lets you immediately merge the text from one file into the text from another. When you select this option, you won't see the name of the file in the Assignment List, and when you load your original file into your word processor, you'll find that the two have been merged. This option has numerous uses, one of which is explained in the following tip.

Tip 8-7

Chaining Text Files Together

By loading a text file into the cursor position at the very end of a chapter, you can chain two text files together within a single chapter. If you also create a tag that contains a Page Break Before and use it to mark the first paragraph of the second file, you can in effect create a multichapter document within a single chapter. For many medium-length documents, this may be more convenient that creating separate chapters and then joining them into a publication.

Tip 8-8

Loading Text from WordPerfect

A trio of utility programs, called WP2VP, VP2WP, and TAGTeam, are available for assisting the work of formatting text in Word-Perfect and then loading it into Ventura. WP2VP gets rid of double spaces at the end of sentences, converts WordPerfect's own footnote commands to Ventura format, and performs other related tasks; VP2WP does just the opposite: it strips Ventura codes from your file, replacing them with the equivalent WordPerfect formatting codes for such things as centering and bold text. TAG-Team automatically converts WordPerfect formats into their Ventura equivalents. For details on these programs, see Chapter 27, "Utilities."

❖ Loading Worksheet Data

There are a variety of tools and methods for loading worksheet data into Ventura documents and formatting it. With most of these methods, you start by setting the margins of the worksheet to 0 and then printing your worksheet to a file (the exception is XVP /Tabs, which lets you load WKS files without first creating a print file). The reason you have to print to a file is that Lotus WKS files can't be loaded directly into Ventura. Having created the print file, you have several options.

◆ Ventura (older versions)

If you are using an older version of Ventura that lacks the PRN-to-Table feature (2.0 base version or earlier), you can select XyWrite format and load the print file into a blank chapter or into an empty frame in a formatted chapter. Since the columns in the print file are separated by spaces rather than tabs, they won't align properly if formatted with a proportional font. Note: Helvetica and Swiss are proportional fonts — Courier is not. You'll have to manually delete all the spaces and insert tabs to separate the columns, a time-consuming process.

◆ Using a Worksheet-Conversion Utility

Manually replacing all the spaces between worksheet columns with tabs is only practical for a very small worksheet. What you need is a tool to make the process automatic. Fortunately, several such tools are available:

CONVERTD: This is a program on the Microsoft Word utilities disk. To prepare a file for CONVERTD, first print your worksheet to disk. To use CONVERTD, you must enter the name of an input file, an output file, a list of the column widths of the spreadsheet, and a delimiter character (Tab). CONVERTD also lets you indicate a list of the rows you wish to convert, and this can be any combination of rows and columns, for example: rows 5, 8, and 16–22. When the program prompts you for the type of file, select the second option (delimited text file).

Tabin and XVP/Tabs: These are two commercial utilities specifically designed to prepare worksheets for importing into Ventura. Besides converting the spaces between columns to tabs, they provide a number of additional features such as adjusting the placement of dollar signs and parentheses around numbers according to accounting conventions. For details on these programs, see Chapter 27, "Utilities."

◆ PRN-to-Table

If you select PRN-to-Table as the text import format, Ventura will automatically create a table to hold your worksheet data. You can then easily adjust the formatting of the table using standard table-editing techniques. If you want to load the worksheet into a separate frame, select "List of Files" for your destination. If you want to place the worksheet directly into your text, select "Text Cursor."

Obviously, the PRN-to-Table feature doesn't give you all the formatting extras that a utility such as Tabin or XVP/Tabs has to offer. If you frequently import worksheet data, you may well find that such a program is well worth the investment.

❖ Ventura's Text Editor

Having loaded a text file into Ventura, you can alter it using Ventura's internal text editor, which is activated when you select the text mode. Note that any changes made using Ventura's text editor will be reflected in your original text file, so if you want to preserve the original version of that file, be sure to make a copy before editing it with Ventura.

The operation of Ventura's text editor is simple and intuitive. To insert text, you place the cursor in the desired spot, click once to insert the text editing cursor, and begin typing. You can move the text editing cursor by using the keyboard cursor keys. Forward deletion is done with the Del key, backward deletion with the Backspace key. To highlight a block of text you hold down the mouse button while dragging it across the desired text. Alternatively, you place the text cursor at one end of the block, then move the mouse cursor to the other end and hold down the Shift key while clicking. Blocks can be cut or copied to the Text Clipboard by pressing Del or Shift-Del respectively, and text in the

Ventura's Text Editing Operations

DEL - Deletes one character to the right of the cursor. Or, if you have selected a passage by dragging a cursor across it, the Del key places the selected passage in the scrap (i.e., saves it for later insertion). You can use this for moving blocks of text.

INS - Inserts material from the scrap at the cursor point.

BACKSPACE - Deletes one character to the left.

CURSOR KEYS - Once you have clicked the mouse while the cursor is within a passage of text, a separate text cursor appears on the screen (a thin vertical line). You can move this with the cursor keys.

HOME AND END - Move you to the first or last page of the document.

PGUP AND PGDN - Move you to the previous page or the next page.

ENTER - Starts a new paragraph.

CTRL-ENTER - Inserts a line break (i.e., starts a new line without starting a new paragraph).

CTRL-HYPHEN - Inserts a discretionary hyphen.

CTRL-SPACEBAR - Inserts a nonbreaking space.

CTRL-SHIFT-F - Inserts a figure space (the width of a numeral in the current font).

CTRL-SHIFT-N - Inserts an En space ($\frac{1}{2}$ the width of an Em space).

CTRL-SHIFT-M - Inserts an Em space (measured as the same size as the current font; for example, in 12-point text an Em space measures 12 points in width, or $\frac{1}{6}$ inch).

CTRL-SHIFT-[or **CTRL-SHIFT-]** Inserts a left or right quotation mark.

CTRL-[- Inserts an En dash

CTRL-] - Inserts an Em dash.

CTRL-SHIFT-T - Inserts a thin space.

CTRL-SHIFT-C - Inserts ©.

CTRL-SHIFT-R - Inserts ®.

CTRL-SHIFT-2 - Inserts ™.

Table 8-7: *Ventura's Text Editing Operations.*

Clipboard can be inserted into a different location by pressing Ins. Table 8-7 summarizes these and other text operations.

Tip 8-9

The Ellipsis Character...

There's a special character in most fonts for typing the ellipsis marks. Use this character (by holding down the Alt key while typing 193 on the numeric keypad) instead of typing three periods.

◆ Inserting Boxes

Many fonts lack the hollow box (□) and filled box (■) characters, so Ventura makes them universally available from the Insert Special Item option of the Edit menu (DOS/GEM version) or the Text menu (Windows version). When you insert them, the boxes take on the font attributes of the tag for that paragraph. To change their size, you can highlight them and use Set Font. To delete a box, place the cursor to the left of it so that the words Box Character are displayed in the Current Selection Box. Then press Del.

◆ Inserting Fractions

To create a fraction, select Insert Special Item from the Edit menu (DOS/GEM version) or the Text menu (Windows version) and select Equation (or Fraction, for the non-EMS version). The equation editing screen will appear. Type the fraction in the form **15 / 16** for a diagonal fraction such as $^{15}\!/_{16}$, or as **15 over 16** for an over-under fraction such as ($\frac{15}{16}$). Then press Ctrl-D to return to the page. The fraction will appear in your text.

Tip 8-10

Adjusting Interline Spacing for Fractions

If you use over-under factions (like $\frac{2}{3}$), make sure you turn on Grow Inter-Line To Fit in the Paragraph Typography menu.

◆ Inserting Page and Chapter Numbers

You can set up Ventura to automatically place the current page number anywhere on the page. The procedure differs depending on which version of the program you're using:

- In the non-EMS version, place the cursor in the desired position in your text, select Ins Special Item from the Edit menu, then select Insert Reference. Select either Page # or Chapter #, and Ventura will automatically make the insertion.

- In the Professional Extension, place the cursor in the desired position in the text, select Ins Special Item from the Edit menu, then select Cross Ref. A dialog box will appear. Don't type anything on the line that says At the Name. Select P# for page number or C# for chapter number. The other options (F#, T#, S*, C*, and V*) do not apply for this purpose.

- In the Windows version, place the cursor in the desired position in the text, select Ins Special Item from the Text menu, then select Cross Ref. A dialog box will appear. Don't type anything on the line that says At the Name. Select P# for page number or C# for chapter number. The other options (F#, T#, S*, C*, and V*) do not apply for this purpose.

❖ Formatting Words within Paragraphs

Most formatting in Ventura is done by means of style sheets, which are discussed in the following chapter. A style sheet is simply a collection of tags, each of which contains the formatting parameters for a particular type of paragraph, such as a subhead or a caption. Tags, however, are of no use for formatting a single character, word, or set of words within a paragraph. To do that, you can use the Assignment List and the Set Font button (DOS/GEM version), or the Text menu and the Set Font Attributes option (Windows version).

◆ Assignment List

When you are in text editing mode in the DOS/GEM version, the Assignment List has the entries shown on the right. These correspond to the attribute options in the Text menu for the Windows version. To apply any of these attributes to a passage of text, you drag the mouse across the passage and then select the appropriate attribute. Note that you can apply more than one attribute, such as combining bold and italic to make bold italic. "Small" switches the font to a smaller size (actually, you can use the "Small" switch to create large text as well — see below). "Upper Case" capitalizes all the characters in the selection; "Capitalize" capitalizes only the first character of each word.

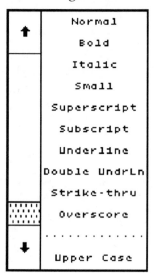

◆ Set Font (DOS/GEM version)

Although tags apply only to entire paragraphs, you can use the Set Font option to make formatting changes within a paragraph. The procedure is as follows:

• Select text mode.

Figure 8-2:
The Set Font
dialog box.

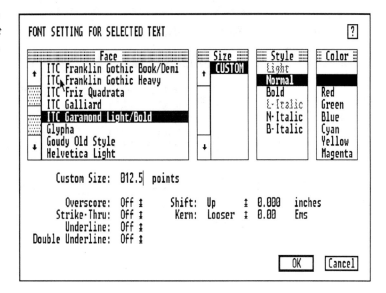

• Select a passage of text by dragging the mouse cursor across it.

• Select the Set Font option.

• Enter the desired font settings in the dialog box shown in Figure 8-2.

◆ Set Font Attributes (Windows version)

You can use the Set Font Attributes option to make formatting changes within a paragraph. The procedure is as follows:

• Select the text icon.

• Select a passage of text by dragging the mouse cursor across it.

• Select the Set Font Attributes option from the Text menu.

• Enter the desired font settings in the dialog box.

Figure 8-3:
The Attribute
Overrides
dialog box.

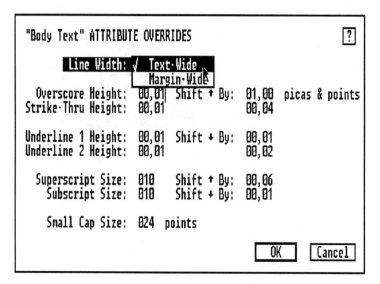

```
"Body Text" ATTRIBUTE OVERRIDES                              [?]

      Line Width: √ Text-Wide
                    Margin-Wide
   Overscore Height:  00,01  Shift ↑ By:  01,00  picas & points
   Strike-Thru Height: 00,01              00,04

   Underline 1 Height: 00,01  Shift ↓ By:  00,01
   Underline 2 Height: 00,01              00,02

   Superscript Size:  010    Shift ↑ By:  00,06
     Subscript Size:  010    Shift ↓ By:  00,01

     Small Cap Size:  024    points

                                        [  OK  ]  [Cancel]
```

◆ Using Attribute Overrides

A feature called Attribute Overrides lets you adjust the thickness and relative position of strikethrough lines, overscore lines, and underscore lines; the size and position of superscripts and subscripts; and the size and position of small caps. It is best described with an example. Let's say that you want all superscripts to be 10 points in size and to be 7 points above the baseline. First, in text mode you highlight the letter or letters you wish to have superscripted, then select Superscript from the Assignment List. Next, switch to tagging mode, click on the paragraph, and select Attribute Overrides from the Paragraph menu (see Figure 8-3). For line width, select Text-Wide, then enter 10 points for size of the superscript and 7 points for the amount to be shifted up. These Attribute Overrides now become a permanent part of the tag that applies to the current paragraph and any other paragraph so tagged.

Column-Wide Underlining

If you want text automatically to be underlined, overscored, etc., across an entire column, (like this line), select Column-Wide in the Attribute Overrides dialog box.

Using "Small Caps" for Big Letters

Using Attribute Overrides, you can specify a point size for Small Caps, and Ventura will always apply that size when you select "Small" from the Assignment List (DOS/GEM) or from Set Font Attributes (Windows). For example, in this paragraph the small cap size was set at 24 points and the first letter of the paragraph was assigned the "Small" text attribute. Note that you can specify a different size for small text for each tag in your style sheet.

◆ Editing Attributes

Any attributes that you apply to text are stored as hidden codes in the text. To locate the attribute codes, place the cursor in the text and watch the Current Selection Box (right above the page number box) as you move the cursor. When the cursor is located at an attribute code, the name of the attribute will appear in the Current Selection Box. To eliminate the attribute, press Del. Another way to eliminate the attribute is to highlight a portion of text and apply the Normal text attribute.

❖ Creating Text within Ventura

Although it is generally recommended that you create text outside Ventura with a word processing program and then import the text file into Ventura, with short documents you can simply create your text directly with Ventura's text editor.

Here's how to proceed. If you've just loaded up the program, you'll be looking at a blank screen. If you're in a different chapter, select New from the File menu to get a blank screen. Now click on the text icon, click on the blank page, and start typing. When you're ready to save your document, select Save As from the File menu and give a name to the new chapter you've just created. Ventura will automatically give the text file the same name and save it in the same directory as the chapter file.

❖ Caption Files

Two kinds of text files are generated by Ventura itself. For every chapter that you create, Ventura creates a file with the same name as the chapter file and the extension CAP. It is somewhat misleading to refer to this as the "caption" file, since it contains not only text you enter for captions but also text you type into box text boxes and blank frames.

Tip 8-13

Making Global Changes in Captions, Box Text, and Frame Text

This tip should only be attempted after you have backed up your CAP file. Since the CAP file is a text file, you can load it into any word processor and use such word processor features as spell checking and search and replace. This can come in especially handy if you want to change a single word that occurs repeatedly in a number of captions, but only minor changes should be attempted, because it is easy to alter the CAP file in such a way that all the captions, box text, and frame text will disappear from your chapter. REPEAT: BEFORE YOU EDIT A CAP FILE IN ANY WAY, MAKE A BACKUP COPY.

❖ Generated Files

This type of file is generated by Ventura when you create an index or a table of contents, or when you select Print Style Sheet in the Update Tag List option (under the Paragraph menu). In each case, Ventura creates a file with the extension GEN. You can load this file back into Ventura and format it, just like any other file. Simply select Generated as your text file type in the Load Text/Picture dialog box.

To format the generated file for a style sheet, use the STYLOG style sheet in the \TYPESET directory.

Tip 8-14

Saving Formatting Information

If your word processing file contains formatting information that Ventura does not recognize when it loads the file, that information will be stripped away and lost during the loading process. If you want to preserve the formats of your original document, save a new copy under a different name before you load it into Ventura.

Tip 8-15

Converting Text Files among Word Processor Formats

A common problem in offices is converting documents from one word processing format to another—for instance, from Multi-Mate to WordPerfect. You can use Ventura for this routine task. Load the text file into a chapter, then select File Type/Rename from the Edit menu (DOS/GEM version) or the Frame menu (Windows version). You'll be given the option to choose a new subdirectory, name, and word processing format for the file.

Suppressing Hyphenation

You can keep Ventura from hyphenating a word by placing a discretionary hyphen (<->) directly in front of the word when you prepare text with your word processor.

Moving Text Files from One Directory to Another

If you have a text file in one directory and want to move it to another directory, select frame mode, then select File Type/Rename from the Edit menu (DOS/GEM) or from the Frame menu (Windows). If the file is currently on the screen, its path and name will be listed on the top line. Otherwise, type in the path and name. Then type in the new path and name and the new format, if you want Ventura to convert it.

Entering Text in a Frame

There are two ways to enter text into a frame. One is to type directly into a frame. The other is to load a text file into the frame. Generally, it's better to load a file into the frame, because then the text in the frame will be saved on your hard disk as a separate text file that can easily be edited with your word processor. If you type text directly into the frame without first loading in a text file, Ventura stores the text in a file with the same name as the chapter file but with the extension CAP. This file also contains the contents of all figure captions and also the contents of any other frames into which you've typed text directly. While using the CAP file to hold your frame text is convenient, a problem arises if you ever want to use the spell checking or search-and-replace features of your word processor, since it's not advisable to do any editing of the CAP file. Also, if the data in your chapter somehow becomes corrupted, it's easier to reconstruct the chapter if each frame has its own separate text file. Of course, this is not a hard and fast rule. For frames with a small amount of text, you may as well enter your text directly into the frame. But for long text passages, it's a good idea to create a separate text file and then load that file. Once the text file is loaded, you can add or delete text from it using Ventura's editing tools.

❖   Questions and Answers

Q: *I drew a frame, selected the File menu, selected the Load Text/Picture option, and selected a text file to load. However, the text did not load into the frame and the frame remained blank. How do I get the text to load into the frame?*

A: After you select the text file to load using the Load Text/Picture option, its name should appear in the Selection List on the left side of the screen (DOS/GEM version) or in the Files window (Windows version). Select the frame you want to pour the text into. When you point at its name in that menu and click with the mouse, it will appear in that frame.

Q: *I'm laying out a newsletter that has articles in several different files. I loaded them into Ventura by selecting the Load Text/Picture option from the File menu. In the Load Text/Picture dialog box I selected # of Files: Several. Then I selected three files. However,*

only one of them appeared in the document.
How do I put multiple text files in a chapter?

A: To create a chapter with multiple text files, such as a newsletter, you have several options. One technique, which is appropriate for newsletters, is to draw a separate frame for each text file. Another technique is to select Load Text/Picture from the File menu and select Text Cursor as the Destination. A third technique is to draw a frame for each column of your newsletter and then load text files into these frames. A fourth technique is to use the Insert Page option from the Chapter menu.

Q: *When I load text into Ventura, some lines are highlighted in black. Why?*

A: Lines shown in black are known as "loose lines," meaning that Ventura has been forced to exceed the Maximum Space Width value in order to justify the line. Several solutions are available to correct a loose line. One is to hyphenate words in adjacent lines. Another is to select the Typographic Controls option from the Paragraph menu, set letter spacing on, and enter an amount to use for adjustment. This causes Ventura to adjust the spacing between characters within words, as described in the Chapter 10, "Formatting Text." Note, however, that after you turn letter spacing on, the loose lines may still be highlighted. If you don't want loose lines to be highlighted, you can select Hide Loose Lines in the Options menu (DOS/GEM version) or the View menu (Windows version).

Q: *Why does text take longer to load with one hyphenation routine than with another?*

A: When Ventura loads a text file, it inserts all possible hyphenation points. The more complete a hyphenation routine, the longer it takes to check all the hyphenation points.

Q: *I tagged some text before loading it into Ventura by typing an @ followed by the name of the tag and an equal sign. However, the effect was that the name of the tag printed rather than causing the text to be formatted. Why?*

A: The most likely reason is that the @ sign was not the first letter of the line (perhaps you preceded it with a space or a tab). To be recognized by Ventura, the @ sign must be the first character in the first line of a paragraph and may not be indented.

Working with Style Sheets

As described in Chapter 2, "How Ventura Works," Ventura stores information about a document in multiple locations: the chapter file (CHP), the chapter information file (CIF), the caption file (CAP), the Ventura information file (INF), the style sheet file (STY), and the various text and graphics files that comprise the contents of the document. Among these files, the style sheet file is especially important, since it contains formatting information for the document as a whole, such as the margins and columns settings, as well as the formatting instructions contained in each paragraph tag. The following are the elements that are stored in each style sheet:

- Page size and layout;
- Chapter typography, except widow and orphan settings;
- Auto-numbering settings;
- Footnote settings;

- Margin and column settings for the base page;
- Printer width table name;
- Formatting information for each tag (font, alignment, spacing, breaks, tabs, special effects, attribute overrides, paragraph typography, and ruling lines).

❖ Ventura's Sample Style Sheets

During the installation procedure for Ventura, you are asked whether you want to have example documents installed on your hard disk. If you answer Yes, the style sheets shown in Table 9-1 are installed in the \TYPESET directory. Most begin with an ampersand (&). The characters immediately preceding the extension (P1, P2, L1, or L2) indicate whether the document is landscape (printed sideways across the page) or portrait (printed up-right on the page), and whether it has one or two columns. To see one of these styles applied to an actual document, you can load one of the chapter files with the same name contained in the \TYPESET directory.

◆ Miscellaneous Sample Style Sheets

In addition to the style sheets that begin with an ampersand, six other style sheets are automatically installed in the \TYPESET directory. These are as follows:

- CAPABILI.STY. This style sheet goes with CAPABILI.CHP, a special page that shows the capabilities and limitations of your printer.
- CHARSET.STY. This style sheet goes with CHARSET.CHP, a chart showing the symbols in the Ventura International character set.
- DEFAULT.STY. This is simply a blank style sheet containing no tags, which proves to be quite handy to use as a starting point when you want to build your own style sheet from scratch.

Ventura's Sample Style Sheets

&BOOK-P1.STY	*A single-column layout for books and reports*
&BOOK-P2.STY	*A two-column layout for books and reports*
&BRO-L2.STY	*A two-column layout in landscape orientation for brochures*
&BRO-P3.STY	*A three-column layout in portrait orientation for brochures*
&INV-P1.STY	*A single-column invoice form*
&LSTG-P2.STY	*A two-column product listing*
&LTR-P1.STY	*A single-column business letter, including letterhead*
&MAG-P3.STY	*A three-column magazine or newsletter*
&NEWS-P2.STY	*A two-column magazine or newsletter*
&NEWS-P3.STY	*A three-column magazine or newsletter*
&PHON-P2.STY	*A two-column directory or phone book*
&PREL-P1.STY	*A single-column press release or announcement*
&PRPT-P1.STY	*A single-column proposal or report*
&PRPT-P2.STY	*A two-column proposal or report*
&TBL-P1.STY	*A single-column financial table*
&TBL2-L1.STY	*A four-column table in landscape orientation*
&TCHD-P1.STY	*A single-column technical manual*
&TDOC-P1.STY	*A single-column technical manual*
&VWGF-L1.STY	*A presentation viewgraph in landscape orientation*
&VWGF-P1.STY	*A presentation viewgraph in portrait orientation*
CAPABILI.STY	*A page that shows the capabilities and limitations of your printer*
CHARSET.STY	*A table showing the characters in the Ventura International and the Symbol character sets*
DEFAULT.STY	*A blank style sheet*
SAMPLE1.STY	*A style sheet with several levels of heads and subheads, used to learn tagging*
SCOOP.STY	*The style sheet that goes with a sample newsletter called Ventura Scoop*
STYLOG.STY	*Formats the generated file that contains the contents of a style sheet*

Table 9-1: The sample style sheets that are provided with Ventura. During the installation process, they are automatically loaded into the \TYPESET directory.

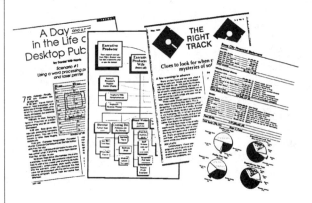

Third-Party Style Sheets

Document Gallery Style Sheets
MicroPublishing
21150 Hawthorne Blvd. #104
Torrance, CA 90503
213/371-5787
This collection includes 50 style sheets. Topics include newsletters, technical documentation, marketing literature, books, directories, and forms.

Style Sheets for Business Documents, Style Sheets for Newsletters, Style Sheets for Technical Documentation
New Riders Publishing
P.O. Box 4846
Thousand Oaks, CA 91360
818/991-5392
Price: $39.95 each
Each set in the New Riders collection includes approximately 20 style sheets. These come bound into a book that explains how to use the style sheets, shows sample printouts, and provides extensive production tips. Included with the style sheets are sample chapters.

Ventura Designer Stylesheets
BCA/Desktop Designs
P.O. Box 2191
Walnut Creek, CA 94595
800/727-8953, 415/946-1716
Price: $149.95 each
There are four "application packs" in this collection. They include the Business (22 style sheets, including financial statements, forms, proposals, letterhead, business

cards), News (11 newsletter style sheets), Corporate (10 brochures, 2 seminars, 1 annual report), and Techdoc (10 technical documentation styles). Each application pack includes chapter files illustrating the style sheets. Separate versions of the packs are provided for LaserJet and PostScript printers.

VPDesigner Style Sheets
HyperFormance, Inc.
4906 Fitzhugh Ave. #107
Richmond, VA 23230
804/355-0083
Price: $129.95
HyperFormance has created a set of over 40 style sheets, each of which is illustrated in an accompanying manual. The sample documents include newsletters, resumes, menus, manuals, books, proposals, forms, annual reports, technical sheets, directories, and catalogs.

Will-Harris Designer Disks
P.O. Box 480265
Los Angeles, CA 90048
Price: $49 for Disks #1 & #2; $39 for Disk #3
Daniel Will-Harris (a contributor to this book), derived the style sheets in this collection from his book **Desktop Publishing With Style**. *For a complete description, see the ad on the facing page.*

Table 9-2: *Third-party style sheets.*

- SAMPLE1.STY. This is a style sheet that you'll use if you follow the tutorial in the training booklet provided with Ventura.

- SCOOP.STY. This is the style sheet that goes with a sample newsletter called Scoop. It's an example of a complex page that includes text and graphics in multiple frames. To see the newsletter, load the chapter SCOOP.CHP

- STYLOG.STY. If you want to print the contents of a style sheet, you'll find this style sheet useful for formatting the printout. The procedure to follow is described later in this chapter.

Tip 9-1

Ventura's Default Style Sheet

Often it's easier to start from a scratch style sheet (i.e., one containing no tags) than to adapt one of the style sheets provided with Ventura. When you need to start with a blank style sheet, select DEFAULT.STY from the \TYPESET directory. This style sheet only contains one tag, the one for Body Text.

❖ Third-Party Style Sheets

A number of companies have gone into the business of selling "prefab" style sheets. You can either put these to use as is, or else customize them for your own particular needs. Table 9-2 lists several sources of these style sheets.

❖ Loading a Style Sheet

When you load Ventura, the most recently used style sheet is automatically loaded as well, and its name is listed in parentheses on the Title Bar. To load a new style, select Load Diff. Style from the File menu, then use the Item Selector to pick the style you want. (For an explanation of how to use the Item Selector, see Chapter 7, "Managing Files.")

Generally, you'll start by loading one of the style sheets in the TYPESET directory, or else by loading a third-party style sheet. The first thing you should do is use the Save As New Style option under the File menu to save your style sheet with a new name. This ensures that the original style sheets will be preserved intact.

Tip 9-2

Keeping Your Original Style Sheets Intact

If you accidentally modify one of the sample style sheets in the \TYPESET directory and wish to restore the original version, delete the modified style sheet and copy the original from the installation disk labeled "Examples."

❖ Tagging

Once you have loaded the style sheet, you're ready to apply tags to paragraphs. There are three ways to do this: with the mouse, with the function keys, and in your word processor prior to loading a text file into Ventura.

◆ Mouse Tagging

In the GEM/DOS version, the way to apply a tag to a paragraph is to select the tag icon, then position the cursor anywhere within the paragraph and click, and then click on the name of a tag in the Assignment List.

In the Windows version, tagging is a bit more flexible. You can be in either tagging or text editing mode. Position the cursor anywhere within a paragraph and click, then click on the name of a tag in the Tag List window.

Note that tags can only be applied to entire paragraphs. (To format a portion of a paragraph, such as changing a single word to a different font, you'll need to select the passage in text mode by dragging the cursor across it with the mouse button held down, then selecting one of the attributes listed in the Assignment List on the left side of the screen (DOS/GEM version), by clicking the Set Font button (DOS/GEM), or by selecting Apply Text Attributes from the Text menu (Windows version). For more information on this topic, see Chapter 8, "Preparing, Loading, and Editing Text.")

Tip 9-3

Speed Up Tagging by Moving the Tag Window (Windows version)

Remember that the Tag Window can be dragged to a new location. So if you want to speed up the tagging process, simply click in the top bar or the window, hold down the mouse button, and drag the window to a position right on top of the page you are working with. To see more tags at once, use the window corners to expand the size of the Tag Window.

Tip 9-4

Tagging Multiple Paragraphs

To tag multiple paragraphs at once, hold down the Shift key while selecting the various paragraphs. They need not be contiguous, but they do need to all be on one page.

◆ Tagging with the Function Keys

You can apply up to ten different tags directly by using the function keys. This works in either tagging or text editing mode. In many cases, this works faster than regular tagging. The procedure is simple: place the text cursor anywhere in the paragraph you wish to tag and press the appropriate function key.

Figure 9-1:
*Function key
assignments for
tags are controlled
through the
Update Tag List
option in the
Paragraph menu.
Note that in the
Windows version,
these menus and
dialog boxes look
slightly different,
but work just the
same.*

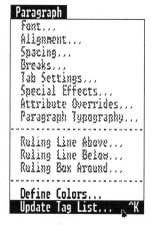

Figure 9-2: *The
Update Tag List
dialog box, which
is used to assign
tags to function
keys, remove tags
from the style
sheet, rename
tags, and save a
style sheet as a
text file with the
GEN extension.*

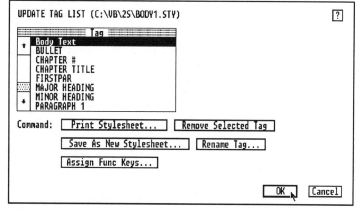

Figure 9-3: *The
Assign Function
Keys dialog box. It
is accessed via the
Paragraph menu
or by pressing
Ctrl-K.*

ASSIGN FUNCTION KEYS

F1:	Minor heading	F2:	Major heading
F3:	Tip #	F4:	Tip Title
F5:	Q	F6:	Question Text
F7:	Bullet	F8:	A
F9:	Answer Text	F10:	Body Text

OK   Cancel

To assign tags to function keys, press Ctrl-K. This puts you into the Update Tag List dialog box. To assign a tag to a function key — or merely to find out which tags are assigned to which function keys — select Assign Func Keys. Of course, no more than 10 tags can be assigned to function keys, so you'll have to make sure that the tags you assign are the ones most frequently needed. Note that in the Windows version, F1 and F10 are reserved for other purposes.

Tip 9-5

A Shortcut to the Function Key Assignment List from Text Mode (DOS/GEM version)

If you're in text mode and want to remind yourself of the function key assignments, there's a slight problem: when you select the Paragraph menu, you'll see Update Tag List shown in light gray, meaning that you can't select it unless you switch to Paragraph Tagging mode.

Here's a trick to find out the function key assignments without leaving text mode. Press Ctrl-K, which is the keyboard shortcut for getting into the Update Tag List dialog box. Surprisingly enough, Ctrl-K works no matter what mode you're in.

◆ Tagging with a Word Processor

As described in the previous chapter, you can attach tags to the elements of a document before importing it into Ventura from any word processor. Simply type the @ symbol, the name of the style in capital letters, a space, the = sign, and another space. Thus, all tags take the form @tagname = . Better yet, use a keyboard macro program such as SuperKey, or use the macro capabilities of your word processor. For example, you can use the macro program to store the phrase "@SUBHEAD = " as Alt-S. To format all subheads, you merely type Alt-S at the beginning of each.

Tip 9-6

Identifying Tags in the Word Processor

When you insert tags with your word processor, the @ sign must be the first character in the line. Otherwise it will not be recognized as a tag.

❖ Tagging with WordPerfect

Although you can enter plain text into Ventura and then do your formatting, one way to save time is to embed Ventura formatting codes in your text files using WordPerfect. An annoying side effect of this technique is that it clutters your text files with Ventura formatting codes. Fortunately, there's a way to avoid the clutter, and that is to use two WordPerfect style sheets. While you're working on your document, you use a style sheet that doesn't put lots of Ventura codes in your document. Just before you load the document into Ventura, you switch to a different style sheet, which produces fully formatted, Ventura-ready files with all the necessary codes embedded. Creating both style sheets is simple.

◆ VPDRAFT.STY

The draft WordPerfect style sheet, called VPDRAFT.STY, allows headlines, subheads, and readouts (or pull-quotes) to stand out from regular text by using extra hard returns, underlines, bold, centers, or indents. Here's how to set it up:

BYLINE (paired):

`[Tab][F6][CursorRight]`

HEADLINE (paired):

`[Enter]`

`[Enter]`

[Shift-F6][F6][F8][CursorRight][Enter]

[Enter]

READOUT (paired):

[F4][F4][F6]

(Note: You can use Shift-F4, which gives you a left/right indent, in place of F4, which gives you a left indent.)

SUBHEAD (paired):

[Enter]

[F8]

TOPPER (paired):

[Shift-F8] L M 1.25" [Enter] 1.25" [Enter] S1.5 [Enter]

UND/ITAL (paired):

[F8]

◆ **VPFINAL.STY**

The final WordPerfect style sheet, called VPFINAL.STY, removes all extra returns and replaces them with Ventura tag names. Even underlines become real Ventura italics codes.

BYLINE (paired):

@BYLINE =

HEADLINE (paired):

@HEADLINE =

READOUT (paired):

@READOUT =

SUBHEAD (paired):

How to Remove Tag Names from Text Files

Like cats, most documents go through many lives. Typically, not long after a technical manual is written and printed, a writer begins work on the next revision.

With Ventura, any changes made up and saved in the chapter file are reflected back in the original document file. That provides a great deal of convenience in keeping the document up to date. The one drawback of Ventura's way of working is that the numerous tags embedded in a document become distracting.

Let's say you've completed printing out a document and now wish to remove all the tags from the original text file so that you can continue editing it without the distraction of the embedded @ signs, tag names, and = signs. Obviously, you could go through the file with your word processing program and manually delete all the tags. But there are several alternatives that may be quicker:

When you set up your style sheet, make sure that all the tags you create are the same length. Since 13 characters is the maximum, you might make that your standard length. If you don't need 13 characters for a tag name, just fill up the remainder with the underline symbol. Having made all tags the same length, you can delete them using a single search and replace by searching for "@????????????? = "

A second method is to retag the chapter, making every paragraph Body Text. Since Body Text is the default tag, there is no embedded tag name in the original document. When you save the chapter (it's a good idea to save it under a new name), the text file will be saved without any embedded tag names.

A third method is to use the macro capabilities of your word processor to automatically delete all tags. In Microsoft Word, the following macro finds a tag string of any length and deletes it. To record the macro, press <F3>, then enter the following string:
<Esc>=<Spacebar>S<Spacebar><Enter><F6><Home><Del>
<Del><Del>
Then press F3 again and provide a name for the macro at the prompt. To execute the macro, press <Esc>I, then type the name of the macro. A shortcut is to type the name of the macro and then press <Shift>-<F3>.

`@SUBHEAD =`

TOPPER (open):

`Shift-F8 L M 1" [Enter] 1" [Enter]`

UND/ITAL (paired):

`<MI>`

`[CursorRight]`

`<D>`

(Note: <MI> stands for Medium Italics, and <D> stands for Default, because it returns text to its normal attribute.)

◆ TAGTeam

There's a utility called TAGTeam that automates the work of pre-tagging a WordPerfect document even more than the WordPerfect style sheets described above. TAGTeam lets you associate certain WordPerfect attributes with Ventura styles and then places those tags in your document. For more on TAGTeam, see Chapter 27, "Utilities."

❖ Tagging with Microsoft Word

When using Microsoft Word to prepare pre-tagged text for Ventura Publisher, the F3 key can be used for rapid tagging of paragraphs. Save each tag name, preceded with an @ and followed by a space, an equal sign, and another space (for example @HEAD-LINE =) in a glossary and assign each glossary entry a one- or two-letter name. To do that, type the passage you wish to assign to a glossary, highlight the passage, and press Esc for the Word command line and then C for the Copy command. When Word prompts you with Copy to:, type a one- or two-letter name. To apply this tag to the passage, place the cursor at the beginning of the first line of the paragraph, press the key combination assigned to that tag, and immediately press F3.

Profile

*Pub*Star*

If you like to enter Ventura tagging information in your word processing file, but have a mind like a sieve (and don't we all at one time or another), Pub*Star just might be the ticket.

Pub*Star is a memory-resident program designed solely to help you place Ventura tagging and code information in your word processing file. Pub*Star provides instant "Macros" which allow you to place tags in a file; it shows you a little bit of information about each tag while you're in your word processing program; it frees you from having to look up the codes for various symbols such as em-dashes, copyright symbols, index entries, and anchor entries; and it allows you to quickly enter repetitive phrases.

Pub*Star reads a Ventura style sheet and extracts the names of the tags. From then on, rather than having to type the full tag name, you press the star on the keypad, press ENTER on "Tag a paragraph," and move the cursor to the tag name you want. Pub*Star will then insert the current tag name, complete with @ and spaces

Figure 9-4: This screen shows you the embedded codes to use for various types of formatting. When you want to place one of these codes in your text file, you simply move to the desired code and press Enter.

```
Ventura & Pub*Star Ventura & Pub*Star Ventura & Pub*Star Ventura & Pub*Star Ven
Pub*Star Ventura & Pub*Star Ventura & Pub*Star Ventura & Pub*Star Ventura & Pub
Ventura & Pub*S                                                  & Pub*Star Ven
Pub*Star Ventur ┌─────────────────────────────────────────────┐ r Ventura & Pub
Ventura & Pub*S │ Discretionary Hyphen                    <->  │ & Pub*Star Ven
Pub*Star Ventur │ Horizontal Tab                          <9>  │ r Ventura & Pub
Ventura & Pub*S │ Line Break                              <R>  │ & Pub*Star Ven
Pub*Star Ventur │ DASH   - En Dash                        <196>│ r Ventura & Pub
Ventura & Pub*S │          Em Dash                        <197>│ & Pub*Star Ven
Pub*Star Ventur │ SPACE  - Thin Space                     <!>  │ r Ventura & Pub
Ventura & Pub*S │          Figure Space                   <+>  │ & Pub*Star Ven
Pub*Star Ventur │          En Space                       <~>  │ r Ventura & Pub
Ventura & Pub*S │          Em Space                       <_>  │ & Pub*Star Ven
Pub*Star Ventur │          Non-Breaking Space             <N>  │ r Ventura & Pub
Ventura & Pub*S │ SYMBOL - Copyright        (C)           <189>│ & Pub*Star Ven
Pub*Star Ventur │          Trademark        TM            <191>│ r Ventura & Pub
Ventura & Pub*S │          Registered Mark (R)            <190>│ & Pub*Star Ven
Pub*Star Ventur │ INDEX  - Entry                        <$I ; >│ r Ventura & Pub
Ventura & Pub*S │          "See" Reference              <$S ; >│ & Pub*Star Ven
Pub*Star Ventur │          "See Also" Reference         <$A ; >│ r Ventura & Pub
Ventura & Pub*S │ ANCHOR - Same Page                  <$&name> │ & Pub*Star Ven
Pub*Star Ventur │          Below                      <$&name[v]>│r Ventura & Pub
Ventura & Pub*S │          Above                      <$&name[^]>│& Pub*Star Ven
Pub*Star Ventur │ Footnote                            <$Ftext> │ r Ventura & Pub
Ventura & Pub*S │ Hidden Text                         <$!text> │ & Pub*Star Ven
                └─────────────────────────────────────────────┘ n 1" Pos 1"
```

before and after the equal sign.

Pub*Star is also smart enough to keep the cursor on the last tag name you used, so you don't have to keep moving the cursor through the list of tag names. Another nice touch permits you to press the first letter of the tag-name and have the cursor jump to the first tag which begins with that letter.

While you can do much the same thing with a macro in your word processing program, Pub*Star works in a more convenient fashion because it reads the latest version of your style sheet and therefore makes all tags automatically available — no need to add them manually. Pub*Star will also show you information about each tag including the typeface, size, attributes (such as italic or bold), alignment, "In From Left" and special effects such as bullets and big first characters. This is a handy reference when you can't remember which tag to use.

For those times when you need to temporarily change typefaces, sizes, attributes or color, additional menus contain all these codes and will place them in your file just by moving to them on the

Figure 9-5: When you need a reminder about which tag to use, Pub*Star can show you the contents of the tag.

```
4 body text      z 1-2-3 plain
4 Bullet         z 1-2-3 table
4 Bullet 1       z 10 on 10
4 heading        z 10 on 11
4 keystroke      z 10 on 12
4 subhead        z 10 on 13
Body no widow    z 10 on 14
Body Text        z 24┌─────────────────────────────┐
Bullet           z 80│        Chap Paragrap        │
Bullet 1         z bo│  Goudy                      │
Caption left     Z ce│  Point Size: 14             │
Chap Paragrap    Z HA│  Attributes: Normal         │
Chapter Numbr    Z Ju│  Alignment:  Justified      │
Chapter Sub      z le│  In From Left:  0.00 Inches │
Chapter Title    z le│              Big First Char!│
Gill Tabs        Z Ra└─────────────────────────────┘
Helvetica        z readout
Keystrokes       Z reverse
Readout          Z Right
Readout centr    z unkearned
Serif            z-boxed
Serif 2          Z_cap center
Sub head         Z_CAPTION
Subhead small    Z_HEADER
Text small       Z_LABEL CAP
```

menu and pressing Enter. The same goes for symbols. Tabs, line breaks, dashes, spaces, symbols, index marks, anchors, footnotes and hidden text are all included in the "Inserts and Symbols menu." Until using this program I didn't know that <9> meant "tab" in Ventura.

While the program is clever and easy to use, if you are a true novice, pre-tagging may be more trouble than it's worth. If you want to pre-tag, Pub*Star can help, but you don't have to, and many people prefer to tag, insert special codes, or change typefaces and sizes using Ventura's own WYSIWYG fashion, rather than by inserting codes.

Despite this complaint, Pub*Star is simple to understand and use. It allows even the less technically inclined to tag in Ventura with ease, and you never have to figure out how to "program" a macro in your word processing program to use it.

*For access information on Pub*Star, see the Utilities section of Appendix A, "Resources."*

❖ Creating a New Tag

No matter how comprehensive the style sheet you're using may be, there comes a time when you'll need to create a new tag. To do so, select tagging mode, select a paragraph to which you want to apply the new tag, and tag it with the tag that is the closest to the new tag you wish to create. Now select the Add New Tag button (DOS/GEM version) or press Ctrl-2 (Windows version). Type the name of the new tag on the top line, and make sure that the tag listed next to "Tag Name to Copy From" is the old tag you wish to alter to create your new tag. Select OK.

Now you'll be back in your document and you can proceed to define your new tag. At the outset, its attributes will be identical to the tag from which it was copied. To change the attributes, select any of the choices in the Paragraph menu, such as Font, Alignment, Spacing, Breaks, and so forth.

Tip 9-7

Copying a Tag to a Different Style Sheet (Windows version)

A feature unique to the Windows version is the ability to copy a tag from one style sheet into another. In tagging mode, click on a tag in the List of Tags window. Then select Copy from the Edit menu, open up a different style sheet, and use Paste to copy the tag in the new chapter's style sheet.

❖   **Naming Tags**

Because Ventura lets you have up to 128 tags in your style sheet, but the Assignment List only can show you 12 at a time, you're going to spend a lot of time scrolling up and down looking for tags unless you pay careful attention to how you name your tags. The following tips will help you keep your style sheet well organized and make tagging go much faster.

Tip 9-8

Organize Your Tags into Groups

In the list of tags, the tag names are shown in alphabetical order, so it's easy to organize your tags into groups. For example, any time you generate a new tag that is specific to a certain document or chapter, give it a unique prefix, such as C5 for chapter five. That way, when you get near the 128-tag limit and want to prune some tags from your style sheet, you'll know which ones to take out and which ones to keep in.

Tip 9-9

Place the Most Frequently Used Tags on Top

*As noted above, Ventura keeps the list of tags in "ASCII-alphabetical" order, i.e., the order in which symbols are listed in the ASCII character set: !, ", #, $, %, &, ', (,), *, +, ,, -, ., /, 0, 1, 2, 3, 4, 5, 6, 7, 8, 9, :, ;, <, =, >, ?, @, A, B, C, etc. You should think carefully about the tags you want to appear at the top of your list, so that you don't have to scroll to get to them. Then name them (or rename them) so that their first character is a number or a punctuation mark like # or +.*

Tip 9-10

Don't Use All Caps in Tag Names

If Ventura loads a chapter that contains an embedded tag name that doesn't happen to be in the current style sheet, it displays this name in the Assignment List in all caps. Some people refer to such tags as "foreign tags." As described in the Tip 9-10, such tags can overload your style sheet and may have to be removed from the text file. The reason you should avoid naming your tags with all caps is that otherwise you won't be able to distinguish them from other tags when you see them in the Assignment List.

❖ Deleting a Tag

The maximum number of tags in a style sheet is 128. If you get close to that number, you'll need to start deleting tags. The procedure is to select Update Tag List from the Paragraph menu (or press Ctrl-K), select Remove Selected Tag, and make sure that the top line of the dialog box names the tag you want to get rid of and that the bottom line names the new tag you want assigned to all paragraphs that had been tagged with the old tag.

D:\TYPESET\&BOOK-P1.STY

Base Page Settings

■ Page Size & Layout	Orientation:	Portrait	■ Ruling Box Around	Color:	Black
	Paper Type & Dimension:	Letter, 8.5 x 11 in.		Pattern:	Solid
	Sides:	Double		Dashes:	Off
	Start On:	Right Side		Space Above Rule 1:	0.750 inches
				Height of Rule 1:	0.010 inches
■ Margins & Columns	# of Columns:	1		Space Below Rule 1:	0.000 inches
	Settings For Left Page			Height of Rule 2:	0.000 inches
	Top:	01.50 inches		Space Below Rule 2:	0.000 inches
	Bottom:	01.17 inches		Height of Rule 3:	0.000 inches
	Left:	01.25 inches		Space Below Rule 3:	0.000 inches
	Right:	01.25 inches			
	Widths/Gutters—1:	06.00 inches			
	Settings For Right Page		■ Vertical Rules	Settings For Left Page	
	Top:	01.50 inches		Inter-Col. Rules:	Off
	Bottom:	01.17 inches		Rule 1 Position:	00.00 inches
	Left:	01.25 inches		Rule 1 Width:	0.000 inches
	Right:	01.25 inches		Rule 2 Position:	00.00 inches
	Widths/Gutters—1:	06.00 inches		Rule 2 Width:	0.000 inches
				Settings For Right Page	
■ Sizing & Scaling	Flow Text Around:	On		Inter-Col. Rules:	Off
	Upper Left X:	00.00 inches		Rule 1 Position:	00.00 inches
	Upper Left Y:	00.00 inches		Rule 1 Width:	0.000 inches
	Frame Width:	08.50 inches		Rule 2 Position:	00.00 inches
	Frame Height:	11.00 inches		Rule 2 Width:	0.000 inches
			■ Frame Background	Color:	White
				Pattern:	Hollow

Color Settings

Screen Display:	Shades of Gray		Color Number 4 (Blue):	(100.0, 100.0, 000.0, 000.0)
Color Number 0 (White):	(000.0, 000.0, 000.0, 000.0)		Color Number 5 (Cyan):	(100.0, 000.0, 000.0, 000.0)
Color Number 1 (Black):	(100.0, 100.0, 100.0, 000.0)		Color Number 6 (Yellow):	(000.0, 000.0, 100.0, 000.0)
Color Number 2 (Red):	(000.0, 100.0, 100.0, 000.0)		Color Number 7 (Magenta):	(000.0, 100.0, 000.0, 000.0)
Color Number 3 (Green):	(100.0, 000.0, 100.0, 000.0)			

Tag Settings

Body Text ───

■ Font	Face:	Times		Hyphenation:	USENGLSH
	Size:	12 points		Successive Hyphens:	2
	Style:	Normal		Overall Width:	Column-Wide
	Color:	Black		First Line:	Indent
	Overscore:	Off		Relative Indent:	Off
	Strike-Thru:	Off		In/Outdent Width:	00.08 inches
	Underline:	Off		In/Outdent Height:	1
	Double Underline:	Off		In From Right to Decimal:	00.00 inches
■ Alignment	Horz. Alignment:	Justified	■ Spacing	Above:	0.000 inches
	Vert. Alignment:	Top		Below:	0.000 inches
	Text Rotation:	None		Inter-Line:	13.98 fractional pts

Figure 9-6: A sample of a style sheet printout.

Tip 9-11

Exceeding the Tag Limit

Sometimes, when trying to load a text file into a chapter, you may get the error message, "You've used 128 tags, files, or chapters" even if there are less than 128 tags in your current style sheet. The reason for this seemingly erroneous error message is that when Ventura counts tags, it includes the tags you created in your style sheet; the tags automatically created by Ventura itself for captions, box text, and other attributes; and any "foreign tag names" it encounters (see Tip 9-9 about foreign tag names). To correct the problem, use your word processor to remove foreign tag names from the text file.

❖ Printing a Style Sheet

Here's a very useful feature — the ability to print out the contents of a style sheet. The procedure is as follows. When you're done, you'll have a printout that looks like Figure 9-6.

- From the File menu, select Load Diff Style and select the name of the style sheet you want to print.

- Press Ctrl-K, then select Print Style Sheet. Or select tagging mode, pull down the Paragraph menu, select Update Tag List, then select Print Style Sheet.

- Type a name for the text file that Ventura will generate to contain the contents of the style sheet. Note: the name can be anything — it doesn't need to be the same as the name of the style sheet itself — but it should end with the extension GEN, indicating that it is a text file generated by Ventura. Select OK.

- Select Cancel to quit the Update Tag List menu.

- From the File menu, select New to clear your screen. When prompted, save your current chapter.

- From the File menu again, select Load Text/Picture. For Type of File, select Generated.

- From the Item Selector, select the name of the generated file that holds the contents of the style sheet. Select OK.
- Select the base page frame, then select the name of the file from the selection list on the left. The contents of the style sheet will now appear on the screen.
- From the File menu, select Load Diff Style. From the \TYPE-SET directory, select STYLOG.STY.
- Your style sheet will now automatically format itself according to the specifications of the tags in STYLOG.STY. To have a paper record of the style sheet, print the chapter.

❖ Generated Tags

When you create text within Ventura using the box text, caption, header, and footer operations, Ventura automatically creates tags called generated tags. These tags all begin with the letter Z and are not listed in the sidebar unless you select Set Preferences from the Options menu and specify Generated Tags: Shown.

Tip 9-12

Changing Generated Tags

You can alter generated tags in the same manner used to alter other tags. You can also assign new tags to boxed text and captions; headers and footers, however, can only be tagged with the generated Z tags. This allows text in two different boxes, or text for two different captions, to be formatted with different fonts and typographic attributes. Thus, text in one box can look one way and text in another box can look another way. That is not the case with headers and footers, however.

Profile

VPToolbox

How many times have you wondered just exactly what all the tags in a Ventura style sheet did? How many times have you wanted to copy all your files to another directory and then delete the old files in one swell foop? How many times have you wanted to change all your Times Roman tags to Garamond, or have a sample of what each tag really looks like? How many times have you wondered why you didn't study the piano, or programming, or something useful like that?

Well, you may never be able to play the piano, but you won't need to know how to program to get out of Ventura vertigo. VPToolbox is an endlessly useful program that integrates the most needed Ventura utilities into one program. Most of its features are oriented toward managing style sheets, allowing you to manipulate tags and style sheets in ways unavailable within Ventura.The capabilities include the following:

- **Keeping Track of Tabs.** VPToolbox can give you a summary of all the tags in a style sheet (Figure 9-8), and also

Figure 9-7: The main menu for VPToolbox. Here, you decide whether you want a detailed listing of text, graphics, style sheet, or chapter files.

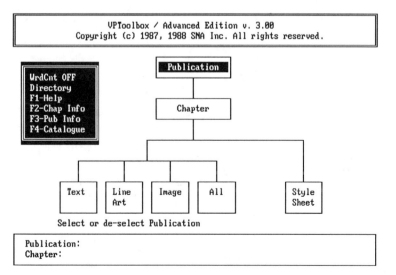

Figure 9-8: This is VPToolbox's list of the tags in a selected style sheet. For each tag, information is provided on font, style, ruling lines, and alignment. In addition, the top of the screen shows number of tags, page parameters, and type of printer.

```
Viewing Style Sheet: C:\VB\2S\TEST3.STY  10/18/88
Output Device:        POSTSCRIPT           Tag Count:  111  XVP version: 2
Page dimensions:      08.50 in. x 11.00 in., 2-sided Portrait, 1 column

Tag Name        Size Face          Style  Rules     Alignment Special

▶ 3 COLUMN       12 Garamond       Normal             Left
  6-BOX TITLE    12 Swiss          Bold               Centered
  A              17 Palatino       BdItal             Centered
  ACCESSBOX      12 Garamond       Normal             Left
  ADDRESS        14 Palatino       BdItal             Left
  ADDWHITE       12 Garamond       Normal             Left
  AFTER BOX      12 Garamond       Normal             Left
  AFTER MINOR    13 Garamond       Normal             Left
  ANSWER         12 Garamond       Normal             Left
  ANSWER TEXT    12 Garamond       Normal             Left
  BIG            12 Dutch          Normal Above       Left
  BIG BOX        12 Garamond       Normal             Left
  BIG HEADER     24 Dutch          Bold   Below       Centered
  BODY TEXT      12 Garamond       Normal             Justified
  BOX AROUND     13 Dutch          Normal Box Around  Justified
  BOXY           11 Helv-Narrow    Italic             Left

[ Zoom  Style Functions  Tag Functions  Output      ]
```

Figure 9-9: The Zoom feature of VPToolbox gives you a detailed description of a tag, including font, alignment, spacing, breaks, tabs, special effects, attribute overrides, paragraph typography, and ruling lines.

```
Viewing Style Sheet: C:\VB\2S\TEST3.STY  10/18/88
Output Device:        POSTSCRIPT           Tag Count:  111  XVP version: 2
Page dimensions:      08.50 in. x 11.00 in., 2-sided Portrait, 1 column

                          3 COLUMN
FONT
     Face: Garamond    Size:  12 Style: Normal    Color: Black
     Overscore:  Off       Strike-Thru:  Off
     Underline:  Off       Double Underline:  Off

ALIGNMENT
     Horiz. Alignment: Left  Hyphens: 1st Dict  (Unlim  successive )
     Vert. Alignment: Top
     Text Rotation: None
     In from Right to Decimal: 00.00 in.
     Overall Width: Column   First Line: Indent , 00.00 in.
     Indent/Outdent height:  1 Relative Indent: None

SPACING
     Above:  0, 11   Below:  0, 0

[ Print   ]
```

lets you zoom in on a tag to find out its specific contents (Figure 9-9). All reports are created as pre-formatted VP chapters, ready to print. Like Ventura, the program lets you print out a list of the tags in a style sheet and a description of the settings for each tag, but VPToolbox goes further in that it can also show you an example of the style sheet applied to a sample chapter.

- **Printing a Sample of Every Tag.** Anyone who's used Ventura on a regular basis has longed for a report which would print a sample of each tag. VPToolbox has this report, and it's invaluable for fast and easy style sheet reference, especially when more than one person must use the same style sheet. This sample report is much more useful than a mere printout of attributes because it's visual and instantly understandable.

- **Copying a Tag from One Style Sheet to Another.** This is perhaps the most useful feature of VPToolbox. The procedure is easy. Just select a tag, select copy, and then select the name of the destination.

Figure 9-10:
The Usage feature tells you which tags are actually used in the current chapter, a good thing to know when you need to delete some tags to make room for more.

```
Viewing Style Sheet: C:\VB\2S\TEST3.STY  10/18/88
Output Device:        POSTSCRIPT           Tag Count:  111  XVP version: 2
Page dimensions:      08.50 in. x 11.00 in., 2-sided Portrait, 1  column

Tag Name       Size Face        Style  Rules       Alignment Special

▶ BIG BOX         12 Garamond     Normal             Left
  BIG HEADER      24 Dutch        Bold   Below       Centered
  BODY TEXT       12 Garamond     Normal             Justified
  BOX AROUND      13 Dutch        Normal Box Around  Justified
  BOXY            11 Helu-Narrow  Italic             Left
  BULLET          12 Garamond     Normal             Justified
  C1              12 Garamond     Normal             Left
  C2              12 Garamond     Normal             Left
  C3              12 Garamond     Normal             Left
  CAPTION BOT     11 Avant Garde  Italic             Justified
  CAPTION RGHT    12 Dutch        Italic             Right
  CENTER 18       18 Suiss        Normal             Centered
  CH3-SYSTEMS     12 Avant Garde  Normal Above/Below Left
  CHAPTER #      150 Garamond     Normal             Centered
  CHAPTER TITLE   30 Garamond     Italic Above       Left
  CITIZENS        12 Garamond     Normal             Left

[ Zoom  Style Functions  Tag Functions  Output    ]
```

- **Comparing Style Sheets.** You can find out which tags are identical between two style sheets, even if they have different names.

- **Finding Out Which Tags Can Be Deleted.** It's easy for a style sheet to swell to the 128-tag limit, but when that limit is reached, it's often difficult to know which tags can safely be deleted. Here's where VPToolbox can play a helpful role by reporting on which tags in a style sheet are actually used by a particular chapter (see Figure 9-10). The tags that aren't used can then be safely deleted. You never know just how useful this is until you've opened an old chapter with 128 tags and can't remember which of them you actually need.

In addition to its style sheet management functions, VPToolbox provides several important chapter management capabilities

- **Copying and Moving Chapters.** You can either copy or move a chapter (and all its associated files) from one subdirectory to another.

- **Deleting Entire Chapters.** With Ventura itself, there's no way to remove a chapter and all its associated files from your hard disk. VPToolbox lets you do it.

- **Cataloging Your Files.** Another new feature is a "catalog" of all your Ventura files, no matter where they reside on the hard disk. This document management feature allows you to enter a descriptive title, name of author, and notes. Times and dates are automatically inserted.

VPToolbox offers an "Advanced Edition." This version of the program includes two important additions. First, it lets you convert the information contained in the document management catalog into dBase III or Comma Delimited ASCII format for use with any database program.

The program also offers "Global Style Sheet Editing." This feature lets you make one change for something such as typeface or leading, and have it affect all tags at once. Suppose you want to change all tags which use the Times Roman typeface and turn them into Garamond. With the Advanced Edition, you can make this change in one keystroke, *no matter how many tags are involved.* Or you could increase the leading in all tags by 10%. These types of changes can be time-consuming to make in Ventura when you have to make them individually for many tags. VPToolbox does it in a flash and this feature is great for major changes.

For access information on VPToolbox, see the Utilities section of Appendix A, "Resources."

❖ Questions and Answers

Q: *Several tag names in the tag list are in uppercase, for example, FIRSTPAR, BULLET, NAME. These tags are occupying precious space in my chapter, because I cannot add new tags beyond 128. When I select Remove Selected Tag from the Update Tag List dialog box, I get this message: "No tag by the name you've typed exists. Therefore, it can't be renamed, removed, or converted to."*

A: If you load a text file into Ventura that contains tag names not in your current style sheet, Ventura will list these in uppercase letters.

To remove them, you need to go into your original document with a text editor and delete the tag names.

Q: *After I tagged some text in a frame, the text disappeared. What happened?*

A: The problem is one of the following: (1) You switched to a font that was too large for the frame. Ventura won't display or print any characters that it can not fit entirely within a frame. (2) You specified additional space above the text, which pushed the text out of the frame. To fix the problem you need to change the specifications associated with the tag. This might seem impossible, however, since the text is no longer visible. If you haven't selected any other paragraphs, the paragraph you were working with should still be selected even though it is not visible. If the paragraph is no longer tagged, you can still fix the problem by tagging another paragraph with the same tag and changing the font or the spacing for that paragraph. The change will automatically apply to the disappeared text and it will appear again.

10 Formatting Text

You're finally ready. You've got a computer, a monitor, a printer, and a mouse. You've learned about how to load a text file into Ventura and how to select a style sheet. Now for the moment of truth, the raison d'être of desktop publishing: formatting text. In this chapter, we'll start with some tips on formatting for those becoming acquainted with Ventura. Then we'll analyze how the options for formatting text can be broken into categories, and examine these categories one at a time.

❖ Advice for Beginners

One of the most difficult aspects of Ventura for beginners is its richness. There are so many menu options, each with so many sub-options, that it's hard to know where to start. In fact, you don't really need to learn all that much to use Ventura effectively.

At least 90 percent of all the formatting work you'll ever need to do with Ventura involves only four menu options: one in the Frame menu (Margins & Columns) and three in the Paragraph menu (Font, Alignment, and Spacing). Once you've mastered this core subset of Ventura's features, you can start experimenting with other features, which are useful for unusual situations or typographic fine-tuning.

The illustrations on the following pages show the four key dialog boxes, with notes on each. The dialog boxes shown here are for the DOS/GEM version. Although the dialog boxes for the Windows version are superficially different, their structure and contents are virtually identical.

Tip 10-1

Work with the Menus from Left to Right

As you format text with Ventura, a logical way of working is to move from the left side of the menu bar to the right side. Start in the File menu to load a chapter or a text file. Next, use the Chapter menu to change the page orientation, if necessary. Then pull down the Frame menu and select Margins & Columns to determine the overall appearance of your page. Then tag a paragraph and begin moving through the options in the Paragraph menu, starting with Font, then Alignment, and working your way down. Of course, as you continue to work on formatting a document you jump around from menu to menu, but the pattern of starting from the left side of the bar is a sound, logical way to get things going.

Tip 10-2

Changing Measurement Units in Dialog Boxes

You can change measurement units in any dialog box merely by pointing the cursor at the measurement units (e.g., inches, picas

The Margins & Columns Dialog Box

In starting a new chapter, the first thing you should do is specify the number of columns. While Ventura can format as many as eight columns of text on a page, it's rare that any layout would have more than four columns.

If you point at the word "inches" and click, the measurement units will change to centimeters. Click again and they change to picas & points, then to fractional points. All the measurements in this dialog box will be translated automatically, but no other dialog boxes will be affected.

```
MARGINS & COLUMNS                                          [?]
# of Columns:   [1] [2] [3] [4] [5] [6] [7] [8]

Settings For:   [Left Page]  [Right Page]

                Widths  Gutters
        Column 1:  06.25           Top:     01.33   inches
               2:  00.00   00.00   Bottom:  01.00
               3:  00.00   00.00   Left:    01.00
               4:  00.00   00.00   Right:   01.25
               5:  00.00   00.00
               6:  00.00   00.00
               7:  00.00   00.00   Calculated Width = 08.50
               8:  00.00   00.00   Actual Frame Width = 08.50

       Inserts:  [Make Equal Widths]  [Copy To Facing Page]

                                        [OK]   [Cancel]
```

Typically, a gutter (the space between two columns) is one to two picas in width. If you set your gutter widths first, then select Make Equal Widths, Ventura will do the work of calculating the widths of the columns so that they fill up the available space.

Most layouts are symmetrical. In that case, you enter the settings for either the left page or the right page (it doesn't matter which you start with), then select Copy To Facing Page. Ventura will create a mirror image of your page layout on the facing page by inverting the left and right margin settings.

This pair of entries tells you whether the numbers you have entered for column and gutter widths match the actual width of the frame.

Figure 10-1

The Font Selection Dialog Box

This list shows the fonts in your printer width table. To print with these fonts, you must also have the necessary printer font files, or else the fonts must be resident in your printer. For example, the PostScript width table lists 42 typeface families, although most PostScript printers only come with 11 resident typeface familiies.

If you have installed a PostScript printer width table, the Size bar will say "Custom," as is the case here. You then type in the desired size in half-point increments up to 255 points. If your width table is for a LaserJet, the available sizes are listed in the Size bar.

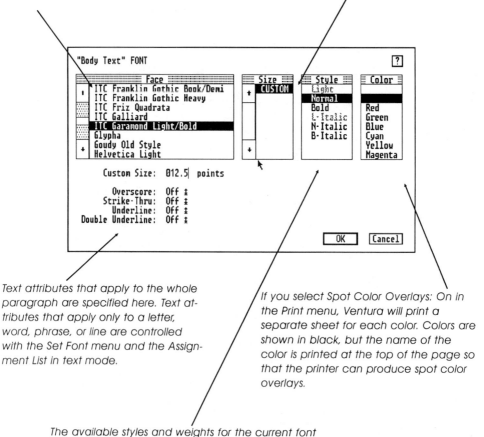

Text attributes that apply to the whole paragraph are specified here. Text attributes that apply only to a letter, word, phrase, or line are controlled with the Set Font menu and the Assignment List in text mode.

If you select Spot Color Overlays: On in the Print menu, Ventura will print a separate sheet for each color. Colors are shown in black, but the name of the color is printed at the top of the page so that the printer can produce spot color overlays.

The available styles and weights for the current font are listed in the Style bar in black. Those styles and/or weights that are not available are shown in gray.

Figure 10-2

The Paragraph Alignment Dialog Box

The options for horizontal alignment are left-justified (also called "rag right," because the right side of the text block is not aligned), centered, justified (aligned with both left and right margins), right-justified, and decimal (aligned with the last period on the line, as in a financial table).

With LaserJet printers, you can print vertical and horizontal text, but not together on the same page.

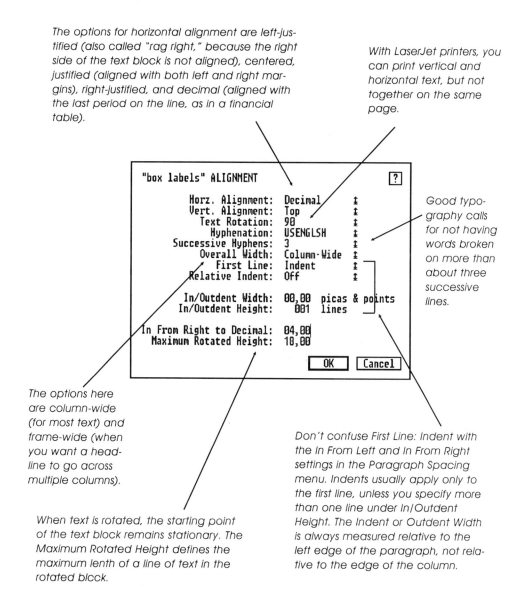

```
"box labels" ALIGNMENT                    [?]

        Horz. Alignment:  Decimal       ↕
        Vert. Alignment:  Top           ↕
         Text Rotation:   90            ↕
          Hyphenation:    USENGLSH      ↕
     Successive Hyphens:  3             ↕
         Overall Width:   Column-Wide   ↕
            First Line:   Indent        ↕
        Relative Indent:  Off           ↕

       In/Outdent Width:  00,00  picas & points
      In/Outdent Height:    001  lines

 In From Right to Decimal: 04,00
   Maximum Rotated Height:  18,00

                              [  OK  ]  [Cancel]
```

Good typography calls for not having words broken on more than about three successive lines.

The options here are column-wide (for most text) and frame-wide (when you want a headline to go across multiple columns).

Don't confuse First Line: Indent with the In From Left and In From Right settings in the Paragraph Spacing menu. Indents usually apply only to the first line, unless you specify more than one line under In/Outdent Height. The Indent or Outdent Width is always measured relative to the left edge of the paragraph, not relative to the edge of the column.

When text is rotated, the starting point of the text block remains stationary. The Maximum Rotated Height defines the maximum lenth of a line of text in the rotated blcck.

Figure 10-3

The Paragraph Spacing Dialog Box

Above adds space above a paragraph; Below adds space below a paragraph. The rule for combining the two is explained in Table 10-2 on page 236. Inter-Paragraph spacing only takes effect between paragraphs with the same Inter-Paragraph setting. Hint: generally, Inter-Paragraph spacing should be set to 0.

If you point at the words "picas & points" and click, the measurement units will change to fractional points.. Click again and they change to inches, then to centimeters. All the measurements in this dialog box will be translated automatically, but no other dialog boxes will be affected.

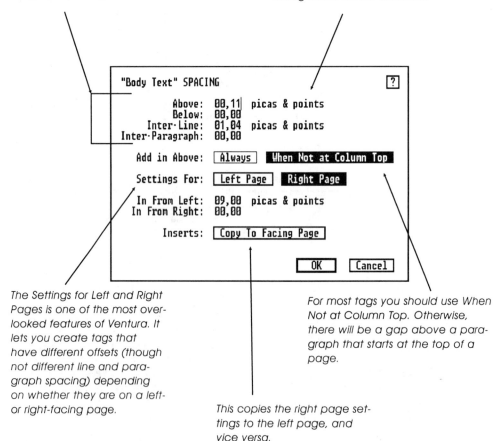

The Settings for Left and Right Pages is one of the most overlooked features of Ventura. It lets you create tags that have different offsets (though not different line and paragraph spacing) depending on whether they are on a left- or right-facing page.

For most tags you should use When Not at Column Top. Otherwise, there will be a gap above a paragraph that starts at the top of a page.

This copies the right page settings to the left page, and vice versa.

Figure 10-4

& points) and clicking. Ventura will automatically make the con-version for all the measurements in the dialog box, but other dialog boxes will not be affected.

Tip 10-3

Making Mistakes with Picas and Points

When you're entering measurements for picas and points in dialog boxes, it's easy to neglect both decimal places reserved for points. For example, you might make the mistake of typing 1,6 instead of 1,06. Ventura will interpret the 1,6 as 1 pica and 60 points.

❖ An Inventory of Ventura's Typographic Controls

Formatting text involves specifying the size, style, and position of each symbol, word, and block of text on the page. In the world of typed and word-processed business documents, the task was relatively simple. The selection of type was generally limited to a single font, and positioning text on the page required setting only a handful of parameters: the margins of the page; the alignment of text (usually flush left, but sometimes centered or justified); the indenting of paragraphs; and the amount of space (in increments of whole and half lines) between lines and between paragraphs.

In Ventura, things become more complex right away, beginning with the selection of type. Hundreds of different fonts are available, each in a wide range of sizes. The options for positioning characters, words, and text blocks are correspondingly rich, providing a full range of typographic controls. The following is an inventory.

- **Page Margins.** For the underlying page, as well as for any new frame you draw on the page, Ventura lets you set the top, bottom, left, and right margins.

- **Margins Around Frames.** Ventura lets you specify an amount of padding around each frame.

- **Columns.** Each page can have up to eight columns of varying widths; the width of the gutters (space between columns) is also adjustable.

- **Horizontal Alignment and Tabs.** Text can be left aligned, right aligned, or centered. Text can also be justified (filling up a defined space) or unjustified (also known as ragged text). You can also align text on a decimal point. You can set up to 16 tabs, aligned either left, right, center, or on a decimal point. A major limitation that still remains is that tabs cannot be placed in justified text.

- **Vertical Alignment.** Text can be top aligned, bottom aligned, or centered. Text can also be vertically justified, so that it fills a page or frame.

- **Offsets and Indents.** Paragraphs of text can be offset from the left, right, bottom, or top margins by a specified distance. One or more lines can also be indented relative to the rest of a paragraph. Text can also be indented by a distance relative to the length of the last line of the previous paragraph.

- **Spacing Between Paragraphs.** The distance between paragraphs can be specified and can vary depending on whether the two paragraphs are of the same type (such as two paragraphs of plain text) or of different types (such as a header followed by a paragraph of text).

- **Spacing Between Lines.** Interline spacing, or leading, can be specified. That distance can also be automatically adjusted to accommodate large characters, fractions, or equations.

- **Spacing Between Words.** Termed spaceband control or space width control, this lets you specify a minimum and maximum amount of space between each word. In addition, Ventura lets you insert a variety of fixed spaces between words.

- **Spacing Between Letters.** This includes adjusting the spaces between pairs of letters to create a better pairwise fit (kerning), globally tightening up the spacing between letters (tracking), and adjusting the spacing between letters on a line-by-line basis to assist the justification process (letter spacing).

- **Ruling Lines.** A close adjunct to text formatting, ruling lines can be placed above, below, or around blocks of text. The thickness of the lines can be specified, and the width can be set either absolutely or relative to the width of the paragraph, the column, or the frame.

- **Special Features.** Ventura provides a number of special formatting features, including bullets, large first character, table formatting, and equation formatting.

While most text formatting is done on a tag-by-tag basis using the options in the Paragraph menu, margins and columns are controlled from the Frame menu. After specifying the number of columns, you enter widths for each of the columns and for the "gutters," or space between each column. Next, you enter values for top, bottom, left, and right margins.

Tip 10-4

Measuring Tabs, Indents, and Offsets

To see the dimensions of your margins, columns, and gutters, use the Options menu (DOS/GEM version) or the View menu (Windows version) to show the column guides. You'll see them represented by dotted lines. Note that all paragraph tag settings, including tabs, indents, and offsets, are measured from the edge of the column, not from the edge of the paper.

Tip 10-5

Changing the Number of Columns for Just One Page

If you want to have a single page with a different number of columns than the rest of your document, select Insert/Remove Page from the Chapter menu, then select Margins & Columns from the Frame menu and designate the desired number of columns. Finally, click on the name of the text file in the Assignment List. The number of columns will change for the inserted page, then resume as normal.

Tip 10-6

The Unprintable Zone

The position of text is always measured relative to the edge of the paper, even if a particular printer is not capable of printing all the way to the edge of the paper, as is normally the case with laser printers. Ventura does not stop you from specifying margins for

Figure 10-5:
When setting text on a skew, draw a diagonal line for a guide, then draw small frames in a stairway pattern.

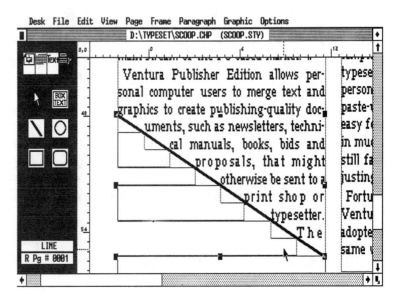

frames that go into the unprintable edges of the paper; if you do so, that portion of your page will simply be cut off.

Tip 10-7

Setting Text on a Skew

To set text on a skew, as shown in Figure 10-1, select graphics mode and select the line drawing tool, then draw a diagonal line to mark the skew. Turn Line Snap on using the Options or View menu. Using the line you have drawn as a guide, you can create a stairway of frames, each one line in height, from the left margin to the skew line. Text will reformat to flow around the stairway and thus will align with the skew line.

❖ Padding around Frames

Putting margins around frames, or frame padding, corrects the problem of text running right up against frames inserted in text blocks containing pictures or tables. To specify padding, select frame mode, select the frame you want to place padding around, select Sizing & Scaling from the Frame menu, and type settings for Frame X Padding and Frame Y Padding. Frame X Padding sets up a "no entry" zone on either side of the frame; Frame Y Padding sets up a "no entry" zone above and below the frame.

❖ Offsets and Indents

Having specified margins for your columns, you can further control the horizontal positioning of paragraphs using offsets and indents. There are several things about these controls that tend to confuse people:

- The first source of confusion is the difference between an offset and an indent. An offset applies to the entire paragraph, while an indent usually applies only to the first line. Usually, but not always: if you want to have more than one

How to Calculate the Position of a Line Relative to the Edge of the Page

In some instances, it is necessary to figure out the location of a particular line relative to the edge of the page. To do this, you can use the following formula:

Distance of a line from left edge of page = A + B + C + D

Where:

A = Upper Left X position of the frame within which the text is located. This is set by selecting frame mode, selecting the frame itself, selecting the Sizing & Scaling option of the Frame menu, and specifying a value for Upper Left X.

B = The Left margin of the frame within which the text is located. This is set by selecting frame mode, selecting the frame itself, selecting the Margins & Columns option of the Frame menu, and specifying a value for Left Margin.

C = The In From Left space specified for the tag of the paragraph of that text. This is set by selecting tagging mode, selecting the paragraph, selecting the Spacing option of the Paragraph menu, and entering a value for In From Left. This indent is referred to as an "offset" or a "temporary indent," since it can change from one paragraph to the next.

D = the Indent Width. This only applies to the first line (or several lines) of a paragraph. To set it, you start by selecting tagging mode, selecting the paragraph, selecting the Alignment option of the Paragraph menu, and entering values for In/Outdent Width and In/Outdent Height. In addition, you can specify a Relative Indent, which causes the line to be indented so that it starts at the point at which the previous line ended.

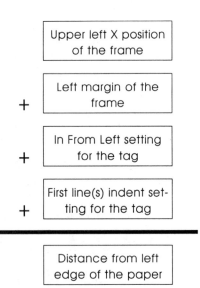

line indented (or outdented) relative to the rest of the paragraph, you can do so by entering the number of lines next to the In\Outdent Height entry of the Alignment menu.

- The second source of confusion arises from the fact that offsets and indents are controlled in different dialog boxes. Controls for offsets are located in the Spacing dialog box under In From Left and In From Right; controls for indents are located in the Alignment dialog box.

- A third source of confusion has to do with the reference point from which offsets and indents are measured. The In From Left and In From Right offsets for a paragraph are measured from the margins of the column. Indents, on the other hand, are measured relative to the rest of the paragraph.

❖ Tabs

The way Ventura handles tabs is quite logical, but since it is different from the methods used by most other programs it tends to cause confusion. Here are some things to keep in mind about Ventura tabs:

- Tabs are measured from the edge of the current column (not the edge of the text in that column). To find out where the edge of the column is located, select Show Column Guides from the Options menu.

- Tabs cannot be set in justified text. For ideas on how to get around this limitation, see the section below on hanging indents.

- Once a tab is set, Ventura no longer performs word wrap for that paragraph. That means you cannot use tabs for first line indents.

- Ventura will preserve tabs set in most word processors but not the settings for the tabs. Instead, it will substitute its own settings.

Tip 10-8

Using the Comma for a Decimal Tab

With decimal tabs, the tab aligns with the decimal, a useful feature for columns of money amounts. In European currencies, a comma rather than a period is used for the decimal point. Since Ventura looks for a period, you need to select Set Preferences from the Options menu (DOS/GEM version) or Edit menu (Windows version) and specify a new Decimal Tab Character. The comma is decimal 44.

Tip 10-9

Using Fixed Spaces Instead of Tabs

Occasionally, you want to tab a line a certain distance that does not correspond to one of the tabs that have been set for that tag. Rather than setting up a new tab (which will affect other paragraphs with the same tag), try using Em spaces (Ctrl-Shift-M)to achieve a tabbing effect. After inserting the Em spaces, use the Set Font button (DOS/GEM version) or the Text menu (Windows version) to convert them to 12-point type. That way their widths will be 12 points, or 1/6 inch.

Em spaces are also handy to substitute for tabs in justified text, since Ventura does not allow tabs in justified text. To insert an indent into a single paragraph without affecting other paragraphs, use Em spaces. For a one-inch indent, insert six Em spaces by pressing the Ctrl-Shfit-M combination six times.

Tip 10-10

Decimal Tab Characters

Normally, when you specify a decimal tab (from the Tab selection of the Paragraph menu), it is for the purpose of aligning columns of dollar figures at the decimal point. Another use of the decimal

The Tab Settings Dialog Box

You can think of each tab stop as an invisible marker. If the tab type is Left, the text will start at the marker; if the tab type is Right, text will end at the marker; if the tab type is Centered, the text will center on the marker. If the tab type is decimal, the decimal point will fall on the marker. Tabs placed in justified text will be ignored by Ventura. Note that tabbed text will not wrap to the next line. Note also that you can designate any character as the decimal character, using Set Preferences in the Options menu.

The space to the tab can be filled with space, with ellipsis marks, with underlining, or with any other character. For example, ASCII 197 will fill the space with Em dashes.

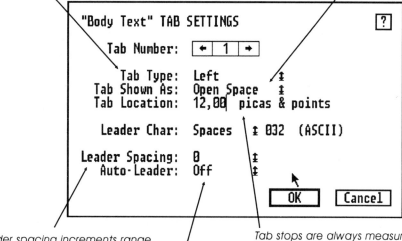

Leader spacing increments range from 0 to 8: selecting 0 means that Ventura will place no spaces between characters, selecting 8 means that it will place 8 spaces between characters. This spacing applies to all tabs.

Tab stops are always measured from the edge of the current column. To locate the column edge, turn on column guides in the Options menu. Measurement units can be changed by pointing at them and clicking. Doing so will not affect the measurement units used in other dialog boxes.

If you turn Auto-Leader on, Ventura will automatically fill any empty space remaining at the end of a paragraph with the leader character. This feature is generally used in tables.

Figure 10-6

tab character is to create an invisible marker to arbitrarily align lines of text. The best character to use for that purpose is | (ASCII 124). You can "hide" this character in a line of text by using Set Font to change its color from black to white (since it takes up barely any horizontal space). By using the decimal tab option in conjunction with this hidden character, you can position horizontal lines freely without using fixed characters or generating multiple tags. Remember that text containing tags must be left justified.

❖ Breaks

Ventura's commands for page, column, and line breaks give you some powerful tools for controlling the placement of text on a page. The most commonly used type of break is the line break, which is used as described below to simulate tabs in justified text. Line breaks are also useful for certain types of tables, as illustrated in Chapter 11, "Tables."

Selecting "Page Break: After" or "Column Break: After" bumps the next paragraph to the following page or column respectively. Selecting "Before & After" makes the current paragraph appear by itself on a page. You can use such a double break in conjunction with Vertical Alignment: Middle to create a section division title that appears by itself in the center of a page.

Setting Next Y Position to Beside Last Line of Prev. Para should be done in conjunction with two other settings:

- Eliminating any line break with the previous paragraph.
- Setting Relative Indent: On in the Alignment dialog box.

The Result The result is a run-in header (such as the one in this paragraph). To create such a header, set the line break for the 24-point run-in to Before and the line break for the text paragraph to After, with Next Y Position for the second paragraph set at Beside Last Line of Prev. Para and Relative Indent for the

The Breaks Dialog Box

A little-known feature of the Page Break option is that it also works as a frame break. If you have a newsletter-style layout and are jumping text from one frame to the next, tagging the last paragraph with Page Break: After causes the next paragraph to jump to the next frame.

The Before/Until Left option forces the current paragraph to jump to the next left-facing page, inserting a blank right-facing page if necessary.

If you select Normal and don't have any line breaks between two paragraphs, the new paragraph will start on the same line as the first line of the previous paragraph. To keep them from overlapping, use the Spacing menu to increase the In From Right spacing for the first paragraph and the In From Left spacing for the second paragraph.

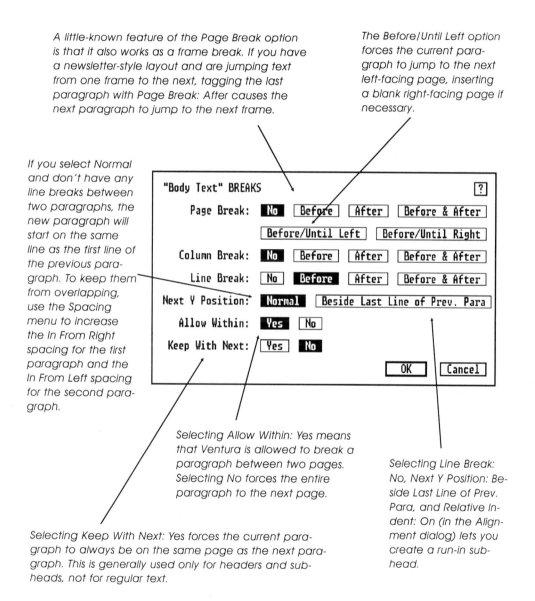

```
"Body Text" BREAKS                                          [?]

      Page Break:  [No]  [Before]  [After]  [Before & After]
                   [Before/Until Left]  [Before/Until Right]

    Column Break:  [No]  [Before]  [After]  [Before & After]

      Line Break:  [No]  [Before]  [After]  [Before & After]

  Next Y Position: [Normal]  [Beside Last Line of Prev. Para]

    Allow Within:  [Yes]  [No]

   Keep With Next: [Yes]  [No]

                                         [OK]   [Cancel]
```

Selecting Allow Within: Yes means that Ventura is allowed to break a paragraph between two pages. Selecting No forces the entire paragraph to the next page.

Selecting Line Break: No, Next Y Position: Beside Last Line of Prev. Para, and Relative Indent: On (in the Alignment dialog) lets you create a run-in subhead.

Selecting Keep With Next: Yes forces the current paragraph to always be on the same page as the next paragraph. This is generally used only for headers and subheads, not for regular text.

Figure 10-7

second paragraph turned on (Alignment dialog box). If you only have to create one run-in header, it's easier to simply use Set Font, but if you have a number of run-in headers it's quicker to use a special tag.

Tip 10-11

Frame Breaks

Ventura has no Frame Break option to let you push subsequent text to the next Frame. To create a frame break effect, create a new tag and call it Frame Break. To create the tag, select text mode, press Enter to create a blank paragraph. You may see a ¶ mark, Ventura's way of marking paragraphs. If not, press Ctrl-T. Select tagging mode, select the paragraph mark (¶), select Add New Tag (Ctrl-2), type Frame Break, select Breaks from the Paragraph menu, and select Page Break: After. Use this tag when you are loading text into multiple frames on the same pages and wish to break text to the next frame on the same page.

❖ Simulating Tabs in Justified Text

Ventura doesn't allow you to place normal tabs in justified text. If you do, the program will simply ignore them. Sometimes, however, it is necessary to format text with a hanging indent, such as the following:

Section I.   The right of citizens of the United States to vote shall not be denied or abridged by the United States or by any State on account of race, color, or previous condition of servitude.

With many word processors, you would format this paragraph by specifying a negative indent for the first line of the paragraph, then creating a tab that is the same as the indent for the rest of the paragraph. With Ventura you need to separate the paragraph into two separate paragraphs, typing them as follows:

`Section I.`

`The right of citizens of the United States to`
`vote shall not be denied or abridged by the`
`United States or by any State on account of`
`race, color, or previous condition of ser-`
`vitude.`

Select tagging mode, select the first paragraph, and select Breaks from the Paragraph menu. If the dialog box shows Line Break: No or Line Break: Before, you don't have to make any changes. Cancel out of the dialog box.

If the dialog box shows Line Break: After or Line Break: Before and After, Cancel out of the dialog box and then press Ctrl-2 to add a new tag. Type the previous paragraph's tag next to Tag Name to Copy From, and type a new tag name next to Tag Name to Add.

Select the Breaks option of the Paragraph menu and change the setting to "Line Break: Before." Press Enter.

Now select the second paragraph, and press Ctrl-2 (Add New Tag). Type the previous paragraph's tag next to Tag Name to Copy From, and type a new tag name next to Tag Name to Add.

Select Spacing from the Paragraph menu and enter the amount of the indent next to In From Left.

Select Breaks and specify Line Break: After.

❖ Ruling Lines

Ventura allows the creation of a variety of ruling lines: horizontal, vertical, surrounding frames, dashed, and shaded. You can add ruling lines to either a frame or a paragraph tag. The choices are either Ruling Line Below, Ruling Line Above, or Ruling Box Around.

The first thing you need to do is specify the length of the ruling line. The choices are Text (the width of the line of text), Margin (the width of the column, minus the In-From-Left and In-From-Right settings for the current tag), Column, Frame, and Custom. With the Custom option, you determine the starting point and the length of the line.

The Windows version provides 16 different predefined ruling line thicknesses and combinations of ruling lines. The options are as follows: hairline, 1-point, 1½-point, 2-point, 3-point, 4-point, 6-point, 8-point, 10-point, 12-point, 18-point, double half-point, thick-thin, thin-thick, triple, and triple half-point. If none of these suits you, the User Defined option lets you specify the line thicknesses yourself.

 In each of these cases, you must specify the line height within the dialog box. You can indicate up to three ruling lines by indicating Height of Rule 1, Height of Rule 2, and Height of Rule 3. If you just want one line, simply specify a Height of Rule 1 and leave the other heights blank. When you specify the Height of Rule, a line or lines with the specified line height(s) will appear smack inside the dialog box. If you do not see a line inside the dialog box, you will not see a line in your document either.

If you have specified Height of Rule for more than one line, you will have to indicate a Space Below Rule dimension also. If you don't, the lines will merge into one thick line. The ruling lines options give you a good deal of feedback right inside the dialog box. You can immediately see the effect of your line height, spacing, and color pattern without even going to the page. However, note that the width of the line shown in the dialog is not the actual width it will appear on the screen. Instead, it is relative to the total amount of vertical space available to the three ruling lines.

Note: In the Ruling Line menus, you must also be sure to specify a line width. If you set the width default to None, your ruling lines will not appear on the page even though you can see them inside the dialog box!

Tip 10-12

Reversed Type with Ruling Line Above

To create white type on a black background, use the Ruling Line Above option and set Height of Rule 1 to a value slightly larger than the point size of the current font. Enter the same value for Space Below Rule 3 and select the minus sign (-). Then change the color of the font to white.

Tips 10-13

Reversed Type with Box Text

Another way to create reversed type is to use the box text tool in graphics mode. Draw a box using the box text tool. Set Fill Attributes to solid black, and use Set Font to change the color of the text in the box to white.

Tip 10-14

Disappearing Rules

If your ruling line doesn't show, you probably forgot to specify height of ruling line. Ventura will show you a ruling line right inside the dialog box once you specify the line height.

Tip: 10-15

Vertical Dashed Lines

Ventura has no command for vertical dashed lines, such as you would use to indicate cutting out a page. Make a frame of zero width and surround it with dashes

❖ Vertical Alignment and Justification

The vertical alignment feature lets you align text with the top or bottom of the current column, or center the text within the column. You have the additional option of vertically justifying text, i.e., of having Ventura automatically add space so that the column fills up the vertical space allotted to it.

Because of the many different kinds of elements that may inhabit a page, the internal logic used by Ventura to vertically justify a column of text is fairly complicated. The goal of the procedure, however, is very simple: to add small amounts of space in the least conspicuous way until the page is filled. Space is first added around frames, up to a specified maximum. Next, it is added between paragraphs, again until a certain limit is reached. Finally, if adding space around frames and between paragraphs is not sufficient, space is added between lines of text.

Tip 10-16

Where to Enter Settings for Vertical Justification

Since vertical justification settings can be entered in the Chapter, Frame, and Paragraph menus, which should you use? The answer is the Chapter menu for all settings except Between Lines of Para, which is specified under Paragraph Typography. The others should only be used if it is necessary to override the chapter menu settings for a particular frame, paragraph, or table.

Tip 10-17

Carding versus Feathering

Under Vert Just Within Frame, you have the option of carding or feathering. Carding adds space in increments equal to the inter-

line spacing; feathering adds the exact amount of space that is needed. The only time you should select carding is if the design of your document requires lines of text to line up in adjacent columns and you have set the spacing for all tags in multiples of the interline spacing. Otherwise, use feathering.

Tip 10-18

Fixed Frame versus Movable Frame

Under Vert. Just. Around Frame, you should generally select Movable Frame rather than Fixed Frame. This allows Ventura to shift frames on the page down as it adds space to justify the page. If you select Fixed Frame, Ventura will only insert space within the portion of the column that is located underneath the frame.

Tip 10-19

No Halfway Justification

Ventura never goes halfway in vertically justifying a page. If it can't add enough space to accomplish the task without exceeding the specified limits for adding space around frames, between paragraphs, and between lines of text, it does nothing.

Tip 10-20

Vertical Justification without the Professional Extension or the Windows version

Even if you don't have the Professional Extension or the Windows version, both of which can automatically perform vertical justification, there are still some techniques that you can use if you need to fill up a certain vertical space. Here are three:

- *To slightly lengthen a column, you can create a tag that adds a small amount of leading between each line. In traditional typesetting, this technique is known as feathering.*

The easiest way to feather a paragraph is to create a tag called One Point. Move the cursor between the paragraphs, press Enter, and select tagging mode. Select the paragraph sign between the two paragraphs, select Add New Tag, name the tag One Point, select the Spacing option in the Paragraph menu, and set interline spacing to one point. The effect will be to add a point of leading between the two paragraphs.

- *Make the tracking looser under Paragraph Typography.*
- *Increase the minimum and normal letter spacing under Paragraph Typography.*

❖ Spacing between Lines and Paragraphs

Spacing between lines and paragraphs, termed leading in typography, is controlled by the Spacing option of the Paragraph menu. For each tag, you can specify the spacing above the paragraph, below the paragraph, between lines of the same paragraph, and between two paragraphs with the same tag. In practice, the interaction of these various kinds of spacing becomes rather complex. But by knowing the rules Ventura uses to combine different kinds of spacing, you can learn to control precisely the desired distance between lines and paragraphs.

Spacing is always measured from baseline to baseline. Thus, the space between two lines is measured from the baseline of the first to the baseline of the second. Similarly, the space between two paragraphs is measured from the baseline of the last line in the first paragraph to the baseline of the first line in the second paragraph.

◆ Interline Spacing

To set the interline spacing for a paragraph, switch to tagging mode and select a paragraph. Select the Spacing option from the Paragraph menu. The Spacing dialog box will appear. Enter the desired figure for Interline spacing. The figure you enter will determine the distance from the baseline of one line to the baseline of the next line. Since type is measured in points, it is generally best to use points as your measurement units. To change measurement units, point at the units themselves with the mouse and click. For example, to change from inches to picas & points, point at the word inches and click.

This Grow Inter-Line to Fit feature is located in the Paragraph Typography dialog box. This should be set to On if you want the program to stretch the leading when a paragraph contains a large element, such as a fraction or a floating frame.

◆ Spacing between Paragraphs

Any two paragraphs will automatically be separated by at least the amount of line spacing specified for the previous paragraph. Additional paragraph spacing can be specified via three controls in the Spacing dialog box. To set these controls, first select tagging mode and then select a paragraph. Select the Spacing option from the Paragraph menu. The Spacing dialog box will appear. The three controls are (1) Above, (2) Below, and (3) Inter-Paragraph.

To master Below, Above, and Inter-Paragraph spacing, you need to know the rules for combining the two. These rules are summarized in Table 10-2.

In working with text, the rule of thumb is that you should set Above and Below Spaces as the amount of additional space (besides normal interline spacing) that you want to have between paragraphs. Set Interparagraph Spacing to 0.

Tip 10-21

Using Ctrl-Enter for New Lines

If you want to start a new line without starting a new paragraph, use Ctrl-Enter rather than Enter. That way, Ventura will not start

How to Calculate Spacing between Paragraphs

Case 1: When paragraph A and paragraph B have the same tag

Case 2: When paragraph A and paragraph B have different tags

	Case 1		Case 2
	Interline space		Interline space for paragraph A
+	Interparagraph space	+	Interparagraph space (only if identical for A and B)
+	Below space for A or Above space for B (whichever is greater)	+	Below space for A or Above space for B (whichever is greater)
+	Width of ruling lines, including space above or below ruling lines	+	Width of ruling lines, including space above or below ruling lines
	Total space between paragraphs		Total space between paragraphs

Table 10-2: The amount of space that Ventura places between two paragraphs is determined by four factors: interline spacing, interparagraph spacing, above/below spacing, width of ruling lines, and spacing above or below ruling lines.

a new paragraph and spacing will remain the standard interline distance. No Space Above or Space Below distance will be added between the lines.

❖ Spacing between Words

When you specify that a paragraph is to be justified (i.e., all lines the same length), Ventura squeezes the amount of space between words or adds space between words. You can keep words from being squeezed too closely together by changing the setting indicated under Paragraph Typography for Minimum Space Width.

While Ventura adheres religiously to the Minimum Space Width, never squeezing words more closely than allowed by the minimum figure, the same is not the case with Maximum Space Width. That setting is merely a guideline: when it must do so to justify a line, Ventura will violate the Maximum Space Width. The result is a "loose line." All loose lines are highlighted when you select Show Loose Lines from the Options menu. To get rid of them, you need to either edit the lines, change the hyphenation points, or turn letter spacing on (see below).

❖ Fixed Spaces

If you want to create spaces that are of a fixed width and will not be squeezed or expanded by Ventura, you can do so using several fixed space options. Ventura provides the following types of fixed spaces: figure spaces, Em spaces, En spaces, and thin spaces.

◆ Figure Space

The width of a figure space is the same as the width of a numeral (traditionally in typesetting, all digits from 0 to 9 are given the same width). Such spaces can be used for aligning tables of numbers. To insert a figure space into a passage using Ventura's text editor, hold down the Ctrl and Shift keys while pressing the F key. To insert a figure space into a passage using your own word processor, type a plus sign surrounded by angle brackets (<+>).

◆ Em Space

The width of an Em space is the same as the point size of the font in use. Thus, an Em space in a passage of 12-point Times Roman is 12 points wide, or ⅙ inch. To insert an Em space into a passage using Ventura's text editor, hold down the Shift and Ctrl keys while pressing the M. To insert an Em space into a passage using your own word processor, type an underline surrounded by angle brackets. (<_>).

◆ En Space

The width of an En space is half the width of an Em space. Thus, an En space in a passage of 12-point Times Roman is 6 points wide, or ¹⁄₁₂ inch. To insert an En space into a passage using Ventura's text editor, hold down the Shift and Ctrl keys while pressing N. To insert an En space into a passage using your own word processor, type a tilde surrounded by angle brackets (<~>).

◆ Thin Space

The width of a thin space is half the width of an En space. Thus, a thin space in a passage of 12-point Times Roman is 3 points wide, or 1/24 of an inch. To insert a thin space into a passage using Ventura's text editor, hold down the Shift and Ctrl keys while pressing the T. To insert a thin space into a passage using your own word processor, type a vertical bar surrounded by angle brackets (<|>).

Tip 10-22

Customized Fixed Spaces

Although Ventura provides four types of fixed spaces, you can create more simply by typing a character and setting its color to white. To do so, select text mode. Then type the character from the keyboard and highlight it with the mouse by dragging the mouse across it while holding down the mouse button. Select the Set Font button. From the font setting dialog box, select White as the color. On the screen the character will not be seen, but its place will be kept in the text.

❖ Spaces between Letters

The spacing between characters is controlled primarily by a width table that is part of a font. Unless you are using a font editor to create entirely new characters, there's no need to worry about this width table. Because of the width table, Ventura automatically performs proportional spacing, assigning more space to a *W*, for example, than to an *i*. For altering the spacing between letters, Ventura provides four types of controls: (1) manual kerning, (2) automatic kerning, (3) tracking, and (4) letter spacing.

◆ Manual Kerning

The procedure for manually kerning a pair of letters is simple and intuitive. To perform manual kerning you select text mode, then hold down the mouse button and drag the cursor across the letter immediately to the left of the letter space that you wish to close up. While holding down the Shift key, press the left arrow key to make the space narrower, or press the right arrow key to make the space wider.

Methods for Controlling Spacing within Words and between Words

- **Kerning** *Adjustments to the space between individual letter pairs.*

- **Letter Spacing** *Uniform addition of extra space between all the characters in a line if the line is "loose," i.e., if the space between the words of that line exceeds the Maximum Space Width.*

- **Tracking** *Uniform tightening or loosening of the space between letters. For most text, tracking should be neither tight nor loose. For headlines and titles, it should usually be tightened up.*

- **Minimum Space Width** *The closest allowable distance between two words in a line. Though Ventura will exceed the Maximum Space Width if necessary to justify a line of text, it will never set words closer together than the Minimum Space Width. A recommended number is 0.6 times the Normal Space Width.*

- **Normal Space Width** *The optimum space that Ventura aims at in justifying a line. Generally, it should be set to 1.0 unless you need to expand a paragraph to fit a particular space.*

- **Maximum Space Width** *The maximum desirable distance between words in a justified line. If Ventura is forced to exceed this figure, the line is considered "loose." To keep the space between words within the Maximum Space Width limit, Ventura will add spaces between letters, provided Letter Spacing is on.*

Table 10-3: Methods for controlling the spacing within words and between words.

Tip 10-23

Kerning Increments

Each time you press the left arrow key, you close the space by .02 Em. Each time you press the right arrow key, you widen the space by .02 Em. In other words, you would have to hit the space bar 50 times to widen the space between two letters the width of a capital letter M.

Tip 10-24

Don't Highlight the Last Letter

When you use the Shift-Arrow combination to widen or tighten kerning, Ventura adds space on the right side of all the letters you have highlighted. So if you're trying to uniformly tighten or loosen the spacing in a word or phrase, don't highlight the last letter. Also, if you're kerning just one letter combination, just highlight the first letter, not both letters.

To find out how much the space has been reduced, select Set Font and check the setting for Kern. The amount of reduction or enlargement in the space between the two letters is measured in Ems, where one Em equals the point size of the font. So if the paragraph is set in 12-point type, an Em is 12 points, or 1/6 inch, wide.

In general, it is easier to adjust the kerning of letters by using the shift and arrow key combination; however, an alternative method is to type the desired amount of tightening or loosening directly in the Set Font dialog box.

If you want to return to the original spacing, simply highlight the character and select Normal from the Selection List.

◆ Automatic Kerning

The manual kerning procedure described above lets you interactively adjust the spacing between any pair of characters. Automatic kerning means that Ventura will use the kerning information contained in your printer width table to automatically adjust all instances of particular letter combinations, such as AV and To.

This assumes, of course, that your printer width table contains a table listing the spacing adjustments for particular character combinations. You can turn automatic kerning on or off either for the chapter as a whole (Chapter menu: Chapter Typography), for the current frame (Frame menu: Frame Typography), or for a single tag (Paragraph menu: Paragraph Typography).

The question, of course, is: which menu overrides which? If you tell Ventura at the chapter level to turn kerning off, at the frame level to turn it on, and at the tag level to turn it off, what will happen? The answer is best summarized in Table 10-5.

Tip 10-25

Font Support for Automatic Kerning

Automatic kerning only works if the width table for the fonts you are using includes kerning information. Ventura's PostScript width table does include such information. The width table for the LaserJet fonts provided with Ventura does also. Many third-party fonts also include kerning information, including LaserJet fonts from Conographic, The Font Factory, Mephistopheles, Soft-Craft, VS Software, and Weaver Graphics. When you buy a font, check with the vendor to see that it includes a width table with a built-in table of kerning pairs.

Kerning Options

Menu/Option	Applies To	Notes
Chapter Menu: Chapter Typography	*Automatic Kerning for All Tags*	*Pair Kerning: On enables automatic kerning if the font width table for your printer includes kerning pair information. It does not affect manual kerning.*
Frame Menu: Frame Typography	*Automatic Kerning for All Tags in the Selected Frame.*	*Pair Kerning: On overrides the Chapter menu for the selected frame.*
Paragraph Menu: Paragraph Typography	*Automatic Kerning at the Tag Level*	*Automatic Pair Kerning: On overrides the Chapter and Frame Typography menus for the selected tag.*
Set Font	*Manual Kerning*	*This option is used in Text mode. It moves the selected characters closer together or farther apart.*
Shift-Arrow Keys	*Interactive Manual Kerning*	*The selected characters are moved closer together (left arrow) or farther apart (right arrow).*

Table 10-4: *Ventura's five methods of kerning.*

Relation between Chapter, Frame, and Paragraph Controls for Automatic Pair Kerning

Chapter Menu Pair Kerning	Frame Pair Kerning	Automatic Pair Kerning	Letters Kerned
On	On	On	**YES**
On	Off	On	No
Off	Off	On	No
On	On	Off	No
Off	On	Off	No
On	Off	Off	No
Off	Off	Off	No
On	Default	On	**YES**
Off	Default	On	No
On	Default	Off	No
Off	Default	Off	No

Table 10-5: *Relation between chapter, frame, and paragraph controls for automatic kerning.*

◆ Tracking

The difference between kerning and tracking is that kerning means tightening up particular pairs of characters whose shapes allow them to fit more closely together, while tracking refers to uniform tightening or loosening of an entire block of text. While kerning is generally used to avoid unattractive gaps between particular characters, tracking is most often used to improve the appearance of passages of text that are set in large type, such as headlines and titles. Generally, while normal spacing looks good in regular text sizes, large type needs to be tightened up to look right.

To change the tracking settings for a single tag, select a paragraph. From the Paragraph menu select the Paragraph Typography option. Select the Looser or Tighter options, and enter an amount (always measured in Ems). As noted above, the size of an Em is relative to the size of the font in the selected paragraph. If you're using 12-point type, setting the tracking to 0.050 Ems tighter would reduce the amount of space between each character by .6 points, or $\frac{1}{120}$ inch.

To change tracking settings interactively for a passage of text, you can switch to text editing mode and select a passage of text by dragging the mouse across it, so that it appears in reverse video on the screen. Now, if you hold down the Shift key and press the left arrow, the space between each pair of letters will be closed up by .02 Em, or about 1/4 point for each letter (assuming 12-point type). In effect, what you're doing is applying the interactive kerning procedure to a group of letters all at once. Remember not to highlight the final letter of the passage you're tracking.

When should you use interactive tracking with the Shift-Arrow combination, versus tag-based tracking with the Paragraph Typography option? Generally, interactive tracking adjustment is better when you need to reduce or enlarge the amount of space taken up by a passage of text. Tag-based tracking is better for uniformly tightening up the passages of text set in large fonts, such as headlines and titles.

Tip 10-26

When to Use Tracking

With normal body type set in wide columns, tracking is usually not necessary. Tracking, which uniformly increases or reduces the spaces between characters, is used in the following situations:

- *To improve the appearance of body copy set in certain fonts. For example, 8.5-point Palatino looks slightly better when the tracking is loosened by .05 Ems.*

- *In headlines and other text that uses large fonts (such as the chapter titles in this book). Normally, large type sizes are too loose without tracking.*

- *To squeeze copy within a given area. This is most often necessary to get rid of a word appearing by itself on the last line of a paragraph. Once you have tightened up the tracking of the text above the solitary word, the word will jump up to join the previous line.*

- *With italic fonts, which sometimes appear too loose without tracking.*

◆ Letter Spacing

The method that Ventura uses to create justified text is to uniformly increase or decrease the amount of space between the words in a particular line. Of course, adding too much space between words may give text an undesirable appearance. Lines in which the amount of space between words exceeds a certain desirable maximum are referred to as "loose lines." To deal with a loose line, a typographic system can resort to increasing the amount of space between letters within words. This is known as "letter spacing."

Here's how Ventura goes about setting lines. First, it tries to justify lines by adding space between words. If the amount of space between words exceeds a specified limit, you have a "loose line." The specified limit is the Maximum Space Width setting shown in the Typographic Controls dialog box, selected from the Paragraph menu. As long as you have chosen not to activate letter spacing, Ventura will go ahead and print loose lines, that is, lines in which spaces between words exceed this maximum. However, if you turn the letter spacing option on, Ventura will attempt to fix the loose line by adding spaces between letters.

To turn letter spacing on, start by selecting a paragraph. From the Paragraph menu select the Paragraph Typography option. Select Letter Spacing: On and enter a figure next to "Up to:" This controls the maximum amount of space that Ventura will add to the already existing spaces between characters to try to fill out the line.

To see which lines in a document are in need of letter spacing, select the Show Loose Lines option of the Options menu.

Tip 10-27

Loose Lines

After you "fix" a loose line by adjusting the letter spacing, the line will still be marked as loose. Table 10-3 compares the various options for controlling spacing within words and between words.

Tip 10-28

Marker Characters

Ventura uses a variety of markers to indicate the hidden characters used for tabs, paragraph endings, discretionary hyphens, etc. These marks will be shown on the page if you press Ctrl-T or select Show Tabs & Returns from the Options menu.

Tip 10-29

Line Snap

To activate line snap, change Line Snap to "On" in the Options menu. Line snap sets up an invisible grid on the page. The width of this grid is the interline spacing used by the Body Text tag. The reference point is the baseline of Body Text set on the base page. You can use line snap for the following:

- *Creating a thin frame that is exactly the same height as a single line. Such a frame can be used to adjust vertical spacing in a column of text.*
- *Making text in adjacent columns line up.*
- *Allowing two frames to adjoin each other exactly.*

❖ Special Effects

Over the years, designers and typographers have developed a repertory of special techniques for enhancing the appearance of text. When used effectively, these effects play not only an aesthetic role, but also serve to accent the underlying organization of a document and make it more effective. In general, you should avoid using special effects such as large first letters merely for decorative purposes. The most commonly used special effects, both of which are easily done in Ventura, are bullets and large first characters. For an explanation of the big first character function, see Chapter 20, "Using Fonts."

◆ Bullets

To create a tag that automatically places a bullet in front of a paragraph, select Special Effects from the Paragraph menu. Note that a bullet can be any character, not just the • mark. Look up the chart of characters (shown on the inside cover of this book) and type the appropriate ASCII character in the Special Effects dialog box. Ventura lets you also use solid or hollow box characters for bullets, even though these characters are not part of either the Ventura International symbol set or the Symbol font. If you have a PostScript printer, you can use character 110 of Zapf Dingbats for a solid box (■) and characters 111 (❑), 112 (❐), 113 (❑), and 114 (❐) for hollow boxes. Use the Set Font Properties option to change the size and font for the bullet.

Tip 10-30

Changing the Size of the Bullet

If you don't like the size of the bullet, you can create a larger one. Tag the paragraph and select Special Effects from the Paragraph menu. Select Bullet and select Set Font Properties. By indicating a larger point size, you'll get a larger bullet even though the size of your text will remain the same. If you select a large point size for your bullet, you'll also have to use the Shift option to nudge it down slightly.

• Small

● Medium

● Large

● Humongous

● Brobdingnagian

Tip 10-31

Using a Picture for a Bullet

You can use a graphic image such as a piece of clip art or a company logo for a bullet. The technique involves loading the graphic into a "floating frame." It is described in Chapter 13, "Pagination."

◆ Small Caps

SMALL CAPS are capital letters set one or two points smaller than the size of current text. Among other purposes, they are useful for making acronyms less conspicuous (e.g., UNICEF instead of UNICEF). In Ventura, creating small caps is easy. Type the text as normal, then highlight it (still working in text mode rather than tagging mode) and select Upper Case and Small from the Assignment List. For an enhanced effect, keep the initial letters of words that would otherwise be capitalized in regular caps, as shown above.

❖ Questions

Q: *How can I make a headline that goes across several columns?*

A: Select tagging mode. Tag the headline. Select the Paragraph menu. Select the Alignment option. Select Overall Width: Frame-Wide.

Q: *I turned kerning on in the Page Layout dialog box of the Page menu, but doing so did not cause the text to be kerned. Why not?*

A: In order for automatic kerning to function, the font you're using must include spacing information for each kerning pair (each pair of characters that is to be automatically kerned). Such information is part of PostScript fonts and the LaserJet soft fonts provided with Ventura.

Q: **What is the difference between tracking and space width?**

A: Tracking is a way of globally tightening up the distance between characters. Space width settings provide a minimum, an optimum, and a maximum allowable amount of space between words.

Q: **Kerning looked fine on the screen but did not print correctly.**

A: This is an unavoidable side effect of the fact that the resolution of graphic displays is so much lower than of output devices. At the level of character spacing, true WYSIWYG is still in the future.

Q: **What does Letter Spacing: On/Off mean in the Typographic Controls dialog box of the Paragraph menu?**

A: As long as letter spacing is turned off, Ventura will only adjust the spaces between words as it justifies lines of text. If the program does not succeed in keeping these interword spaces within the limits you have specified for maximum spaceband values, it will highlight the line as a "loose line." By turning on letter spacing, you can then allow the program to adjust the spacing between letters within words, so that the spaces between words can be narrowed. Note that even after you turn letter spacing on, the lines will still be highlighted as loose.

Q: *Some of the measurements in the menus are shown as ~~.~~ rather than as numbers. What is the meaning of these marks?*

A: They denote that the measurement is out of range. Generally, this occurs when you are using fractional points as your measurement units. Any number larger than 99.99 points (about 1.4 inches) will be shown as ~~.~~ fractional points. The solution is to change measurement units, which is done by pointing directly at the words "fractional points" and clicking with the mouse.

11

Tables

The easiest way to format tables and forms is to use Ventura's powerful and flexible table generator, which is available in the Windows version and in the Professional Extension with the DOS/GEM version. Most of this chapter is devoted to explaining the table generator, but we will also look at four other ways of setting up tabular material: using tabs, using breaks, using ruling lines, and using box text.

❖ Tabs

Tabs should be used to separate columns when the material in each column can fit on one line and does not need to wrap to the next line within that column. For the tabs to work, the paragraph must be formatted as left or right aligned — not justified. Note: *Tabs are always measured from the edge of the current column.*

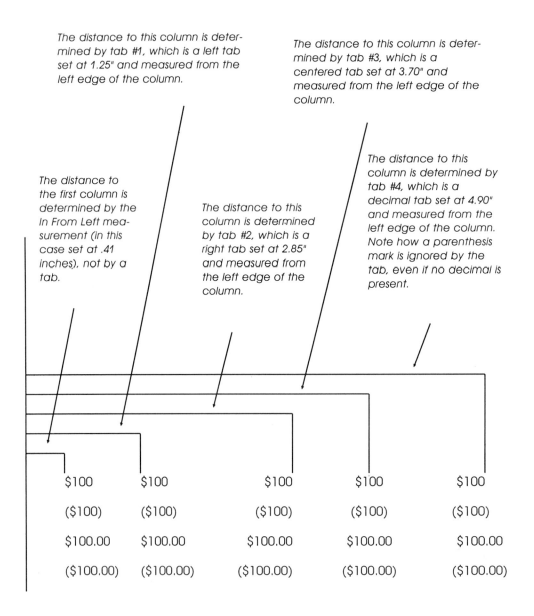

The distance to this column is determined by tab #1, which is a left tab set at 1.25" and measured from the left edge of the column.

The distance to this column is determined by tab #3, which is a centered tab set at 3.70" and measured from the left edge of the column.

The distance to the first column is determined by the In From Left measurement (in this case set at .41 inches), not by a tab.

The distance to this column is determined by tab #2, which is a right tab set at 2.85" and measured from the left edge of the column.

The distance to this column is determined by tab #4, which is a decimal tab set at 4.90" and measured from the left edge of the column. Note how a parenthesis mark is ignored by the tab, even if no decimal is present.

$100	$100	$100	$100	$100
($100)	($100)	($100)	($100)	($100)
$100.00	$100.00	$100.00	$100.00	$100.00
($100.00)	($100.00)	($100.00)	($100.00)	($100.00)

Figure 11-1: *Examples of left, right, centered, and decimal tabs.*

In Figure 11-1, the edge of the column is shown by the vertical line. The first column is set not with a tab but with the In From Left setting for the paragraph. The other four columns show the placement of various number formats for left, right, centered, and decimal tabs.

❖ Breaks

Breaks rather than tabs should be used when the material in each column needs to wrap. This method is also referred to as "vertical tabs." To set up such material you proceed one step at a time. The first step is to type the three paragraphs, tagging them with the Body Text tag. The second step is to create a new tag for each column and adjust the settings for In From Left and In From Right so that they won't overlap after you line them up next to each other. The final step is to adjust the settings for Line Breaks so that the three columns line up next to each other. These three steps are illustrated in Figure 11-2.

❖ Box Text

Complex tables are most easily handled by using the Box Text tool in graphics mode, typing text into the boxes, and then setting Line Attributes at None to eliminate the boundaries of the boxes. The drawback of this method is that surrounding text does not flow around boxes, so you'll have to create empty space or draw a frame to contain the boxes. If you want to make the table move with text, create it within a frame and then make the frame a floating frame.

❖ Ruling Line Below

Here's a quick way to create a simple table. Draw a box using either the Box Text tool or the Add New Frame button. Place the

This is the first column. It will be positioned on the left side of the page.¶

This is the second column. It will be positioned in the middle of the page.¶

This is the third column. It will be positioned on the right side of the page☐

Step 1: Type each column as a separate paragraph, using the standard Body Text tag.

This is the first column. It
will be positioned on the
left side of the page.¶

This is the second column. It will
be positioned in the middle of
the page.¶

This is the third column. It
will be positioned on the
right side of the page☐

Step 2: Create three new tags, one of each of the paragraphs. Use the In From Left and In From Right settings of the Paragraph Spacing menu to position the paragraphs horizontally.

This is the first column. It will be positioned on the left side of the page.¶	This is the second column. It will be positioned in the middle of the page.¶	This is the third column. It will be positioned on the right side of the page☐

Step 3: Use the Paragraph Breaks menu to position the paragraphs side by side. Set the Line Breaks for the first paragraph to Before, for the second paragraph to None, and for the third paragraph to After.

Figure 11-2: *The three-step method for using line breaks to place text in adjacent columns.*

cursor inside the box or the blank frame and press Enter several times.

Now switch to tagging mode and create a tag with Ruling Line Below width set to "Frame." Your box or frame will instantly fill up with evenly spaced lines. You can then type text on any of the lines and create additional tags to change the spacing for a particular line or to align it left, right, or center. If you use a frame, you can even make it a floating frame so that the table always remains in the same position relative to the surrounding text, just as though you were using the table generator in the Professional Extension. You can also use Margins & Columns to create multiple columns within the frame, and use Vertical Rules to set up vertical ruling lines between the columns. To align your block of ruled lines relative to other such blocks, set up the underlying page so that it has a large number of columns, then set Column Snap and Line Snap on. If you're using box text to create your lined blocks, also set Grid Snap on.

❖ The Table Generator

In the Windows and DOS/GEM versions (Professional Extension only), the table generator is accessed by first clicking in front of a paragraph, then selecting the Table icon. The generator lets you do the following:

- Quickly set up a table with a specified number of rows and columns.
- Add or delete rows and columns.
- Use thin, thick, or double lines to set off parts of the table.
- Hide some or all of the ruling lines.
- Create complex tables by merging cells.
- Type text directly into cells or else load it from a spreadsheet.
- Use shading to highlight selected cells.

Insert/Edit Table Dialog Box

Ventura will create the number of rows and columns you specify here. If you change your mind later and want to add more rows and columns, use Ins Row and Ins Column in the Assignment List.

If you select Overall Width: Column, Ventura will make the table fit the width of the column. The other option is Custom, which lets you type in a figure for width.

The table can be aligned with the left or right margin, or indented a specified amount. If you allow the table to break across pages, you can cause a specified number of the header rows to be repeated on the second page.

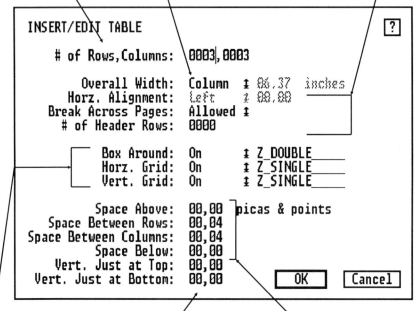

```
INSERT/EDIT TABLE                                    [?]

    # of Rows,Columns:  \0003|,0003

        Overall Width:  Column  ± 06.37  inches
      Horz. Alignment:  Left    ± 00.00
   Break Across Pages:  Allowed ±
      # of Header Rows: 0000

           Box Around:  On      ± Z_DOUBLE____
           Horz. Grid:  On      ± Z_SINGLE____
           Vert. Grid:  On      ± Z_SINGLE____

          Space Above:  00,00  picas & points
  Space Between Rows:   00,04
Space Between Columns:  00,04
          Space Below:  00,00
    Vert. Just at Top:  00,00
 Vert. Just at Bottom:  00,00        [  OK  ]  [Cancel]
```

Box Around controls the outer perimeter of the table; Horz. and Vert. Grid control the internal lines. You can override these settings by selecting a vertical or horizontal line and applying attributes from the Assignment List.

The figures for Vert. Just at Top and Bottom control how much space Ventura can add above and below the table to vertically justify a page.

Space Above and Space Below control the distance to adjacent paragraphs. Space Between Rows is measured from the baseline of one row to the baseline of the next.

Figure 11-3

- Apply any tag to text in cells, and thus easily control such parameters as font, alignment, and spacing within cells.

- Change the width of a cell by holding down the Alt key while dragging the edge with the mouse.

- Use absolute measurements to specify the width of a cell, or set its width relative to other cells.

To show these capabilities in action, let's try creating a table from scratch. The first thing to do is to select table mode by clicking on the table icon. Next, position the mouse at the top of a page (if the page is blank) or just above a paragraph (if the page contains text) and click. You'll see a horizontal gray line on the screen. Now click on the Ins New Table button (DOS/GEM version) or the Insert New Table option of the Table menu (Windows version). The dialog box shown on the following page will appear for the DOS/GEM version. For the Windows version, the dialog box looks superficially different but provides the same functions.

At this point, you don't have to worry about what settings to enter. Just accept the defaults and select OK. An empty grid will appear on your screen, like this:

◆ Adjusting the Size of the Cells

Let's start by learning how to adjust the size of the cells. In editing tables, there are two ways to do this. One is to set the size of each column in proportion to other columns. To select a column, first select table mode, then click anywhere in the column. Now select Set Column Width from the Edit menu (DOS/GEM version) or the Table menu (Windows version). If you don't see that as an option in the DOS/GEM version, make sure you're in table mode. The Table icon should be highlighted.

```
┌─────────────────────────────────────────────────┐
│  TABLE COLUMN WIDTHS                        [?]   │
│                                                   │
│     Column Number:   [ ← │  1  │ → ]              │
│                                                   │
│     Width Setting:   Variable  ↨                  │
│                                                   │
│        Fixed Width:  00.00   centimeters          │
│     Variable Width:  0001|   proportions          │
│                                                   │
│                      [  OK  ]    [ Cancel ]       │
└─────────────────────────────────────────────────┘
```

Having selected Set Column Width, you'll see the dialog box shown above.

If you select variable width in the dialog box, the columns will be related to each other in size according to each column's setting for variable width. Let's set the proportions to 2 for the first column and 1 for the other two columns. The result looks like this:

¶	¶	¶
¶	¶	¶
¶	¶	¶

Now let's try something different. We'll use the other option, which is to designate the width of a column using absolute measurements. We'll set the width of the first column to 1.5 inches.

As you can see, when the first column got narrower, the other columns got wider to fill the page column, retaining their proportions relative to each other. As the example shows, you can mix variable and fixed width settings for columns within the same table.

Let's add a fourth column to the table. To do this, select column mode and click anywhere in the third column. Then select Ins Column from the Assignment List. Ventura will make the new Column 3 the same width as the current Column. The current Column 3 will become Column 4. If you end up with a column that's too wide for your page, go back to the Set Column Width and make the columns narrower, or change them all to variable width.

Now let's add a fifth column.

We're ready to add text to the table:

Product	BIOS Seek	Disk Access	Short File Access	Long File Access
Flexo 240	60.11	51.09	34.90	216.00
SemiPac A	41.50	39.80	35.00	201.97

Text added to a table is automatically assigned the Table Text tag. Let's create a new tag, called Table Center. As the name implies, any text tagged with Table Center will be centered. It will also be centered vertically in its cell. Space Above, Space Below, In From Left, and In From Right for Table Center are all set at one pica.

As you can see, Ventura automatically adjusts the height of each row to accommodate the text within. The widths of the columns, however, are not automatically adjusted.

Let's now add a title to this table. To do so, we need to start by adding a row on top that extends across the width of the table. Select Table Edit mode, click on the top line of the table, and then click on Ins New Row in the Assignment List. The table now looks like this.

Product	BIOS Seek	Disk Access	Short File Access	Long File Access
Flexo 240	60.11	51.09	34.90	216.00
SemiPac A	41.50	39.80	35.00	201.97

The next step is to merge the blank cells into a single cell. To select the entire row of cells, select Table Edit mode, then point at the left side of the top left cell and hold the mouse button down while you move the cursor up the side of the upper left cell and across the top of the five blank cells, then down the right side of the upper right cell. You'll know that the top row has been selected when it is entirely surrounded by a dotted or broken border. Now select Join Cells from the Assignment List. Switch to text mode and type in the title, then use Set Font to change the font. The table looks like this:

Storage Device Performance Tests				
Product	BIOS Seek	Disk Access	Short File Access	Long File Access
Flexo 240	60.11	51.09	34.90	216.00
SemiPac A	41.50	39.80	35.00	201.97

As a final enhancement to the table, let's hide the vertical lines separating the cells and change the line under the title to a double line. To hide a line or make it double, select the line with the mouse, then click on Z_HIDDEN or Z_DOUBLE in the Assignment List (GEM/DOS version), or Z_HIDDEN or Z_DOUBLE under the Custom Rules option of the Table menu (Windows version). The tricky part is selecting vertical lines (horizontal ones are easy). If you point at a vertical line and click, you'll almost always select an adjacent horizontal line, not the vertical line you intended to select. The secret is explained in the following tip.

Tip 11-1 ———————————————————————————

Selecting Vertical Lines in Tables

To select a vertical line, don't just point at the line and click. Instead, point at one end of the line, then hold down the mouse button while you move the cursor along the line to the other end.

Storage Device Performance Tests				
Product	BIOS Seek	Disk Access	Short File Access	Long File Access
Flexo 240	60.11	51.09	34.90	216.00
SemiPac A	41.50	39.80	35.00	201.97

Tip 11-2

Controlling the Height of a Cell

Rows of cells automatically grow to fit the largest amount of text within any cell in the row, but what if you want to make a cell especially tall, even though it has little or no text? This is frequently necessary in formatting forms. If you try to change the setting for Space Between Rows, the entire table will be affected. The solution is to create a new tag for the particular cell you want to make tall, and give it a large Space Below setting in the Paragraph Spacing menu. Note that only one paragraph of text is allowed per cell.

Tip 11-3

Controlling the Position of Text in a Cell

If you want to precisely control the vertical position of text in a cell, set the Space Between Rows setting in the Edit Table Settings dialog box to 0 and use the Space Below and Space Above settings in the Paragraph Spacing menu. This is especially important if you want to make your text flush with the top or bottom line of a cell.

Tip 11-4

Making a Table Start on a New Page

Suppose you want a table to start at the top of a page. The Edit Table Settings dialog box does not have an option that lets you force a table to start on a new page, but there's another way to get the same effect. Place the cursor at the end of the paragraph that precedes the table and press Enter once to create a blank paragraph. Now press Ctrl-2 to select Add New Tag and create a tag for this blank paragraph called Table Break. Set the Above, Below, Interline, and Interparagraph settings for the tag to zero, and set the breaks to Page Break: Before. The table will now start on its own page, aligned with the top margin.

Tip 11-5

A Quick Way to Delete a Row

Click on the top line of the row and press Del. You don't have to drag the cursor around the whole row. If you accidentally delete the wrong row, press Ins to make it reappear.

Tip 11-6

Adding Margins around a Table

Conspicuously absent from the Edit Table Settings menu is any way to set top, bottom, left, and right margins for a table. There are two ways to make up for this deficiency:

- *Create the table within a frame and use the Margins & Columns controls. Placing a table in a frame has the added benefit of holding your frame in a fixed location of the page (unless you make the frame a floating frame).*

- *Create blank rows on the top and bottom, and blank columns on either side. Join the cells to create the appearance of a margin.*

12

Equations

The equation generator is standard with Windows Ventura, but with the DOS/GEM version it is only available if you have EMS memory and install the Professional Extension. The equation generator works like this. You begin by locating the text cursor at the spot where you want an equation to begin. From the Edit menu (DOS/GEM version) or the Text menu (Windows version), select Ins Special Item and then select Equation. Ventura switches to a special editing screen, which looks like a blank page with a double horizontal line near the top.

To create an equation, you use a special formatting language called EQN. As you type EQN commands above the double line, Ventura shows you the formatted equation generated by those commands underneath. If you modify the commands above the line, Ventura waits a few seconds, then updates the equation. When the equation is satisfactorily formatted, you press Ctrl-D, which takes you back to your page and shows you the equation embedded in your document.

❖ EQN Syntax

Table 12-1 lists the commands in the EQN language. In applying these commands, the rules are simple:

- Every command applies to the expression that follows it. An expression is anything that is contained within braces, or anything that is clumped together without a space.

- Each element in a string of EQN commands and symbols must be set off by spaces on either side. If you want the formatted equation to contain a space, type a tilde (~) for a normal space and a caret (∧) for a thin space.

- You can use pairs of left and right braces ({ and }) to group expressions together. When you do that, the command operates on the entire group.

Tip 12-1

Equation Alignment

Paragraphs containing equations should always be left-aligned or justified; otherwise, formatting is not reliable.

Tip 12-2

Wrapping

Equations do not wrap; however, the code strings you enter in the equation formatting screen can wrap to the next line, if necessary. By nature, the EQN code strings tend to take up much more room than the equations they represent.

Table 12-1
EQN Formatting Commands

Command	Effect
above	This command is used in piles and matrices. It puts the preceding expression directly above the following expression.
back *x*	Moves the following expression to the left by x tenths of a point. (Similar to up, down, and fwd.)
bold	Changes the following expression to bold.
ccol	Used in a matrix to specify that the following group of expressions should be centered within a column. (Compare to lcol and rcol.)
cpile	Aligns a stack of expressions one above the next and centered. Note: unlike ccol, cpile is not used with the pile command. Pile and cpile are synonymous.
down *x*	Moves the following expression down by x tenths of a point. (Similar to back, up, and fwd.)
fat	Same as bold.
font *x*	Changes the following text to font x, where x is the ID number of the font (for a list of ID numbers, see Appendix K of the Ventura manual).
fraction bar (/)	Formats two expressions as a diagonal fraction, superscripting the first and subscripting the second.
from	Used in conjunction with sum, prod, and union (with int you use sub and sup). Places the following expression underneath the sign.
fwd *x*	Moves the following expression to the right by x tenths of a point. (Similar to back, down, and up.)

Command	Effect
lcol	Used in a matrix to specify that the following group of expressions should be left-aligned within a column. (Compare to ccol and rcol.)
italic	Changes the following text to italic.
lineup	Used in conjunction with the mark command to control the alignment of multiple lines. You place the mark anywhere in the first line, then place the lineup command in subsequent lines. The starting point of the expression that follows lineup or mark is the alignment point.
lpile	Same as cpile, but left-aligned rather than centered.
mark	See lineup.
matrix	Used in conjunction with lcol, ccol, and rcol. Creates a matrix in which all the rows are the same height. All columns must have the same number of rows.
over	Creates a horizontal-bar fraction, with the preceding expression the numerator and the next expression the denominator.
pile	Same as cpile.
rcol	Used in a matrix to specify that the following group of expressions should be right-aligned within a column. (Compare to ccol and lcol.)
roman	Changes the following text to roman (i.e. normal) type.
rpile	Same as cpile, but right-aligned rather than centered.
size x	Changes the point size of the current font to x.
sub	Causes the following expression to be subscripted. Also used to set the lower limit for the integral sign.
sup	Causes the following expression to be superscripted. Also used to set the upper limit for the integral sign.
up x	Moves the following expression up by x tenths of a point. (Similar to back, down, and fwd.)

❖ Entering Symbols

◆ Method 1: Spelling Out the Greek

There are several ways to enter symbols into equations. The easiest is to type out the name of a Greek character; the equation generator then converts the name into the corresponding symbol. In some cases, such as pi and PI (π and Π), there are both uppercase and lowercase versions. Table 12-2 shows the full Greek character set.

◆ Method 2: Using the Symbol Command

Another way to enter a symbol into an equation is to enter the character in the Ventura International symbol set that corresponds to the desired symbol, preceded by the expression "symbol," which switches the following text to the symbol font. For example, typing **symbol p** results in ρ. To use this approach, you need to know which keyboard character corresponds to the symbol you need. You can find this out from the chart in Appendix E of the Ventura manual, or by printing out the chapter called CHARSET.CHP in the TYPESET directory.

Table 12-2: Greek Characters

alpha	α	lambda	λ	sigma	σ	LAMBDA	Λ
beta	β	mu	μ	tau	τ	OMEGA	Ω
chi	χ	nu	ν	theta	θ	PHI	Φ
delta	δ	omega	ω	upsilon	υ	PI	Π
epsilon	ε	omicron	o	xi	ξ	PSI	Ψ
eta	η	phi	φ	zeta	ζ	SIGMA	Σ
gamma	γ	pi	π	DELTA	Δ	THETA	Θ
iota	ι	psi	ψ	EPSILON	E	UPSILON	Y
kappa	κ	rho	ρ	GAMMA	Γ	XI	Ξ

◆ Method 3: Symbol Combinations

A third way to enter symbols is to type symbol combinations, such as ==, which Ventura converts into ≡ . Table 12-3 provides a complete list of the available combinations.

◆ Special Symbol Commands

The integral ($\int$), sum ($\sum$), product ($\prod$), sqrt ($\sqrt{}$), and union ($\bigcup$) symbols require special treatment, since they are used in conjunction with other symbols. For example, integrals, sums, and products involve limits placed above and below the symbol. The square root sign must extend so that the horizontal bar covers the entire argument to which the function is to be applied. EQN provides a special set of commands for handling these symbols, as listed in Table 12-3.

❖ Font Changes

You can't use any of Ventura's text formatting options within an equation. To select a typeface, point size, or weight, use the following commands:

- **bold** or **fat** (either command changes the following text to boldface);
- **font** *number* (changes the font for the following text, with *number* standing for the ID number of the font, as listed in Appendix K of the Ventura manual);
- **italic** (changes the following text to italic);
- **roman** (changes the following text to normal type);
- **size** *number* (changes the following text to the point size given by *number*);
- **symbol** (changes the following text to the symbol font, equivalent to font 128).

Tip 12-3

Getting Help with Ctrl-C

When you are in the equation-editing screen, pressing Ctrl-C shows you a list of common commands associated with the ten function keys. If you select one of these function keys, Ventura will automatically enter an example of the use of that command. Table 12-4 lists the function keys, the command associated with each, the complete EQN string that Ventura inserts when you select one of these function keys, and the formatted result.

❖ Italicized Variables and Romanized Functions

In mathematical typesetting, the default convention is to format variables in italics and function names in roman (i.e., unitalicized type). As a rule, EQN sets any individual letter or word in italics unless you preface the letter or word with the roman command.

However, EQN does have an exception dictionary of common function names, and it will automatically set these in roman. If you are setting a function that is not on this list, you'll have to use the roman command.

The functions that are automatically romanized are as follows: Im, Re, and, arc, cos, cosh, cot, coth, det, exp, for, if, lim, ln, log, max, min, sin, sinh, tan, tanh.

Table 12-3:
EQN Symbol Commands

Command	Effect
approx	Creates an approximation symbol ($\approx$).
cdot	Creates a centered dot ($\cdot$).
ceiling	Creates a ceiling symbol ($\lceil$).
del	Creates a delta sign (∂).
floor	Creates a floor sign ($\lfloor$).
grad	Creates a gradient sign (∇).
inf	Creates an infinity sign (∞).
int	Creates an integral sign ($\int$). Use sub and sup to set the limits for the integral.
inter	Creates an intersection symbol ($\cap$). Use the from and to commands to place text above and below.
left	Used in conjunction with a parenthesis, bracket, brace, bar, floor, or ceiling character. It causes the character to grow to fit the expression.
partial	Creates a partial derivative sign (∂).

Command	Effect
prime	Creates a prime mark (').
prod	Creates a product symbol ($\prod$). Use the from and to commands to place text above and below.
right	Used in conjunction with a parenthesis, bracket, brace, bar, floor, or ceiling character. It causes the character to grow to fit the expression.
sqrt	Creates a square root symbol ($\sqrt{}$) that encompasses the following expression.
sum	Creates a summation sign ($\sum$). Use the from and to commands to place text above and below.
times	Creates a multiplication sign ($\times$).
union	Creates a union symbol ($\cup$). Use the from and to commands to place text above and below.
,....,	Creates comma-bracketed ellipsis marks (,....,).
!=	Creates a not equal sign ($\neq$).
...	Creates ellipsis marks (...).
+-	Creates a plus-or-minus sign ($\pm$).
->	Creates a right arrow ($\rightarrow$).
<-	Creates a left arrow ($\leftarrow$).
>>	Creates a greater-than sign (>).
<=	Creates a less-than-or-equal sign ($\leq$).
>=	Creates a greater-than-or-equal sign ($\geq$).
==	Creates a logical equal sign ($\equiv$).

Table 12-4:
Results of the Choose Equation Text Menu

Function Key	Command	EQN String	Result
F1	fraction	1/2	$\frac{1}{2}$
F2	over	1 over 2	$\dfrac{1}{2}$
F3	sub/sup	x sub {i^+^1} sup {n^+^1}	x_{i+1}^{n+1}
F4	square root	sqrt x	$\sqrt{x}$
F5	summation	sum from 0 to inf i	$\sum_{0}^{\infty} i$
F6	integral	int sub 0 sup 1 {x^dx}	$\int_{0}^{1} x\, dx$
F7	matrix	matrix{ccol{a above b}~ccol{c above d}}	$\begin{matrix} a & c \\ b & d \end{matrix}$
F8	center column	ccol{a above b}	$\begin{matrix} a \\ b \end{matrix}$
F9	center pile	cpile{a above b above c}	$\begin{matrix} a \\ b \\ c \end{matrix}$
F10	left/right	left ({x} right)	(x)

❖ Quotation Marks

If you want a string of text to appear exactly as is, place quotation marks around it. This prevents EQN from interpreting the string as a command.

❖ Diacritical Marks

In contrast to other commands, which always precede the expression they modify, the commands that produce diacritical marks come after the expression. Eight diacritical commands are recognized by EQN: bar, dot, dotdot, dyad, hat, tilde, under, and vec. The following is an example of the use of these commands and the results.

Command	Result
x bar	$\bar{x}$
x dot	$\dot{x}$
x dotdot	$\ddot{x}$
x dyad	$\overset{\leftrightarrow}{x}$
x hat	$\hat{x}$
x tilde	$\tilde{x}$
x under	$\underline{x}$
x vec	$\vec{x}$

❖ How to Build an Equation

While the EQN language looks difficult at first glance, it's easily mastered if you build your equations one step at a time. The following is an example of the construction process. As the example in Table 12-5 illustrates, a good way to work is to start in the middle and build outward.

Table 12-5: How to Build an Equation

EQN String	Result	Notes
10 sup -x	10^{-x}	
sum from {x~=~1} to 4 10 sup -x	$\displaystyle\sum_{x=1}^{4}10^{-x}$	The ~ inserts a normal space.
left { {^ ~ sum from {x ~= ~ 1 } to 4 ~~10 sup -x}} right }	$\left\{\displaystyle\sum_{x=1}^{4}10^{-x}\}\right\}$	The command "left" or "right" indicates that the brace that follows is to actually appear in the equation.
left { {^ ~ sum from {x~=~1} to 4~~10 sup -x} right }~+~3^cos^ x	$\left\{\displaystyle\sum_{x=1}^{4}10^{-x}\right\} + 3\cos x$	
{ left { {^~sum from {x~=~1} to 4~~10 sup -x} right }~ +~ 3^cos^ x} over sum	$\dfrac{\left\{\displaystyle\sum_{x=1}^{4}10^{-x}\right\} + 3\cos x}{\displaystyle\sum}$	The entire denominator is placed in braces.
y~~=~~{ left { {^~sum from {x~=~1} to 4~~10 sup -x} right }~+~3^cos^ x} over sum from {x~=~0} to 3 {~x sup 3}	$y = \dfrac{\left\{\displaystyle\sum_{x=1}^{4}10^{-x}\right\} + 3\cos x}{\displaystyle\sum_{x=0}^{3}x^{3}}$	The equation is now almost complete. The only remaining problem is that the braces overlap the fraction bar.

y~~=~~{ left { {^~sum from {x~=~1} to 4~~10 sup -x} right } sub nothing ~+~ 3^cos^ x} over sum from {x~=~0} to 3 {~x sup 3}	$$y \ = \ \frac{\left\{\displaystyle\sum_{x=1}^{4} 10^{-x}\right\} + 3\cos x}{\displaystyle\sum_{x=0}^{3} x^3}$$	To create some space between the braces and the fraction line, we use the command "sub nothing" after the right brace.

Tip 12-4

Keeping Track of Braces

When you want to apply a command to an expression, you need to demarcate that expression by surrounding it with braces. A good procedure to follow, whenever you type a left brace, is immediately to go to the end of the expression you are setting up and type a right brace. If you always work with braces in pairs, you won't have the problem of "hanging braces."

Tip 12-5

LaserJet Users

When EQN creates subscripts, superscripts, and fractions, it automatically selects a point size that is appropriate relative to other symbols in the equation. This means that your printer must be capable of printing a range of sizes for each font you use in equations. With PostScript printers, that's not a problem, since the printer can automatically scale its master outlines to whatever size you need. In the case of the LaserJet Plus or Series II, the only sizes provided for Dutch and Swiss are 6, 8, 10, and 12; for Dutch bold and Swiss bold 8, 10, 12, 14, 18, and 24; for Dutch italic and Swiss italic 10 and 12; for Symbol 8, 10, 12, and 24; and for Courier 10 and 12. However you can generate the missing sizes (most importantly 7-, 9-, and 11-point Dutch and Swiss; 6-, 7-, 8-, 9-, and 11-point Dutch and Swiss italic; and 6-, 7-, 9-, and 11-point Symbol), using the Bitstream Fontware package, which is bundled with Ventura.

Tip 12-6

Elevating the Numerator

Occasionally, a portion of the numerator will overlap the fraction bar. To fix this, you can't use the Up command, because that moves the fraction bar along with the numerator. Instead, add a "null subscript" (using the command "sub nothing"). This adds the extra room you need between the numerator and the fraction bar. For an example of this technique, look at the last step in Table 12-5.

Tip 12-7

Making Head Room Under a Square Root Sign

Sometimes, the argument of the square root function will be too crowded underneath the square root sign. To make some head room under the square root sign, add a null superscript, using the command sup nothing.

Tip 12-8

Null Superscripts and Subscripts

The previous tips are examples of a technique that can be generalized and used in a variety of contexts. The technique is to create space above and below expressions with null superscripts. Add the command "sup nothing" when you want to create space above an expression (such as some head room between a variable and the square root sign) and "sub nothing" when you want to create space below an expression.

13 *Pagination*

In the jargon of word processing, pagination refers to the capability of a program automatically to print a page number on each page. In publishing parlance, however, the word refers more broadly to the process of assembling the parts of a page and then assembling pages together into chapters and entire documents. While many other desktop publishing programs leave you to handle the pagination task more or less manually, Ventura automates the work to a large degree. The elements that make up the process are as follows:

- headers and footers
- footnotes
- automatic numbering
- frame anchoring
- automatic text insertion

- indexing
- automatic generation of a table of contents
- cross referencing (Professional Extension only)

❖ Headers and Footers

You can create a header or a footer at any point after loading a document. Both headers and footers are limited to two lines of text. To create a header, select Headers & Footers from the Chapter menu. Select whether the header/footer is for a right or left page, select Usage: On, and type the material you want contained in the header/footer. The three lines — left, center, and right — are for material that will be aligned left, centered, or aligned right in the header. If you select Chapter # or Page #, Ventura will insert the chapter or page number within the header/footer.

The 1st Match and Last Match commands allow you to select material from your page to include in the header. This is especially useful in references such as product catalogs where you want

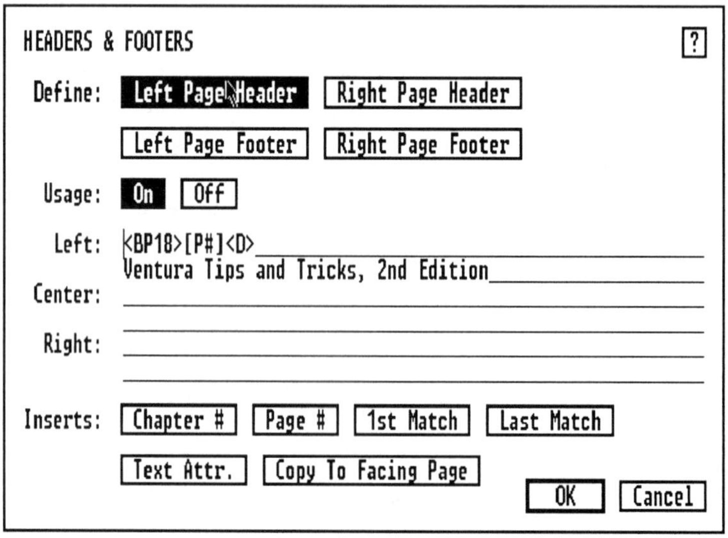

Figure 13-1:
Headers & Footers
dialog box

```
┌─────────────────────────────────────────────────────────┐
│ HEADERS & FOOTERS                                    [?]  │
│                                                          │
│  Define: [Left Page Header]  [Right Page Header]         │
│          [Left Page Footer]  [Right Page Footer]         │
│                                                          │
│   Usage: [On] [Off]                                      │
│                                                          │
│    Left: <BP18>[P#]<D>_____ │
│          Ventura Tips and Tricks, 2nd Edition_____ │
│  Center: _____ │
│                                                          │
│   Right: _____ │
│          _____ │
│                                                          │
│ Inserts: [Chapter #] [Page #] [1st Match] [Last Match]   │
│          [Text Attr.] [Copy To Facing Page]              │
│                                          [OK] [Cancel]   │
└─────────────────────────────────────────────────────────┘
```

the name of the first product listed on the page to be shown in the header for that page. If you select 1st Match or Last Match, Ventura inserts a marker that contains the words "tag name." You must backspace across these words and type the name of the tag that you wish to have as the 1st Match or Last Match.

When you select Text Attr, Ventura inserts a D surrounded by angle brackets (<D>). You can replace the D with any of the text attribute codes listed in Appendix D of the Ventura manual or Chapter 8 of this book. These codes allow you to change the font or type attributes of a single word within a header. For example, to make a single word appear in bold weight, include a <B> on the left side of the word and an <M> (to return to medium) on the right side of the word.

When you select Copy To Facing Page, Ventura translates your header to the opposite page, switching the left and right entries of the header/footer to make facing pages symmetrical.

❖ Tagging Headers and Footers

Once you have created a header or footer, Ventura automatically creates a tag, either Z_Header or Z_Footer. The Z marks it as a "generated tag." Such tags can be altered by means of the same procedure used for altering any other tag. If you do not see any generated tags in the Assignment List when in tagging mode, select Set Preferences from the Options menu and then select Generated Tags: Shown.

Just as with any other tag, you can alter the font, alignment, spacing, and other features of the header or footer tag. The only limitation is that a header or a footer can have no more than two lines of text.

❖ Header and Footer Spacing

The relation between header or footer spacing and the margins set for the rest of the page can be confusing. Generally, you should think of the two as being completely separate. No matter what you specify as the spacing above and below a header, the margin for the rest of the page will continue to be constant. In other words, once you set the margins for the rest of the page, they will not be affected no matter what settings you choose for the header or footer.

Tip 13-1 ————————————————————————

Page Margins and Header/Footer Margins #1

There is one exception to the independence between headers or footers and the rest of the page. It is that if the above and below space set for the header exceeds that of the margin, the margin will be expanded.

Tip 13-2 ————————————————————————

Page Margins and Header/Footer Margins #2

One source of confusion for those setting header/footer margins is that the Z_Header and Z_Footer tags alone do not completely determine the distance between the tags and the top of the page. For every header and footer, Ventura also generates a new frame and automatically sets up top, bottom, left, and right margins for that frame. So the margin above the header is the top margin of the header frame (set by selecting the Frame function, selecting the header frame, and selecting Margins & Columns from the Frame menu) plus the Space Above setting in the Z_Header tag (set by selecting the Tag function, selecting the header, and selecting Spacing from the Paragraph menu).

❖ Footnotes

Ventura's footnote feature is easy to use, though it does have some limitations:

- The size of a block of footnotes is limited to half a page;

- Only text on the underlying page can have footnotes; text in box text or frames cannot;

- A footnote cannot extend from one page to the next (there's a trick to overcome this limitation — see below).

To insert a footnote in your text, switch to text mode and place the cursor at the desired location in your document, pull down the Edit menu (DOS/GEM version) or Text menu (Windows version), select Ins Special Item, and select Footnote. A footnote mark (either a symbol or a number) appears at the designated point, and Ventura creates a frame at the bottom of the page containing the footnote mark or number and the words "Text of Footnote."

To enter the text of your footnote, place the cursor at the end of the words "Text of Footnote," backspace across them, and type the text of your footnote. Like captions and box text, that text will be stored in a file that has the same name as your chapter but uses the GEN extension.

To format your footnote, select Footnote Settings from the Chapter menu. Under Usage & Format, you have a choice of footnotes that are numbered sequentially starting at the beginning of a chapter, footnotes that are numbered sequentially starting at the beginning of a page, and footnotes that are designated with asterisks, plus signs, or whatever character or symbol you wish to use. You can also specify whether the footnote is to be superscripted, subscripted, or neither. (Note: this applies to the footnote mark in the text, not at the bottom of the page. To superscript or subscript the number at the bottom, refer to Tip 13-3.)

Using the Number Template, you can specify two characters that will automatically accompany your footnote number or mark.

Usually, these are used to place a period after the footnote number or to place parentheses around the footnote number.

Tip 13-3

Superscripting a Footnote Number[1]

To superscript the footnote number at the bottom of the page (as shown below), you have to change the parameters for both the Z_FNOT # tag and for the Z_FNOT ENTRY tag. To change Z_FNOT #, create a footnote, tag the number, and change the parameters to the following:

- *Line Breaks: None.*

- *Ruling Line Above: Set Space Below Rule 3 to 4 points and select the minus sign, but set the height of all rules to 0 and set Line Width to to none.*

- *Font size: to 8 or 9 points.*

- *Above Spacing: 1 pica.*

Now tag the text of the footnote and change the parameters to the following:

- *Line Breaks: Before and After*

- *In From Left spacing: 0*

- *Relative Indent: On (Alignment menu)*

- *Interline Spacing: 4 points*

Tip 13-4

Deleting a Footnote

To get rid of a footnote from the bottom of the page, you need to delete the footnote reference mark in your text. When you're in

---

[1]Text of Footnote

The Footnote Settings Dialog Box

In order for the footnote text to appear, you have to select one of these options. Numbering can be sequential throughout your chapter or can start anew on each page. A third option is to define your own footnote characters below under "Character-Defined Strings."

The Number Template lets you specify characters that will always accompany the footnote; for example, #.

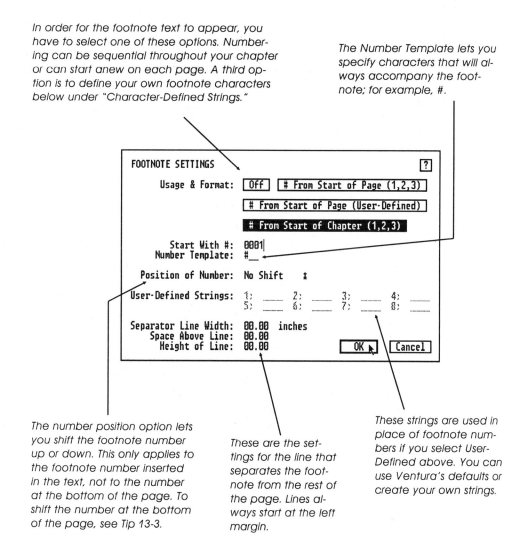

```
FOOTNOTE SETTINGS                                      [?]
         Usage & Format:  [ Off ]  [ # From Start of Page (1,2,3) ]
                                   [ # From Start of Page (User-Defined) ]
                                   [ # From Start of Chapter (1,2,3) ]

            Start With #:  0001
         Number Template:  #__

     Position of Number:  No Shift    ↕

    User-Defined Strings:  1: _____  2: _____  3: _____  4: _____
                           5: _____  6: _____  7: _____  8: _____

    Separator Line Width:  00.00  inches
         Space Above Line:  00.00
         Height of Line:    00.00        [ OK ▶ ]  [ Cancel ]
```

The number position option lets you shift the footnote number up or down. This only applies to the footnote number inserted in the text, not to the number at the bottom of the page. To shift the number at the bottom of the page, see Tip 13-3.

These are the settings for the line that separates the footnote from the rest of the page. Lines always start at the left margin.

These strings are used in place of footnote numbers if you select User-Defined above. You can use Ventura's defaults or create your own strings.

Figure 13-2

the right location, the word "Footnote" will be displayed in the Current Selection Box (underneath the Assignment List on the left side of the screen).

Tip 13-5

Moving a Footnote to a New Page

When you delete a footnote, the footnote number and text remain in the clipboard. To move them to a new position or page, simply insert the cursor at the new position and press Ins.

Tip 13-6

Extending a Footnote to a Second Page

If you have to extend a footnote to a second page, there's a way to do it — quite awkward, but occasionally necessary. Change the color for the Z_FNOT # tag to white so that it becomes invisible. Change the Indent for the Z_FNOT ENTRY tag to 0, so that it is flush left. The result is that the text of the footnote covers up the number or footnote mark, so you'll have to insert the footnote number or mark manually. Type a portion of the footnote on the first page, breaking it off at the end of a line. Go to the next page and insert a footnote mark into text at the end of a line, then use Set Font (DOS/GEM version) or the Text menu (Windows version) to change the footnote mark to white so that it is invisible. Type the remainder of the footnote from the previous page in the footnote box at the bottom of the page.

❖ Widows and Orphans

Another function of the pagination process is making sure that isolated lines do not appear at the top or the bottom of the page. Such lines are referred to as widows when occurring at the top of the page, or as orphans when occurring at the bottom. The Chapter Typography dialog box allows you to specify the minimum number of lines that may be isolated at the top or the bottom of the page. Normally, this should be set to 2 for both orphans and widows, since this will prevent single isolated lines.

❖ Automatic Numbering

With Ventura, you have the ability to automatically number chapters, pages, subheads, and captions. These options are controlled with the Update Counter, Auto-Numbering, and Renumber Chapter options, which are located under the Chapter menu in the DOS/GEM version and under the Paragraph or Edit menus in the Windows version. Of these, the most important dialog box is Auto-Numbering.

Although it is straightforward, the autonumbering process requires a good deal of attention to detail. The procedure is as follows:

- Select Auto-Numbering from the Chapter menu (DOS/GEM version) or Paragraph menu (Windows version).

Figure 13-3: The Auto-Numbering dialog box

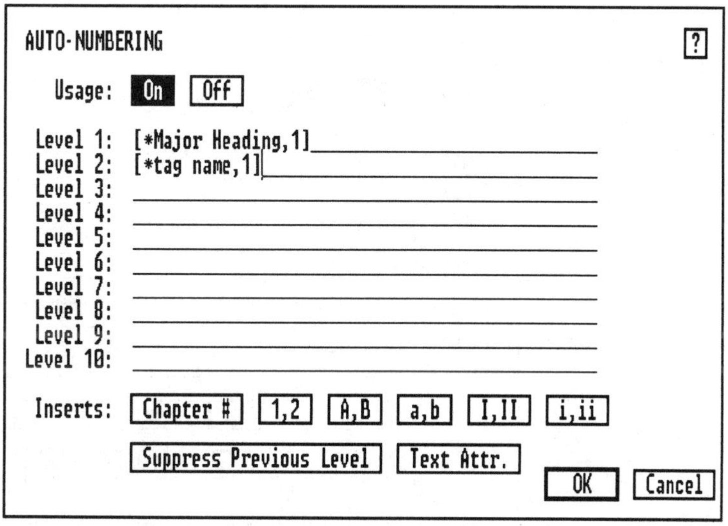

```
AUTO-NUMBERING                                          [?]

    Usage:  [On]  [Off]

  Level 1:  [*Major Heading,1]_____
  Level 2:  [*tag name,1]_____
  Level 3:  _____
  Level 4:  _____
  Level 5:  _____
  Level 6:  _____
  Level 7:  _____
  Level 8:  _____
  Level 9:  _____
  Level 10: _____

  Inserts:  [Chapter #]  [1,2]  [A,B]  [a,b]  [I,II]  [i,ii]

            [Suppress Previous Level]  [Text Attr.]
                                          [OK]  [Cancel]
```

- Select Usage: On.

- Select 1,2; A,B; a,b; I,II; or i,ii to indicate the type of numbering you want.

- Replace the words "tag name" with the name of the tag you wish to have numbered in your document.

- If you wish to start numbering at a number other than 1, type a comma and the number (as an Arabic numeral, e.g., 3) just inside the right bracket.

- If you wish to have any text or punctuation accompanying the number, type it to the right or left of the bracketed portion.

- If you want to have part of the automatically generated material appear in a different font, select Text Attr. Ventura will insert a D surrounded by angle brackets (<D>). You can replace the D with one of the formatting codes shown in Chapter 8 of this book or in Appendix D of the Ventura manual.

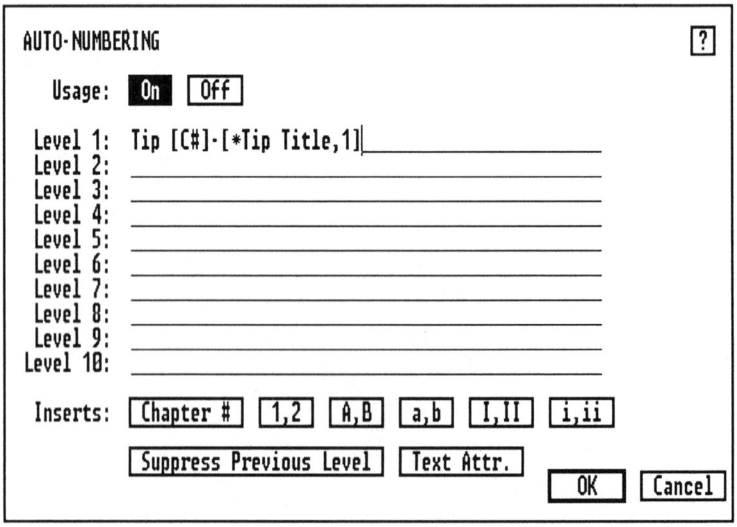

Figure 13-4: The autonumbering dialog box, as used to automatically number the tips in this book.

AUTO-NUMBERING [?]

Usage: [On] [Off]

Level 1: Tip [C#]·[*Tip Title,1]|_____
Level 2: _____
Level 3: _____
Level 4: _____
Level 5: _____
Level 6: _____
Level 7: _____
Level 8: _____
Level 9: _____
Level 10: _____

Inserts: [Chapter #] [1,2] [A,B] [a,b] [I,II] [i,ii]

[Suppress Previous Level] [Text Attr.]

[OK] [Cancel]

- If you don't want the number for a higher level combined with the number for a lower level, move the cursor to the beginning of the line and select Suppress Previous Level.

- Once you have completed filling out the lines of the Auto-Numbering dialog box, select OK or press Enter. Figure 13-4 shows how the autonumbering dialog box was set up to automatically number the tips in this book.

- If you wish to change the font or spacing of the number, select tagging mode and select the number. It will have a tag such as Z_Sec1. Using the options in the Paragraph menu, you can change the font, the spacing, the alignment, and other features of the number.

- If you want the number to appear on the same line as the following text, select tagging mode, select the number, select Breaks from the Paragraph menu, and set Line Break to Before. Then select the following paragraph and set Line Break to After. Adjust the indentation of the first line of the paragraph to avoid overlap. Next, change the tags of other paragraphs to Line Break: After, to avoid overlaps with those paragraphs.

- Automatic numbers are not automatically adjusted if text is edited. If you do perform any text editing, such as deleting a few paragraphs, select Renumber Chapter from the Chapter menu (DOS/GEM version) or the Edit menu (Windows version). Better yet, use the keyboard shortcut: Ctrl-B.

Tip 13-7

Renumbering with Ctrl-B

Any time you add or delete an item that is automatically numbered, press Ctrl-B. This not only removes the number for the item you just removed, but also adjusts the numbers of every subsequent item.

❖ Frame Anchoring

Frame anchoring lets you keep illustrations with the text that they relate to. You can force a picture to always appear on the same page as the text reference, to always appear immediately above or below the line containing the anchor, and even to always appear in the same line as the text reference. The latter makes it possible to have a symbol or a logo in a small frame that always "floats" within the text, no matter how many times you reformat your document.

The procedure for anchoring a frame to a passage of text is as follows:

- Select the frame you want to anchor, and select Anchors & Captions from the Frame menu. Type the Anchor name. (Note: Ignore the remainder of this dialog box; the above, below, left, right selections apply to captions rather than anchors.)

- Select text mode.

- Place the cursor in the paragraph to which you want to anchor the frame and click.

- Select Ins Special Item from the Edit menu (DOS/GEM version) or Text menu (Windows version).

Figure 13-5: The *Insert/Edit Anchor dialog box*

```
┌─────────────────────────────────────────────────────────────┐
│  INSERT/EDIT ANCHOR                                      [?]  │
│                                                              │
│    Frame's Anchor Name:  Figure 3|_____                    │
│                                                              │
│    Frame's New Location:  ▓Fixed, On Same Page As Anchor▓     │
│                                                              │
│                          ┌ Relative, Below Anchor Line ┐      │
│                                                              │
│                          ┌ Relative, Above Anchor Line ┐      │
│                                                              │
│                          ┌ Relative, Automatically At Anchor ┐│
│                                                              │
│                                      ┌ OK ┐  ┌Cancel┐         │
│                                                              │
└─────────────────────────────────────────────────────────────┘
```

- Select Frame Anchor. You'll now see the dialog box shown in Figure 13-5.

- The Anchor name you typed above will appear. Select one of the four location options, described below.

◆ Four Kinds of Anchors

There are four ways to anchor graphics. The first, Fixed On Same Page As Anchor, should be used when you want to keep a picture at the same place on the page (usually on the top of the page or on the bottom of the page). The picture will move to a new page if the anchor point moves to a new page, but it will always retain the same location on the page. In other words, the frame will never shift up, down, left, or right. Note that if the anchor point moves to a new page, the picture will not move spontaneously; to make the picture move, you have to select Re-Anchor Frames from the Chapter menu (DOS/GEM version) or Edit menu (Windows version).

The second and third kinds of anchors — Relative, Below Anchor Line and Relative, Above Anchor Line — should be used if you want Ventura to position a picture just below or above a line of text. Note that if the anchor point moves, the picture does not move until you select Re-Anchor Frames from the Chapter menu.

The fourth option — Relative, Automatically At Anchor — makes the frame "float" with the anchor point, immediately repositioning itself whenever the anchor point moves. If you use this option, you should turn on Grow Inter-Line to Fit in the Paragraph menu. This type of frame anchoring is particularly useful if you have a small illustration that you want to include within a paragraph.

Tip 13-8

Frames in Margins

Frequently, frame anchoring causes frames to be placed in the margins of the page. When that occurs, you have to adjust them manually.

Tip 13-9

Attaching Graphics to Text

Let's say you want to use Ventura's drawing tools to draw an ellipse (like this), a rectangle (like this), or an arrow (like this) directly on your text so that it remains in the same relative position as the paragraph moves. Create a small frame and insert it at the end of the paragraph, and attach it as a relative anchor. Then draw your graphics.

Tip 13-10

Using Floating Frames for Bullets

Besides making Ventura's internal graphics float, you can make any imported graphics float with a frame. The applications of this feature are endless. A few ideas:

♿ *Number your lists with fancy clip-art numbers or decorative bullets*

♿ *Highlight important text with symbols (such as the wheelchair access symbol shown here)*

♿ *Mark official policy with the company logo.*

❖ **Automatic Text Insertion**

You can use the autonumbering feature of Ventura to place a standardized passage of text in front of every paragraph with a designated tag. By deleting the number within the brackets, no numbering will occur; however, any text you print on that line will be printed at the beginning of every paragraph with that tag. Up to 35 characters of specified text can be automatically inserted using this technique.

The Insert/Edit Index Entry Menu

```
┌─────────────────────────────────────────────────┐
│ INSERT/EDIT INDEX ENTRY                      [?] │
│                                                   │
│      Type of Entry:  See      ↨                   │
│     Primary Entry:  Paper jams_____ │
│   Primary Sort Key: _____ │
│                                                   │
│    Secondary Entry: Troubleshooting|_____ │
│  Secondary Sort Key: _____ │
│                                                   │
│                            [ OK ]  [ Cancel ]     │
└─────────────────────────────────────────────────┘
```

```
                    ┌─────────────────────────────────────────────┐
                    │ INSERT/EDIT INDEX ENTRY                      │
                    │                                              │
                    │     Type of Entry:  Index    ↨               │
                    │    Primary Entry:  Paper sizes|_____   │
                    │  Primary Sort Key: _____   │
                    │                                              │
                    │   Secondary Entry: _____   │
                    │ Secondary Sort Key: _____   │
                    │                                              │
                    └─────────────────────────────────────────────┘
```

Paper jams, See Troubleshooting

Paper sizes, 405

Parallel interface, 4, 261–265
 advantage over serial interface, 262
 switching to serial interface, 263

Pascal, 417–419, 455

The Pascal Reader, **455**

```
┌─────────────────────────────────────────────────────┐
│ INSERT/EDIT INDEX ENTRY                          [?] │
│                                                       │
│      Type of Entry:  Index    ↨                       │
│     Primary Entry:  Parallel interface_____ │
│   Primary Sort Key: _____ │
│                                                       │
│    Secondary Entry: advantage over serial interface|_ │
│  Secondary Sort Key: _____ │
│                                                       │
│                                [ OK ]  [ Cancel ]     │
└─────────────────────────────────────────────────────┘
```

```
┌─────────────────────────────────────────────────┐
│ INSERT/EDIT INDEX ENTRY                      [?] │
│                                                   │
│      Type of Entry:  Index    ↨                   │
│     Primary Entry:  The Pascal Reader_____ │
│   Primary Sort Key: Pascal Reader|_____ │
│                                                   │
│    Secondary Entry: _____ │
│  Secondary Sort Key: _____ │
│                                                   │
│                            [ OK ]  [ Cancel ]     │
└─────────────────────────────────────────────────┘
```

Figure 13-6

❖ Indexing

When they hear that Ventura has an "automatic indexing capability," most people get the impression that they can simply browse through their document, marking key words as they go, and then sit back while Ventura searches for each instance of each key word throughout the document, compiles a database of the page number on which it occurs, merges all these together, and generates a formatted index.

In fact, the indexing procedure is a good deal more tedious than that. It's a three-step procedure that works as follows:

◆ Step One: Inserting Index Marks

- You work in text mode, starting at the beginning of your document. When you see a word or a concept that you want to include in your index, place the cursor in the word or near it, select Ins Special Item from the Edit menu (DOS/GEM version) or Text menu (Windows version), and select Index Entry. (The shortcut for this in the DOS/GEM version is Ctrl-C F3. In the Windows version the shortcut is Alt-TCI, though you can make the shortcut even shorter in the Windows version by creating a two-key macro with the Windows Macro Recorder. In the process of creating an index for a long document such as this book, pressing the insert index shortcut hundreds of times, I assure you that this particular key combination will wear a deep crease in your brain.)

- You'll now see the Insert/Edit Index Entry screen, shown in Figure 13-6. The figure illustrates the main types of entries in any index. Every entry must contain a Primary Entry. In addition, you can also add a Secondary Entry, which will be indented below the Primary Entry. If the phrase you are indexing starts with *and* or *the*, you need to tell Ventura how to alphabetize it. As shown in Figure 13-6, if the entry is called *The Pascal Reader*, you type **The Pascal Reader**

The Generate Index Dialog Box

Ventura automatically creates a name for the text file it generates. To load the file, select Text/Generated under the Load Text/Picture option of the File menu. If you want to, you can change this name to something else.

If you set Letter Headings: On, Ventura will place a solitary letter to mark each section of the index.

The arrow indicates that Ventura will place a tab between each index entry and the list of page numbers. You may want to delete this and replace it with a comma followed by a space.

This is the title for your index. You can change it to something else.

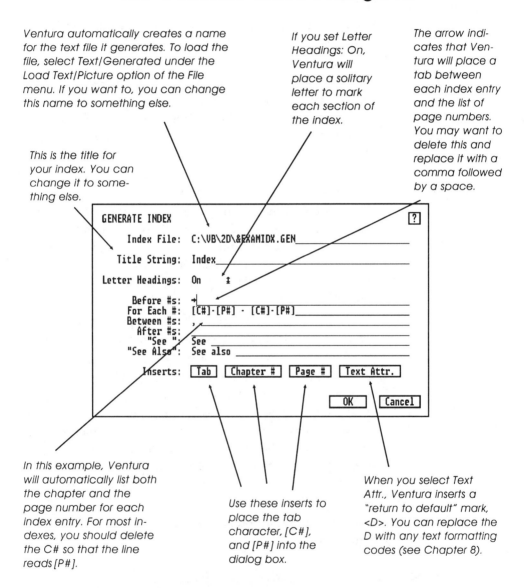

GENERATE INDEX　　　　　　　　　　　　　　　　　?

Index File:　C:\VB\2D\&EXAMIDX.GEN

Title String:　Index

Letter Headings:　On

Before #s:
For Each #:　[C#]-[P#] - [C#]-[P#]
Between #s:　,
After #s:
"See ":　See
"See Also":　See also

Inserts:　[Tab]　[Chapter #]　[Page #]　[Text Attr.]

[OK]　[Cancel]

In this example, Ventura will automatically list both the chapter and the page number for each index entry. For most indexes, you should delete the C# so that the line reads [P#].

Use these inserts to place the tab character, [C#], and [P#] into the dialog box.

When you select Text Attr., Ventura inserts a "return to default" mark, <D>. You can replace the D with any text formatting codes (see Chapter 8).

Figure 13-7

next to Primary Entry and **Pascal Reader** next to Primary Sort Key.

- If you want the index entry to refer to a different index entry, select See or See Also rather than Index.

- Select OK or press Enter to return to your document. By checking for a small bubble, you can see where your index mark is embedded in the text. If you can't see the bubble, press Ctrl-T or turn on Show Tabs and Returns in the Options menu (DOS/GEM version) or the View menu (Windows version).

◆ Step Two: Generating the Index

- When you've finished inserting index entries for all the chapters in your publication (including the Secondary, See, and See Also index variations discussed above), select Multi-Chapter from the Options menu and select New (DOS/GEM version), or select File/Manage Publication/MultiChapter/New (Windows version).

- Select Add Chapter and then select a chapter name. Repeat this step until all the chapters for your publication are listed. Use Save As to name the publication.

- Select Make Index. You'll now be presented with the intimidating dialog box shown in Figure 13-6. Don't worry — usually it's only necessary to make a few changes in the default settings. Usually you'll want to replace the tab (the right arrow) for Before #s: with a comma followed by a space (don't forget the space!). You may also want to delete the [C#] references next to For Each #: and simply have each index entry listed by page number.

- Place <I> and <D> around "See" and "See" also to put these terms into italics.

◆ Step Three: Formatting the Index

- Once you have made the changes you wish to make in the Generate Index dialog box and selected OK, Ventura sets to work creating an ASCII text file with the extension GEN. The end result is a text file with the same first five letters as the name of your publication, then the letters IDX, and finally the extension GEN. For example, if the publication is called MANUAL01.GEN, the index text file will be called MANUAIDX.GEN.

- Select New from the File menu.

- Select Load Text/Picture from the File menu.

- Select Text, Generated as the type of file. Select the index file.

- When the text loads onto the screen, you'll see that each index entry is ended with a line break, and each separate alphabet group is ended with a paragraph break. You'll also notice that Ventura has automatically tagged each index entry with a generated tag. To finish formatting your index, keep these tags, adjusting their settings as necessary.

Tip 13-11

Formatting Secondary Entries

When Ventura generates the index, it automatically inserts a tab in front of all secondary index entries, i.e., entries that fall under another index entry. That works fine if the entry is only one line long, but if the line wraps around it will align to the left margin and the entire secondary entry will no longer be offset from the left margin, as standard practice requires. The solution is to delete the tab mark, and replace the line break at the end of such secondary entries with a paragraph break. Then create a new tag for such secondary entries (i.e., ones that wrap) and set the In From Left setting for this tag equal to the width of the tab for regular entries.

Tip 13-12

Beware of Placing Index Marks within Text with Special Attributes

Don't place index marks in text that is marked with text attributes such as italic or bold, or which has been changed using Set Font. If you do, the next time you load your chapter, you'll find that all text following the inserted index point has reverted to regular formatting.

Tip 13-13

Moving and Deleting Index Marks

Index marks look like little bubbles inserted in your text. If you can't see them, go into the Options or View menu and select Show Tabs & Returns. To move an index mark, first place the cursor directly in front of the mark. You'll know you're in the right place when the word "Index Entry" appears in the Selection Box (on the lower left side of the screen). Press Del to delete the index mark, then move to the new location and press Ins.

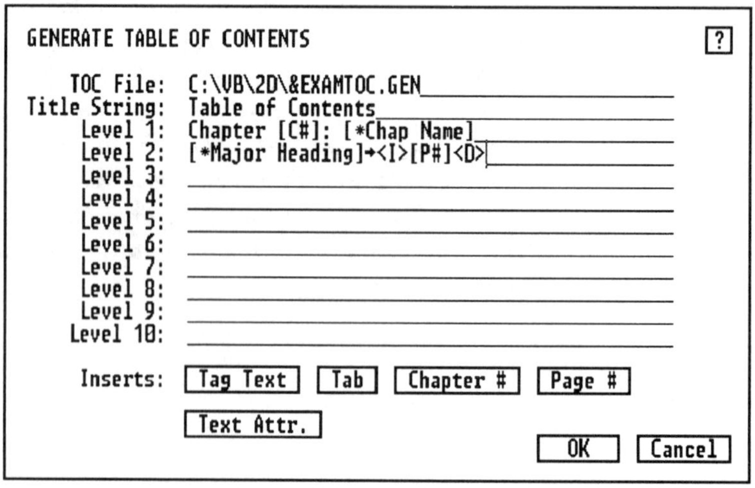

Figure 13-8: The Table of Contents generating menu.

```
GENERATE TABLE OF CONTENTS                                    [?]

      TOC File:  C:\VB\2D\&EXAMTOC.GEN_____
   Title String: Table of Contents_____
       Level 1:  Chapter [C#]: [*Chap Name]_____
       Level 2:  [*Major Heading]→<I>[P#]<D>|_____
       Level 3:  _____
       Level 4:  _____
       Level 5:  _____
       Level 6:  _____
       Level 7:  _____
       Level 8:  _____
       Level 9:  _____
       Level 10: _____

       Inserts:  [Tag Text]  [Tab]  [Chapter #]  [Page #]
                 [Text Attr.]
                                              [OK]  [Cancel]
```

Tip 13-14

Always Spell Check Before Indexing, Not After

If you use the spell checking feature of your word processor, you probably like to wait to do spell checking until after you've imported the text file into Ventura, so that you're able to check any last-minute editing you did in Ventura. Make sure, however, that you spell check your document before you insert the index marks. If you spell check after indexing, your spell checker will query you about every index mark and about every word that has been divided by an index mark. Spell checking will take three times as long as it otherwise would.

Tip 13-15

Keep Track of Your Indexing Terms

As you index a document, keep a sheet of paper or a box full of index cards handy to record frequently used reference. Otherwise, you may enter the same reference in slightly different ways throughout your document, causing there to be multiple index entries, each slightly different, for a particular concept.

Tip 13-16

One More Indexing Tip

When a group of index references crops up on several pages, draw a small box text on one page and fill it with some spaces, then put the index marks between the spaces. Then copy the box onto all the other pages.

◆ No Pain, No Gain

While Ventura's index generator may seem difficult and unwieldy the first time around, it's worth the effort. Once you've set up the index format and saved it, you don't have to repeat the process when you revise your document. All the index marks are still in the text, so even though the page numbering may have changed completely, it's simple to generate a new index.

❖ Generating a Table of Contents

To generate a table of contents, you follow a procedure that is similar to that used in creating an index. In this case, there are two steps.

◆ Step One: Generating the TOC Text File

- Before you go into the Multi-Chapter menu, make a note of the names of the tags for your chapter titles as well as the tag names of any other text elements (such as subheads) that you want to include in the table of contents.

- Next, make sure your publication file is complete. In the Multi-Chapter dialog box, use the Add Chapter command to add any missing chapters to your publication, then use Save As to name the publication.

- Figure 13-8 shows the dialog box where you enter the tag names for the text elements you want included in the table of contents. Note that tabs are represented by the right-facing arrow. Use the Text Attr. insert to format any text,

Figure 13-9:
The Insert/Edit
Marker Name
dialog box.

```
┌────────────────────────────────────────────────┐
│  INSERT/EDIT MARKER NAME              [?]        │
│                                                  │
│  Marker Name:  Table 1|_____                  │
│                                                  │
│                                                  │
│                                                  │
│                      [  OK  ]   [ Cancel ]       │
└────────────────────────────────────────────────┘
```

such as putting chapter numbers in bold or page numbers in italic. Refer to Chapter 8, "Preparing, Loading, and Editing Text," for more information on embedded formats.

◆ Step Two: Formatting the File

- Once you've let Ventura generate the table of contents file, you can load it into a blank chapter as a generated text file.

- You'll see that every element has been given a tag by Ventura. To format the table of contents, simply adapt these tags to match your particular design.

Tip 13-17

Save the Publication

After you amend the defaults in the table-of-contents generating menu, make sure to save your publication one more time. That makes the defaults permanent for this publication.

❖ Cross Referencing

◆ Inserting Page and Chapter Numbers

Ventura's cross referencing capability lets you automatically insert the current page or chapter number anywhere on the page. (Pre-

Figure 13-10:
The Insert/Edit
Reference dialog
box

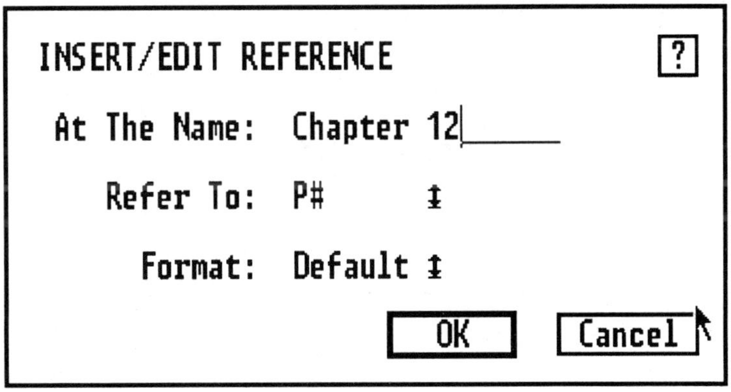

```
INSERT/EDIT REFERENCE            [?]

At The Name:  Chapter 12|_____

    Refer To:  P#      ↕

      Format:  Default ↕

                        [  OK  ]  [ Cancel ]
```

viously, you could only reference the page number in headers and footers.)

The procedure to insert the page or chapter number in your text is as follows:

- Select text mode and click on the desired location in your text.
- From the Edit or Text menu, select Ins Special Item and then select Cross Reference.
- Select Page # or Chapter #.

Keep the line that reads At The Name blank. (In the non-EMS version, that line is not present in the dialog box.)

◆ Cross Referencing with Markers

In addition to making it possible to insert the current page number in your text, Ventura lets you insert a marker in one part of a document and refer to the location (page number, chapter number, and section number) of that marker in another part of the same document. The procedure is as follows:

- Place the text cursor in the location to be referenced.
- From the Edit or View menu, select Ins Special Item.

```
┌──────────────────────────────────────────────────────────┐
│ INSERT/EDIT VARIABLE DEFINITION                      [?] │
│                                                          │
│   Variable Name:  Company_____                        │
│                                                          │
│ Substitute Text:  Whimple, Pfister, and Schudd|_____ │
│                                                          │
│                                         ┌────┐  ┌──────┐ │
│                                         │ OK │  │Cancel│ │
│                                         └────┘  └──────┘ │
└──────────────────────────────────────────────────────────┘
```

Figure 13-11: The Insert/Edit Variable Definition dialog box.

- Select Marker Name. You'll now see the dialog box shown in Figure 13-9.
- Type the name of your marker.
- Go to the page where you want the page, chapter, or section number inserted.
- From the Edit or View menu, select Ins Special Item.
- Select Cross Reference. The dialog box shown in Figure 13-10 will appear.
- In the Refer To line, select P# (Page number), C# (Chapter number), or S* (Section Number)
- Type the name of the marker.
- DOS/GEM version: Select Options/Multi-Chapter, and select Renumber. Windows version: Select File/Manage Publication/Multi-Chapter, and select Renumber.

◆ Cross Referencing with Frame Anchors

Although Ventura's manual is usually very complete, it fails to mention that you can use frame anchors as markers. In fact, referencing frame anchors is the only way to cross-reference figure numbers, table numbers, and caption text.

To use a frame anchor for a cross reference, do the following steps:

- If the frame which you are referencing does not have an anchor name, use Anchors & Captions from the Frame menu to give it one.
- Use Ins Special Item, Cross Reference to place a reference mark in your text.
- In the Insert/Edit Reference dialog box, type the name of the anchor on the At The Name line.
- Depending on what you select in the Refer To line, you can reference either P# (the page number of the frame), C# (the chapter number of the frame), F# (the figure number of the frame), S* (the section number that precedes the frame), or

C* (the caption text for the referenced frame, which is the text that is typed into the Anchors & Captions dialog box on the Label line).

• DOS/GEM version: Select Options/Multi-Chapter, and select Renumber. Windows version: Select File/Manage Publication/Multi-Chapter, and select Renumber.

◆ Variable Text

One of the most versatile aspects of cross referencing is the ability to reference a variable. The best procedure is to insert the text of the variable at the beginning of the chapter, since that's the easiest place to find it later.

• Place the cursor in the location in which you want to substitute text.

• From the Edit menu, select Ins Special Item, and select Cross Ref.

• Place the cursor at the beginning of the chapter and select Ins Special Item from the Edit menu.

• Select Variable Def.

• Type the name of your marker in the Variable Name line, and type the text you want to replace it with in the Substitute Text Line (see Figure 13-11).

• DOS/GEM version: Select Options/Multi-Chapter, and select Renumber. Windows version: Select File/Manage Publication/Multi-Chapter, and select Renumber.

14

Document Layout Strategies

You can use Ventura to produce virtually any type of document: forms, business reports, books, technical manuals, business letters, brochures, catalogs, newsletters — the list is endless. Fortunately, you don't have to master a completely different set of techniques for each document.

There are three basic layout strategies that apply to almost all documents. Each strategy is appropriate for certain types of materials but not for other types. A large part of mastering Ventura is knowing how to classify a job and then bringing the right set of techniques to the task.

This chapter starts by describing three layout strategies. It then reviews the procedure to follow in laying out several types of documents, and finally includes some layout tips.

❖ **Base-Page Strategy**

Although one might devise other terms, we'll refer to the three layout strategies as *base page, newspaper style,* and *freeform.*

The most common type of documents are those in which you use a word processor to create text, then load the text directly onto the base page. Ventura then automatically creates as many pages as are needed to hold the entire text file. Any settings you specify for number of columns, margins, headings, and so forth are automatically reflected throughout the document.

The base page layout method is appropriate for books, technical manuals, catalogs, magazines, and other lengthy documents that can be divided into chapters and in which each chapter contains a single long text file. It also works surprisingly well for many short documents, such as newsletters and single-page ads and flyers. The longer you use Ventura, the more you'll find yourself doing everything with this approach. For example of the base-page strategy, see Chapter 28, "Label Sheets."

❖ **Newspaper-Style Strategy**

Some documents differ from base page documents in that they require text from several different files to be joined up on the same page, and frequently to leapfrog each other; for example starting on page 1 and jumping to page 7.

This need for stories to temporarily pause on one page with a "continued on..." and then resume on a different page calls for a special strategy. The method used to format newspaper-style documents is to draw frames, using the column boundaries on the base page as guidelines. You then load text into these frames rather than directly onto the base page.

When asked to load text into a frame, Ventura loads as much of the text file as will fit and then stops. To continue the file into a new frame you select that frame and then select the name of the file from the list. Ventura starts where it left off and continues loading text into the second frame until it again runs out of space.

The newspaper-style layout strategy is appropriate for news-papers, newsletters, and magazines, and sometimes for books and brochures.

❖ Free-Form Strategy

While the newspaper-style strategy provides more layout flexibility than the base-page method, some documents require even more flexibility. For example, in flyers, small blocks of text and even individual words are arranged freely on the page. Some-times the text is surrounded by boxes, as in tax forms; other times it accompanies graphics, as in the typical flyer.

For such documents it would be impractical to create each piece of text as a separate file and import each into its own frame. Instead, the free-form strategy calls for the use of Ventura's Box Text tool, which allows text to be entered in boxes and then moved freely around the page.

Of course, you could do roughly the same thing by drawing small frames on the page and entering text in these, but entering text in boxes has a couple of advantages over entering it in frames. First, with the Select All option of the Graphic menu, you can select groups of boxes and move them together, a process that is more difficult in the case of multiple frames. Second, with the Box Text feature you can change the default line and fill attributes of a box and use the new defaults to make numerous matching boxes.

❖ Designing Documents

The three strategies outlined above all beg the more fundamental question of document design. Although a full-blown discussion of that topic is obviously outside the scope of this book, before proceeding we'll now take a summary look at it and list some reference materials on the subject.

In traditional publishing, the job of designing a document is kept rigidly separated from the jobs of typesetting and pasteup. The organization of labor is this: First the designer creates a set of specifications for all the elements of the document, based on his or her own sketches and dummies. Next, the typesetter creates galleys according to the specifications, and the pasteup artist — also following the directions of the designer — cuts and pastes these onto boards along with illustrations.

Books about Graphic Design

Desktop Publishing By Design
Ronnie Shushin and Don Wright
Microsoft Press
1113 Heil Quaker Blvd.
LaVergne, TN 37086-7005
800/677-7377
List price: $24.95

Layout
Allen Hurlburt (1977)
Watson-Guptill Publications
1 Astor Plaza, 1515 Broadway
New York, NY 10036
800/526-3641, 212/764-7518
List price: $22.95

Do-It-Yourself Graphic Design
John Laing (1985)
Macmillan Publishing
Front and Brown Streets
Riverside, NJ 08370
800/257-5755, 212/702-2000
List price: $9.95

Editing by Design
Jan V. White (1986)
R.R. Bowker
245 W. 17th St.
New York, NY 10011
800/521-8110, 212/916-1600
List price: $29.95

The Graphic Designer's Handbook
Alastair Campbell (ed.) (1983)
Running Press
125 S. 22nd St.
Philadelphia, PA 19103
800/428-1111, 215/567-5080
List price: $14.95

Looking Good in Print, 2nd Edition
Roger Parker (1990)
Ventana Press
P.O. Box 2468
Chapel Hill, NC 27515
919/490-0062
List price: $23.95

Table 14-1

Those new to publishing often tend to minimize the importance of having a formal design for a document. Frequently, the attitude is: "I'll feel my way through, designing as I go along."

A compromise between ad lib designing and the formal design approach is to use Ventura itself to design your document, creating dummies of each different kind of page that the document will contain.

As the designer, there are two kinds of consistency that you must enforce: first, consistency within pages; second, consistency from one type of page to the next. For example, even though index pages are quite different from chapter title pages, the margins and the placement of headers and page numbers must be exactly the same in both.

If you've never designed documents before, the best way to learn the basics is simply to copy the designs of existing documents. In addition, there are a number of books on the subject, some of which are listed in Table 14-1.

❖ Universal Procedure

Assuming you have at least a preliminary design for your document and have determined which of the three layout strategies to use, the next step is to get to the work of setting up the appropriate file structure, style sheets, frames, etc. — in short, laying out the document. The procedure is basically the same no matter what type of document you are creating.

- Prepare text and graphics, as described in Chapter 8, "Preparing, Loading, and Editing Text," and Chapter 15, "Using Graphics."

- Prepare a directory structure to hold Ventura's own files and the text and graphics files. This is covered in Chapter 7, "Managing Files."

- Design the document. Some documents are laid out according to precise specifications created by a designer. For others, no formal design is ever done. With most documents, some sort of design is done in advance and then adjusted and fine-tuned as the document is tagged and draft copies are printed.

- Load Ventura.

- Establish a new style sheet. Load one of the style sheets provided with Ventura (located in the Typeset subdirectory and designated with & as the first character), and save it under a new name in a different subdirectory. Always work with the style under its new name, so that you don't alter the original style sheet.

- Select the desired defaults under the Options menu (DOS/GEM version) or View and Edit menus (Windows version).

- Select a paper size, using the Page Layout option of the Chapter menu. Note: this is the size of the paper you are using in your laser printer, not the final size of the pages of your document. For now, ignore the other selections from the Chapter menu.

- Select Reduced View or Facing Pages View so that you can view the entire page as you prepare the grid.

- Remove any ruling lines or boxes from the base page. This is done from the Frame menu.

- If necessary, use the Sizing & Scaling option of the Frame menu to change the size of the base page frame to match the trim size of your final document. Use the Set Ruler selection of the Options or View menu to change the 0,0 point of the ruler so that it begins at the corner of the base page frame.

- Establish a grid, i.e., the margins, columns, alleys between columns, and gutters for the page (see "Notes on the Grid" below).

- If working with a newspaper-style layout, draw a frame for each column.

- Load text onto the base page (in a base page layout) or into each separate frame (in a newspaper-style layout).

- Tag text and use Add New Tag (Ctrl-2) as needed to create new tags. Use the options from the Chapter and Paragraph menus to change the formats stored in each tag.

- Add headers and footers (Chapter menu).

- Draw frames to hold pictures or special text such as tables.

- Add captions to frames (Frame menu).

- Use Ventura's internal graphics tools to add arrows, labels, and other enhancements to imported graphics. Make sure that the correct frame is selected when you create these added graphics, so that if you have to move the frame the arrows and labels will maintain their positions relative to the graphics.

- Print a draft of the chapter.

- If this is the first of a multi-chapter document, save it as CHAPTER1.CHP, then convert it into a template for other chapters. To do that, remove the text and graphics files from the chapter using the Remove Text/File option of the Edit menu (DOS/GEM version) or Frame menu (Windows version), and save the chapter as TEMPLATE.CHP.

- Load the text for the next chapter into the template chapter. Save it as CHAPTER2.CHP.

Tip 14-1

Ventura's Default Style Sheet

Often it's easier to start from a scratch style sheet (i.e., one containing no tags) than to adapt one of the style sheets provided with Ventura. Use the DEFAULT.STY style sheet, located in the \TYPSESET directory. If you alter DEFAULT.STY, don't forget to use Save As to rename it so that the original is preserved.

Tip 14-2

Headers and Footers

Headers and footers are not automatically stored with the style sheet. So when you are doing a book and create the master page and the style sheet, you still have to create the headers and footers independently for each chapter.

On the other hand, when you create headers and footers, Ventura automatically creates the tags Z_Header and Z_Footer. These tags, as well as any adjustments you make to them, are stored with the style sheet.

❖ Components of the Page

◆ The Grid

The grid is the invisible set of lines that guides the layout process, allowing different types of pages to fall within standard boundaries. In setting up your grid, you'll find it easier to work in picas than in other measurement units, since you can usually do everything in single picas and avoid the need for working with fractions. For example, an 8½- by 11-inch page comes to 51 by 66 picas.

TRIM SIZE: The trim size is the final size of the pages after they are printed, bound, and then trimmed. With technical manuals, the base page is frequently the standard 8½- by 11-inch sheet.

CROP MARKS: When you take the camera-ready pages to a printer, they must each have four crop marks indicating the corners of the trimmed page. At the printer, a film negative will be made of each page, and the crop marks will provide reference points for the stripper.

There are two ways to place crop marks on your printed pages. One is to have Ventura automatically generate the crop marks by selecting the Print option from the File menu and then selecting the Crop Marks: On option in the dialog box. When you select this option you won't actually see the crop marks on the screen, but they will appear on the printed page.

Crop Marks and the Base Page

Automatic crop marks are placed outside the base page frame, so they won't appear when your base page frame is the same size as your paper. In particular, when you are printing on 8½- by 11-inch paper and not altering the size of the base page frame, you won't be able to use the automatic crop mark feature. In that case, you'll need to draw crop marks manually. For more information on crop marks, see Chapter 25, "Printing Tips."

Incidentally, here's how to change the size of the base page frame. Select frame mode and then select the base page. Select the Sizing & Scaling option of the Frame menu. Enter values larger than 0 for the Upper Left X and Upper Left Y settings and values smaller than 8½ inches for Frame Width and smaller than 11 inches for Frame Height.

The other way to create crop marks is to draw them using Ventura's graphics tools. Select graphics mode, then select Grid Settings from the Graphic menu. Set Grid Snap On and set horizontal and vertical spacing to approximately .250 inches.

Draw a horizontal line at one of the corners. Select Line Attributes from the Graphic menu and choose settings for the line. Then select Defaults: Save To to make these settings apply to the remainder of the crop marks you draw. Draw a vertical line to define a corner, then repeat the process for the other three corners.

Fortunately, you only have to draw the crop marks once — on the first page. If you select the crop marks and then select Show On

All Pages in the Graphics menu, Ventura automatically copies any graphics placed on the base page onto all subsequent pages.

◆ Inside Margin versus Outside Margin

To compensate for the portion of the page hidden by the binding, the inside margin should be given a little extra width, say ¼ inch or so. According to publishing convention, documents start on a right page and all right pages have an odd number. From the Frame menu select Margins & Columns. Set the Right Margin equal to the outside margin and the Left Margin equal to the inside margin. Select Copy To Facing Page and press Enter. Now the dotted lines that indicate the column or margin also indicate the active area.

◆ Margins and Vertical Justification

In traditional book design, margins are sized so that the bottom margin is the largest, the outside margin the next largest, the top margin the next largest, and the inside margin the smallest. (These days, of course, those guidelines are routinely ignored by designers.) The top margin normally marks the top of text, and the header is placed within this margin. Likewise, the bottom margin marks the bottom of text, and the footer is placed within this margin. No matter what type of publication you are working with, the top margin should be fixed, with text columns hanging from it like curtains. The bottom margin is much more open to adjustment. While Ventura's vertical justification feature gives you the capability to maintain a constant bottom margin on every page, doing so is actually not necessary for most designs. For example, many magazines and newsletters run "ragged bottom."

◆ Active Area

The active area is the area within the margins. The active area is the portion of the page on which text and graphics are normally placed (on occasion something may be placed outside this active area, but normally the active area is not exceeded). Headers, footers, and page numbers, however, do fall outside the active area.

◆ Gutters

The gutter, also called alley, is the small gap separating adjacent columns. It is set using the Margins & Columns option of the Frame menu. One pica is normally sufficient for the alley.

◆ Columns

The width of the columns is set under Margins & Columns. The maximum and minimum desirable width for text columns depends on the size and typeface of the font. For multicolumn documents, designers recommend a minimum line length of 20 characters, an optimum of 40 or 50 characters, and a maximum length of around 60 characters. Lines longer than 60 characters are occasionally used in book designs; however, text set in long lines can be difficult to read because of the tendency of the eyes to lose their place when they complete one line and scan back to the left for the next.

If you do need to set wide lines, use a wide font that has a small

Table 14-2:
Average character counts per pica for Helvetica and Times Roman

Helvetica (Swiss)

Point Size	Characters/Pica
10 point	2.68
11 point	2.46
12 point	2.24

Times Roman (Dutch)

Point Size	Characters/Pica
10 point	2.86
11 point	2.62
12 point	2.38

number of characters per pica. Typefaces whose designs make them suitable for wide columns include Schoolbook, Goudy, and Korinna. Faces with more narrow characters include Times and Galliard. Table 14-2 shows the average character counts per pica (including uppercase and lowercase letters) for the two typefaces provided with Ventura.

Books and Manuals

❖ Overview

The procedure for laying out books and manuals is the same, except that with manuals there is more use of Ventura's automatic numbering feature. As described above under "Universal Procedure," the basic strategy is to work on the first chapter until you are satisfied with the appearance, then remove the text and graphics from the chapter and save it as a template for the rest of the manual or book. Once you have created the initial style sheet and template chapter, laying out additional chapters is merely a matter of loading them into the template, tagging text from the style sheet, and adding graphics.

At first you may wonder why it is necessary to create a template chapter in addition to a new style sheet. After all, doesn't the style sheet contain all the formatting information necessary to make every chapter look the same? Not quite. What's lacking from the style sheet are the margins and contents for headers and footers (although the tags for the headers and footers are saved in the style sheet). Also, if your document contains a number of illustrations all the same size, the template file is a useful place to store properly sized and captioned master frames.

❖ Preliminaries

As described above under "Universal Procedure," the first thing you need to do after creating the text and graphics for your document is to organize your directories. You should create a new subdirectory to contain your book or manual. We'll call it BOOK. Within this directory you should create three subdirectories, BOOK\DOCS (for text files), BOOK\ILLUS (for graphics files), and BOOK\VEN (for chapter files, style sheet files, and other files generated by Ventura). By copying all your text and graphics files from their original locations into the appropriate directories, you'll have duplicate copies of each, including copies of your text files that don't include any tags.

❖ Starting a New Style Sheet

Load Ventura and start a new chapter. From the File menu, load either Ventura's one-column or two-column style sheet (&BOOK-P1.STY or &BOOK-P2.STY). Save the style sheet under a new name, let's say MYBOOK.

You can now change the size of the base page frame, if desired, using the Sizing & Scaling option of the Frame menu and entering new values for Upper Left X and Upper Left Y and for the page height and width.

Another option is to produce the master pages of your book at an enlarged size. This method was used in producing the book you are reading in order to sharpen the appearance of the laser-generated type.

❖ Establishing the Grid

Assuming you don't alter the size of the base-page frame, the next series of steps is to place crop marks on the base-page frame, and select margins for your columns and alleys between the columns. Note that the top and bottom margins are measured from the edge of the page to the top and bottom of your text. Headers and footers have separate margins from the base page and are positioned within the base-page margins. Left and right margins will normally be different to allow extra room on the spine side of the page. By selecting Copy To Facing Page from the Margins & Columns menu, you can have your settings for right pages mirrored in left pages, and vice versa.

❖   Headers and Footers

Once you have set up your margins and columns, use the Headers & Footers option of the Chapter menu to select the content of your headers and footers. Ventura will create frames to hold these elements. To specify margins for those frames you need to select the frames themselves and then use the Margins & Columns option of the Frame menu.

❖   Using the Template

Having created the headers and footers, the next step is to load the text for your first chapter and tag the text, experimenting with the various options for indents, fonts, ruling lines, leading, etc. When text is formatted to your satisfaction, draw and size frames to hold the graphics, using the Line Snap and Column Snap options to align these frames with the text columns.

Graphics should be added quite late in the process, after the text is tagged to your satisfaction. Often in technical manuals, there is a standard-size graphic that is used over and over again. Rather than draw and size the frame to hold this standard size over and over again, you can create it once and then cut and paste it as needed.

When the chapter is completely formatted and proofed, save it, then use the Remove Text/File option of the Edit menu (DOS/GEM version) or the Frame menu (WIndows version) to remove all the graphic and text files. The headers and footers will remain, as will the frames that contained graphics. You can now save this skeleton chapter as a template. For the next chapter, load the text file into the template, then copy the frames for graphics wherever needed (or delete them if not needed). Save this chapter under a new name and start the third chapter, again, from the template.

❖ Ancillary Sections

Although most of the work that goes into laying out a book or a manual is in creating the chapters, such a document is actually a set of designs: cover, copyright and permissions page, acknowledgments, preface, table of contents, section division pages, index pages, appendix pages, and other front and back matter. Each separate ancillary section requires its own design and style sheet.

For the table of contents, you can use Ventura's automatic TOC generator to create the text, then load the file created by Ventura (using the Generated File option in the Load Text/Picture dialog box) and format it with a style sheet.

Newsletters

Unlike books, most newsletters use standard letter-size paper, making it unnecessary to change the size of the base-page frame from 8½ by 11, and also making it unnecessary to draw crop marks. What makes newsletter layouts different from books and manuals is that various text files must be merged within a single chapter.

The basic procedure for setting up a newsletter is as follows:

- Follow the universal procedure described at the beginning of this chapter to set up a file structure, establish a style sheet, remove any ruling borders or vertical lines from the page, and select a page size.

- Select the base-page frame and indicate the number of columns that the newsletter will contain. Enter the desired widths for these columns, the gutters between them, and the top, bottom, left, and right margins for the page. Make sure that the calculated width — the sum of the widths and gutters — equals the actual frame width.

- Select Show Column Guides, Turn Column Snap On, and Turn Line Snap On in the Options or View menu.

- Select Add New Frame and draw a horizontal frame to hold the newsletter headline. Then draw two vertical frames to hold articles.

- Select Insert/Remove Page from the Chapter menu to create the second page of the newsletter (still blank). Create more pages, if desired. You may have to remove vertical lines again. Draw frames on these columns.

- Press PgUp to return to the first page.

- Select the first frame and load a text file into it. Ventura will load as much of the file as it can into that frame.

- Press PgDn to go to the jump page. Select a frame and select the text file name from the Assignment List to continue the article. Ventura will continue placing text, starting where it left off. You can keep on going in this manner for as many frames as you want.

- Add a headline by using a large font (with scalable font printers) or a scanned graphic of a typeset headline (if your printer lacks large type).

- Add a thin horizontal frame to contain the date, issue number, etc. Type this directly into the frame.

- Add headers and footers.

Tip 14-4

Reusing a Layout

If you use the same format over and over, such as printing a monthly newsletter, you can save time by reusing your layout. Most newsletters are best formatted by setting up a two- or three-column master page, and then drawing a frame for each column. After printing an issue, use the Remove Text/File option of the Edit or Frame menu to save the layout as a template for the next issue. Next time you format the newsletter, you merely insert new text files into frames and adjust the lengths of the frames.

❖ Continued On ..., Continued From...

When a newsletter story jumps to a new page, you have to insert the phrase "continued on" at the bottom of one frame and "continued from" at the top of another. It's possible, but rather nerve-racking, to attempt to embed the phrase directly in the text at the end of the column. The problem is that if you adjust the text in any way you'll find that the phrase will have moved and you have to repeat the process. A better way is to create a caption for the frame and type Continued On... as the caption. Select Below for the caption's position. Then tag the caption and create a new tag to substitute for the automatically generated caption tag. Call your substitute tag "Continued On." Follow the same procedure for the Continued From... but position the caption above the frame this time and create a new tag called "Continued From."

Forms

The quickest way to create most forms is with the table generator. If you're using DOS/GEM Ventura without the Professional Extension, the best way to create most forms is with the free-form method. Set up the base page frame with no ruling boxes or lines, one column, and column guides not showing. If the form consists of a single clump of continuous boxes, you can use the Box and Box Text tools from the graphics palette to draw the boxes you need directly onto the base page. In most forms, however, there are groups of boxes clumped here and there on the page. In that case, the best way to work is to create a frame for each group of boxes and then draw your boxes within that frame.

The advantage of this way of setting up the page is that if you have to reposition a group of boxes you can do so easily by dragging the frame they belong to. The drawback is that you have to make sure that you keep the correct frame selected while you draw its contents. Every time you print the document or switch from graphics mode to one of the other modes, the selection switches back to the base page and you have to once again select the frame you're working with.

The basic procedure is as follows:

- Create a frame for each group of boxes.
- Create the boxes with the Box Text tool.
- Add text to the boxes.
- Specify shading and borders for the boxes.
- Create tags for the text in the boxes and tag the text.

Using this method, you can create extremely complex forms, moving into enlarged mode when necessary for detail work.

Ventura generates a tag called Z_BOXTEXT, and initially all boxes are assigned this tag. However, you can tag the text within a box with any other tag. The best way to work is to create a special Box Text style sheet, complete with an array of tags for different sorts of alignments and fonts.

❖ Box Text Style Sheet

None of the style sheets provided with Ventura really lends itself to the special requirements of tagging forms created with the box and box text commands. You'll need to create your own Box Text style sheet. To do so, load the DEFAULT.STY style sheet from the TYPESET subdirectory. Save it under the new name: BOXTEXT.STY.

In a typical form, you'll have some text right aligned within boxes, some left aligned, and some centered. Various fonts may be used, but sans serif faces such as Swiss (Helvetica) and Avant Garde are the most common. What you need in your style sheet is a tag for each kind of alignment and typeface, as shown in Figure 14-1.

To create the first tag, use the Box Text tool to draw a box containing text. Select tagging mode and tag the box. Select Add New Tag. Name the tag Swiss 10b lft (or Helv 10b bft).

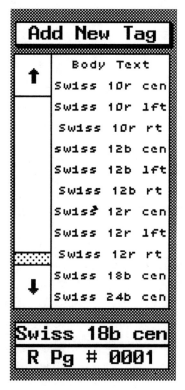

Figure 14-1: In working with forms, it helps to have a tag for each kind of alignment and typeface.

Set the font to 10-point bold Swiss (or Helvetica) and choose Horizontal Alignment: Left and Overall Width: Frame-Wide for Alignment. Set In From Left and Above spacing at one pica (more or less depending on your taste and the size of the boxes) so that the text does not run flush against the edges of the box.

Tip 14-5

Saving and Applying Default Line and Fill Attributes

Typically, you'll be drawing a number of boxes with the same line and fill increments. To make this easy, select the Save To option from the Line Attributes and Fill Attributes dialog boxes after drawing the first box. This lets all the other boxes you draw have the same attributes. If there's a box you've already drawn and you want to apply the new default attributes to it, select Load From. Remember that boxes don't have to have any lines, making the Box Text tool useful as well when you simply want to place a piece of text at an arbitrary location on the page.

Tip 14-6

Drawing Multiple Boxes

Once you've saved your line and fill attributes, you can speed up the process even more by holding down the Shift key while you draw multiple boxes. That way you won't have to reselect the graphics tool each time.

Tip 14-7

Choosing Grid Settings

When creating forms, it's a good idea to set the vertical grid to 1 pica. That way, the boxes you create will be on an invisible grid with 6 lines per inch, which just happens to match the line spacing used by typewriters, thus making it easy for anyone filling out the form with a typewriter to stay in alignment.

Tip 14-8

Form Letters

Although Ventura lacks a mail merge feature, you can achieve the same effect. Use the mail merge feature of your word processor and print to disk. Then load the file into Ventura for formatting.

❖ Questions

Q: *I have created the first page of my newsletter and am now ready to create the second page. However, when I press PgDn, Ventura won't go to the second page. Why not?*

A: PgDn will only take you to the next page if one exists. If not, you can create a new page using the Insert/Remove Page option of the Chapter menu.

Q: *I am creating a form using the Box Text feature of graphics mode. I want text in one box to be 12-point bold and centered, and text in another box to be 10-point normal and left-aligned. How can text in one box be made different from text in another? Both have been automatically tagged with the Z_BOXTEXT tag.*

A: Z_BOXTEXT is the tag that is automatically assigned to any text type with the Box Text operation. However, it is perfectly all right to assign a different tag to text typed into a Box Text box. Switch to tagging mode, select the text, select Add New Tag, name the new tag, and format it as you wish using the selections in the Paragraph menu.

Q: *How can I create a page that is entirely blank?*

A: You can create a new page using the Insert/Remove Page option of the Chapter menu. Make it blank by turning off headers and footers.

Q: *How do I change the order of frames?*

A: This might be desirable in order to change the way text flows from one frame to the next in a newspaper-style layout. You change the order by selecting a frame, pressing Delete, and then immediately pressing Insert. The frame most recently inserted becomes the last frame. Note: you can't use this technique to flow text to an earlier page.

Q: *In a multiple-column layout, how can I make a headline that goes across several columns?*

A: Select tagging mode. Tag the headline. Select the Alignment option of the Paragraph menu. Select Overall Width: Frame-Wide.

Q: *What do "1st Match" and "Last Match" mean in the Headers & Footers dialog box of the Chapter menu?*

A: When you select 1st Match, the first occurrence of text tagged with the tag name you specify will be shown in the header or footer. This is useful for dictionary or phone book printing.

Q: **Sometimes I need a one-column first page in an otherwise two-column-per-page document. I know this can be accomplished by placing a frame over the entire page and setting it in a single column, but how can I do it so text flows from page 1 without interruption?**

A: After setting the base frame for two columns, go to the first page of your document and select Insert/Remove Page from the Chapter menu. Then select Insert New Page Before Current Page. Ventura will create a new, blank page 1 for your document. With the new first page created, select frame mode, then click on the underlying page. From the list of files, select the name of your text file. It will load onto the page in two columns. From the Frame menu, select Margins & Columns, and in the dialog box change the number of columns to one. This will apply only to the new page you have created; the rest of the document will still be in a two-column format.

Graphics

15 Using Graphics

Ventura is designed with the assumption that you will generally create the illustrations for your documents with a graphics program and then import them. Ventura does provide a set of graphics tools, but these are limited in functionality and are mainly used for drawing lines, arrows, and boxes.

In working with graphics, the first distinction to keep in mind is the difference between two categories: bitmapped graphics (referred to as "images" by Ventura) and object graphics (referred to as "line art" by Ventura).

◆ Bitmapped Graphics

Bitmapped graphics are stored in the computer as patterns of 0's and 1's. The digital pattern in the computer has a one-to-one correspondence to the pattern of dots in the image. Some alternative terms for bitmapped graphics are paint graphics, images, and pixel-based graphics. Bitmapped graphics in a Ventura document may originate in three places:

- "Paint" programs such as PC Paintbrush or GEM Paint
- Scanners
- Clip art collections

◆ Object Graphics

Object graphics, also called draw art or line art, are stored by the computer in the form of a compact mathematical description. (Ventura's use of the term "line art" to refer to object graphics is unfortunate, because in the graphic arts the term line art refers to any black-and-white illustration.) Object graphics have several origins:

- "Draw" programs such as GEM Artline, Adobe Illustrator, Micrografx Designer, and Corel Draw
- CAD programs such as AutoCAD
- Business graphics programs such as Freelance
- Clip art
- Ventura's drawing tools

◆ Comparative Advantages

Object graphics have several advantages over bitmapped graphics. When printed on a high-resolution output device such as a typesetter, diagonal lines in object graphics become smooth, whereas such lines in bitmapped graphics show noticeable "jaggies." Object graphics also have the advantage that they can be scaled to any size and still look equally good, while bitmapped deteriorate markedly when they are scaled to a larger size.

Figure 15-1 shows the effect of scaling a bitmapped graphic versus an object graphic. As you can see from the top pair of pictures, the two Peachpit logos look about the same at the original

Fiigure 15-1: *The Peachpit logo on the left (above and below) was scanned into the computer and saved as a PCX file, a bitmapped format. The logo on the right was drawn with Adobe Illustrator and saved as an Encapsulated PostScript (EPS) file, an object graphics format. At this relatively small size there is no apparent difference in quality between the two. The difference becomes noticeable when they are scaled to a larger size, as shown below. On the left, the logo in PCX format now has quite noticeable jaggies; the logo in EPS format looks equally good no matter what size it is scaled to.*

Figure 15-2: To
scan a picture,
you select the Scan-
ning command
from the PC
Paintbrush IV Plus
or Publishers
Paintbrush Page
menu.

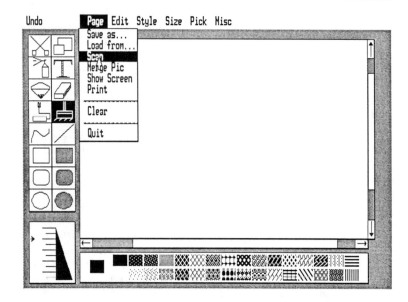

size of the drawing. But when they are scaled to a much larger
size, the image version gets a severe case of the jaggies.

❖ Scanning Images

In conjunction with 300-dpi laser printers, digital scanners provide
a great deal of utility but also pose some distinct drawbacks.
These devices are of greatest use in converting pictures that are
black and white with no intermediate shades of gray. The quality
of such images stands up well when converted into a computer
file by the scanner and printed on the laser printer. As explained
in Chapter 6, "Scanners," you shouldn't attempt to include grayscaled images in your documents unless you are outputting to a
Linotronic 300 or to a LaserJet II with an Intel Visual Edge board.

To be imported into Ventura, a scanned image must be in one of
the formats recognized by Ventura — either PC Paintbrush (PCX),
GEM Paint (IMG), MacPaint (PIC), or Tagged Image File Format
(TIFF). Most PC scanners can be operated by software that
generates files with the PCX or the GEM extension. For example,
the Eye-Star software that drives the Microtek MS-300A scanner

Figure 15-3: After you scan the graphic, it appears on the PC Paintbrush screen as shown here.

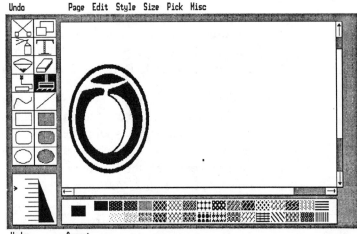

Figure 15-4: PC Paintbrush has two magnification options, zoom-in and ZOOM-IN. After you select the zoom-in option from PC Paintbrush's Misc menu, you can edit individual pixels.

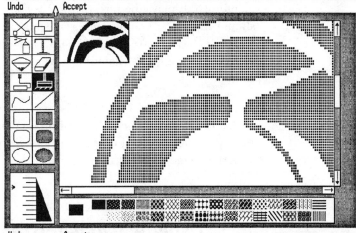

Figure 15-5: With the ZOOM-IN option, you can work even more closely at the pixel level. The portion of the picture being enlarged is shown in the upper left.

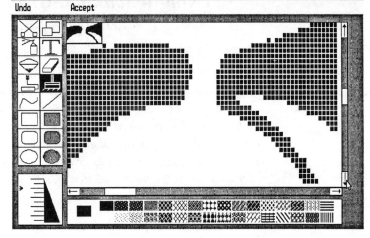

can produce either GEM or PCX format. The Publish Pac software that drives the Dest Corporation PC Scan Plus scanner can produce PCX files. In addition, PC Paintbrush IV Plus, Publisher's Paintbrush, and Halo DPE can all drive scanners directly.

To digitize the Peachpit Press logo shown above, I used PC Paintbrush Plus to drive a Canon IX-12 scanner. To operate the Canon (or other scanners supported by PC Paintbrush, such as the Dest PC Scan, the ShapeScan, the Datacopy 730, and the HP ScanJet), you select the Scanning option from the Page menu, as shown in Figure 15-2. You then select a scanning area, at which point the scanner automatically feeds the page past its optical sensors and digitizes the picture. When that is complete, PC Paintbrush displays the final picture, as shown in Figure 15-3. You should make the scanning area as small as possible, since each square inch of an image can take up as much as 11K on your hard disk, even though PC Paintbrush performs some data compression.

As shown in Figures 15-4 and 15-5, you have two levels of zoom available for editing the individual pixels that make up the image. After you alter or clean up the image with pixel editing, you can save the image as a PCX file.

Tip 15-1

Using a Scanned Graphic for Large Type

Many non-PostScript printers cannot print large type. For example, HP LaserJet Plus compatibles are generally limited to type of 30 points or smaller. If you were printing a monthly newsletter and wanted very large type for your masthead, you could have the masthead prepared at a typeshop, use a scanner to convert it into a graphic image, and then load it into Ventura as an image. This option, of course, is only practical for something that is used over and over, like the newsletter masthead.

❖ Loading Graphics

Once you have created a graphic using a scanner or drawing program, you're ready to load it into a Ventura document. Follow these steps:

- Load Ventura and open the chapter into which you want to place the graphic.
- Create a new frame for the graphic by selecting frame mode, selecting Add New Frame, and then drawing the frame on the page.
- Select Load Text/Picture from the File menu. The Load Text/Picture dialog box will appear.
- Select Line-Art or Image, then select the appropriate format. The Item Selector dialog box will appear.
- Enter the name of the path and extension on the Directory line, and enter the name of the file on the Selection line. For shortcut methods of selecting paths, extensions, and file names, refer to Chapter 7, "Managing Files."

❖ Types of File Formats

A large number of formats are used for storing both object graphics and bitmapped graphics. The good news is that Ventura can cope with a large number of these formats, giving you access to the great bulk of graphics programs as well as to virtually all the clip art available on PC disks. The bad news is that most graphics formats are not standardized. In some cases you may not be able to load a graphic at all, even though the format in which it is stored is one that is supposedly recognized by Ventura. In other cases you may be able to load a graphic, but the picture won't look right. For example, black and white may be reversed, dark shades may be too light and light shades too dark, etc. When such problems occur, there's usually no easy solution, except to see if you can use an alternate format. For example, if you create a drawing in GEM format and then find that you can't load it into

Ventura, go back to the graphics program and see if you can store it in HPGL or EPS format, then try loading again.

At least in theory, Ventura can import object graphics stored in the following formats: GEM Draw (GEM), AutoCAD SLD, Lotus and Symphony PIC, Mentor Graphics, VideoShow, MacDraw and other Macintosh PICT, Computer Graphics Metafile (CGM), Encapsulated Postscript Standard Format (EPS or EPSF), and Hewlett-Packard Graphics Language (HPGL). It can import bit-mapped graphics stored in these formats: PC Paintbrush (PCC or PCX), GEM Paint (IMG), MacPaint, and Tagged Image File Format (TIF). Appendix B, "Graphic File Compatibility," lists programs that can produce files in CGM, DXF, HPGL, and VideoShow format.

Let's now look at some of the pros and cons of some of the graphics formats recognized by Ventura.

◆ PCX

PCX is the format developed by ZSoft for its PC Paintbrush family of products. (The letters refer to the file extension used by such files — alternatively, they sometimes have the extension PCC.) A great deal of clip art is available in PCX format. It's a bitmapped format, which means graphics are stored as patterns of dots and therefore appear jagged when scaled to larger sizes. Generally, you should have no problem importing anything in PCX format into Ventura.

◆ IMG

This is the extension used by GEM Paint for its files. Like PCX, this is a bitmapped format. When you import a PCX file into Ventura, it is automatically converted into an IMG file. IMG files are well standardized and always load into Ventura without any problem.

Tip 15-2

Clearing Space on the Hard Disk By Deleting Duplicate PCX Files

When Ventura imports a PCX or PCC file, it automatically converts it into an IMG file and stores that IMG file alongside the PCX or PCC file in the same directory. In order to avoid having duplicate copies on your hard disk of every PCX image you import (one with the PCX extension, the other with the IMG extension), you should use the Remove Text/File command from the Edit menu to remove the PCX file from the list of files. Then load the matching IMG file into the same frame. Having done so, you can later delete the PCX file from your hard disk and save some room on the disk.

◆ TIFF

TIFF, which stands for Tagged Image File Format, is a recent format that was developed mainly for supporting scanned images, including grayscaled scanned images.

◆ CGM

CGM, which stands for Computer Graphics Metafile, is an object graphics format, which means that it stores pictures as geometric shapes. Since they are stored in object format, CGM graphics can be scaled in any way without losing quality. Unfortunately, the CGM "standard" isn't really standardized, even though it's been around for years. Freelance has one kind, Harvard Graphics another, Arts & Letters yet another. Micrografx has gone so far as to say they'll have menu options for each of the major CGM variants. Arts & Letters' CGM is actually quite reliable; it seems to read into other programs more accurately and more often than anyone else's. As for CGM files produced by other programs, you may be able to import some files but not others, depending on the contents of each file.

For example, colors in CGM files translate differently depending on which program created the file.

For a list of programs that can create files in CGM format, see Appendix B, "Graphics File Compatibility."

◆ HPGL

HPGL stands for Hewlett-Packard Graphics Language. It's an object graphics format developed for plotters and therefore works well for importing CAD graphics into Ventura. Because of its plotter heritage, HPGL doesn't do a good job of storing shades and patterns, so it isn't a good format for storing the sort of graphics created by the newer drawing programs such as Artline, Corel Draw, Illustrator, and Designer.

For a list of programs that can create files in HPGL format, see Appendix B, "Graphics File Compatibility."

Tip 15-3

Importing from AutoCAD, Generic CADD, and Design CAD

When you install your CAD program, tell it you have an HP 7475A plotter. You don't have to actually have one attached. From the plot menu, double the paper size dimensions (both X and Y). Ventura prints HPGL graphics with thick lines when the default paper size is used. Doubling the paper size makes the lines look thinner and more well defined.

◆ EPS

The main drawback of EPS, which stands for Encapsulated PostScript Standard, is that it's only useful if you have a PostScript printer. Otherwise, it's an excellent object graphics format, well standardized and capable of storing shades and patterns.

◆ DXF

This is the object graphics format used by AutoCAD and other CAD programs. It stands for Data Exchange Format. The main drawback of DXF is that AutoDesk keeps changing the format as it releases new versions of AutoCAD, so there's little chance for a true standard to develop. Also, DXF isn't very good with line widths, fills, and drawings that have been rotated or scaled. Ventura includes a utility called DXFTOGEM.EXE on the Utilities disk for converting DXF files into GEM Draw files, which you can import into Ventura. (Note: It can take a long time for DXFTOGEM.EXE to convert a file, so don't think the program has locked up just because you don't get quick results.) However, if you want to import CAD drawings, you're probably better off with the HPGL format than DXF format anyway.

For a list of programs that can create files in DXF format, see Appendix B, "Graphics File Compatibility."

◆ Windows Metafile

Windows Metafiles are simply inadequate. While the format is capable of containing all the information that the new generation of sophisticated drawing programs can create, the files become unbearably huge and unmanageable. Color is a real problem, since different programs interpret the colors in metafiles differently. This means that if you export a graphic to a metafile, it's WYSMBNRTWYG (what-you-see-may-bear-no-relation-to-what-you-get) time. It's not a good situation and the picket line forms to the right at the Microsoft entrance.

◆ VideoShow

This is an object graphics format that is supported by a large number of programs. For a list of programs that can create files in VideoShow format, see Appendix B, "Graphics File Compatibility."

◆ **AutoCAD SLD**

Since this format was created for storing slide files from AutoCAD, it's better to use other formats, such as HPGL, if possible.

❖ **Format Translators**

For bitmapped graphics, numerous tools make it easy to convert files among formats. These include Hotshot Graphics, which can convert among IMG, PCX, and TIFF. Even more versatile is HiJaak from Inset Systems, which can convert among Amiga IFF, CCITT FAX, CompuServe GIF, Dr. Halo CUT, GEM IMG, HP LaserJet PCL, Windows Paint MSP, MacPaint, NewsMaster SHP, PCX, and TIFF.

For object graphics, the tools for converting from one format to another are few and far between. One is a program called Micrografx X-Port, which translates between Micrografx Draw format and MAC PICT, CGM, and DXF.

Tip 15-4

Placing and Removing Graphics

After you load a picture, it may not immediately appear on the screen. You'll notice that its name is shown in the Assignment List, however. To make the picture appear, select the Frame icon, select the frame into which it is to be loaded, and select the name from the Assignment List.

To remove a picture from a frame, select the Frame icon, select the Frame containing the picture, select Remove Text/File from the Edit menu, and indicate List of Files or Frame. If you choose List of Files, the image will be entirely removed from Ventura. If you choose Frame, the image will still be listed in the Assignment List and you can reload it by selecting its name.

Tip 15-5

Lotus 1-2-3 Graphics

With most laser printers, the Lotus 1-2-3 PrintGraph module is limited to a crude 75-dot-per-inch resolution. However, once a graph has been loaded into Ventura it will print at a full 300 dpi. Simply draw a frame on a blank page, load the Lotus graph, and then stretch the edges of the frame to make it any size you want. If you're not satisfied with the chart labels and titles imported from Lotus, create your own with Ventura's Box Text tool, format them using tags or Set Font, choose an opaque white background, and drag them into place to cover up Lotus's labels.

❖ Cropping, Panning, and Scaling

Once a graphic has been loaded into a frame, you can proceed to crop, pan, and scale it. Select frame mode and select the frame containing the graphic. Next, select the Sizing & Scaling option of the Frame menu. All the controls for manipulating imported graphics are located in this dialog box, which is shown in Figure 15-7.

Cropping is done by panning (i.e., moving) the graphic so that part of it is hidden by the boundary of the frame or by the frame margin. To pan a graphic, hold down the Alt key, place the cursor inside the graphic, hold down the mouse button, and drag the mouse.

Tip 15-6

Understanding the Sizing & Scaling Dialog Box

Here's a rule of thumb for understanding the Sizing & Scaling dialog box: you control the position and dimensions of the frame itself using the controls on top, and you control the position and dimensions of the graphic using the controls on the bottom. Just

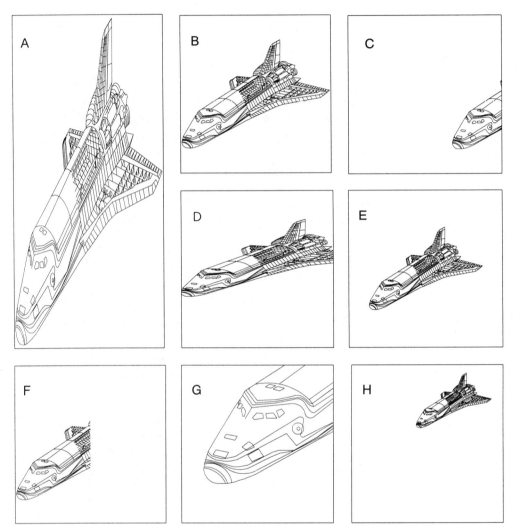

Figure 15-6: *By entering different settings in the Margins & Columns and in the Sizing & Scaling dialog boxes, you can scale, distort, pan, and crop any graphic. The settings for each picture are shown in the table on the next page. In **A**, the dimensions of the shuttle are distorted to fill the frame. In **B**, the shuttle fits the frame but is not distorted. In **C**, the shuttle has been panned (using the Alt-Mouse combination) so that only part of it appears in the frame. In **D**, the shuttle has been distorted by lengthening the width but leaving the height unchanged. In **E**, the shuttle is automatically reduced in size to fit within ¼-inch margins. In **F**, a 1-inch right margin has been used to crop the shuttle. In **G** and **H**, the shuttle has been scaled and panned, but the proportions have been preserved.*

	A	B	C	D	E	F	G	H
SIZING & SCALING								
Fit in Frame /By Scale Factors	F	F	F	S	F	S	S	S
Asp.Ratio Maintained /Distorted	D	M	M	D	M	M	M	M
X Crop Offset	0	0	−1.32"	0	0	0	.25"	−.82"
Y Crop Offset	0	0	0	1.32"	0	0	2.75"	.05"
Scale Width	N/A	N/A	N/A	2.50"	N/A	2.00"	5.00"	1.00"
Scale Height	N/A	N/A	N/A	1.00"	N/A	N/A	N/A	N/A
MARGINS & COLUMNS								
Top	0	0	0	0	.25"	0	0	0
Bottom	0	0	0	0	.25"	0	0	0
Left	0	0	0	0	.25"	0	0	0
Right	0	0	0	0	.25"	1.00"	0	0

Table 15-1: *The settings in this table apply to the shuttle pictures on the facing page. Note that in positioning a graphic, you won't normally need to enter figures for the X and Y Crop Offset, since you can more easily pan a graphic using the Alt-Mouse combination. Entering offsets is useful when you need to position a graphic more precisely.*

remember: frame controls on top, picture controls on bottom.

◆ Positioning and Sizing the Frame

Underneath the text flow control, which allows you to specify whether you want text to make room for the new frame, the next set of controls is for changing the position and size of the frame itself and for creating a margin around the frame.

The figures shown for Upper Left X, Upper Left Y, Frame Width, and Frame Height are the current parameters of the frame you have drawn. The Upper Left X coordinate measures the distance of the upper left corner of the frame from the left side of the page and the Upper Left Y coordinate measures the distance of the frame from the top of the page. By entering new settings for the upper left corner of the frame and for its width and height, you can move a frame or position it more precisely. By using the two settings for padding, you can create additional space around the frame.

To the right of Vertical Padding is the measurement unit that applies to all settings in the Sizing & Scaling dialog box. You can change this by placing the cursor directly on top of the unit of measurement (i.e., the word *inches, picas & points,* etc.), and clicking the mouse button.

◆ Positioning and Scaling the Picture

Underneath the settings that control the position and size of the frame are settings that let you scale and crop the graphic. If you choose Fit in Frame, Ventura will make the picture as large as possible without exceeding the boundaries of the frame. If you also choose Distorted, Ventura will enlarge it to both the horizontal and the vertical edges of the frame; if you choose Maintained, the program will preserve the original ratio of its horizontal and vertical dimensions.

Selecting the By Scale Factors option lets you crop an image and manually enter its width and height. The X Crop Offset moves the picture to the left if you select the plus sign, and to the right if you select the minus sign. The Y Crop Offset moves the picture up if you select the plus sign and down if you select the minus sign.

A much easier way to crop a picture is to hold down the Alt key while holding down the mouse button and moving the mouse. The cursor takes the shape of a hand and you can move the graphic in any direction. You can also use this method to adjust the position of a graphic within the frame.

Tip 15-7

Use the Hand, Not the Crop Offset Commands

Using the "hand," the cursor shape that appears when you hold down the Alt key and the mouse button at the same time and start moving the cursor, is much easier than positioning a graphic using the X Crop Offset and Y Crop Offset settings in the Sizing & Scaling dialog box. It's like the difference between kerning with the Shift-Arrow combination and kerning by entering settings in the Set Font dialog box. So make life easy on yourself and use the hand! Note: when you hold down the Alt key and press the mouse button, you won't immediately see the cursor change into a hand. Not to worry: as soon as you move the mouse, the hand will appear.

Figure 15-7: *The Sizing & Scaling dialog box.*

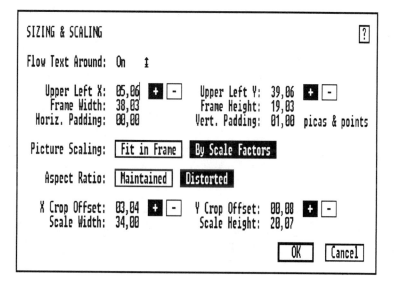

Tip 15-8

Scaling Object Graphics versus Scaling Bitmapped Graphics

When it comes to scaling, there's a big difference between object graphics and bitmapped graphics. With object graphics, such as the shuttle shown in Figure 15-7, you have freedom to scale and distort the image any way you like without losing quality. That's because object graphics are stored as geometrical shapes. With bitmapped graphics, you generally should not have to do any scaling at all. If you must scale a bitmapped graphic, do so carefully, as described in the next tip.

◆ How to Scale a Bitmapped Graphic

After you load a bimapped graphic, go into the Sizing & Scaling dialog box and click on By Scale Factors. Now take a piece of scratch paper and write down the settings next to Scale Width and Scale Height (Scale Width will probably be in black; Scale Height in gray). These are the true dimensions of your picture. If the picture is too big or two small, avoid using Fit in Frame. Instead, enter values for Scale Width that are integer multiples or quotients of the size you wrote down. For example, if the width you wrote down was 2.44 inches, then try to stick to the following sizes: 0.61, 1.22, 2.44, 4.88, etc. When you use an integer multiple to increase the size of a bitmapped graphic, Ventura simply doubles each pixel. Hence the only reduction in quality is that the picture becomes coarser. However, if you use something other than an integer multiple, Ventura doubles some pixels and not others, causing the quality of the picture to diminish and introducing moire patterns. If an integer multiple isn't going to work, try to stick with even proportions such as 1.5, 2.5, etc.

If you have chosen Aspect Ratio: Maintained, then Ventura will automatically scale the height as you scale the width. If you wish, you can select Distorted and apply different scaling ratios to the height and the width. Once again, you should try to stick to proportions such as ½, 1, 1½, 2, and 2½ times the original width.

Tip 15-9

Finding Out the True Dimensions of a Bitmapped Image

If you forget the true dimensions of the picture, you can always regain them again by clicking on Fit in Frame and then Clicking on By Scale Factors.

Tip 15-10

Speed Up Ventura By Hiding Pictures

After loading a picture on a page, you should activate the "Hide Pictures" option in the Options menu. This allows Ventura to perform scrolling and other operations more quickly. You can even keep the pictures hidden while drawing labeling arrows and working on captions.

❖ Captions

Having loaded a graphic into a frame, you can attach a caption frame to it using the Anchors & Captions option in the Frame menu. The following are some tips on working with captions.

Tip 15-11

Don't Enter Text in the Captions Dialog Box

In the Anchors & Captions dialog box, there is a line for entering caption text. Don't use it. Instead, type your caption text directly into the frame itself. The reason this is better is that text entered from within the menu can't be edited without going back into the menu, which makes it awkward to work with. Also, you can only enter a small amount of text, whereas you can enter any amount of text you wish if you type directly into the caption frame.

Tip 15-12

Creating Your Own Caption Tags

When you create a caption frame, Ventura automatically sets up a caption tag called Z_LABEL.CAP. It's OK to use that tag if you only have one kind of caption in your document. However, if you have two kinds of captions (e.g., some on the left side of a picture, some on the bottom of a picture), you can create your own caption tag and name it anything you like.

Tip 15-13

Treat the Caption Frame Like a Separate Frame

The main condition on caption frames is that they remain attached to the frame they are labeling. You can stretch them, give them margin settings different from those of the picture frame, and also give them padding.

Tip 15-14

Create a Master Caption

Setting up a caption, complete with correct margins and padding, and correctly tagged, takes some time. Fortunately, you only have to do the work once. You can copy a frame to the clipboard (using Shift-Del) and then place it on a new page by pressing the Ins key. The caption will remain attached to the frame. You can then load a different picture into the frame and type over the old caption. All the tags and settings will remain intact.

❖ Ventura's Drawing Tools

To use Ventura's own drawing tools, switch to graphics mode and then select one of the five drawing tools from the sidebar. After creating the graphic, such as a line or a box, select the Line Attributes or Fill Attributes to set the thickness, color, or end styles (in the case of lines) or color, fill pattern, and opaqueness or transparency (in the case of boxes and circles).

◆ Changing Graphic Defaults with *Save To*

Ventura keeps track of default parameters for each kind of graphic: lines, ellipses, box text, regular rectangles, and rounded-corner rectangles. For example, in the case of lines, it remembers the thickness, color, and end styles. In the case of rectangles, it remembers the border line thickness, border line color, fill color, fill pattern, and whether the fill is transparent or opaque. This ensures that if you draw a series of graphics of the same type, they will all have a consistent appearance.

To change the default attributes, draw a graphic, use the Line Attributes or Fill Attributes selection to select attributes, and then click on Save To.

◆ Applying Graphic Defaults with Load From

After you establish the desired defaults using Save To, they will automatically apply to any new graphic of the same type that you draw. But what if you have previously drawn a graphic with parameters that are different from the current defaults and now want to apply those defaults to it? You can do it by selecting the graphic and then selecting Load From. Note that you'll have to do this twice (except for lines), once for Line Attributes and once for Fill Attributes.

Tip 15-15

Drawing Multiple Graphics

After you use a graphic tool, the selection defaults to the selector arrow. If you want to quickly draw several lines or boxes without selecting the line or box key each time, hold down the Shift key while you draw the graphics.

❖ Selecting Graphics

Having drawn a graphic, you can always go back and change its appearance, stretch it, or move it. Select the pointer icon (the one that looks like an arrow) and point at the graphic. Eight small black boxes will appear around the graphic to indicate that it is selected.

Once selected, a graphic can be stretched by selecting one of the edge boxes, holding down the mouse button, and dragging that edge inward or outward. It can be moved by placing the cursor within the graphic, holding the mouse button down, and dragging the graphic to a new location. Finally, once selected, you can change the settings for the graphic from the Graphic menu.

It is possible to select multiple graphics. This allows you to change all their settings together or to drag them as a group. To select multiple graphics, hold down the Shift key while selecting them one at a time. To select all the graphics associated with one frame, choose Select All from the Graphic menu. You can then move the graphics as a group by pointing inside one of the graphics, holding down the mouse button, and dragging the graphic. The others will move with the graphic you are dragging.

If you used Select All to select all the graphics on the page, you can turn off the selection by clicking somewhere on the page outside any graphic.

Tip 15-16

Trouble Selecting Graphics

In graphics mode, if you have trouble selecting a graphic element such as a box or a circle, select Frame mode, select the frame to which the graphic is attached, then return to graphic mode and try again.

Tip 15-17

De-selecting Graphics One at a Time

Let's say you have a large number of graphics on a page and want to move all but one. From the Graphic menu, choose Select All. To de-select one of the graphics, point the cursor at it, hold down the Shift key, and click.

❖ Graphics and Frames

Every graphic you draw is "attached" to the frame that you most recently selected. However, the graphic does not have to actually be within the boundaries of the frame. This means that you can draw arrows pointing at items inside frames, or place "Post-It" notes on frames; later, if you move the frame, the arrows and labels will move along with it.

In early versions of Ventura, any graphic attached to the base page frame would automatically repeat on every page of the document. Needless to say, this caused a great deal of confusion, so Ventura 2.0 and later versions let you select either Show On All Pages or Show On This Page. In the former case, the graphic will be repeated throughout the document; in the latter case, it will appear only on one page.

Figure 15-8: This
scanned image
provides a
template for
tracing using
Ventura's graphics
tools.

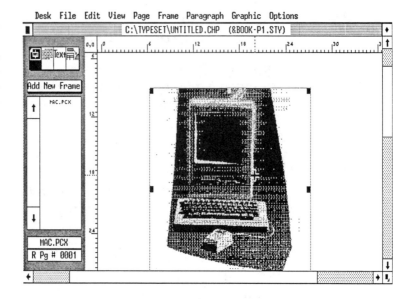

Figure 15-9: After
using Ventura's
graphics tools to
trace the image,
you can remove it
from the page
using the Remove
Text/File option of
the Edit menu.

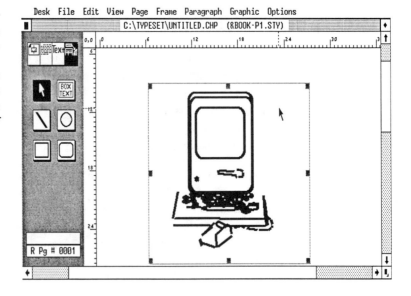

Tip 15-18

Making Room around Graphics

Ventura automatically flows text around graphics frames, but the fit may be too tight for your liking. To create some extra space, use the padding option of the Sizing & Scaling menu.

Tip 15-19

Using a Tracing Template

It is possible to load a scanned image into a frame and then trace on top of it using Ventura's drawing tools, as shown in Figures 15-8 and 15-9. After you finish tracing, you can then select Remove Text/File from the Edit menu to remove the image. By holding down the Shift key while drawing with the Line tool, you can rapidly generate a traced sketch on top of the scanned image.

Tip 15-20

Precise Positioning of Graphics

If you want to precisely position a graphic, one way is to use the rulers. An even more precise method, however, is to create a special position marker on the page. To do so, draw a small frame. From the Frame menu, choose the Sizing & Scaling option. Type the coordinates you wish to mark next to Upper Left X and Upper Left Y. You now know the precise location on the page of the upper left corner of this "positioning frame." Deactivate the frame by clicking on a different one, so that the positioning frame will be used for reference purposes only, rather than to hold the graphic you are about to draw. After drawing the graphic, you can reactivate and delete the frame, which has served its purpose as a reference point. This is a handy trick for placing crop marks at odd locations, like 1.3 inches from the top and left sides of the paper.

Tip 15-21

Working with Groups of Graphics

If you want to create a group of graphics that you can select and move as a group, "tie" the group to a frame. They don't actually have to be placed within that frame, and the frame can be very small. In fact, you can place the actual frame off to the side and then draw the graphics directly on the page. To select the group as a whole, you can activate the frame, then select graphics mode, and type Ctrl-Q to select the group as a whole.

Tip 15-22

Making a Do-It-Yourself Eraser

You can use opaque white boxes as erasers to cover up small portions of text or graphics. Select graphics mode, and select the box tool. Draw a box. From the Graphic menu select Line Attributes and set Thickness to None. From the Graphic menu select Fill Attributes and set Color to White, Pattern to Solid, and Result to Opaque. (Unfortunately, this tip doesn't apply to all printers.)

Tip 15-23

Moving a Small Graphic

Sometimes it is difficult to move a small graphic. Every time you point at it and click, the pointing finger symbol (for stretching) appears rather than the four-way arrow symbol (for moving). Here's a trick for moving such a graphic: Create a larger box near the small graphic. Then hold down the Shift key while you select both. Now, when you move the larger box, the small box will move with it. You can use this technique to move the small box into the exact location you want.

Tip 15-24

Moving Graphics between Documents

You can copy any frame and its contents from one document to another. Select frame mode, select the frame to be copied, press Shift-Delete, load the new chapter, and press Ins.

❖ Box Text

The Box Text drawing tool allows you to draw boxes that also contain text. To use box text, select the Box Text tool, move the cursor to the page, press the mouse button, and hold it down while you draw the box. You'll now see a hollow box character, Ventura's end-of-paragraph mark. This character doesn't print—it just shows you that you can put text in the box. To add text, switch to text mode, place the cursor next to the hollow box character, and type.

Figure 15-10: By substituting other tags for the Z_BOXTEXT tag, you can vary the format of text contained in boxes on the same page.

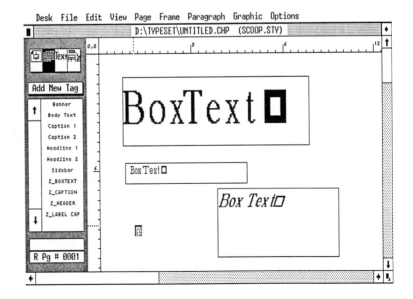

Initially, Ventura generates its own tag, Z_BOXTEXT, for the text you type in a box. However, you can label boxes with other tags instead of Z_BOXTEXT, just as you would tag any other text. In fact, if your box contains two paragraphs, you can use two different tags within the box, as shown in Figure 15-10.

◆ Labeling Graphics

Box text is especially useful for labeling graphics, as shown in Figure 15-11. Notice that it is not necessary for the boxed text to be within the frame containing the graphic. After you create the box, you can specify Line Attributes: None so that the box itself disappears and only the frame is left. If you select the frame containing the graphic while drawing the boxes and arrows, the labels and arrows will move if you move the frame to a new location.

Figure 15-11: Labeling graphics with box text "Post-Its."

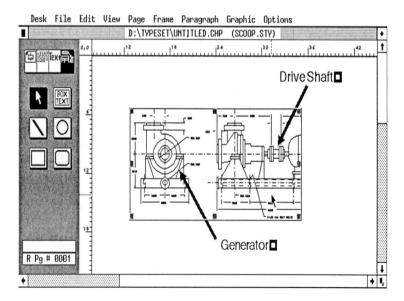

❖ Creating Tables

Another useful application of box text is for creating forms and complex tabular material. When using box text for forms and tables, you can have the option of using different line and fill attributes, or alternatively of eliminating the box lines entirely.

❖ Frames or Box Text?

When should you use frames and when should you use box text? Generally, you should only draw a frame on a page to hold text when you are loading text from a word processed file, when the text must be in multiple columns, or when the text must jump to another frame. Otherwise, you should use box text because of the greater control provided by the grid settings feature and because a group of boxes can all be moved together, retaining their relative positions, when you select and drag the frame to which they are attached.

❖ Questions

Q: *I'm making a crossword puzzle and want to create numerous boxes identical in size. How do you make multiple copies of a graphic such as this?*

A: The method for making copies of frames and of graphics is exactly the same. Select the frame or the graphic. Press Shift-Del. Now drag the frame or graphic to the location you want to copy it to. Press Ins. The frame or graphic will reappear at its old location and you'll now have two copies.

Q: *What's the difference between line snap and grid snap?*

A: Line Snap applies to text and frames placed on a page, which will automatically be aligned to the nearest text baseline, based on the leading set in the Body Text tag. Grid Settings sets up an invisible grid that applies only to graphics.

Q: *I created a graphic, labeled it with arrows, then moved it. The arrows stayed behind. How can I get the arrows to move with the graphic?*

A: Make sure that when you are creating them, the same frame is selected at all times. If they are all attached to the same frame, they will all move together when you reposition the frame.

Q: *I need vertical dashes to indicate a cutout page in a book, but the graphic menu doesn't have a dashed-line option. How can I make them?*

A: The usual method for generating vertical lines is with the Vertical Rules option of the Frame menu. However, it does not allow dashed lines to be specified. The way to create a vertical dashed line is by creating a frame with no width and surrounding it with a dashed boundary. Draw a thin, tall frame. From the Frame menu, select Sizing & Scaling, and set Frame Width to 0. From the Frame menu, select Ruling Box Around and set Width: Frame and Dashes: On. To select the frame "holding" the dashed line, select frame mode, hold down the Ctrl key while pointing close to the frame, and keep clicking until that frame has been selected.

Q: **The type of a Lotus graphic is tiny.**

A: Ventura substitutes its own fonts to match those of Lotus 1-2-3. When a graph is imported into the program, the font it picks is a 2-point Helvetica (Swiss). You cannot tag this text. The only way to make it larger is to cover it up with larger type that you create using Box Text.

Q: **Is it possible to place padding around captions?**

A: Yes. Switch to frame mode and select the caption frame (not the picture frame). Now select the Sizing & Scaling option of the Frame menu, and specify padding settings.

Q: **I want two pictures to overlap, but I can't load them into the same frame.**

A: You can't load two pictures into one frame, but you can draw two overlapping frames and load a picture into each.

Q: **When I loaded the graphic into the document, I couldn't see it anymore.**

A: Select frame mode, select the frame where the graphic is supposed to be located, and select the name of the graphic from the list of files. If the graphic still doesn't appear in the frame, select Sizing & Scaling from the Frame menu and check the settings for X Crop Offset and Y Crop Offset. If these settings are too large, the picture will have been pushed out of the frame.

Q: *What's the largest graphic I can print with a 512K LaserJet Plus or LaserJet II?*

A: In the best possible case, where no fonts have been loaded into the printer, the largest graphic you can print is 32 square inches. You can exceed that maximum by using the LaserTORQ print spooling utility (see Chapter 25, "Printing Tips"). Without LaserTORQ, you can print graphics larger than 32 square inches if you select the 150-dpi LaserJet Plus option when you install Ventura. (If you didn't install this option the first time around, place disk #1 in the computer and type A:VPPREP, then answer No when Ventura asks if this is your first time installing the program. Select the 150-dpi LaserJet Plus option and don't select any other printers.) Once you've installed the 150-dpi option, you can switch to that option from the Options menu by selecting Set Printer Info.

Q: *I use a PostScript printer and am finding it takes much too long to print pages containing graphics. What are my options for speeding things up?*

A: The first thing to do is to make sure you're using the parallel port of your printer (assuming your printer uses both a serial and a parallel port). The next step is to get a spooling program such as PrintCache (see Chapter 25, "Printing Tips").

Q: *I set margins for the frame but the graphic didn't fit within them.*

A: From the Frame menu, select Sizing & Scaling. Set Picture Scaling to Fit in Frame.

Q: *I selected the Graphics icon and then selected the arrow tool, but was unable to draw arrows.*

A: There is no arrow tool per se. The tool that looks like an arrow is actually the selection tool, which is used for stretching or moving graphics. To draw arrows, select the line icon, then use the Line Attributes option of the Graphic menu to specify an arrow line end.

Q: *Often, when I select a left-pointing arrow in the Line Attributes dialog box, I end up with an arrow that points to the right. Is this a bug?*

A: Ventura always considers "left" to be the starting point of the arrow and "right" to be the ending point. If your arrow is pointing in the wrong direction, draw it over again, this time starting at the other end.

16

Graphics Tools

As everyone knows, desktop publishing originated on the Macintosh with PageMaker, and until Ventura was released, the best page layout software remained on the Macintosh. Even after Ventura arrived, PC graphics programs lagged behind those on the Mac.

But new versions of paint programs and a new batch of draw programs rival and even surpass their opposition on the Mac. These programs include Micrografx Windows Designer, Adobe Illustrator, Corel Draw, and GEM Artline.

Before I go into detail about them, let's figure out what exactly draw programs do. In the world of computer graphics, there are two types of programs: "paint" (bitmapped) and "draw" (line art or object-oriented). In a paint program, everything is made up of tiny dots, or pixels. This is the kind of program the master pointillist artist, Seurat, might have used.

Using a paint program, if you draw a circle overlapping a square and then want to move the circle, you have to erase something and draw it in again. If you try to increase or decrease the size or the picture, the quality deteriorates, edges become jagged, and solid grays can become unwanted tartan plaids. Many paint programs can also be used to edit scanned images, even if they are grayscale photographs. The files created by paint programs are also known as "bitmapped."

Draw programs treat what you draw in a completely different fashion. In a draw program, each object you create is a distinct, unique item. If you draw a same circle overlapping a square, you can move the circle independently at any time. Every object you draw remains a separate piece unless you specifically "combine" it with another. Objects can be moved, colored, filled with patterns, sized, stretched, squeezed — anything you want. And because they are made of outlines rather than dots, they never get jagged.

The printed output from a draw program is also sharper, no matter what it's printed on, because, once again, you aren't dealing with dots, but with shapes. A graphic created in a draw program will print at the highest resolution your output device can offer: from 300 dpi on a laser printer up to 2450 dpi on a Linotronic imagesetter.

A draw program is the right tool for producing any type of illustration that requires the utmost precision and ability to revise. Such software can be used for anything from the simplest word charts, flow charts, or organization charts, to the most detailed, complex technical illustrations, to gloriously artistic pictures.

Profile

The PC Paintbrush Family

The granddaddy of PC paint programs is still the greatest. With support for almost every conceivable monitor, mouse, and printer, and the industry-standard PCX file format, PC Paintbrush, now in its fourth major release, is the most flexible and useful paint program for the PC. It provides the most control in creating or editing graphics scanned from within the program. The interface is intuitive, the performance is good, and the "spray paint" feature is a godsend for lightening overly dark scanned images. Also, a large amount of PC clip art is in the PCX format used by the Paintbrush family.

PC Paintbrush IV is the newest low-end version, with PC Paintbrush IV Plus being the more powerful choice. Both of the programs can edit line art or gray scale images. The Plus version adds scanning, advanced grayscale editing, and large image support to its repertoire of features. Both programs can now edit TIF files — the only format Ventura supports for grayscale images.

The Pbrush program included with Windows 3 is a stripped down version of PC Paintbrush, and a more powerful Windows version

Figure 16-1: PC Paintbrush is closely patterned after the seminal Mac-Paint program. On the left are drawing tools and shapes. On the bottom are fill patterns. In the lower left, you specify the width of your lines.

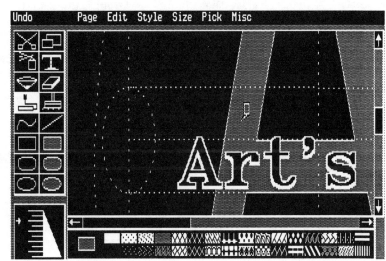

is also included with the HP ScanJet Plus.

As with any paint program, you'll need more than the minimum 512K of memory in your LaserJet if you want to print graphics larger than a third of a page. The rule of thumb is that a full-page image at 300-dpi resolution requires a megabyte and a half of free memory in the printer.

Even if you never create a graphic with PC Paintbrush, you may still need one of the program's most important features: the ability to grab, right off the screen, graphics created by other programs. This makes it an indispensable tool for integrating the graphics from many non-compatible programs, but does not work with all the monitors the program supports. (Keep in mind that the resolution of graphics PC Paintbrush reads from the screen will only be as high as that of the monitor they were taken from. Most often, this is lower than graphics created directly by a graphics program.)

❖   A New Generation of Drawing Programs

We live in a 3-D world, but everything on paper is 2-D. Every piece of 2-D art in the world is made up of lines and curves, color or gray. That's it, just four things. But until now, computers were unable to accurately create half of those four. You couldn't get good curves or color. That made most computer art rather flat and uninspiring. Programs such as Illustrator and Freehand on the Mac side started to change this, but the PC side was still severely limited in the graphics department.

But a new breed of software for the PC has changed all that. Micrografx Designer was the first high-powered drawing package for PCs. It now has even more new tools, reads and writes more formats, and has learned a few tricks from the competition. But the competition is fierce.

Adobe Illustrator, originally released on the Macintosh, now runs under Windows. This means that if you have a 386 (nothing less need apply) you can achieve precisely what you can achieve with a Mac. The Arts & Letters Editor, another powerful Windows-based line-art editor, joins the fray, complete with thousands of pieces of clip-art.

Corel Draw also runs under Windows and lets you do what Illustrator does, but much more quickly and with more command over type. In addition, Corel has a significant advantage in that it is not limited only to printing on PostScript printers.

Artline differs from the other programs in that it doesn't run under Windows. Like Ventura, Artline runs under GEM, and it takes advantage of GEM's speed and compatibility with Ventura. If you don't have a 386 computer, it is probably your best bet, at least from the standpoint of speed.

GEM Artline was the first draw program to give users the power to manipulate true foundry type, but Corel Draw soon appeared and set the standard for PC-based draw programs. Corel Draw can use fonts from *any* foundry: Adobe Type 1, PostScript Type 3, Bitstream Fontware, Compugraphic Intellifont, Digifonts, or Z-Soft Type Foundry. Corel's exceptional abilities with type caused other programs to follow suit. Micrografx Designer added the ability to work with fonts from Bitstream and URW, and Artline added Type 1 support. Corel has even affected the Mac, where Adobe Illustrator can now manipulate Type 1 fonts.

These "tools" help you to put down on paper just exactly what you see in your mind. If you have artistic talent, they are like a set of electronic pens, pencils, brushes, and paint. However, if you're like most people, you can't draw worth beans. You may have tried, but everything you do looks like it was produced by a third grader.

The most exciting aspect of these new programs is that they offer so many tools, even the artless can produce high-quality art. What's more, these tools allow you to create graphics that would be nearly impossible (or at least just very expensive and time-consuming) with traditional graphic arts tools.

◆ Tracing

All of these programs also allow you to take a scanned image and
turn it into high-quality line art using a feature called "autotrace."
Here's how it works: first you scan an image. With "autotrace,"
you merely point to an edge of the drawing and the program
automatically traces its own lines over the scanned image. This
feature means you don't have to spend your time doing the basic
work. You will almost certainly need to clean up the line art or do
detail work, but the autotrace feature is a real timesaver. Corel
also includes a separate tracing utility that gives you the fastest,
most accurate tracing.

◆ Fun with Type

For the most exciting and professional type manipulation available on any microcomputer, you're going to want Corel Draw or
GEM Artline. For type fanatics, these are two of the most exciting
programs ever created for the PC. They're the kind of programs
that make you remember how much fun and how truly revolu-
tionary computers can be.

These programs are a dream come true for anyone who realizes
that type itself is art. You may never have noticed, but virtually
every company logo, every advertisement, every package, has
some kind of emblem that uses type. In almost every case, the
type has been manipulated in subtle or glaring ways. The type has
been stretched, or squashed, or connected, hollowed out, rotated,
skewed, shadowed, filled with gray, or color, or set in a circle.

In the past, you needed press-on type, an X-ACTO knife, a Rapid-
O-Graph pen, and a lot of skill, time, and patience to create some
of these effects. Both Corel Draw and GEM Artline allow you to
take standard text, break it apart until you are working with the
basic Bezier curves which form the letters, and reshape them to
suit your needs.

Micrografx Designer also gives you control over type, and even
works with Bitstream fonts, but the number available is limited.

The Arts & Letters Composer also has powerful type capabilities, although the number of available typefaces is likewise limited.

Despite the competition (or perhaps because of it), Corel Draw is the single best program for manipulating type. Its kerning control is exceptional, and because it works with all major typeface formats, it gives you access to the largest number of typefaces as well.

These programs allow you to do something as complicated as disassemble the characters of a typeface into their most basic elements and have your way with them, or something as simple as create type in circles, big headlines, or reverse type that will print on a LaserJet.

Profile

GEM Artline

Artline has one advantage over the rest — GEM graphics. It runs under GEM, just as Ventura does. While the other programs can import and export GEM format graphics, Artline uses GEM as its

Figure 16-2: GEM Artline is the only program that can manipulate standard Bitstream typefaces. Most graphics programs can only manipulate the fonts that are provided with the software.

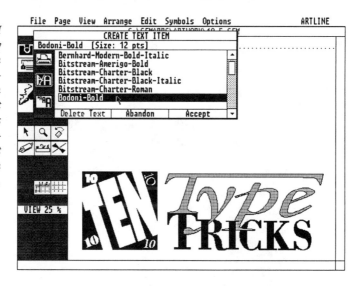

standard format, so importing graphics into Ventura is simple.

Artline comes standard with versions of 35 basic PostScript type-faces: Times, Helvetica, Helvetica Narrow, Avant Garde, Palatino, Century Schoolbook, Bookman, Dingbats, and Zapf Chancery. If you tire of these, Artline can convert both Fontware and Adobe Type 1 fonts, so there's a huge selection of typefaces available.

While Artline 1.0 was fast and Ventura compatible, it lacked some features that Corel Draw made standard. So Artline 2 added auto-trace, fountains, 16 million colors, masking, blending, layers, undo, and text-to-path.

But Artline also forges new ground with its highly customizable user-interface which allows you design your own icons and designate their functions. The toolbox can be resized, and it can contain as few or as many tools as you want. The tools can even be macro-like, automatically performing several functions. In a few years you're going to be seeing interfaces this innovative from everyone else, but this is just plain great today.

On the type front, this new version of Artline matches Corel Draw in that you can still edit text even after you stretch, rotate, or set it

Figure 16-3: This figure illustrates GEM Artline's skewing capability, which lets you distort a letter or a passage of text by stretching its boundaries.

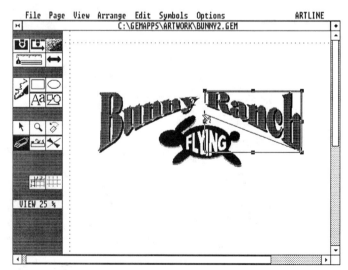

to a path. It's only when you convert the type to graphic curves that you can no longer edit it. Artline's text-to-path feature will automatically size or space text so that it perfectly matches the length of the path.

Artline has the best built-in autotrace feature yet. Of course it can just plain autotrace like othr programs. It can also trace interactively, allowing you to change the level of precision based on the graphic itself. If one part of the graphic needs few points and long curves, you set the trace to a low number. If you then reach a part of the graphic where you want super precision and many points, you stop, change the precision setting, then let it go. Artline has taken a feature that other programs let run wild, and turned it into a precise, interactive tool. This interaction means less need for editing later on. It even has a unique halftone trace mode. This mode allows it to trace images from other programs, which even Adobe Streamline would choke on.

Another example of Artline's thoughtful design is the way that it keeps track of complex paths and prevents you from creating one that is too complex to be printed by a PostScript printer. PostScript has serious limits, and while other programs blithely allow you to create paths that can't be printed, Artline won't.

Artline 2 includes a sophisticated layering feature, which helps you work on extremely complex drawings by letting you view or edit just the layer you're working on. The View Bookmarks command lets you jump to commonly used views in a drawing. Unlike other programs, which send you to the very back or front in one jump, Artline lets you step in back or front one level at a time. Finally, the program shows the actual object outline during moving and rotating, rather than just a bounding box.

Artline still has its excellent Illustrator-inspired Bezier drawing quill tool, and like Corel it now includes a pop-up menu for editing Beziers. The only thing it can't do is combine bitmaps with line art.

All this runs in 640K with no EMS required. CCP, the German software company that authored Artline, has taken Artline from an efficient but limited program to a complete, powerful, Ventura-compatible contender.

Profile

Corel Draw

Corel Draw changed the face of computer graphics. While draw-type programs first appeared on the Mac, Corel introduced important features, including its power to manipulate fonts, that took a year and a half to appear on the Mac. By the time you read this, Corel will have released Draw 2.0 which is supposed to add to Corel Draw's considerable powers.

Corel Draw may very well change the way you think about PCs for desktop publishing. No longer will you think: "Maybe I should have a Mac for the art," because you will no longer need it. Corel Draw's features include fountains (a smooth progression of gray tones or color), auto-trace, and the ability to automatically fit text to a path, such as a circle or curve. In fact, Corel Draw probably has every feature you've ever dreamed of in a draw program. And even with all these features, Corel Draw doesn't feel complex.

◆ Intuitive Drawing

While Corel is strong in freehand drawing, it is weak in structured drawing because of the lack of a curve-drawing tool. Without this tool you lack the power to draw smooth curves — try drawing a curve by hand and what you'll get is as bumpy as what you'd draw on paper without the aid of a compass. The 2.0 release is expected to correct this omission.

But even the manipulation of curves is easier and more powerful. You can add or delete points to a curve anywhere you want. You can transform curves into lines and vice versa. In a thoughtful touch, the "points" menu appears right at your mouse cursor when you double click, which eliminates the need to move the mouse all over the screen.

◆ Auto-Tracing Scanned Images

No auto-trace is perfect, but Corel Trace comes close. While it doesn't offer the interactive control of Artline, it's so accurate that it rarely needs human intervention. Corel Trace is a separate utility program which does nothing but trace. You give it a list of paint-type files (either scanned, created in a paint program, or from a clip art package) and it zooms though them, tracing everything in sight. It's sort of like the beginnings of one of those old Disney movies where you saw a hand drawing the landscape — it looks like magic and it probably is. Best of all, it's included in the standard package for free.

◆ Type Handling

Corel is number one with type, and to make it even better, the program comes with over 100 typefaces. One of the great conveniences of the program is that even after you've rotated or stretched type, Corel still treats it as text. This means that you can correct typos, change typefaces, or do anything else you'd want to do with text. Corel Draw includes a unique feature that allows easy custom kerning of a single letter or an entire string of letters, and this gives you impressive control. While 1.0 is limited to a few hundred characters at a time, 2.0 should handle larger blocks of text.

◆ Jumping to a Shape

Corel Draw's power with type doesn't stop there. Draw a circle, curve, rectangle, or any other shape, and then watch in amazement as the line of text jumps to the shape. The letters remain perfectly kerned. Text can fit inside or outside the circle or shape, and you can even straighten it out at any time.

Text can be filled with any color or pattern, including fountains. Fountains are available in both linear (where the progression is in straight lines) and radial (where the progression occurs out from a point). Fountains can consist of varying shades of gray, or even progressions of color.

◆ Calligraphic Pen Shapes

Corel Draw is unique in that it has calligraphic pen shapes. These pen shapes are unusual in a draw program and help add character and realism, bringing a human touch to Corel Draw artwork. They make the difference between lines being static and animated.

Corel will also automatically change line widths so they are proportional when you enlarge or reduce a drawing. The only other PC program that does this is Illustrator, and it's important because even thin lines can seem thick when you reduce the size of a graphic.

◆ Color Support

Corel includes full Pantone color support with an almost unlimited choice of colors, and special effects for PostScript printers. Currently Corel Draw will not color separate scanned images, but this feature may appear in 2.0.

And once you've selected all the attributes of an item (color, line, fountain, whatever), you can select another item and have all the attributes copied — another nice touch which ensures precision and saves time. Corel Draw even has macros to let you automate tedious and repetitive tasks, something that no other program profiled here has.

◆ No Speed Demon

While not as fast as Artline, Corel still manages to be much faster than any other Windows draw program. Still, like all Windows applications, you need a very fast 286 or a 386 to make it run out-and-out fast.

Figure 16-4: *These examples of graphics created with Corel Draw show the program's ability to apply special effects to type, and to mix type and graphics.*

◆ Import/Export

Early versions of Corel were less than ideal for use with Ventura, but as additional import and export filters were added, the program became an excellent companion for Ventura.

Corel's own file format isn't directly used by Ventura, so luckily Corel's GEM export is exceptional. Because GEM itself is limited in the number and complexity of elements it can handle, Corel can take the most complex graphics and break them into pieces small enough for Ventura to deal with.

The only feature that doesn't translate well to GEM is fountains. Yet even fountains work if you're using the Windows version of Ventura. All you need to do is cut or copy the graphic from inside Corel, then switch to Ventura and paste the graphic. Ventura will ask you to give the Windows Metafile (the Windows Clipboard file) a filename, and insert the graphic. If you can see it on screen in Corel, you can get it on-screen and on paper in Windows Ventura.

Corel can also export to Autocad DXF, CGM (produced by countless programs including Harvard Graphics), HPGL (a plotter format created by most graphics programs), GDF, EPS (Encapsulated PostScript), AI (Adobe Illustrator), Mac PICT, SCDOL (for creating slides), VOS (another slide format), and WPG (WordPerfect graphics).

Corel can read files in the following formats: GEM, DXF, CGM HPGL GDF, EPS, AI, Lotus PIC, and Mac PICT.

◆ The standout

Overall, Corel is an approachable, feature-packed, and thoughtfully designed graphics program. It doesn't overwhelm you with technicalities, and it always seems to be able to do what you want. As far as artistic ability, Corel is the clear standout among PC illustration programs.

Profile

Micrografx Designer

This is probably presumptuous of me, but I've started to think of all these Windows-based graphics programs as being a bit like Charlie's Angels. Corel is the "pretty" one with its calligraphic line shadings and decorative type. Arts & Letters is the "street-wise" one with all its clip art. And Designer is the "smart" one.

◆ Technical Orientation

Designer's own package calls it "the technical illustration program for Windows," and that's exactly what it is. It includes technical, CAD-like necessities that the other lack, such as layers, automatic dimensioning, a customizable interface, even import and export of DXF, a standard CAD format. In fact, Designer is a sort of cultured CAD program, and in fact it did come from a CAD background.

That's not to say that Designer can't be artistic. That point has been proved by thousands of users and Micrografx's own talented art department.

The latest version of the program adds text control similar to (yet different from) Corel's, and handles long blocks of text with ease. Designer also allows you to manipulate type from Bitstream and URW.

◆ Space and Format

None of the other programs offers such a huge workspace: 48 pages. When you're not using it with Ventura, you can create billboards.

Designer imports Micrografx Draw and Graph, PCX, TIF, Ansi text, Windows Metafile, GEM, and Mac PICT. Designer exports to EPS (with or without header), PCX, TIFF, CGM, WMF, GEM, and Mac PICT.

◆ Powerful Tools

Designer is designed well for the most complex drawings. Its layers feature is especially useful because it helps you isolate elements on separate drawing planes. You can view or edit these as you choose, or view and edit all layers at once.

There are fifteen different line endings: squares, circles, triangles, arrows, etc. There are pie slices and a "library window" that allows you to easily choose from your own custom symbol sets — great when composing complex images which use repetitive elements. You can name elements and keep a log of them and how often they're used. Designer simply has more features than any of the others. This is both good and bad. If you're the kind who wants every feature under the sun, you'll love it. If you're the kind who's easily intimidated, you'll run screaming from the room. There is so much to choose from that you can get bogged down.

Designer isn't difficult to use, but like any software with a multitude of features, it can be complex. Make no mistake about it. Designer is a power program and if you're a power user, you'll like it. Even though this is the oldest program of the group, Micrografx has really kept it competitive. They've added an "array"

Figure 16-5:
Micrografx Designer lets you control combinations of color applied to both text and graphics, as shown here.

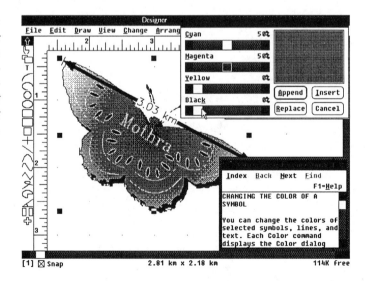

feature that allows you to copy an item repeatedly, gradually changing the color or pattern. They've added fountains, auto-trace, and color support (RGB and CYMK) as well as full color separations.

Designer includes a huge collection of useful clip art, and has the advantage of working with Micrografx's own presentation graphics program, Charisma, as well as their charting and graphing program, Windows Graph.

Micrografx has been working in the Windows environment longer than anyone else, and they really make the most of it. If you primarily do technical illustrations, Designer is the choice.

Profile
Arts & Letters Editor

In the beginning there was nothingness and you really had to put forth some effort to produce anything. Think of how much time God (or whoever) could have saved if he/she/it had used clip art. With evolution and a few billion years, just think of how advanced we might be now.

Well, the Arts & Letters Editor is the world according to clip art. Of course, you can do freehand drawing as well, but the basis of A&L is clip art. The clip art is so important (and useful) that it's cross-referenced by subject matter.

That's right, no shuffling through pages of a catalog thinking, "I know I saw a tube of toothpaste somewhere, maybe near the back of the book." Instead, just look in the index and find it fast. Type in the number and the clip art appears on-screen, ready and waiting for you to add your own personal style. This is A&L's most important advantage.

Arts & Letter's Graphic Composer (the lower-end sibling) uses the same clip art, but while it lets you assemble, move, color, rotate and otherwise create drawings, it can't actually edit the clip art itself. The A&L Editor can. It can take the pre-defined clip art and work with it as curves, like the other programs described here.

Recently, A&L has upgraded its arsenal of tools to match Corel and Designer. This means it includes such feature as: auto-trace, fountains, text to path, join styles, and color separations. In fact, A&L can even produce color separations from scanned color images.

◆ A Zillion Images

About 1,000 pieces of art are included with the program, and for another $295 you can get the complete collection of fifteen zillion images. No, it just seems like zillions — it's really just 2,000 more. The clip art is clean and modern, and while it is sometimes a bit simplistic, it's obvious that much time was spent in careful planning so that the graphics cover frequently-used topics and are genuinely useful.

A&L is no slouch when it comes to typefaces either. It comes with fifteen, and another thirty are available at a reasonable $25 per typeface. A&L *can't* use foundry type from Adobe or Bitstream, so

Figure 16-6: Arts & Letters not only lets you use graphics tools to modify clip art, but also assists you in managing your clip art collection.

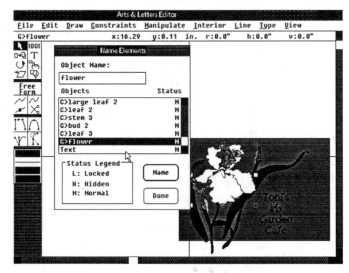

the choice of typefaces is limited. Still, the limited number of typefaces available are good quality, and the program can do lots of fascinating things with them. Type can be rotated, filled with patterns and colors, and taken apart, as in Corel Draw. Computer Support has had the same selection of typefaces for the last few years, but has announced they will be adding a considerable number of new typefaces.

◆ Unique Features

In addition to the expected features, A&L offers some unique touches designed especially for creating clip art. You can name items for easier selection in complex drawings, and a unique Angle-Matching command helps you create precision drawings where one angled line needs to perfectly match another. This may seem like an esoteric feature, but in reality it can genuinely help illustrations have a more precise and professional appearance. A&L also has a useful Distribute feature that creates a smooth progression of shape and color between two items.

A&L Editor has a truly excellent manual and book-based tutorial. The two-volume set is thorough, well-designed and easy to read, and includes complete information about exporting files for use with other programs. The help system is semi–context-sensitive: you go into help mode, then point at the menu you need help with. The help information is not as complete as Designer's, but better than Corel and Artline, which have no on-screen help.

A&L Editor's CGM files import perfectly into Ventura. This means that LaserJet users can effectively use files created by the A&L Editor.

◆ Conclusions

While Arts & Letters has many unusual features, it lacks a few of the basics. Its undo feature is not as useful as the others because it only brings back what you just deleted, and it doesn't undo moves or changes in size.

Still, many people find A&L the ideal program because of its comprehensive collection of clip art. If you need to jump start your graphics, take a look at A&L.

17

Clip Art

There are two kinds of clip art: the regular kind sold in graphic arts stores and the electronic kind. If you have a scanner, you can digitize illustrations from collections such as that produced by Dover Publications. Dover sells a huge line of clip art that you can scan to your heart's content. The company even publishes a series of wonderful and sometimes weird alphabets, which can be used as initial caps or even as electronic "press-on" letters. Save each letter in its own file, and then load it into a frame to create fancy headlines letter by letter.

If you don't have a graphics program or a scanner, but still want some graphic images on your pages, electronic clip art is the way to go. This chapter shows a couple of examples from each of the leading clip-art libraries. Since taste and style are always subjective, you should obtain catalogs from the vendors, and choose the ones that match your style.

◆ Formats

There are two types of clip art files: object-oriented (geometrically based, called "line art" by Ventura), and bitmapped (saved as patterns of dots, called "images" by Ventura). Since object-oriented clip art is stored as a geometrical description, it can be scaled and distorted without any loss in quality. It also takes full advantage of the resolution of the output device, whether that happens to be a 300-dpi laser printer or a 2,540-dpi phototypesetter. Bitmapped clip art is less versatile: you can't scale it without a deterioration in quality, and 2,540-dpi output looks no better than 300-dpi output.

Chapter 15, "Using Graphics," provides notes on various graphic file formats. For bitmapped graphics, all file formats are equally satisfactory. For object graphics, the EPS format is best if you have a PostScript printer (it won't work on other printers), and CGM is best if you have a LaserJet printer. *For access information on the various clip art packages described in this chapter, see Appendix A, "Resources."*

❖ Object-Oriented Clip Art

◆ Publisher's PicturePak

One of the most important things about clip art is that it's useful. It's not enough just to be pretty. Publisher's PicturePak is one of the most useful collections of clip art I've seen. There are three collections, and each collection has a different business theme: Executive & Management, Finance & Administration, and Sales & Marketing. They may sound dull, but they aren't. They range from totally serious to light-hearted and fun, and they

can enhance a wide variety of publications.

All three collections are available in CGM or PCX format. PCX format is a paint-type format, which means it's the easiest to edit. The CGM files can be edited in Lotus Freelance, or Harvard Graphics. I recommend the CGM format because it can be scaled without distortion.

These graphics are simple, but professional and up to date. They come with a spiral bound booklet which shows all the available images, and information on how to use them. But don't take my word for it, look for yourself.

◆ ClickArt EPS Illustrations

If you own a PostScript printer, you might be interested in T/Maker's ClickArt EPS Illustrations files. The collection includes 180 Encapsulated PostScript files. One nice feature of the collection is that each graphic includes a bitmap and thus can be seen onscreen. Since these are PostScript graphics, they will not print on a LaserJet or any other non-PostScript printer.

Each set of EPS files includes 180 images.

The designs tend to be emphatically modern, and the files include screen versions which help in placing, sizing, and cropping the images. I have only two complaints about this collection. First, not all the images are useful. Publisher's PicturePak's selection is more versatile. Second, many of the files don't really take full advantage of the EPS file format. Many of the images are just black and white, with no shades of gray, even though the format supports gradation well. Still, some of the images are quite attractive and print beautifully.

◆ Image Club

Image Club represents a New Wave entry into the clip art scene. The pictures are all contemporary, some reminiscent of airbrushed illustrations, others cartoony. In general, the quality is

excellent. All the art in the collection is in EPS format. Currently five "volumes" are available, each containing approximately 100 pieces of clip art. Subjects include travel, sports, construction, entertainment, people, symbols, cartoons, logos, line

tapes, template pages, certificates, special occasions, business, food, animals, and objects.

When you buy a clip art volume, the art on each disk is compressed into a single file, which you can decompress using a special utility that is supplied along with the clip art. The process is simple and straightforward. A major problem, however, is that the company does not provide a clear catalog showing you which picture is associated with which

file name. Since Image Club's EPS files are represented onscreen with a large X, you're left guessing about what a particular frame contains until you actually print it out.

◆ Other Sources for Object-Oriented Art

A number of Macintosh clip art vendors with large, high-quality collections have now converted their libraries of object-oriented (generally EPS) art to PC format. For phone numbers and addresses, see Appendix A, "Resources." The vendors include:

- **Artbeats.** Several volumes of patterns ("Dimensions" collection) as well as some very interesting natural images ("Natuaral Images" collection), such as tree silouettes, wood grain patterns, mountain ranges, wheat silouttes, droplets, and marble.

- **Casady & Greene.** An amusing EPS collection called "Vivid Impressions: Cats Disk" that consists entirely of decorative letters created from the shapes of cats.

- **Hired Hand Design.** This company's Moonlight ArtWorks EPS collection provides a number of simple, business-oriented images such as credit cards, flags, and banners.

- **MicroMaps.** Detailed maps of states and continents in EPS format.

- **Multi-Ad Services.** Traditional business illustrations and silouetted symbols in EPS format.

- **Studio Advertising Art.** This company has a large number of simple, clean, EPS images of common items and symbols—everything from fingerprints and fire extinguishers to piggybanks and pizza slices.

- **T/Maker.** In addition to the bitmapped clip art described below, T/Maker has a growing collection of high-quality commercial illustrations in EPS format. Things like phones, sneakers, and wine bottles.

- **3G Graphics.** This company's EPS graphics include basic business symbols as well as unusual borders.

- **Underground Grammarian.** This company has an exceptional EPS collection called "Typographers' Ornaments" that would can enhance almost any newsletter, book, or catalog. From an artistic standpoint, this is probably the finest clip art available from any source.

❖ Bitmapped Clip Art

The next three packages are all in bitmapped format. These clip-art packages allow you to use a program such as PC Paintbrush to manipulate the clip art (change its size, add text, invert it, stretch it, etc.). Remember: most bitmapped graphics can't be enlarged much or they get jagged.

◆ ClickArt Series of Image Portfolios

These pieces of clip art are lively but low-resolution (only 75 dpi). This means you must use them in small sizes or they will get a severe case of the jaggies. Five sets are now available: Business Images (presentation art, arrows, com-puters, of-

fice equipment, logos, arrows, logos, communications), Personal Graphics (cars, celebrities, cartoons, animals, billboards, sports, statues, Americana, political figures), Publications (borders, calendars, credit cards, alphabets, desk items, dingbats, headlines, maps, marquees),

Holidays (Christmas, New Year, Hanukkah, etc.), and Christian Images (crosses, biblical characters, etc.). Each set contains from 13 to 21 files; each file consists of anywhere from 1 to 25 different images. Since there are so many images in one file, they are not always practical unless you have first edited them with a program such as PC Paintbrush.

◆ Desktop Art

Desktop Art is the electronic wing of Dynamic Graphics, another large clip-art company. At last count there were eight art-on-disk packages, including Business, Four Seasons, Education, Graphics & Symbols, Sports, Artfolio, Health Care, and Borders & Mortices. The style of these packages ranges from ultra-modern to traditional. They include realistic line illustrations, cartoony-type drawings, and decorative elements.

While the art itself is excellent, the packaging leaves something to be desired. A paint program such as PC Paintbrush is a virtual necessity for using Desktop Art, because so many images are contained in a single file. Unfortunately, because you cannot crop these images adequately from within Ventura, you need to go into the paint program and save the image you want to a separate file. This takes a bit more time and effort, but the wide variety of subject matter and graphic styles offered by Desktop Art may be worth it for your publication.

◆ Metro ImageBase

A late entry into the electronic clip art fray, Metro obviously has learned from the mistakes of its predecessors. To begin with, each file has a single image, so you don't need a paint program to edit them before you can use them. Next, each file is very large, often over 100K; even though the files are bitmapped, they offer high resolution and print a sharp image, even on Linotronic typesetters.

Most packages include three or four high-density 5¼- or 3½-inch disks (360K disks are available upon request). This means each package contains about 4.8 megabytes of art. But the art on these disks is "arced," which means you often get as much as twice that amount. I'm not one to buy anything artistic by the pound (or megabyte), but the sheer size of the files tells you how sharp it's going to be on the printed page.

Most importantly, the art is wonderful. This is the most contemporary, most attractive clip art I've seen yet for computers. The best thing you can say about clip art is that it doesn't look like clip art, and Metro ImageBase art doesn't. The styles include (just to be able to talk about styles in clip art is something of an accomplishment) woodcuts, pen and ink, charcoal, and pointillist. It's the first clip art collection with so much style that you can actually say there's as much art as clip. As well as being appealing, the images are genuinely practical. Metro ImageBase is not unlike having an in-house artist.

Each package contains 100 images. Fourteen packages are now available, including Newsletters, Business Graphics, Art Deco, Four Seasons, Reports, Borders and Boxes, Exercise and Fitness, Nine to Five, Food, Weekend Sports, Team Sports, Computers, People, and Travel.

❖ Other Sources

Some graphics programs will come bundled with a collection of clip art. You can either insert these pictures directly into your documents, or else use the drawing tools provided by the graphics program to alter them.

◆ GEM Draw

This graphics program comes with a modest clip art collection in GEM line art format (GEM extension). In addition, you can buy a larger collection separately from Digital Research. In general, this set of clip art is not as good as most other collections. Having been created with GEM Draw, it has a distinct computery flavor.

◆ Micrografx Designer

This collection consists of over 400 useful symbols such as maps, landmarks, furniture, computer components, animals, planes, borders, flags, familiar objects, signs of the zodiac, and space vehicles. The drawings are remarkably intricate and well rendered, and they offer a wide variety. Micrografx also sells over 3,000 professional images in separate collections. Each collection costs $50 and contains about 400 pictures. For moving its clip art files into other formats, Micrografx also sells a program called Convert Plus for $100, which translates pictures among the following formats: CGM, DXF, EPS, GEM, PCX, TIFF, and MacDraw.

◆ Hewlett-Packard Graphics Gallery

This program comes with 600 images, ranging from simple shapes to an elegant set of fancy capital letters. Thousands of additional clip art images are available for $95 per set. Graphic Gallery can save pictures in HPGL, VideoShow, PCX, or TIFF format.

◆ Arts & Letters

This program comes with over 2,200 professionally drawn pieces of clip art. It allows you to manipulate the images by sizing, slanting, flipping, rotating, etc. Images can be converted into EPS (with a bitmap for the screen) or CGM, either of which can be loaded into Ventura.

18

Encapsulated PostScript

For those with PostScript printers, Ventura's ability to import Encapsulated PostScript (EPS) files provides dramatic capabilities. Encapsulated PostScript merely means that a PostScript file is in a format that allows it to be embedded within another file.

There are several ways to take advantage of Ventura's EPS capability. First, an increasing number of PC graphics programs can save pictures in EPS format. Second, a large amount of clip art is now available in EPS format. Third, you can create your own EPS files if you know how to program in PostScript. Finally, from within Ventura you can save your current page as an EPS file.

Once you have created an EPS file using any of these methods, you can load it into Ventura. Draw a frame, select Load Text/Picture from the File menu, select Line Art and PostScript format, and select OK. In most cases, the file will not be shown on the screen, but will be indicated with a large X; it will appear when printed. However, if an EPS file includes a bitmap representation of the graphic in TIFF or Windows Metafile format, Ventura can display the bitmap.

Just like other graphics, EPS pictures can be scaled, cropped, and distorted by selecting the Sizing & Scaling option from the Frame menu.

❖ Using Ventura Print Files

Let's take a closer look at using Ventura's print-to-file capability as a way of creating EPS files. This technique can be used to take snapshots of pages that can then be incorporated as illustrations in other pages. This method can only be used for saving a single page.

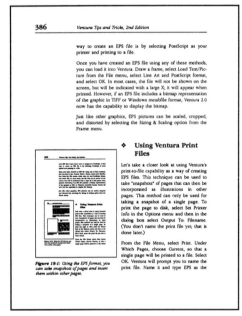

Figure 18-1: Using the EPS format, you can take snapshots of pages and insert them within other pages.

◆ DOS/GEM Version

To print a page to disk in EPS format, first select Set Printer Info from the Options menu and then in the dialog box select Output To: Filename. (You don't name the print file yet; that is done later.)

From the File Menu, select Print. Under Which Pages, choose Current, so that a single page will be printed to a file. Select OK. Ventura will prompt you to name the print file. Name it and type EPS as the extension. A typical page containing no graphics takes up 20K when printed to disk as an EPS file. You can reduce that amount by removing the PS2.PRE file, as described in the tip below. Having created the print file on disk, you can load the EPS picture into a Ventura frame.

◆ Windows Version

To print a page to a file in the Windows version, select Print from the File menu and then select Setup. In the Setup dialog box select Options and then select PostScript as your printer driver. Select the Encapsulated PostScript File option and type the name you want for the EPS file. Now print the page.

❖ The EPS Format

You can write your own PostScript programs to create special effects using a word processor or text editor, saving these effects in ASCII (i.e. nondocument) format and giving them the extension EPS. For diagnostic assistance while working with PostScript, the Ventura Utilities disk contains a helpful file called ERHANDLR.PS, located in the POSTSCPT subdirectory. Once you have copied that file to the printer, the printer will provide feedback on program errors.

When you create EPS files on your own, such as those shown in Figures 18-2 and 18-3, you must make sure that the PostScript program abides by the rules set forth for EPS files.

The rules are explained in "Encapsulated PostScript File Format," a six-page document available from Adobe Systems. Call Adobe

```
%!PS-Adobe-2.0 EPSF-1.2
%%BoundingBox: 210 300 420 420
%%EndComments
newpath
250 320 moveto
300 400 lineto
```

Figure 18-2: This EPS file creates a diagonal line.

Technical Support at 415/961-0911 or write to Technical Support, Adobe Systems, 1585 Charleston Rd., P.O. Box 7900, Mountain View, CA 94039-7900.

Basically, EPS files are normal PostScript files, with these minor differences:

- First, every EPS file is required to include the following two lines in its header:

  %!PS-Adobe-2.0 EPSF-1.2

  %%BoundingBox: x1 y1 x2 y2

```
%!PS-Adobe-2.0 EPSF-1.2
%%BoundingBox: 180 300 350 520
200 350 translate
/Roman /Times-Italic findfont 6 scalefont def
/Bold /Times-Bold findfont 200 scalefont def
/strg (XEROX VENTURA PUBLISHER XEROX VENTURA PUBLISHER
XEROX VENTURA PUBLISHER XEROX VENTURA PUBLISHER) def
/crlf
{ currentpoint 6 sub
exch pop 0 exch moveto } def
/prtstring { strg show crlf } def
/Background
{ 25 { prtstring } repeat } def
gsave
newpath 0 0 moveto
8 setflat
Bold setfont (V) true charpath clip
0 133 moveto
Roman setfont Background
grestore
```

Figure 18-3 (above) and Figure 18-4 (facing): The PostScript program shown above generated the graphic shown on the following page. Note the two header lines that distinguish this as an EPS file.

EROX VENTURA PUBLISI   X VENTURA PUI
  OX VENTURA PU   'TURA '
   ' VENTURA P   TUR
    VENTURA PU   TUI
     'ENTURA PU   'TU'
      'NTURA PUB   .NT'
       'NTURA PUBL   ENT
        'TURA PUBL   'EN
         'URA PUBLI   VE'
          'URA PUBLIS   ' VF
           'RA PUBLISH   X V
            RA PUBLISH   )X '
             'A PUBLISHE   .OX
              ' PUBLISHE   RO)
               PUBLISHER   'RO
               'UBLISHER .ER(
                'UBLISHER XEF
                 'BLISHER XE'
                  'BLISHER XF
                   'LISHER X
                    'ISHER '
                     'SHER
                      'HE'
                       'F

where x1 and y1 are replaced by the lower left coordinates of the bounding box of the EPS file, and x2 and y2 are the upper right coordinates.

- Second, every EPS file must end with a return or linefeed character.

- If fonts are included in the EPS file, the following command may be necessary:
  %%DocumentFonts: font1 font2 ...
  where font1 is replaced by a name such as Times Roman or Helvetica.

- Finally, the following PostScript operators should not be included in EPS files: grestoreall, initgraphics, initmatrix, initclip, erasepage, copypage, banddevice, framedevice, nulldevice, renderbands, setpageparams, note, and exitserver.

Tip 18-1

Rotating EPS Pictures

To print a rotated EPS picture, load the EPS graphic onto a page in landscape orientation, then print to a file. This will produce an EPS file with the extension C00. Now load this file into a page in portrait orientation. When you print, the picture will be rotated.

❖ Editing EPS Files Within Ventura

Because EPS files are not WYSIWYG — all you usually see on the screen is a large X — you'll find it necessary in most instances to modify your program a few times before you have it completely to your liking. Unfortunately, exiting Ventura and loading your word processor merely to edit a line or two of the EPS file is a cumbersome procedure. An alternative is to load the EPS file as a PostScript graphic in Frame A and as a text file in Frame B. Although the file is in plain ASCII format, you should load it as a

XyWrite file rather than as an ASCII file, since Ventura strips carriage returns out of ASCII files but not out of XyWrite files, though the latter also use ASCII format. To change the appearance of the EPS graphic, you can make changes in the EPS listing with Ventura's text editing controls and save the chapter, then print the chapter. Each time you print the chapter, the latest changes you make in the EPS listing in Frame B will then be reflected in the picture in Frame A.

❖ Removing the PS2.PRE File (DOS/GEM Version)

If you are creating print files, you can reduce the amount of storage they require by temporarily renaming or deleting the PS2.PRE file from the \VENTURA directory. Renaming or deleting this file also allows your regular printing to go faster, since Ventura will no longer have to download PS2.PRE prior to printing a chapter. To provide your laser printer with the necessary preparatory information, you'll need to copy the file PERMVP.PS from the \POSTSCPT directory of the Utilities disk to the \VENTURA directory on your hard disk. Then, each time you turn the laser printer on, copy the file to the printer by typing

COPY C:\VENTURA\PERMVP.PS COM1:

❖ PostScript Resources

An increasing number of books, journals, and classes are available for those seeking to learn elementary and advanced PostScript.

◆ Books

PostScript Language Reference Manual by Adobe Systems (Addison-Wesley, Reading, Massachusetts), 1985; *PostScript Language Tutorial and Cookbook* by Adobe Systems (Addison-Wesley, Reading, Massachusetts), 1985; *PostScript Language Program*

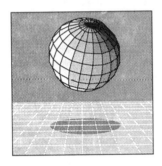

Figure 18-5: *When we wanted an EPS version of our Peachpit Press logo, we contacted a custom PostScript graphics specialist, Mark Powell at WordScapes in Los Altos, California (415/968-8737). We sent Mark a stat of our logo, and a week later he sent back a flawless EPS rendition—on a Macintosh disk—and a bill for $30. For another $5, our local desktop publishing shop converted the file to PC format. Shown here are examples of WordScape's work for various clients.*

Design by Adobe Systems (Addison Wesley, Reading, Massachusetts), 1988; *Learning PostScript: A Visual Approach* by Ross Smith (Peachpit Press, Berkeley, California), 1990; and *Real World PostScript*, edited by Stephen F. Roth (Addison-Wesley, Reading, Massachusetts), 1988.

◆ Publications

Colophon, published by Adobe Systems and free upon request (415/961-4400); *PostScript Language Journal,* published by Pipeline Associates four times per year (201/334-0772).

◆ Electronic Bulletin Boards

CompuServe has an extensive PostScript forum run under the auspices of Adobe Systems. To find out how to subscribe to CompuServe, call 800/848-8199 or 614/457-0802 in Ohio. Once you've logged onto CompuServe, you can access the PostScript forum by typing GO ADOBE from the CompuServe prompt. Other PostScript-oriented bulletin boards include the Byte Information Exchange or BIX (603/924-9281), and the National Independent PostScript Support Board (409/224-4075).

◆ Custom PostScript Graphics

If you have to turn your corporate logo into a format that can be used by Ventura, the easiest method is to scan the logo and save it as a PCX or IMG file. Unfortunately, the quality of such a graphic deteriorates when you scale it to different sizes. The answer is to use a drawing program like Illustrator or Corel Draw and render the logo in EPS format, a task that takes a good deal of graphics expertise. An alternative is to find a service bureau or a graphic artist specializing in custom PostScript graphics. Figure 18-5 shows examples of logos converted into EPS format by one such service bureau.

19

Screen Snapshots

In preparing technical documentation, training materials, and books about software (such as this one), a common task is to take snapshots of the computer screen — also known as screen shots — and insert them in documents. Fortunately, this proves to be relatively easy with Ventura.

Let's start with an overview of the entire process of importing a screen snapshot into Ventura. This process is as follows:

- Load a screen snapshot utility into the computer's memory. Such utilities are small programs devoted specifically to the task of capturing a screen; several are discussed below.

- Load the program you want to take a screen snapshot of, prepare the screen, and activate the screen snapshot utility. With some utilities a menu will be shown on screen; with others the key combination that activates the utility also automatically creates a file containing the screen snapshot on your hard disk.

- In most cases, the screen snapshot utility will save the file with a PCX (PC Paintbrush) extension. In other cases, the screen snapshot utility will save the file in a proprietary format.

- (Optional) Load a bitmapped graphics program, such as PC Paintbrush IV Plus or HotShot Graphics, and edit the screen snapshot. The editing that can be done might include cropping the image (that can also be done in Ventura itself, but you save file space by cropping the graphic before importing it), making alterations using the graphics tools in Paintbrush or HotShot Graphics, and using zoom mode to edit individual pixels. Note that if you edit an image in Paintbrush, its extension may be changed to PCC.

- (Optional) If the screen snapshot is not saved in IMG format, convert it to IMG format. Your screen snapshot utility should have a conversion routine. After converting to IMG, delete the original file to conserve space on your hard disk.

- Load Ventura. Open the document into which you want to load the screen snapshot. Create a new frame of approximately the right size for your screen snapshot. From the File menu select Load Text/Picture. Select Image and select GEM / HALO DPE (for IMG files), PC PAINTBRUSH (for PCC or PCX files), or TIFF (for TIF files) as your format. If necessary, change the extension on the directory line (the top line in the selection box) from PCX to PC?, so that any PCC files will be listed along with any PCX files. The file name containing the screen snapshot will now appear in the Assignment List. Select the name; the screen snapshot will now load onto the page.

- From the Frame menu, select Sizing & Scaling. In the Sizing & Scaling dialog box, select By Scale Factors and Maintained.

- Adjust the size of the screen snapshot, the margins of the frame, and the padding around the frame using the Sizing &

Scaling dialog box. Crop the screen snapshot if desired, either by entering values in the Sizing & Scaling dialog box for Crop Offset or by holding down the Alt key while moving the image with the mouse.

- Add enhancements such as borders, captions, arrows, background shades, and boxed text.

❖ Choosing a Screen Snapshot Utility

Currently, there are a number of screen snapshot utilities on the market, including HotShot Graphics, HotShot Grab, HiJaak, Snap, Tiffany Plus, and Pizazz Plus. In addition, screen capture utilities are provided with the PC Paintbrush family of programs. *(For access information on all the screen snapshot utilities discussed in this chapter, see the Utilities section of Appendix A, "Resources.")*

The main criteria for comparing screen snapshot utilties are as follows.

◆ What Displays Do They Support?

There are five major display standards: the IBM Monochrome Display Adapter (MDA), the Hercules Graphics Card (HGC), the IBM Color/Graphics Adapter (CGA), the IBM Enhanced Graphics Adapter (EGA), and the IBM Video Graphics Adapter (VGA).

Most screen snapshot programs support all these standards. In addition, some programs support less common video formats. HotShot supports the Wyse 700, Amdek 1280, Vega Deluxe, and AT&T 6300. HiJaak supports the AT&T DEB, Wyse 700, Amdek 1280, Genius, and Toshiba. To be sure your monitor is covered, contact the vendor.

◆ Do They Allow Editing of the Image?

The main difference among the utilities listed above is in how much they allow you to edit the image. At one end of the spectrum is HotShot Grab, which merely performs screen captures with no alteration. Likewise, Snap provides no editing features. At the other end are Hotshot Graphics, HiJaak (via Inset), and PC Paintbrush, which allow you to treat the screen snapshot as a graphic image. With these high-end programs you can add text to a screen snapshot, crop it, convert colors to gray shades, change some portions to reverse video, draw arrows, erase portions of the picture, change the size of the screen snapshot, and even draw your own graphics on top of the screen snapshot.

Note that if the utility supports PCX format, you can also export the screen snapshot into PC Paintbrush or Publisher's Paintbrush for extensive editing.

◆ What Formats Do They Create?

You can load a screen snapshot into Ventura if it is in GEM Paint format (IMG extension), PC Paintbrush format (PCX or PCC extension), or Tagged Image File Format (TIF extension). IMG format is preferable, because if you load a PCX, PCC, or TIFF file into Ventura, Ventura will automatically convert it into IMG format anyway but will still look for the original file on your hard disk. The result of this program idiosyncracy is that your hard disk space is wasted on redundant files. Most screen capture utilities either save directly in IMG, TIFF, or PCX format, or else they save captured screens in a proprietary format and then allow you to convert from that format into IMG, TIFF, or PCX.

◆ Can They Capture Windows Screens?

In the past, many screen snapshot utilities did not allow you to take snapshots from within Microsoft Windows. If that capability is important to you, make sure the utility you select allows it. The most sophisticated Windows snapshot utility is Tiffany Plus, which is newly designed for Windows 3.0. It allows you to specify whether you want to capture the entire window, the entire screen, the client window, or a designated rectangular area. You can also set a monochrome threshold for converting intermediate gray levels to black or white. Formats for storing Windows snapshots include gray and color TIFF, monochrome and color PCX, and color or monochrme BMP. Unfortunately, neither DOS/GEM nor Windows Ventura are yet able to import BMP files.

Other utilities that can capture Windows screens incude Pizazz, HotShot Grab, and HotShot Graphics.

◆ How Extensive Are the Controls over Parameters?

All the screen snapshot utilities listed above provide some control over parameters such as aspect ratio, reverse video, and cropping. Of these, reverse video (being able to switch black pixels to white and white pixels to black) is the most important feature to have in a screen snapshot utility, because it cannot be done by Ventura. Both the aspect ratio and the cropping can be controlled from within Ventura. Note that aspect ratio becomes important if you're using a monitor with rectangular rather than square pixels (Hercules, Wyse 700). For example, since each pixel on the Hercules monitors is taller than it is wide, screen snapshots appear too flat when they're printed on a laser printer, since laser printer pixels are always square. To make up for the difference in pixel dimensions, you need to increase the height of the image relative to its width.

◆ What Are the Memory Requirements?

The less memory required by a screen capture utility, the better. HotShot's Grab program uses 25K and its WinGrab program uses 28K. HiJaak uses 40K. Tiffany Plus uses 25K. Pizazz Plus uses 40K to 50K, depending on the configuration.

❖ Text Screens

HotShot, HiJaak, and Snap can all make snapshots of text screens, but the quality of the resulting image varies. HotShot does the best job, followed — in order of quality — by HiJaak and Snap.

For those who already have Sidekick, a cheap method for making screen snapshots is to capture the screens in SideKick and then convert them into PCX files using a program called TXTTO-PCX.EXE, which is provided on Ventura's Utility disk. One limitation of the utility is that it does not work in conjunction with the Hercules Graphics Board.

Here's the procedure. First pop up the Sidekick menu, then open Notepad with Alt-N. Press F4 and the original screen appears again. Press Ctrl-KB before moving the cursor away from the upper left corner, then cursor down to the lower right corner and press Ctrl-KK. Now you're back in Notepad with the image. Save it as a file and leave Sidekick. Type

TXTTOPCX filename

to convert the file into PC Paintbrush (PCX extension) format. Before loading Ventura, you should de-install Sidekick. To load the snapshot into a frame, use the PC Paintbrush option in the Load Text/Pictures dialog box.

❖ Keeping Track of Screen Shots

Generally, it's convenient to create a set of screen shots in the program you are documenting, rather than creating only one. Some screen snapshot utilities, including Frieze, will automatically create sequentially numbered files, one for each snapshot. Others, such as HotShot, let you assign a name to a snapshot at the time you capture it.

A good way of working is to use one subdirectory as a staging ground to temporarily hold newly created screen shots and another subdirectory as a permanent storage location for keeping screen shots you intend to use later. If you use just one subdirectory both for initially creating and for storing screen shots, you may find that in making your second set of screen shots you have inadvertently copied over your first set (since the screen snapshot utility will restart its numbering at 1 each time you use it).

❖ Scaling Screen Snapshots

After you load a screen snapshot into a frame, you should use the Sizing & Scaling option of the Frame menu to set the picture scaling to By Scale Factors and the aspect ratio to Maintained. That way, the screen snapshot will be at its "true pixel count." True pixel count means that every pixel in the onscreen image will be translated into one printed pixel by the laser printer. Since laser printer pixels are smaller than screen pixels (about 1/4 as wide), this means the printed version of the screen snapshot, if shown at true pixel count, will be quite small.

The best way to scale up the picture is to multiply the pixels by integer amounts. Otherwise, you'll notice stripes and moiré patterns in the printout, caused by the program's attempt to scale the picture to fractional specifications. Scale the picture by entering new values for Scale Width and Scale Height, after first noting the original values. Since some screens will appear too wide and flat when printed, you may want to scale the height by a greater factor than the width. You don't need to keep the aspect ratio constant as long as you work in integer amounts.

Profile

Frieze

For screen shots of graphics screens, another option is the Frieze utility, a built-in option of the PC Paintbrush family.

To use Frieze, you load Paintbrush and press Shift-PrtSc. A menu then appears at the top of the screen indicating your setup options. At this point Frieze is loaded into the computer's RAM. You can exit Paintbrush and load the program from which you wish to make the screen shots; Frieze will remain loaded in RAM. When you have prepared the screen, press Shift-PrtSc to see the Frieze menu again. One of your options will be to draw a border around the portion of the screen you want to capture, using the cursor keys. To speed up this process, hold down the Shift key while you move the cursor keys. After you have adjusted one border, press the Spacebar to adjust another, then push the Spacebar again, etc.

Profile

HotShot Graphics

HotShot Graphics is actually four programs in one: a screen capture utility, a screen annotating utility, a paint program, and a graphics conversion program.

◆ Screen Capture

The center of HotShot Graphics is a screen-capture utility that can capture either text screens or graphics screens on a variety of monitors: CGA, EGA, VGA, Wyse 700, MCGA, Hercules, AT&T 6300, and Vega Deluxe. If you're just interested in this aspect of the program, you can purchase HotShot Grab separately. Unlike some other screen-capture programs, this one can handle regular

Figure 19-1: With HotShot Graphics, when you're editing a text screen such as this spreadsheet, you can pop up a table of special symbols. These can then be inserted into the captured screen.

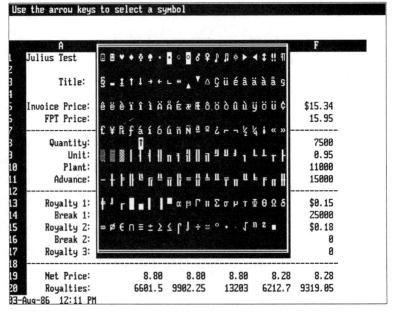

text screens (such as the Lotus spreadsheet shown in Figure 19-1) and Microsoft Windows screens (as shown in Figure 19-2).

◆ Legal Graffiti

Once you've captured a screen, HotShot lets you modify it in numerous ways. You can draw arrows, type notes, and otherwise mark up a captured screen. You can also erase portions of the screen. Not only does the utility faithfully reproduce any inverse video portions of the screen, but it also allows you to "paint" inverse video onto the screen to highlight particular passages. In addition, HotShot will automatically print a border around the screen dump if you want one. You can also add a title to the screen dump. As shown in Figure 19-1, HotShot can provide a table of special symbols that you can insert into a captured screen. For example, you might want to insert the British pound sterling sign (£) into a spreadsheet.

Figure 19-2: You can edit with 16 colors and add text in four sizes. Here's a screen dump from Windows.

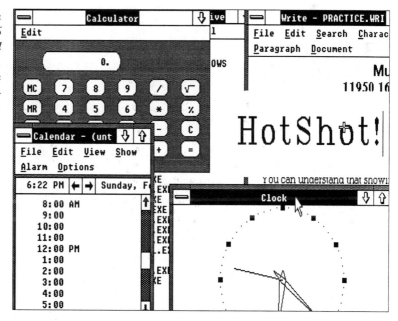

◆ More Legal Graffiti

While annotating a screen is well and good, HotShot Graphics goes even further, providing a full-fledged paint program, whose drawing tools include lines, boxes, curves, arcs, and circles, and functions such as inverting, flipping, mirroring, ellipses, pixel editing, cropping, panning, and zooming. Not quite all the features are there that you might find in PC Paintbrush, but the capabilities are impressive when you consider that HotShot is primarily a screen-capture program.

◆ File Conversions

Less flashy than HotShot's abilities to sling a paintbrush are its workaday file conversion features. You can convert captured screens to ASCII, PCX, GEM IMG, TIFF, and EPS formats. With the PCX and IMG formats, you can then load captured screens into Ventura (as we've done throughout this book).

◆ Hotshot Grab

If you don't need all the graphics-editing capabilities of HotShot Graphics, but simply want to make screen snapshots, you can get the much cheaper HotShot Grab. This package includes WIN-GRAB, a screen-capture utility specifically for Microsoft Windows. It can take snapshots of text or graphics screens, can convert captured screens to different formats, and can reverse black and white in a snapshot.

Tip 19-1

Problems Using HotShot with Hercules Clones

While HotShot works quite well with most monitors, a big exception is Hercules clone boards. If you have such a monitor, don't use HotShot.

Tip 19-2

Using HotShot with a Wyse or Amdek High-Resolution Monitor

When you press Alt-H to capture a graphics screen with HotShot on a Wyse WY-700 or Amdek 1280 monitor, the picture may suddenly turn into gibberish. To fix the problem, press F2.

SECTION FIVE

Fonts

20

Using Fonts

For anyone attempting to master Ventura, the subject of fonts represents a variety of challenges. First, you have to figure out which fonts to buy — and with literally thousands of fonts now available, that's not always easy. Next, you have to figure out how to install the darned things, both for your printer and for your screen. Having installed the fonts in your computer, you still may confront the problem of downloading, that is, figuring out how to get the fonts from your computer into your printer in a reasonably expeditious fashion. Now the fonts are ready to be used, but you're still only halfway home, because having the technical ability to print fonts is not the same as having the knowledge of typography and design to use them correctly. In this chapter and in the following two chapters, we'll be concentrating on the technical aspects of installing and using fonts. It's beyond the scope of this book to teach typography and design, but fortunately, some good books are now available on those topics.

As desktop publishing products go, Ventura's support for fonts is excellent, especially for non-PostScript printers. For HP-compatible laser printers the program provides a set of high-quality fonts from Bitstream, guaranteeing all users — no matter what printer they're using — a solid typographic foundation. Those with HP-compatible printers can also generate additional fonts using Bitstream's Fontware, which is bundled with Ventura. If your printer isn't PostScript or HP compatible, you still have many options for printing, due to the availability of excellent printer utilities such as Atech's PC PowerPak (see the printer utility listings in Appendix A, "Resources," for access information).

In this chapter it's assumed that you've installed Ventura for at least one printer and thus have a set of fonts to work with. The next chapter explores ways of increasing the number of fonts at your disposal.

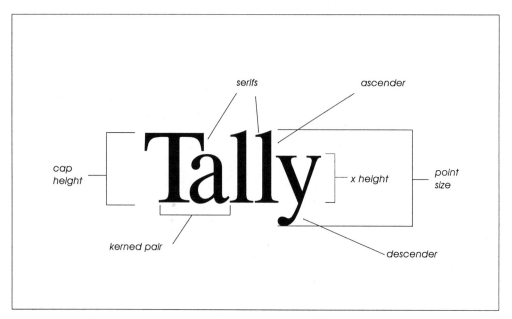

Figure 20-1: *Elements and standard measures of type.*

❖ Font Terminology

Generally, the word *typeface* refers to a particular type design, such as Palatino Italic or Helvetica. *Font,* on the other hand, refers to the source from which type is generated, usually a file on a computer disk. Traditionally, a font was a particular set of characters in a particular typeface and a particular size. The traditional definition is still used in reference to bitmapped fonts, which are always a particular size. However, a revised definition is also in use — a font as a set of scalable outline characters that are not tied to any particular size. A *typeface family* refers to variations on a typeface, such as black (very bold), demi (midway between black and bold), bold, light, book, roman (i.e., regular), compressed, extended, obliqued (i.e., slanted), and italic.

Typefaces can be divided into several groups. Display faces are specially designed for use in titles and headlines. Generally, such faces are bold and dramatic. Decorative faces are highly distinctive and are used for special purposes such as advertisements and diplomas.

Text faces are designed for maximum readability. In most cases, text should be in a serif face. (At one time it was thought that serifs enhance readability by providing the eye with helpful visual "clues." More recently, studies have shown that serif type is more readable for those who grew up with serif type, and sans serif type is more readable for those who grew up with sans serif. In this country, of course, virtually everyone is accustomed to reading text set in serif type.)

The standard unit of font measurement is the *point* (1/72 inch). The point size of a font is generally measured from the top of the highest ascender to the bottom of the lowest descender.

Tip 20-1

X-Height versus Point Size

While point size is the standard way of describing the size of fonts, it can be deceptive in that it understates the size of fonts with short ascenders and descenders, and overstates the size of fonts with tall ascenders and long descenders. For example, notice the difference between the following two lines, both of which are set in 16-point type:

This is 16-point Avant Garde Gothic.

This is 16-point Palatino.

❖ Bitmap Fonts and Outline Fonts

Both laser printers and digital typesetters are raster devices. That is, the text and images they print are actually patterns of dots on a very fine rectangular grid. Prior to being printed, the arrangement of dots that constitutes a single character is stored as a corresponding arrangement of digital bits, or bitmap, in the memory of the laser printer.

Laser printers with sophisticated page description languages such as PostScript and PCL Level 5 (used in the LaserJet III) store type as sets of mathematic descriptions of the character outlines. When called upon to print a 12-point Times Roman italic, the printer uses the outline to generate the appropriate bitmap.

One advantage of the outline method is that type of any size can be generated from a single set of outlines, thereby providing the ultimate in flexibility while consuming relatively little storage space. A disadvantage of the outline method is that the computations necessary to generate bitmaps from outlines exact a toll on printer performance; however, PostScript automatically stores bitmaps generated from outlines in a temporary font cache, which generally makes it unnecessary for the system to generate a new bitmap each time a particular character is needed.

A second advantage of outline fonts is that they can be resolution-independent. The same fonts can be used on a 300-dpi laser printer or a 2400-dpi typesetter; in either case, type will be printed at the maximum resolution available.

The alternative method of storing fonts, used by most non-Post-Script printers, is to work with a separate set of bitmaps for each font size, rather than generate all sizes of a font from a single master outline. The advantage of the bitmap method is that size-specific bitmaps can produce higher quality than fonts generated from outlines. The drawback of the bitmap method is storage space, since you must use a separate file for every font.

Let's say that you want the roman, italic, bold, and bold italic versions of Garamond in every size from 6 points to 36 points. With a printer that uses the outline method, you have to store four outline files: one for roman, one for italic, one for bold, and one for bold italic. With a printer that uses the bitmap method, how-ever, you'd need 124 separate fonts (31 sizes times 4 styles). The size of a single bitmap file ranges from about 12K for a 6-point font to 32K for a 12-point font and 105K for a 24-point font. Notice that the amount of memory increases faster than the point size. Above 30 points, bitmap font files become so large as to be unwieldy.

Generally, printers that use bitmapped rather than outline fonts are a good deal less expensive than PostScript and other printers that use outline fonts, but the drawback of using such printers is that your range of sizes and styles is more restricted.

One way around the restriction, if your printer uses bitmapped fonts and you do have an occasional need for type larger than 30 points, is to use a font generator such as FaceLift, Glyphix, or Type Director. These tools are discussed in Chapter 21, "Adding New Fonts," and Chapter 22, "Font Tools."

❖ Font Storage Locations

The file containing a font outline or bitmap may be stored in one of several locations: in the printer, in a plug-in cartridge, or on the

Table 20-1: Standard PostScript Typefaces

Times Roman

Times Roman Italic

Times Roman Bold

Times Roman Bold Italic

Helvetica

Helvetica Oblique

Helvetica Bold

Helvetica Bold Oblique

Courier

Courier Oblique

Courier Bold

Courier Bold Oblique

Palatino

Palatino Italic

Palatino Bold

Palatino Bold Italic

New Century Schoolbook

New Century Schoolbook Italic

New Century Schoolbook Bold

New Century Schoolbook Bold Italic

ITC Avant Garde Gothic Book

ITC Avant Garde Gothic Book Oblique

ITC Avant Garde Gothic Demi

ITC Avant Garde Gothic Demi Oblique

Helvetica Narrow

Helvetica Narrow Oblique

Helvetica Narrow Bold

Helvetica Narrow Bold Oblique

ITC Bookman Light

ITC Bookman Light Italic

ITC Bookman Demi

ITC Bookman Demi Italic

ITC Zapf Chancery Medium Italic

ITC Zapf Dingbats:
✿╋⭒╉⭒✛✦✧★☆✪

Symbol: ΑΒΧΔΕΦΓΗΙϑ

computer's hard disk. Some fonts, designated as resident, are permanently stored in printer ROM and hence are always available for use. In most PostScript printers, for example, the following typeface families are resident in the printer: Times Roman, Helvetica, Helvetica Narrow, ITC Bookman, ITC Zapf Chancery, Courier, Palatino, Avant Garde Gothic, New Century Schoolbook, and Symbol. Table 20-1 shows a complete list. The HP LaserJet Plus and Series II store Courier 12-point medium and bold, and 8-point Line Printer.

A closely related method of font storage is plug-in ROM cartridges. In the past, these were used more commonly with word processing programs than with desktop publishing programs due to the limited number of typefaces and point sizes on each cartridge, but new cartridges with more typefaces and scalable sizes may change that.

A third method of storing fonts is on floppy or hard disks in the computer. These are called *soft fonts*. A set for HP-compatible printers is provided with Ventura. Additional soft fonts can be purchased or generated.

The amount of storage space you'll need on your hard disk for font files varies considerably, depending on whether the fonts are in outline or bitmapped format. In the case of the HP LaserJet

Figure 20-2:
The Font Setting dialog box for the PostScript width table.

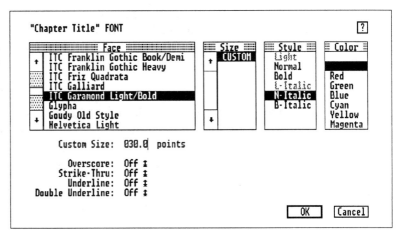

Series II, the amount of storage necessary is about 2.4 megabytes, but for the IIP and III the amount of storage is about half that, because these printers don't require separate files for portrait and landscape fonts.

❖ Selecting Fonts in Ventura

There are two ways to specify type characteristics within Ventura — we'll call them the Paragraph Method and the Text Method. The Paragraph Method uses a tag and sets the font for the entire paragraph; the Text Method sets the font for a portion of the paragraph, such as a single letter, a word, or a group of words. You can also use your word processor to embed the codes used by Ventura for specifying type.

◆ Paragraph Method

When you select a paragraph in tagging mode and then select a tag, the font characteristics stored in that tag are automatically applied to the entire paragraph. To change the font information stored in a tag, select a paragraph, select the Font option from the Paragraph menu, and choose the Face, Size, Style, and Color from the dialog box. You can also select overscore, strike-through, underline, and double underline.

Under Face, the menu displays the typefaces available for the width table you are currently using. Note that the width table need not be the same as the printer you are using. We'll discuss the implications of that later in this chapter.

With printers that use bitmapped fonts, the menu shows the available options. With PostScript or the LaserMaster card, you can select any custom size (Figure 2). Under the Styles heading, those styles that are available in a particular size are shown in black; others are shown in gray. For other printers, the size options are listed in the scroll bar.

You can also use this dialog box to indicate the color of type. Selecting white causes Ventura to save the amount of space that would be taken up if the text were printed, or prints the characters in white if the background is gray or black. This is an extremely useful capability with many possible applications, such as preparing color separations or printing white on black.

◆ Text Method

Use this method when you want to change a single letter, word, or group of words within a paragraph to a different font.

Select text mode, then hold down the mouse button while you drag the mouse across the characters you wish to select. Alternatively, click the mouse button once at your starting point, then hold down the Shift key while you move the cursor to your ending point and click again. The passage, which must be contiguous text, will be highlighted in black. Now select Set Font (DOS/GEM version) or the Text menu (Windows version). The dialog box that appears is similar to the dialog box used by the Tag method, except that now it also includes the shifting and kerning controls.

Shifting means simply that the selected characters are moved up or down the specified distance. Kerning means that characters are moved to the left to tighten up spaces within the word. The most frequent use of kerning is in situations where large type is used, such as titles.

When using the shift or kerning controls, you should normally work in fractional points. If the measurement units are different, change them to fractional points by pointing the cursor directly at the word "inches," "centimeters," or "picas & points" and clicking. With kerning, the number you type determines the distance that Ventura will move the two characters closer together.

Manual kerning should not be confused with automatic kerning, which is also possible in Ventura provided that the font vendor has included the relevant kerning information in the font width

Figure 20-3: The unmodified *HPLJPLUS.CNF* file, which is automatically installed in the \VENTURA directory when you install the program for the HP LaserJet Plus printer. You should save this as *HPLJPLUS.OLD.*

```
permfont(1 EXAMPLE1.SFP)¶
fontspec(HELUTINY,2,2,0,0)¶
fontspec(HLUN3006,2,6,0,0)¶
fontspec(HLUN3008,2,8,0,0)¶
fontspec(HLUB3008,2,8,1,0)¶
fontspec(HLUN3010,2,10,0,0)¶
fontspec(HLUB3010,2,10,1,0)¶
fontspec(HLUI3010,2,10,4,0)¶
fontspec(HLUN3012,2,12,0,0)¶
fontspec(HLUB3012,2,12,1,0)¶
fontspec(HLUI3012,2,12,4,0)¶
fontspec(HLUB3014,2,14,1,0)¶
fontspec(HLUB3018,2,18,1,0)¶
fontspec(HLUB3024,2,24,1,0)¶
fontspec(TMSRTINY,14,2,0,0)¶
fontspec(TMSN3006,14,6,0,0)¶
fontspec(TMSN3008,14,8,0,0)¶
fontspec(TMSB3008,14,8,1,0)¶
fontspec(TMSN3010,14,10,0,0)¶
```

Figure 20-4: The same file after being modified for automatic downloading of 10-point Swiss and 24-point Swiss bold, which are located in the \JETFONTS directory of the D: drive.

```
downpath(D:\jetfonts\)¶
permfont(1 HLUN3010.SFP)¶
permfont(2 HLUB3024.SFP)¶
fontspec(HELUTINY,2,2,0,0)¶
fontspec(HLUN3006,2,6,0,0)¶
fontspec(HLUN3008,2,8,0,0)¶
fontspec(HLUB3008,2,8,1,0)¶
fontspec(HLUN3010,2,10,0,0)¶
fontspec(HLUB3010,2,10,1,0)¶
fontspec(HLUI3010,2,10,4,0)¶
fontspec(HLUN3012,2,12,0,0)¶
fontspec(HLUB3012,2,12,1,0)¶
fontspec(HLUI3012,2,12,4,0)¶
fontspec(HLUB3014,2,14,1,0)¶
fontspec(HLUB3018,2,18,1,0)¶
fontspec(HLUB3024,2,24,1,0)¶
fontspec(TMSRTINY,14,2,0,0)¶
fontspec(TMSN3006,14,6,0,0)¶
fontspec(TMSN3008,14,8,0,0)¶
```

This line tells Ventura where the fonts are located (in this case, in the \JETFONTS directory).

These two lines tell Ventura the names of the fonts that are to be automatically downloaded. They are assigned font ID numbers 1 and 2 respectively.

table. Note that there's also a keyboard shortcut, Shift Left-Arrow or Shift Right-Arrow, that is usually an easier way to kern a pair of letters or a group of words than to enter kerning values in the dialog box. The dialog box, however, can give you precise quantitative feedback on how much you have tightened or loosened the kerning of the letters in your selection using the keyboard shortcut.

◆ Using Embedded Font Codes

An additional way to specify type is to embed codes directly in text files using a word processor. This option is described in Chapter 8, "Preparing, Loading, and Editing Text."

❖ Downloading Fonts

Since soft fonts are not resident in the printer or stored on cartridges, they must be downloaded from your hard disk into the printer each time the printer is turned on. Ventura handles this task automatically: each time you print a chapter the program will download the fonts used in that chapter.

While the automatic downloading feature is certainly convenient, you may want to turn it off. For example, typically it is necessary to print a document several times before you finally get it just right. Particularly if your printer uses a serial port, you'll find that waiting for the fonts to be downloaded each time is too time-consuming. A way to speed things up, which is explained below, is to download all the fonts you need at the beginning of your work session and then turn off automatic downloading.

◆ Downloading LaserJet Fonts (DOS/GEM Version)

If you have a LaserJet compatible, downloading fonts into the printer once at the beginning of a work session, rather than letting Ventura automatically download fonts each time a chapter is

Figure 20-5:
Change the word
Download *(at the*
bottom of the style
list) to ***Resident***
for those fonts that
are listed in the
HPLJPLUS.CNF file.

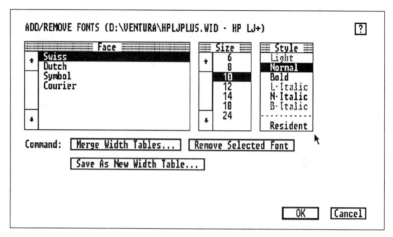

Figure 20-5:
Change the word
Download *(at the*
bottom of the style
list) to ***Resident***
for those fonts that
are listed in the
HPLJPLUS.CNF file.

printed, can save a good deal of time. Ventura comes with a utility called HPDOWN.EXE, located on the Utility disk. Copy this utility into your \VENTURA directory.

Load your word processing program, and load the file HPLJPLUS.CNF from the \VENTURA directory. The file will look like Figure 20-3. Before you modify this file, save a backup of it under the name HPLJPLUS.OLD. Now you can modify the file. If the fonts you want automatically downloaded are in a directory other than \VENTURA, add the following line at the top of the file:

downpath(drive\directory)

Next, add the following line for each font you want downloaded:

permfont(ID# fontname)

Make sure that the only space is between the ID# and the filename of the font. Give the first font you want downloaded the ID# 1, the second font ID# 2, and so forth. Finally, delete the sample line that reads **permfont(1 EXAMPLE1.SFP)**. Save the file in ASCII format under the name HPLJPLUS.CNF.

Figure 20-4 shows an example of a modified HPLJPLUS.CNF file, which names two fonts for automatic downloading, 10-point and 24-point Swiss. Both are located in the \JETFONTS directory.

Now that you've modified the HPLJPLUS.CNF file, you can download the fonts listed in the file by typing

\VENTURA\HPDOWN

Alternatively, you can include that command as a line in your AUTOEXEC.BAT file, VP.BAT file, or VPPROF.BAT file. You'll know the fonts are being downloaded if the green light on the LaserJet control panel starts blinking.

The final step in using your pre-downloaded fonts is done from within Ventura. From the Options menu, select Add/Remove Fonts. Select each of the fonts that you included in the HPLJPLUS.CNF file for automatic downloading, and click on the word **Download** (at the bottom of the Style menu) so that it is changed to **Resident**. When a font is marked as Resident, Ventura doesn't bother to download it to the printer each time a document is printed. As a result, documents are printed a good deal faster than before.

Figure 20-6: The JetScript font downloading program. The fonts already loaded or resident in the printer are listed on the right. On the left are the downloadable fonts contained in the font directory.

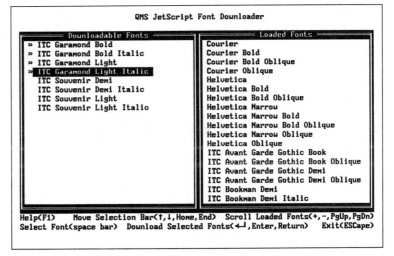

◆ Downloading PostScript Fonts (DOS/GEM Version)

As is the case with LaserJet compatibles, you can download fonts to your PostScript printer at the beginning of a work session and then turn off Ventura's automatic downloading feature for those fonts. The procedure is simpler for PostScript printers, because you don't have to modify the CNF file.

If you purchased your fonts from Adobe Systems, they'll come with a program called PSDOWN.EXE. Follow the directions in the manual provided with the fonts for downloading them to the printer.

Some PostScript printers provide their own downloading programs. For example, if you are using the JetScript controller, use the program JetFonts, which is located in the \QMSJS directory. With JetFonts, you are shown a list of the available typefaces on the left. To select a font for downloading, you press the Spacebar and then cursor down to the next font. When you've finished selecting the batch of fonts to download, press Enter. The JetFonts screen is shown in Figure 6. Note that due to printer memory limitations, you should probably download no more than three or four fonts.

Normally, you download the set of fonts you wish to use at the beginning of your work session. Then you load Ventura. The final step in the procedure is to select Add/Remove Fonts from the Options menu and make sure that the fonts you have downloaded are listed as Resident (as shown in Figure 20-5).

❖ Draft and Ultimate Printing

One of the benefits of PostScript printers is their device independence. This means that you can generate draft copies on a PostScript laser printer and then print the final copy of the same document on a PostScript typesetter. Except for the higher resolution of the typesetter, the two copies will be identical. Thus, the draft copy will give you an accurate preview of your final master.

What if you don't have access to a PostScript printer, but instead are using a more inexpensive laser printer such as a LaserJet Series II? With Ventura, there is still a way to produce draft copies on the LaserJet that will closely match the final output of the PostScript typesetter. Letter spacing will not match up, but line breaks will be the same.

The first thing you have to do is make sure that Ventura is configured to print to both PostScript and LaserJet Plus printers. From the Options menu, select Set Printer Info and check to see whether both options appear next to Device Name. If not, go to the DOS command line, place Ventura disk #1 in drive A, and type **VPPREP.** When Ventura asks you whether you're installing the program for the first time, say No. When it asks you what printer you want to use, select the printer you want to add. When it asks if you want to install any other printers, say No.

Having installed the second printer, you should see two names listed next to Device Name in the Set Printer Info dialog box. For Device Name, pick HP LJ+, 300 dpi, then select Load Different Width Table and select PostScript from the Item Selector box. In other words, you're going to print to a LaserJet Plus (or LaserJet II), using the PostScript font width table. Since you've selected a PostScript width table, the space allotted to each character will be the same as if you were using a PostScript laser printer or typesetter. Thus, line breaks will all be the same as on your final PostScript output device.

21

Adding New Fonts

If you're reading this chapter, you probably have ambitions beyond the basic set of fonts built into your PostScript printer or provided by Ventura for your LaserJet printer. To install new fonts, you need to understand something about Ventura's font management system. Ventura stores font information in three types of files: printer fonts, screen fonts, and width tables.

When you first install Ventura, the installation procedure copies a width table onto your hard disk for each printer that you opt to use with the program. Later, when you add more fonts to your system, you need to revise that width table to incorporate the necessary information on the new fonts. The width table for a printer provides Ventura with the character spacing data it needs to properly position text on the screen and on the printed page. This information is different for every font installed in your system, so when you add a new font, you have to obtain or generate

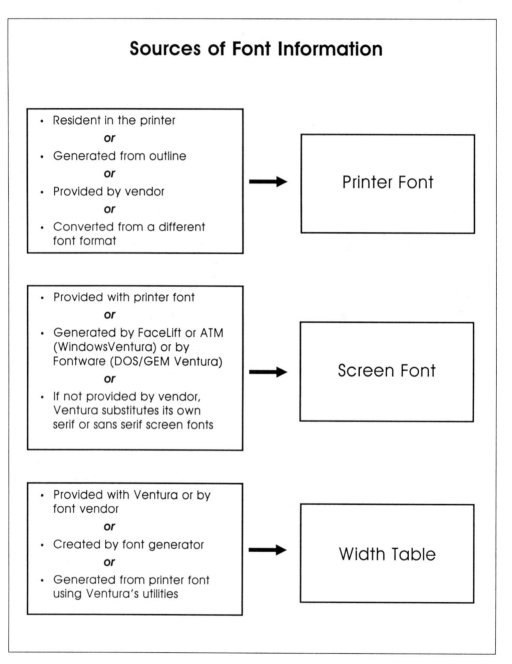

Figure 21-1

a new width table for that font and merge it into your current width table. Because both the display and the printer rely on the same width table for character spacing data, you can be sure that line and paragraph endings will always match up between the display and the printed page.

Whenever you add new fonts to Ventura, you have to consider all three factors: printer fonts, screen fonts, and the width table. The exact steps that you'll need to perform will vary depending on the type of fonts and the type of printer, but the basic procedure, which is outlined in the "road map" on the following pages, is common to all printers and fonts. The remainder of this chapter is devoted to elaborating on that road map by adding relevant details regarding each step for particular printers and particular font categories.

Tip 21-1

Recognizing Font File Extensions

You can usually tell whether a file is a printer font, a screen font, or a width table by looking at the size of the file and at its extension (the three characters following the period in the font file name). Width tables all have the WID extension. Screen fonts usually have the extension EGA, VGA, or CGA, to indicate the type monitor for which they were intended. Adobe's screen fonts to match its PostScript printer fonts have the extension PSF. Printer fonts have a variety of extensions.

❖ Step One: Buy the Fonts

◆ Building Your Personal Font Library

Before you start adding fonts, it's worthwhile to take an inventory of what fonts are already available to you. If you're using a Post-Script printer, you're in luck. Most PostScript printers include a standard set of 35 built-in typeface outlines, which can be scaled

Adding New Fonts: A Road Map
(DOS/GEM Version)

STEPS

NOTES

1 Take an inventory of your current fonts. Make a list of vendors that supply fonts for your printer. Request catalogs and font samples. Purchase fonts.

Most PostScript printers come from the factory with 35 resident fonts, each of which can be scaled to any point size. For non-PostScript printers, such as the LaserJet II, Ventura provides a small set of fonts in the Swiss and Dutch families. To identify sources of additional fonts, use the listings in Appendix B, "Resources."

2 Run the font installation program.

If you have a good installation program, such as the one provided with PostScript's fonts or Bitstream's FaceLift utility, which works with Windows, you may be able to skip all the rest of the steps described below.

■ ━

3 Create size-specific fonts from master outlines, if necessary.

This step is applicable only if you are using Fontware, Glyphix, or another font generator. It does not apply to PostScript printers.

4 Convert fonts to your laser printer's format, if necessary.

This step is necessary if you are using the JLaser board, AST TurboLaser, or Cordata laser printer. For those printers, you can buy fonts in LaserJet format and then convert them using utilities supplied with Ventura.

5 Generate width tables (WID files), if necessary.

This step is only necessary for fonts that do not come with a width table. To generate a width table for these fonts, you need to use the VFMTOWID.EXE utility provided with Ventura. You do not have to generate a width table if you're installing the following kinds of fonts: (1) Most PostScript fonts from Adobe, since a large number of Adobe fonts are included in Ventura's PostScript width table; (2) Fonts generated with Bitstream's Fontware (Fontware automatically generates a WID file when it generates your size-specific fonts); (3) Most LaserJet soft fonts sold by third-party vendors (the vendor usually provides a WID file for each font).

6 Generate screen fonts, if necessary.

It's not necessary to have a screen font for every printer font you install in Ventura. If a screen font is not present for a particular typeface, Ventura will substitute its own generic serif or sans serif screen font. Screen fonts are necessary for fonts whose character sets are different from the Ventura International set (such as foreign language and symbol fonts). For the 35 resident PostScript fonts, you can obtain matching screen fonts from Adobe Systems. For other Adobe fonts, the font installer provided with the fonts you purchase will normally generate and install screen fonts. Many LaserJet fonts are accompanied by screen fonts. If not, you can use SoftCraft's WYSIfonts! utility to generate screen fonts from any LaserJet printer font.

7 Copy printer fonts to the appropriate directory, if necessary.

Normally, PostScript fonts are stored in the \PSFONTS directory, and non-PostScript fonts in the \VENTURA directory. However, if you add a new line to the CNF file for your printer, you can use a different directory. Note that this step may be done automatically by the installation program provided with your fonts.

8 Copy screen fonts to the \VENTURA directory, if necessary.

You can also copy screen fonts to the \VEN-TURA\VPFONTS directory. Note that although you can have screen fonts with different extensions (e.g., VGA, EGA, PSF) stored in the same directory, Ventura can only recognize fonts with one extension at a time. The type of screen fonts currently being used is determined by the extension listed in the Options menu under Set Printer Info. This step may be done automatically by the installation program provided with your fonts.

9 Copy the WID file(s) for your new fonts to the \VENTURA directory and merge them with your current width table.

With many PostScript fonts, this step is not necessary because they are already part of Ventura's POSTSCPT.WID file. To find out which fonts are already in that file, switch to tagging mode, select a paragraph, select Font from the Paragraph menu, and scroll through the list of fonts. Use the Add/Remove Fonts selection from the Options menu (DOS/GEM version) or the Manage Width Table option from the File menu (Windows version) to merge the width table for the new fonts with your current width table.

to any size. These are shown in Table 20-1 in Chapter 20, "Using Fonts." Note that the 35 outlines represent eight complete typeface families (roman, italic, bold, and bold-italic) and three single typefaces. They include five popular serif text faces (Times Roman, Palatino, New Century Schoolbook, and ITC Bookman Light), two sans serif text faces (Helvetica and Avant Garde Gothic), a compressed face for squeezing text into tight spaces (Helvetica Narrow), a script face (ITC Zapf Chancery), a typewriter face (Courier), and two sets of symbols (Symbol and ITC Zapf Dingbats). All in all, it's a strong, balanced set of fonts that can take you a long way, especially when you consider that each font can be scaled to any size.

In contrast to the rich font collection built into every PostScript printer, most non-PostScript printers offer a paltry set of resident fonts. The HP LaserJet II, for example, has 12-point Courier and 12-point Courier Bold. (It also has 8.5-point Line Printer Medium, but that font is not recognized by Ventura.) To supplement the resident fonts of non-PostScript printers, Ventura provides 6-, 8-, 10-, 12-, 14-, 18-, and 24-point Swiss, Swiss Italic, and Swiss Bold; 6-, 8-, 10-, 12-, 14-, 18-, and 24-point Dutch, Dutch Italic, and Dutch Bold; and 8-, 10-, 12-, and 24-point Symbol. (If Swiss and Dutch look familiar, it's because Swiss is a clone of Helvetica and Dutch is a clone of Times Roman.) That amounts to a decent set of fonts, though it will soon seem confining to anyone interested in headlines larger than 24 points.

◆ Sources for PostScript Fonts

The first step in purchasing PostScript fonts is to contact a number of font companies and request the latest catalogs. Each font catalog will show you the company's fonts, the prices for those fonts, and any special features. Typically, PostScript font companies print their catalogs on a PostScript imagesetter, which is misleading if your final output will be on a 300-dpi laser printer. This leads to the following note of caution.

Tip 21-2

Judge Fonts at 300 DPI

Many fonts look great in a catalog but disappointing when you actually use them. Why? The reason is that most PostScript font companies print their catalogs on a high-resolution imagesetter rather than at the 300 dpi of a laser printer. If you really want to know what you're buying, ask for output samples printed on a laser printer.

It used to be that Adobe had a monopoly on good-looking Post-Script fonts because of the fact that the "hints" built into Adobe Type 1 fonts used Adobe's own secret algorithms. In late 1989, however, Adobe was forced to release the hinting technology to other companies in response to the announcement that Apple and Microsoft were joining forces to develop a competing font standard called TrueType. Adobe's fonts are still first rate, but you now have a better chance of finding top-notch fonts at lower cost from smaller companies.

Several dozen companies produce PostScript fonts, with prices per typeface family ranging from $25 to $150. Some shareware fonts are as cheap as $10. Each small font vendor has its specialty: decorative fonts, foreign language fonts, scientific fonts, etc. A number of PostScript font companies are listed in Appendix A, "Resources."

If you find yourself becoming obsessed with wanting to know about *all* the Postscript fonts in existence, you'll want to get hold of *The MacTography Book,* a multi-volume loose-leaf book that includes thousands of fonts from over 25 different companies. (To purchase the book, contact MacTography, 326D North Stonestreet Ave., Rockville, MD 20850; phone: 301/424-3942.)

Most of the companies selling PostScript fonts originally developed these fonts in Macintosh format. Many now offer the identical typefaces on PC disks. If not, it is possible to make the conversion yourself, but I don't advise it unless you're well-versed in the specific differences between Macintosh and PC file formats.

◆ Sources of LaserJet Fonts

There are three sources for LaserJet fonts:

- On-the-fly font generators such as Bitstream's FaceLift.
- Font generators that generate bitmap fonts, such as Bitstream's Fontware and Hewlett-Packard's Type Director.
- Size-specific bitmap fonts available from third-party font companies such as SoftCraft and VS Software. For access information on third-party fonts, see Appendix A, "Resources."

Of the three, the on-the-fly font generator option is the most convenient and flexible, because it lets you create any size you need at the moment without using up space on your hard disk.

Tip 21-3

Get Fonts with WID Files

If you do buy size-specific bitmap fonts, make sure that a width table, also known as a WID file, is provided with each font. If not, you can generate your own WID files as explained later in this chapter, but it's a somewhat difficult procedure. Fortunately, most font vendors do provide WID files.

◆ Other Non-PostScript Printers

Because of the dominance of the HP LaserJet in the printer market, a large selection of fonts are available for that printer. Not so with other non-PostScript printers. Fortunately, Ventura provides utilities that can help you convert LaserJet fonts for use with several printer models.

- **LaserMaster:** LaserMaster boards come with a utility for converting any Bitstream or PostScript font into Bitstream's LXO outline format. You can't use ordinary bitmapped LaserJet fonts, however.

- **AST, Cordata, and JLaser:** With these printers, you'll need to purchase HP LaserJet fonts and then convert them using utilities provided by Ventura. For more details, see "Step Four: Converting the Fonts to Your Printer's Format." .

- **Xerox 4045:** There are two sources of fonts for the 4045. One is Xerox itself. The other is the vendors who sell fonts in HP LaserJet format, since you can convert these fonts to 4045 format using the HPTOXRX and HPTOXRXL utilities on Ventura's Utility Disk. As is the case with the AST Turbo-Laser, the Xerox 4045 is a write-white printer, so fonts converted from LaserJet format (which uses write-black technology) may be slightly lower in quality.

❖   Set Two: Run the Font Installation Program

If you're lucky enough to have a good font installation program, you may be able to skip all the rest of the steps described in this chapter. For example, if you purchase any Bitstream fonts and have the FaceLift utility for Windows 3.0, FaceLift will automatically install the fonts and create screen fonts on the fly whenever you run Ventura. Likewise, if you purchase PostScript fonts from Adobe, the installation program provided with those fonts takes care of all the housekeeping details of installing the fonts, creating and installing the screen fonts, etc.

❖   Step Three: Generate Bitmapped Fonts from Master Outlines

If you are using a PostScript printer or an on-the-fly font generator with a LaserJet, or if you have purchased size-specific LaserJet fonts, you can skip this section.

Because of the flexibility offered by font generators and the fact that Bitstream's Fontware is now bundled with Ventura, many

VENTURA TIPS AND TRICKS

Ventura Tips and Tricks

Ventura Tips and Tricks

VENTURA TIPS AND TRICKS

Ventura Tips and Tricks

Figure 21-2: *Some of the fonts from Image Club's Hot Type collection. From top to bottom, the faces shown here are Lynz, Castle, Fina Bold, Paintbrush Italic, and Sofa Bold.*

people may be content to rely exclusively on Bitstream for their font needs, especially since Bitstream's fonts are unsurpassed in quality. Master outlines for Swiss (Helvetica) and Dutch (Times Roman) are bundled with Fontware; additional outlines can be purchased from Bitstream.

- *For more information on Fontware and other font generators, see Chapter 22, "Font Tools."*

- *For a walk-through demonstration of using Fontware, see "Example 1" later in this chapter.*

❖ Step Four: Convert the Fonts to Your Printer's Format, If Necessary

You can convert any fonts from HP LaserJet format to JLaser, Cordata, AST TurboLaser, or Xerox 4045 format. Copy the HPLTOFNT.EXE utility (for JLaser, Cordata, and AST) or the HPTOXRX.EXE and the HPTOXRXL.EXE (for Xerox 4045 portrait and landscape fonts) from the Utilities Disk to the \VENTURA directory.

To convert a font, the command from the DOS prompt is

HPLTOFNT fontname.SFP [*switches*]

The information needed for the switches is provided in Appendix F of the Ventura manual and is also shown if you type

HPLTOFNT

without naming a font. You'll also need to provide an ID number from the chart of typefaces in Appendix K of the Ventura manual.

Tip 21-4

Convert One Font Before Converting a Batch

If you are adding a number of fonts to your system at once, which is generally the case, it's a good idea to create a batch file rather than attempting to enter the lengthy conversion syntax over and over directly from the DOS prompt. However, before you attempt to set up such a batch file, you should go through the entire process of adding just one font to the system. Once you've sorted through the process with a single font, you have a much greater chance of running a batch file successfully. In other words, start simple before you get ambitious.

❖ Step Five: Generate WID Files, If Necessary

It is rare these days to encounter fonts that don't come with matching width tables (WID files), but if you do, here's what to do. One option is to buy WYSIfonts, which will generate not only the width table but also screen fonts to match the printer fonts.

The other option, which takes extra work, is to use several utilities provided with Ventura to build the WID files. The procedure is as follows:

- Generate a VFM file for each font. Copy the HPLTOVFM.EXE utility from the \HPLJPLUS subdirectory of the Utilities Disk to the \VENTURA subdirectory. If you type

  HPLTOVFM

  without specifying a file to convert, the utility will provide a more detailed set of syntax instructions.

- Using a word processor, create a list of the VFM files. Save it as an ASCII file. Give this file the same name as the width table you plan to create, but use the extension LST.

Type

VFMTOWID filename.LST

to convert the LST file to a new width table.

❖ Step Six: Generate Screen Fonts (DOS/GEM Version)

When you install Ventura, a set of screen fonts are automatically placed in the \VENTURA directory. They match the Dutch and Swiss typefaces provided with Ventura, and they also include a Courier screen font and a screen font for the Symbol font. If you installed Ventura for a VGA or a CGA monitor, the screen fonts will have the extension VGA or CGA respectively. For most other monitors, the screen fonts will have the extension EGA.

When you add new printer fonts, you have to decide whether to also install matching screen fonts. Here are two things to keep in mind:

- **Screen fonts aren't always necessary.** If a screen font for a particular font is not present on your hard disk, Ventura will simply substitute its own Helvetica or Dutch screen fonts.

- **Screen fonts can be a drag.** Why? Because they use up valuable system memory. Ventura normally reserves 64K of RAM for screen fonts. If you install too many screen fonts, the program will take a long time to load (and in some cases may not be able to load at all) and will have slower performance in general.

Having (hopefully) persuaded you to be somewhat judicious about installing too many screen fonts on your hard disk, let's now consider a few situations in which installing screen fonts makes sense.

- If the character set of the printer font you are installing is something other than the Ventura International set (the character set normally used by most Ventura fonts), you'll need to install a screen font if you want to see the same symbols on the screen that will appear in your printed document. If the character set of the printer font is the Ventura International set, you can usually skip installing screen fonts and let

Ventura use its default Helvetica and Times Roman screen fonts with no ill effects.

· If you need to do manual kerning, you should install screen fonts. If you don't install a screen font to match your printer font, line endings and paragraphs will still be accurate on your display; however, manual kerning will be more difficult because adjusting the amount of spacing that is desirable between a given pair of characters depends on the relative shapes of those characters in a particular typeface.

Most third-party fonts come with matching screen fonts, and all you have to do is copy the screen font files into the \VENTURA directory. If you are generating fonts for the LaserJet using Fontware, you'll also have to take the additional step of generating the screen fonts you wish to use. If you are installing Post-Script fonts, you'll have to use the ABFTOFNT.EXE utility to convert the ABF files provided with the Adobe fonts into Ventura screen fonts. These screen fonts will have the PSF extension, but you can change that extension to VGA or EGA and use them with your other screen fonts. Note that these screen fonts are designed for displays with square rather than rectangular pixels.

Tip 21-5

The Maximum Number and Size of Screen Fonts

The absolute maximum number of screen fonts that may be installed is 700 (with a 35K limit on the size of any one screen font file), but the practical limit is much lower.

Tip 21-6

Create Screen Font Ensembles

Having a large number of active screen fonts can slow the process of loading Ventura considerably. If you do have a large collection of screen fonts, try separating them into sets, each with a different extension. For example, if you use one set for flyers and another for memos, change the extension for the first set to FLY and the extension for the second set to MEM. (As you can see, the extensions don't have to be EGA and VGA.) When you want to change to a different set, go into the Set Printer Info dialog box and enter the new extension. You can go even further and "attach" each set of screen fonts to its own batch file. Here's the procedure to create a batch file that automatically loads the FLY screen font set when you load Ventura:

- *Using the DOS Copy or Rename commands, give all the screen fonts that you want included in the FLY set the extension FLY.*

- *Load Ventura, and from the Set Printer Info dialog box, change the screen extension to FLY.*

- *Save your current document and quit.*

- *Use the DOS Copy command to make a copy of VP.INF called FLY.INF.*

- *Using a text editor, copy the VP.BAT file to FLY.BAT and add the line* **copy FLY.INF VP.INF**, *like this:*

```
C:
cd \VENTURA
copy FLY.INF VP.INF
drvrmrgr VP %1 /S=SD_WY700.VGA/M=32
```

Your screen driver and mouse (i.e., everything listed after the %1) may be different, but the technique will be the same. By having a separate batch file like this for each of your screen font ensembles, you'll immediately have the right kind of screen fonts ready to go when you start the program.

Tip 21-7

Ventura's Generic Screen Fonts

You always have to have Times (a.k.a. Dutch) and Helvetica (a.k.a. Swiss) screen fonts in your system. The reason is that those two fonts play the role of generic serif and sans serif screen fonts, respectively.

Tip 21-8

Adjusting Buffers for Screen Fonts

If you're using screen fonts, make sure that the buffers statement in your CONFIG.SYS file is set to 30. For optimum performance, you can even experiment with setting the buffers as high as 50. If you're using a disk-caching utility, however, you should always set the buffers to 3 or 4.

Tip 21-9

Filling In for Missing Screen Fonts

Ventura provides screen fonts for common text sizes, including 10, 12, 14, 18, 24, and 36 points. If you're editing text in other point sizes, however, the characters may look rough and you may run into difficulties positioning the cursor. To overcome those problems, you can use DOS's Debug utility to generate fonts in odd sizes such as 9, 11, and 13 points.

The procedure to create a 13-point font for Times Roman is as follows:

- *Locate the file IBMET12I.EGA in the VENTURA directory.*
- *Type*
  COPY IBMET12I.EGA IBMET13I.EGA
- *Type*
  DEBUG IBMET13I.EGA
- *Debug will provide you with a new prompt (–). Type*
  –d *and press <Enter>*
  –e 0102 *and press <Enter>*
- *You'll now see* **0C.** *Type*
  0D *and press <Enter>*

following the **0C**. *What you're doing is substituting hex 13 for hex 12 in the third byte of the file.*

Now type
-w *and press <Enter>*
-q *and press <Enter>*
to save your work and quit. Follow the same procedure to create 9- and 11-point type from 10-point, 15-point type from 14-point type, etc. Don't create unnecessary screen fonts, however, because each screen font in the system reduces the amount of memory available for holding text and graphics.

Tip 21-10

One Extension at a Time

You can only use screen fonts with one type of extension at a time. For example, if most of your screen fonts use the EGA extension and you then add PostScript screen fonts with the PSF extension, you can use one or the other, but not both at the same time. It's possible, however, to combine two types of fonts, as described in the next tip.

Tip 21-11

Changing Screen Font Extensions

This tip may not work under all circumstances, but it's worth trying if you have screen fonts from two different sources that you'd like to use in the same document. Rename the screen font files so that they share the same extension. For example, give them the common extension 001, then change the screen font extension in the Set Printer Info dialog box to 001.

❖ Step Seven: Copy Printer Files to the Correct Directory

Normally, PostScript fonts are stored in the \PSFONTS directory, and non-PostScript fonts in the \VENTURA directory. However, if you add a new line to the CNF file for your printer, you can use a different directory. Note that the installation program provided by Adobe handles this step automatically.

For LaserJet compatibles, use your word processor or ASCII text editor to add the following line to the top of the HPLJPLUS.CNF file, which is located in the \VENTURA directory:

downpath(C:\JETFONTS\)

For more details on adding that line to HPLJPLUS.CNF, see Figures 20-3 and 20-4 in Chapter 20, "Using Fonts."

For PostScript printers, if you want to store your fonts in a directory other than \PSFONTS, add the following line to the top of the POSTSCPT.CNF file, which is located in the \VENTURA directory:

downpath(C:\JETFONTS\)

For more details on editing CNF files, see Figures 20-3 and 20-4 in Chapter 20, "Using Fonts."

❖ Step Eight: Copy Screen Fonts to the \VENTURA Directory

You can also copy screen fonts to the \VENTURA\VPFONTS directory. Note that although you can have screen fonts with different extensions (e.g., VGA, EGA, PSF) stored in the same directory, Ventura can only recognize fonts with one extension at a time. The type of screen fonts currently being used is determined under Set Printer Info in the Options menu. As explained in the tip above, you can change the screen font extension to organize your screen fonts into sets.

❖ Step Nine: Copy the WID File(s) for Your New Fonts to the \VENTURA Directory and Merge Them with Your Current Width Table

With many PostScript fonts, this step is not necessary because they are already part of Ventura's POSTSCPT.WID file. To find out which fonts are already in that file, switch to tagging mode, select a paragraph, select Font from the Paragraph menu, and scroll through the list of fonts. Use the Add/Remove Fonts selection from the Options menu (DOS/GEM version) or the Manage Width Table option from the File menu (Windows version) to merge the width table for the new fonts with your current width table.

For each font that you add, the final step is to make sure that Ventura marks it with "Download" under Add/Remove Fonts (unless you want to download each font manually, using the procedure described in Chapter 20, "Using Fonts").

❖ Example One: Generating and Installing a Fontware Font

Now let's look at an actual example of generating and installing a new font, going through all the steps from installing the Fontware utility to merging width tables. Generally, in using Fontware, you'll generate a number of fonts in a batch, possibly leaving the computer over your lunch break or even overnight to perform the time-consuming process of creating size-specific bitmaps from its master font outlines. The first time you use Fontware, however, it's a good idea to just generate a single font and test out all the steps of the installation procedure. That way, if you make a mistake and have to backtrack, you'll waste a lot less time.

◆ Installing Fontware

- Place Fontware Installation Kit Disk 1 in the A: drive of your computer.

- Type **A:Fontware**

- Select a directory for the Fontware program. Normally, this will be C:\FONTWARE.

- Select the directory that contains Ventura. This will normally be C:\VENTURA.

- Select the type of display you are using.

- Select a character set for your display fonts (i.e., screen fonts). Normally, you should choose VP International. For more information about character sets, see "Character Sets" below.

- Select the type of printer you are using.

- Select the character set for your printer fonts. Normally, you should choose VP International.

- At this point, the screen will look like Figure 21-3. Press F10 to accept the settings for monitor, printer, and symbol sets.

◆ Making the Fonts

- You should now be in the Fontware Typefaces menu. If you aren't, press Esc to go to the Main Menu and select Add/Delete Fontware Typefaces.

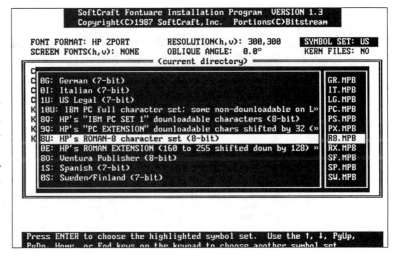

Figure 21-3: The Fontware Control Panel shows you what directories contain Fontware and Ventura, what display and printer you are using, and what character sets you want to use for your screen fonts and printer fonts.

- Press F3 to add a new typeface.
- Place the typeface disk for Dutch in drive A and press Enter.
- Select Dutch roman only. Don't select italic, bold, or bold-italic.
- Select F10 to copy the Dutch roman master outline to your hard disk.
- Select F10 to go to the Make Fonts menu.
- Press Enter to verify Dutch roman as your selection, then type 11 and press Enter. The screen should look like Figure 21-4.
- Press F10 to make the font. Fontware will tell you how much time the procedure will take.

◆ Installing the Fonts into Ventura

- Whenever it generates a font or set of fonts, Fontware automatically creates a Ventura width table to match what it has generated. At the end of the generation process, Fontware will display the name of the new width table. Copy the name onto a piece of paper. In this case, it's HP_LJ000.WID.
- Now quit Fontware and type
  DIR C:\VENTURA*.SF?

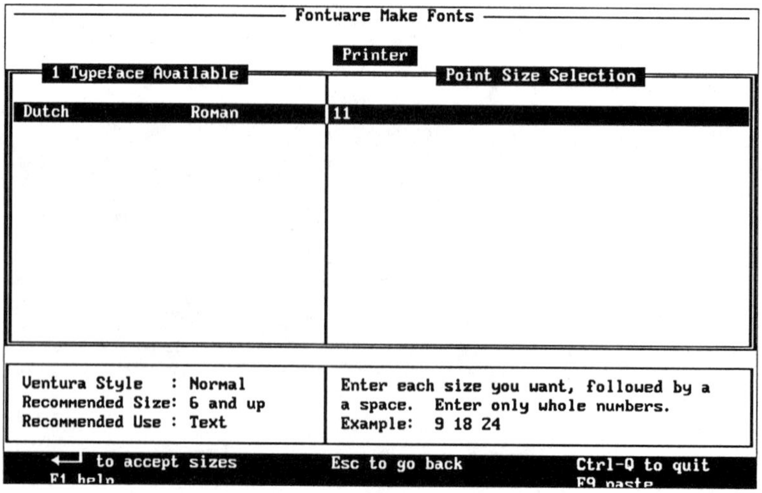

Figure 21-4: The Make Fonts menu shows what fonts you want Fontware to generate.

DOS will list all the LaserJet fonts that are in your Ventura directory. Portrait fonts have the extension SFP, and landscape fonts have the extension SFL. Among the fonts in the directory should be 110IHP.SFP and 110IHP.SFL, the portrait and landscape versions of the 11-point Dutch roman font, which you just generated.

- Before you load Ventura, you need to copy the new width table into the Ventura directory. Type
  COPY C:\FONTWARE\HP_LJ000.WID C:\VENTURA
- Now load Ventura.
- From the Options menu, select Set Printer Info.
- Make sure that the current width table is HPLJPLUS.WID. If not, select Load Different Width Table and select HPLJPLUS.WID from the list. When you've done that, select OK to leave the Set Printer Info menu.
- From the Options menu, select Add/Remove Fonts.
- Select Merge Width Tables.
- From the list of width tables, select HP_LJ000.WID.
- Select OK.

Now the new font should be installed along with the rest of your LaserJet fonts. To check whether the installation worked, tag a paragraph, select Font from the Paragraph menu, and see if Dutch 11-point Normal is on the list.

◆ Adding Screen Fonts

In the example above, we didn't generate and install a screen font to match the 11-point Dutch roman printer font. If you want to create screen fonts to match your printer fonts, you can do so either at the same time that you generate your printer fonts or at a later time. To go back and forth from the printer font menu to the screen font menu, press F2.

Once you have generated screen fonts, there is no need to install them. Ventura will automatically use them as long as the exten-

Character Sets

In deciding which fonts to purchase and add to your system, the most important factors are obviously the design of the typeface and the point sizes available in that typeface. But don't overlook the matter of what character set is included in the font. Unless the font includes characters such as the cent sign (¢) or true quotation marks (" and "), there is no way that you'll be able to print those characters in the desired typeface.

ASCII (or US ASCII)

The most basic character set is the ASCII set (American Standard Code for Information Interchange). Numbers 0 to 31 of the ASCII set are reserved for unprintable control characters. Number 32 is the space character. Numbers 33 through 127 include the standard upper- and lowercase letters of the English alphabet as well as the punctuation marks and symbols found on a standard computer keyboard—92 characters in all. Most other character sets (except those made up entirely of special characters, like Ventura's Symbol font) are supersets of the ASCII set. They fill out the ASCII set with characters in the range above 127. Because numbers up to 127 can be represented by 7 binary bits, the ASCII set is referred to as a 7-bit character set. To represent numbers above 127 you need 8 binary bits; hence, such sets are referred to as 8-bit sets and the characters numbered above 127 are called "high-bit" or "extended ASCII" characters.

Many fonts, especially in large point sizes, include only the ASCII character set. This applies to many third-party fonts for the HP LaserJet as well as to Hewlett-Packard's own soft fonts numbered 33412AC (TmsRmn/Helv), 33412AE (TmsRmn/Helv), 33412RA (ITC Garamond), 33412SA (Century Schoolbook), 33412TA (Zapf Humanist 601), and 33412UA (Headline Typefaces).

Conspicuously absent from the ASCII set are any typographic symbols not found on the keyboard. These include true left and right quotation marks (" and "), the em dash (—), copyright and trademark symbols (©, ®, and ™), European characters (such as ä, à, and å), commercial symbols (such as ¢, £, and ¥), and typographic symbols (such as ‡ and ¶).

The Ventura International Set

The character set used by the printer and screen fonts provided with the Ventura package is referred to in the Ventura manual as the International set and by others as either the International or the Ventura character set. It is an 8-bit character set that includes a full complement of typographic symbols missing from the standard computer keyboard, as well as characters needed by some European languages: Spanish, French, Italian, and German. The full set is shown in Appendix E of the Ventura manual.

The Roman-8 Set

The Roman-8 set is an 8-bit character set used by Hewlett-Packard for many of its cartridge and soft fonts. Since Roman-8 is the character set provided on the F cartridge, it is the only character set available to you if you use Ventura with a plain HP LaserJet. It is also the character set used on Hewlett-Packard's soft fonts numbered 33412AD (TmsRmn/Helv), 33412AF (TmsRmn/Helv), 33412DA (Letter Gothic), and 33412EA (Prestige Elite).

The high-bit characters of the Roman-8 set are mainly European and currency symbols. Missing are a number of important typographic and commercial symbols, including ", ", §, ‡, †, ¶, ©, ®, and ™. Finally, the set lacks a satisfactory bullet character.

The Symbol Font Character Set

The Symbol font is also an 8-bit font. It includes a number of scientific and mathematical symbols, the Greek alphabet (uppercase and lowercase), and a variety of miscellaneous symbols. The set matches Adobe's Symbol character set through character 207, at which point it diverges slightly.

The VP US Character Set

This symbol set has fewer characters than the VP International character set, so fonts that use it take up significantly less room on the hard disk. However, unlike ASCII or Roman-8, the VP US character set includes a number of useful typographic symbols, including true ", ", §, ‡, †, ¶, —, ©, ®, ¢, ‰, and ™. The VP US character set is an option with Bitstream's Fontware and also with Hewlett-Packard's Type Director.

sion of the fonts matches the Ventura's default screen font extension. If you want to find out what extension Ventura is using, select Set Printer Info from the Options menu. The extension CGA, VGA, or EGA will be listed next to Screen Fonts.

❖ Example Two: Installing a LaserJet Font

Now that we have seen how to generate and install fonts with Bitstream's Fontware, let's look at a different example. This time, we'll describe a worst case situation: where you bought a font that does not have a matching WID file.

The first order of business is to copy the font conversion utilities from Ventura's Utility Disk to the \VENTURA directory.

- Place the Utility Disk in drive A.
- Type
  COPY A:\HPLJPLUS\HPLTOVFM.EXE C:\VENTURA
- Type
  COPY A:\HPLJPLUS\VFMTOWID.EXE C:\VENTURA

Next, copy the font (for our example we'll use 30-point Garamond Bold, which is contained in a file called GA300BPN.USP) into the same directory and rename it to meet Ventura's specifications.

- Put the disk containing the font in drive A.
- From DOS, type
  COPY A:GA300BPN.USP C:\VENTURA
- Type
  RENAME GA300BPN.USP HPLJG30B.SFP
  This is not documented in the manual, but it is necessary. The HPLJ must be the first four characters of the font, the G stands for Garamond (the initials for other characters are in Appendix K of the manual), 30 is for the point size and b for bold. For more instructions on renaming fonts, type
  HPLTOVFM

without naming a font. Ventura will produce a screen describing the correct naming conventions.

Now you can run the conversion utilities to create a VFM file.

- Type **HPLTOVFM**
  This produces a screenful of instructions explaining what switches to use with HPLTOVFM.EXE.

- Type
  HPLTOVFM HPLJG30B.SFP/F=GARAMOND/N=22/T

The N=22 is the typeface identification number for Garamond, derived from the table in Appendix K of the Ventura manual. The T means that since there is no screen font for Garamond, Ventura is to use Times (i.e., Dutch) to represent it on screen. The result of this conversion is a file called HPLJG30B.VFM

Next, convert the VFM file to a WID file (a width table).

- Type
  COPY CON HPLJG30B.LST

- Type
  HPLJG30B.VFM

- Type
  Ctrl-Z

- Type
  VFMTOWID HPLJG30B.LST

Now you can load Ventura, try out the new HPLJG30B width table, then merge it with the existing LaserJet Plus width table.

- Load Ventura, and from the Options menu select Set Printer Info. Next, select Load Different Width Table and select HPLJG30B.WID.

- Type a word or two and print it out to check that the width table is working.

- Select Load Different Width Table and select HPLJPLUS.WID.

- From the Options menu select Add/Remove Fonts.

- Select Merge Width Tables.
- Select HPLJG30B.WID.
- Save As New Width Table.

You now will find that 30-point Garamond Bold is one of the regular selections for fonts with your LaserJet Plus driver.

22 Font Tools

The purpose of this chapter is to give you an overview of the variety of font tools on the market. The programs we'll look at fall into several categories:

- **On-the-Fly Windows Font Generators**. These programs, which include Adobe Type Manager for Windows, Bitstream's FaceLift, MoreFonts, PowerPak, and SuperPrint, provide a variety of capabilities for the Windows version of Ventura, including on-the-fly generation of screen fonts and faster printing.

- **Other Font Generators.** These programs offer less convenience than the on-the-fly font generators, but they are still quite useful, since they create fonts for LaserJet and other non-PostScript printers from master outlines. They include Fontware, MoreFonts, Type Director, and Publisher's PowerPak.

- **Font Editing Software.** These programs allow you to modify the appearance of your fonts. They include Publisher's Type Foundry, SoftCraft Font Editor, Font Effects, and fontART. Over the past few years, the state of the art in font editing software has advanced greatly. Unfortunately, many obsolete programs are still on the market, waiting to snag the unsuspecting buyer. The crudest programs are those that must be used in conjunction with an ASCII text editor or word processing program. With the editor, you create each character as a pattern of dots or asterisks. You then save this pattern as a text file and merge it into an existing font using the font-editing program. Obviously, using this sort of font-editing system is tedious and slow. An example is SoftCraft's Efont program. In contrast, the newest font-editing programs work much like painting programs. Using a mouse (or, alternatively, the keyboard), you draw your character on the screen using pens or brushes of adjustable thickness, line-drawing tools, and even tools to automatically create circles, ovals, and polygons.

- **Other Font Tools.** The final utilities discussed in this chapter are a screen font generator called WYSIfonts! and a font compression program called FontSpace.

On-the-Fly Windows Font Generators

What goes from 2 to 254 in 45 seconds? What's able to create tall type in a single bound? Is it bird? Is it a 747? No, it's the high-flying world of fonts-on-the-fly for Windows.

It wasn't so long ago that if you wanted the ease and flexibility of scalable fonts you had to buy a PostScript printer. Now any old LaserJet Plus or Series II (or DeskJet or dot-matrix printer for that matter) can print any size font, any time. This mean there's no need to generate bitmapped fonts in advance or fill your hard disk with megabytes of the pesky things. You're free — as a bird.

That is, a bird with a 386 computer and two megabytes of memory (theoretically you *can* use a 286, but only if you have the patience of an ostrich waiting to fly), a copy of Windows 3.0 and one of the following: Adobe Type Manager (ATM); Bitstream FaceLift; MicroLogic Software's MoreFonts; Atech's Publisher's PowerPak; or Zenographics' SuperPrint. All these programs can give you screen and printer fonts on the fly from scalable outline fonts.

The whole trend started with ATM on the Mac. ATM eliminated inaccurate, jagged screen fonts and replaced them with smooth, WYSIWYG fonts that made the screen look more like the printed page. The same technology that displays fonts on-screen also sends them to non-PostScript printers — not as normal downloadable fonts, but as graphics. The surprise here is that not only does it work, but it works *great* — sometimes faster than traditional downloadable fonts.

But it's not so much the similarities of these programs but the differences that are important. And, as with birds, they all fly, but they all do it differently and have their own special advantages and disadvantages. Let's take a look at them one by one (in alphabetical order).

Profile

ATM (Adobe Type Manager)

Adobe's offering is the simplest, yet surprisingly, it also tied for second *fastest* of the bunch (and actually the fastest for any program using true bold and italic foundry fonts). You heard right. PostScript has never been known for its speed, but Adobe has optimized its Type 1 font format rasterizing to the point where it's a standout for speed — both on-screen and on-paper. Even with the normal 96K font cache (the area in memory reserved for storing fonts), ATM was faster than FaceLift with a 256K cache.

Screen scrolling is very fast. You hardly have to wait as the fonts are created for the screen. Scrolling is smooth, and doesn't have the slight delays you can experience with some of the other programs.

The printed quality isn't just indistinguishable from what would come out of a PostScript printer — it can be sharper than what came out of many PostScript printers. In the past you could always spot pages output on a PostScript laser printer because they tended to be a little darker and more jagged than LaserJet bitmaps. But with ATM, the fonts print light and clean — really top quality. ATM comes with Times Roman, Helvetica, Courier, and Symbol, and uses *any* Type 1 font, from any font foundry (including, of course, Adobe).

If you want the rest of the standard 35 fonts that are resident in most PostScript printers, Adobe sells its Plus Pack for $198. To help you build your type library, Adobe offers extra value through three reasonably priced TypeSets. The two display sets each contain seven display faces, and cost only $99. Set 1 includes: Bodoni Poster, Cottonwood, Freestyle Script, Hobo, Linotext, Trajan, and VAG rounded. Set 2 contains Cooper Black, Copperplate Gothic 31AB, Franklin Gothic No. 2 Roman, Juniper, Lithos Bold, Peignot Demi, and Present Script. Set 3 contains eleven text faces and costs $198: Adobe Garamond (Regular, Italic, Semi-bold, Semi-bold-italic), Helvetica Light (Light Oblique, Black, Black Oblique), Helvetica Compressed, Tekton, and Tekton Oblique.

If you have a PostScript printer, ATM is the *only* program to consider. If you have a LaserJet it's still a good bet. Adobe has the largest font library available for the PC, many new original typefaces, and the only caveat is that they also have the highest font prices (4-weight packages cost $185).

Despite rumors to the contrary, ATM does work with Ventura for Windows. It works best when you use the ENVIRONMENT.WID width table (generated automatically by Ventura) rather than older Ventura width tables.

One important point to remember — ATM's magic only applies to fonts, not graphics. Even though ATM can print PostScript fonts on non-PostScript printers, it won't let you print PostScript graphics on a LaserJet. To do that, you'll have to upgrade your printer to full PostScript capability by adding a PostScript cartridge or software interpreter such as GoScript.

Profile

Bitstream FaceLift

FaceLift, Bitstream's entry into the Windows screen font fray is based on its fast new "Speedo" font format. Despite the name, "Speedo" is not necessarily faster than older technology. For example, a page that took 60 seconds to print using pre-made font bitmaps took 90 seconds to print the first time with FaceLift and 80 seconds the second time.

While ATM puts a high priority on simplicity, FaceLift goes for control. It allows you to create disk-based bitmapped fonts to improve performance, control the number and size of fonts that will be cached, specify whether or not you want to save the cache to disk so the fonts don't have to be rebuilt each session, and control print quality on inkjet and dot-matrix printers.

While FaceLift doesn't beat ATM, the speed is still acceptable. Screen fonts appear quickly and cleanly, and they scroll smoothly. The Speedo format fonts share the same font metrics (widths) as Bitstream's Fontware typefaces, so your documents should not require reformatting.

FaceLift comes with a larger assortment of fonts than ATM, including Swiss (Helvetica), Dutch (Times Roman), Park Avenue, Bitstream Cooper Black, Formal Script (Ondine/Mermaid), Brush Script, and Monospace (Helvetica Monospace).

Bitstream has lowered the prices of its font packages from $195 to $129, and its "Collections" (a bundle of type packages) from $299 to $199. This makes Bitstream fonts an even better value.

abcdefghijklmnopqrstuvwxyz
ABCDEFGHIJKLMNOPQRSTUVWXYZ
1234567890&$£%.,:;-!?"

abcdefghijklmnopqrstuvwxyz
ABCDEFGHIJKLMNOPQRSTUVWXYZ
1234567890&$£%.,:;-!?"

abcdefghijklmnopqrstuvwxyz
ABCDEFGHIJKLMNOPQRSTUVWXYZ
1234567890&$£%.,:;-!?"

abcdefghijklmnopqrstuvwxyz
ABCDEFGHIJKLMNOPQRSTUVWXYZ
1234567890&$£%.,:;-!?"

Figure 22-1: *The Bitstream Charter family, a new set of typefaces designed by Bitstream's Matthew Carter for optimal appearance on a laser printer.*

Bitstream is also offering three special Companion Packs for Face-Lift: The Companion Value Pack is a terrific value because it contains 24 typefaces (the equivalent of six regular packages) and costs only $199. It includes: Bitstream Amerigo (Roman, Italic, Bold, Bold-Italic); Bitstream Charter (Roman, Italic, Black, Black-Italic); Century Schoolbook (Roman, Italic, Bold, Bold Italic); Futura Light (Light Italic, Condensed, Extra Black); Swiss Compressed and Extra Compressed; Exotic Bold and Demi-bold; Coronet Bold; ITC Zapf Chancery; Clarendon and Clarendon Bold. Bitstream also offers a Companion Pack for PostScript (the standard 35) for $179, and a Companion Pack for the LaserJet III for $99.

As always, Bitstream's font quality is first rate, and the Bitstream library for the PC has long been known for its variety and excellence.

An important note: FaceLift only works with the latest Fontware outlines (the ones with the silver diamond on the label). However, Bitstream does let you upgrade any of your Fontware fonts to the new Speedo format. The price is $30 for the first package you upgrade and $15 for each additional package.

Profile ———————————————————————————————

MicroLogic MoreFonts

While the other packages in this article assume that your entire life will revolve around Windows and solid black fonts, More-Fonts takes a different approach. The standard package also includes scalable font solutions for WordPerfect, LetterPerfect, and Microsoft Word — as well as terrific special effects.

The install program doesn't run under Windows, so it's a little trickier to install than the others. But this same install program can create truly dazzling special effects — outlines, shadows, gray fills, and pattern fills, including some that look like they were airbrushed. It displays the special effects on-screen and then creates bitmapped fonts (special effects aren't available in scalable format). On a 386 in enhanced mode, this install program *can* run inside a window.

Like ATM and FaceLift, MoreFonts creates screen fonts on the fly, but unlike them it requires its own screen drivers. Still, the program can take *any* existing Windows driver and automatically convert it for its own use. MoreFonts also uses its own special printer drivers. These drivers worked fine with everything tested, but they printed graphics just a bit slower than the standard drivers.

MoreFonts is fast, taking about a third less time than FaceLift to print the same page. Screen fonts are created very quickly and scrolling is smooth. The program comes with the standard Times and Helvetica clones (called Geneva and Tiempo), and a very useful selection of display fonts: Pageant (Coronet — much nicer than Park Avenue); Opera (University Roman); Showtime (Broadway); Burlesque (Cooper Black); along with a monospaced font called Financial.

Type quality is surprisingly good, considering the fonts are not from a "major" foundry. MoreFonts will only use additional faces from MicroLogic Software, but they are high-quality and low-priced. At $70 each, "Display" packages contain five different faces and "Classic" packages contain four weights of one typeface. You can purchase packages in groups of three for $100, or all six display packages together for $150; all 20 "Classic" packages cost $250, and the entire library of 26 packages can be had for $300 (about the price of two packages from a big font foundry).

MoreFonts is also the only program in this group that can create LaserJet III format downloadable fonts so that the printer can do the font scaling for added performance. Because of its great performance, special effects, and low add-on font prices, MoreFonts means more value.

Profile

Atech's Publisher's PowerPak

Fast and cheap are the words that describe Publisher's PowerPak. In our tests, it was over twice as fast at printing as FaceLift. But there are strings attached, mainly that the page did not include real italic or bold fonts, but was printed with electronically slanted and bolded fonts. These may be acceptable for casual use, but not if you need professional quality.

Except for the lack of true italic and bold, PowerPak's type quality is very good. Like MoreFonts, PowerPak uses its own screen driver to create screen fonts, but PowerPak can't convert existing drivers and will only work with systems that use CGA, EGA, VGA,

CGA, EGA, EGAmono, VGA, VGAmono, MCGA, Hercules, Plasma, and 8514. Screen fonts are created quickly and scrolling is smooth.

PowerPak is the least expensive of the bunch ($79) but comes with fewest fonts: Dixon (Helvetica), Marin (Times), and Cobb (Courier). While the number is small, these faces can be electronically condensed or expanded into countless variations including thin, condensed, wide, expanded, and hollow (outline) versions.

PowerPak's add-on faces are also inexpensive, costing a mere $30 for each set of standard faces (each package includes one weight of two typefaces; PowerPak will slant and bold them), and $79 for faces licensed from the respected Monotype foundry (four weights of a single typeface or four display faces).

PowerPak also offers foreign language faces, including Cyrillic, Greek, Hebrew, IPA Roman, Transliterator, Korean Gwang Ju, Korean Inchon, Korean Pusan, Korean Seoul, Thai Bangkok, Thai Chiang Mai, Thai Sara Buri, and Thai Sukanya.

The program uses its own printer drivers and includes support for over 300 models of laser, inkjet, and 8- or 24-pin dot-matrix printers. PowerPak's LaserJet driver printed graphics just a bit slower than the standard drivers.

Profile

SuperPrint

Alphabetically last, but certainly not least, is Zenographics' SuperPrint. True to its name, it's Super. Printing an example page took 60 seconds, but because of SuperQue (a print caching program included in the package) we were able to get back to work in only 10 seconds. While SuperQue printed in the background, we were able to continue working in Ventura with no loss of performance. So while the program isn't the "fastest," it *is* the most productive because you don't have to wait around while your pages print. This is especially important for multiple-page documents. While your 30-page report prints in the background, you can go back to work on your computer instead of waiting.

SuperPrint offers two more unique and important features: First, it supports *all* major font formats — simultaneously. It works with Adobe's Type 1, Bitstream's Speedo *and* Fontware (so you don't have to upgrade your Fontware fonts), Compugraphic's Intellifonts, Digital Typeface Corp's Nimbus-Q, and LaserJet format bitmapped fonts (for those special faces that may not have been duplicated in outline format). At last you can choose the faces (and versions) you like best, regardless of the format. And your previous investment in fonts is preserved.

Second, while the other programs only deal with text and print graphics like the standard Windows drivers (or slower), Super-Print actually improves the quality of graphics, giving them a more PostScript-like look, especially in fountains and fills (it doesn't however, print PostScript graphics). It also prints graphics significantly faster than other printer drivers. Since one of the reasons you're using Windows may be that you want to include graphics in your documents, SuperPrint's approach makes perfect sense.

While the other programs use RAM to create and cache screen fonts, SuperPrint uses less memory by creating disk-based screen fonts. Of course, this means you'll need to reserve more disk space (at least 512K or 2MB for best performance). Screen fonts take a few seconds longer to create than with the other programs, but once created, they display and scroll quickly.

At the end of each session SuperPrint will delete the fonts unless you ask to save them (so they don't have to be created again next time). This all works fine, except that there's a bug in Windows 3 (not in SuperPrint): in enhanced mode (the preferred mode for 386s), Windows will not display screen fonts larger than 64K, so if you're working with a lot of large type you'll have to do it in standard mode until this bug is fixed. Microsoft acknowledges the bug and has promised to fix it as soon as possible.

SuperPrint supports the LaserJet, DeskJet, and PaintJet printers. PaintJet and DeskJet support are exceptional, printing much faster than standard drivers, and, in the case of the PaintJet, producing better colors. Versions are also available for many color laser printers.

The program includes the follow fonts: Nimbus Sans (Helvetica); Nimbus Roman (Times), Nimbus Mono (Courier), URW Symbols, Nimbus Century Schoolbook, Compugraphic Futura, and a single weight of Bitstream Charter. Zenographics offers a "SuperFonts" package that rounds out the standard 35 from the DTC/Nimbus library. The Nimbus font quality is adequate, but not exceptional, so if you buy SuperPrint, purchase your fonts from Bitstream or Adobe.

Unless you have a PostScript or LaserMaster printer, SuperPrint is the best way to print from Windows.

So there you have it. Whichever of these programs you decide on, they'll help make what you see what you get — and help your imagination take flight.

Other Font Generators

Not quite as convenient to use as the on-the-fly font generators, the programs described below require you to think ahead, anticipating what sizes of fonts you'll need prior to working in Ventura. You'll also need to reserve 5MB, 10MB, or even more space on your hard disk to hold the fonts you're generating. Finally, you'll need to be somewhat judicious in generating screen fonts, since having too many screen fonts in use with Ventura at the same time can slow the program down considerably.

Because of the new generation of on-the-fly screen and printer font generators for Windows, you'll generally be using the programs discussed here if you're working with the DOS/GEM version.

Fontware

Give 'em the razors, then sell 'em the razor blades. That's the tried and true strategy being used to promote Fontware. Because it has been bundled with the DOS/GEM version of Ventura since release 2.0, Bitstream's Fontware is the most familiar font generator for most people. Along with the free installation package, you're provided with two or three sample font outlines. Additional outlines can be purchased from Bitstream.

◆ Background

The development work behind Fontware actually predates desktop publishing. Bitstream, the company that created Fontware, was organized in 1981 as the world's first digital type foundry. Initially, the company concentrated on supplying type for expensive typesetting equipment, but with the arrival of laser printers it began supplying type to the manufacturers of those systems. For example, most of the cartridge and downloadable fonts sold by Hewlett-Packard were developed by Bitstream.

The technology embodied in Fontware actually amounts to a set of artificial intelligence algorithms that check the results of the outline-to-bitmap conversions and make minor revisions, just like a typographic expert. Other font-generating programs now incorporate similar algorithms, but the technology developed by Bitstream is still unsurpassed. Outlines are available for scores of typeface families, and within most of these families there are four variations: roman, italic, bold, and bold italic. Most of these typefaces are already popular in commercial typography. In addition, Bitstream's Matthew Carter has developed the Charter family, which is designed to be especially crisp and legible when rendered by a laser printer (see Figure 22-1).

◆ Storage Requirements

To generate Fontware fonts, you need to specify the sizes you want. Because of the amount of memory each font requires once you have generated it, you'll need to be judicious and not clog your hard disk with too many sizes. Note that the largest Font-ware font you can use with a LaserJet Plus is about 36 points; with a LaserJet II it is about 72 points.

◆ Character Set or Symbol Set

The character sets generated by Fontware all include the English alphabet, but they differ in the remaining characters they provide, such as punctuation marks, special symbols, and foreign accented characters.

With the version of Fontware bundled with Ventura, you can generate the VP US character set (116 characters), the VP International character set (190 characters) or the PostScript Outline character set (186 characters).

The VP International set is the character set used by the fonts that come with Ventura; however, for large fonts used in headlines, you're probably better off choosing VP US. Here's why:

- As Table 22-1 shows, fonts with the VP US character set require about 47 percent less storage space on your hard disk than fonts that use the VP International character set. At 116 characters, it requires only slightly more storage space than US ASCII, which has 95 characters.

- Unlike other reduced character sets (such as US ASCII), the VP US character set includes the most frequently required typographic symbols (", ", §, ‡, †, ¶, ©, ®, ™, ..., ‰, •, –, —, ˙, and „). What's lacking are some of the less frequently used typographical symbols (¤, ‹, ›, -, ., and /) and accented characters (Á, ã, À, Ã, etc.).

◆ Fontware for the LaserJet III

While not included in the standard Fontware package, a new module is available that allows you to transform Fontware outlines into LaserJet III outlines which the printer will scale (as a PostScript printer does).

This module won't create a Ventura width table; instead it creates "Autofont" files. This is a new system designed by HP so that any program with AutoFont support can automatically install LaserJet III fonts. Hewlett Packard is distributing this conversion program *for free*, and they can be contacted at 303-353-7650.

Ventura does not come standard with a driver for the LaserJet III, however. If you want to buy one, the best available comes from VPUG (the Ventura Publisher Users Group, 408/227-5030). This VPUG driver supports AutoFont and will be able to install the fonts created by the Fontware LaserJet III module.

Profile

SoftCraft's Fontware

The Fontware kit provided with Ventura is fine for most people, but those with special requirements may want to buy a slightly different version from SoftCraft. This version of Fontware uses the same technology as the version of Fontware that is bundled with Ventura but has several extra features. Unlike the bundled version of Fontware, SoftCraft's version can generate obliqued versions of fonts, i.e., fonts uniformly slanted at a specified angle. Another advantage of the SoftCraft version is that it provides a wider selection of character sets, including USASCII, ECMA, UK, French, German, Italian, Spanish, Swedish/Finnish, Danish/Norwegian, Legal, SoftCraft, IBM PC, HP Roman-8, HP Roman Extension, Windows/ANSI, Ventura International, HP IBM PC, and HP IBM PC Extension. Last but not least, the SoftCraft Fontware Program can create larger fonts than the bundled version of the program — up to 240 points.

In selecting which character set to generate, you can refer to complete tables of characters in the back of the FontWare documentation. For example, if you want true typographic quotation marks, you should avoid the Roman-8 or IBM PC sets.

SoftCraft's Fontware does not install the fonts it generates into Ventura. For that, you'll need SoftCraft's WYSIfonts program (described below), which also takes care of Microsoft Windows installation.

◆ Storage Requirements

The amount of storage required for various fonts is shown in Table 22-1 on the next page. Notice how storage increases much faster than the point size. For example, the amount of storage needed for a 12-point font is about two times as much as for a 6-point font, for a 24-point font it is eight times as much, for a 48-point font it is 29 times as much, and for a 72-point font it is 64 times as much. Fortunately, FontSpace, the font compresssion program profiled later in this chapter, is able to compress large fonts to a greater degree than small fonts — as much as 97 or 98 percent.

Figure 22-2: SoftCraft's version of Fontware provides a larger number of character sets than the version bundled with Ventura, including character sets for a number of European languages.

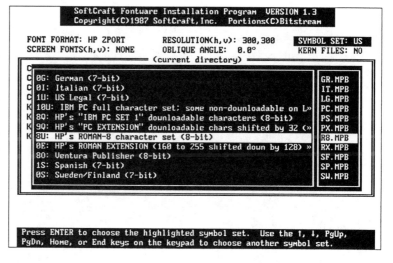

Tip 22-1

Limiting Character Sets for Headline Fonts

Generally, large fonts are used for titles and headlines and hence do not require special characters. So, to save the amount of storage needed, you should choose VP US or USASCII, the character sets with the smallest number of elements. If you frequently use large fonts, look into SoftCraft's Fontware and HP's Type Director. Both allow you to create character sets containing just the characters you need and thereby drastically reduce the amount of storage space needed for the font.

Font Storage Requirements (Kilobytes)

Font	VP International Character Set	VP US Character Set
6-pt Dutch	12	7
12-pt Dutch	29	16
24-pt Dutch	94	49
48-pt Dutch	344	184
72-pt Dutch	764	405

Table 22-1

◆ Installation

Once you've generated a font, you'll still need to download it to the printer and install it for Ventura. For a step-by-step explanation of this process, see Chapter 21, "Adding New Fonts."

Profile ─────────────────────

Type Director

Type Director is Hewlett-Packard's answer to Bitstream's Fontware. While the program had a lot of early promise and included several features not found in Fontware, it was hobbled by the fact that the Compugraphic fonts it generates simply don't look as good as Bitstream's. Now Fontware has improved but the inferior fonts generated by Type Director have not. Verdict: stick with Fontware. Besides, it's free!

Profile ─────────────────────

MoreFonts

MoreFonts is a very versatile program. You read earlier in this

Figure 22-3: As shown here, with Type Director you can either select a standard symbol set such as Ventura International or Ventura US, or else define your own custom symbol set. Custom sets are especially useful for generating large headline fonts.

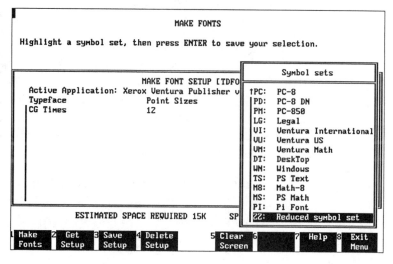

chapter about how it can generate printer and screen fonts on the fly for Ventura under Windows, but it can *also* generate bit-mapped screen and printer fonts and install them into Ventura for GEM.

MoreFonts has two big advantages: First, it creates dazzling special effects fonts; and second, the fonts themselves are very good and reasonably priced — you can purchase their entire line of 26 packages for about $300.

MoreFonts is also a good value because it supports on-the-fly fonts under Windows, WordPerfect, and Microsoft Word, as well as the bitmapped fonts and special effects for Ventura.

Profile

Z-Soft SoftType

Another interesting alternative is SoftType from Z-Soft, the PC Paintbrush people. Although this is a Windows program, I include it in this section because it does not generate fonts on-the-fly like ATM, FaceLift, or SuperPrint. SoftType does, however, offer a great deal of convenience. Remarkably, it manages to run in the *background* under Windows, even on a slow 286 with Windows 2.1, so you can be generating downloadable printer or screen fonts without having to stop everything and go to lunch.

SoftType comes with 29 different typefaces (62 when you count each weight) from URW. While these typefaces aren't as good as those from Bitstream or Adobe, the entire package costs the same thing as one of the Adobe's type packages (or one of Bitstream's Collections). It's even a good deal if you only use the eleven display faces. SoftType can also generate fonts from Z-Soft's Publisher's Type Foundry outline format.

Not content with merely generating fonts, SoftType also enables you to create custom special effects, and displays them (using the generic Sans typeface) in real time so you can see how effective the effect is going to be.

SoftType can generate fonts for the LaserJet including compressed (not scalable) bitmaps for the LaserJet III, PostScript Type 3 (non-encrypted), Publisher's Type Foundry scalable outlines, and PC Paintbrush bitmapped fonts. It can automatically generate Windows screen fonts and Ventura screen fonts at the same time. SoftType also installs the fonts for both Windows and Ventura. One thing to remember: SoftType does *not* create fonts on the fly à la ATM or SuperPrint.

Font Editors

Type is the Achilles' heel of any laser printer. You might spend hundreds of dollars assembling a collection of fonts and then find that it is useless because it lacks a character you need, such as the trademark symbol, the ballot box symbol, or true typographic quotation marks (ones that open and close).

Basically, a font is nothing more than a collection of one or two hundred pictures, each assigned a numerical code. A font editor is a software tool that lets you blow up individual characters on your computer display and change or replace them. In the past, font-editing software tended to be so difficult to use that few people took advantage of it. Now the programs are getting easier and more powerful, though they still require some dedication to master.

Here are some of the things one might do with a font-editing program:

- Add your corporate logo to an existing font. For example, you could replace a little-used keyboard character such as ~ or ∧ with the logo. Using the revised font, you could insert the logo into a document simply by typing that character.

- Add typographic characters such as true quotation marks or the registered trademark symbol to a font (such as any of the Hewlett-Packard fonts that use the ASCII character set) that lacks these elements.

- Add dingbats — special symbols such as the pointing hand frequently used in advertisements — to an existing font.
- Create an entirely new font for a non-European language.
- Design a new typeface.

As you can see, the tasks that might be attempted with a font-editing program range from simple tasks, like adding a single new character for an existing font, to complex projects, like creating an entirely new font from scratch.

Profile——————————————————————————

Publisher's Type Foundry

This extremely powerful program has two modules. One lets you work with outline fonts, which can then be used on PostScript printers. The other works with bitmapped fonts, which can then be used on PCL LaserJets. The remarkable thing is that it lets you move things back and forth between the two.

Figure 22-4:
Publishers Type
Foundry has two
modules, one for
bitmaps, the other
for outlines. You
can operate the
Bitmap Editor and
the Outline Editor
in tandem by
having them open
in adjacent win-
dows and moving
characters back
and forth from
one to the other.

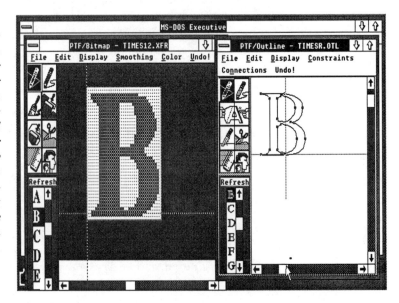

In order to be usable with all types of laser printers, a font editor must be a switch-hitter. Printers that incorporate the PostScript page description language work with characters stored in outline format, i.e., as scalable mathematic descriptions. Other printers, including the LaserJet, work with characters stored as bitmaps, i.e., as stored patterns of dots that cannot be scaled.

◆ Switch-hitting

While previous font editors have been available on the PC, all have worked exclusively with bitmapped fonts. Type Foundry is new in that it lets you work with either outlines or bitmaps.

Surprisingly, the Bitmap Editor and the Outline Editor actually are best used in tandem, whether your final product happens to be a bitmap font or an outline font.

This pooling of talents is the most interesting feature of Type Foundry. For example, you might start in the Outline Editor drawing outlines of the characters you wish to add to a font, then switch to the Bitmap Editor for final cleanup. Alternatively, you might start by scanning in characters from paper, load them into the Bitmap Editor, automatically generate outlines, resize these outlines, then transfer them back to the Bitmap Editor for cleanup.

◆ Windows Interface

Whether you start with the Bitmap or the Outline Editor, the basic interface is similar. On the upper left are your drawing tools, on the lower left a scroll bar from which you select your font. On top are the menus. Most of the screen is devoted to a drawing area. If this area is not enough for your character, you can use scroll bars on the right and on the bottom. Because this is a Windows application, you can have more than one application open at a time, and the design of the program makes it feasible to have both the Outline Editor and the Bitmap Editor on the screen side-by-side.

In the simple case of altering a single character in an existing font, you begin by loading that font into the program. Most laser printer font formats are acceptable, including those sold by Bitstream and by the numerous third-party vendors that specialize in Laser-Jet fonts. The major exception is the PostScript fonts from Adobe Systems, which use a proprietary format. As with all other procedures in Type Foundry, loading a new font is done from a menu. Once a font is loaded, the characters it comprises can be seen in a scroll bar on the left side of the screen. Clicking on one of these with the mouse causes the character to appear, enlarged, in the work area, where it can be altered using various drawing tools.

◆ Editing Tools

With the Bitmap Editor, those tools include a straight-line drawing tool, a freehand drawing tool, a tool for drawing blocks, a fill tool that pours pixels into any enclosed area, a tool for drawing polygons, a cut and paste tool, a tape measure, and a zoom feature. With the Outline Editor, the tools are a line-drawing tool, a tool for drawing Bezier curves, a tool for changing the shape of other tools, a tool for selecting sections of the font, a tool for dividing one curve into two separate curves, a tool for moving parts of the font, a tape measure, and a zoom view.

Like many crafts, that of creating laser printer fonts combines some art and some attention to technical nuts and bolts. Using the graphics tools is the fun part of Type Foundry. The knuckle-skinning part comes in determining technical parameters, such as font spacing and position, that make a font internally consistent and that allow it to be identified and used in the laser printer.

◆ Technicalities

For dealing with the technical side of things, Type Foundry provides several dialog boxes. In the Font Description dialog box, you classify your font according to family, weight, character set, point size, and the resolution of your laser printer. In the Font Parameters dialog box, you specify the standard character pixel height, the numerical encoding of the font, the vertical space to be stored with the font, the maximum pixel width of the font, etc.

Finally, a Global Changes dialog box allows you to apply scaling, slanting, and rotating uniformly to all characters in a font.

Collectively, the various obscure font manipulations possible with these dialog boxes amount to a large degree of power. It's a mixed blessing, because with this many options, you'll probably find that mastering Type Foundry is an even greater challenge than mastering Ventura. Fortunately, Type Foundry provides not only sheer font manipulation power but also some clever touches. One such innovation is the tape measure, with which you can quickly measure not only horizontal and vertical distances in your work area but also any diagonal distance. Another is the "Gadget Box," a set of tools for flipping, rotating, stretching, and scaling a character. A third is the "Gravity" feature of the Constraints Menu, which allows you to precisely connect line and curve segments. As a well-conceived Windows application, Type Foundry should slide smoothly into your font toolbox.

❖ Special Effects

Where would George Lucas be without special effects? Probably still eating at Taco Bell (not Rancho Nicasio). That's not to say there's anything wrong with Taco Bell, but special effects can make the difference between something being ordinary and extraordinary, much like the difference between fast food and nouvelle cuisine.

Man does not live by Times Roman alone (or even Helvetica). While special typographic effects can easily be overused, they can also give a publication a special identity, or draw attention to important information. If you look at the printed material all around you, you'll rarely see effects other than outline, shadow fonts, or gray type. These are the simplest, most popular, and perhaps the most effective effects, but certainly not the only ones. Others include stripes, checkerboard squares, air-brush, pattern fills, slanting, and rotation. You can also shrink, stretch, reverse, or slant a font.

❖ Draw Programs

If all you want is a single fancy headline or running head, the fastest, easiest, most accurate way to produce it is by using a draw program, such as Artline, Corel Draw, Designer, or Arts & Letters. These programs allow you to interactively create special effects, then export the results to a CGM or GEM file which will print as sharp as any font.

◆ Black Turning Gray Over You

If you have a PostScript or LaserMaster printer (or LaserJet III printer with the VPUG driver), then you can easily create gray type from inside Ventura. All you do is tag the text and select a color from the Font dialog box in the Paragraph menu. Then go into the Define Colors dialog box and change the setting for Screen Display from Color to Shades of Gray. If you have a color display you may see a difference, if you have a monochrome display you may not. But when you go to print you should see the results.

If the shade of gray is too dark or too light, you can adjust it in the Define Colors menu.

Profile

fontART

Quark can do it. PageMaker can do it. Ventura can't do it. What is *it?* Compress and expand typefaces. But you can do it with fontART.

fontART allows PostScript users to manipulate their fonts visually, using a simple program with pull-down menus. The program can use any Type 1 fonts, and even retrieve fonts from your PostScript printer. You see the actual font change as you apply the special effects.

Once you have the effect you were after, fontART will create a new WID table for DOS/GEM or Windows Ventura.

fontART can perform the following effects: Baseline rotation of fonts up to 180 degrees, character rotation, slanting forward or backward up to 89 degrees, outlining, filling fonts with any shade of gray, filling fonts with fountain fills starting and ending at any percentage of gray, up to five levels of drop shadows with different effects for each shadow, and strokes around characters. Finally, the program gives you the ability to shrink, expand, or scale drop shadows in any combination.

In addition to fontART, Creative Software also has a whole slew of utility programs in the works. Among these is 321, a font converter that changes PostScript Type 3 and Type 2 fonts into Type 1 fonts.

The program was still in beta testing as this was being written, but is was scheduled for release early in 1991. Call Creative Software for details. *(For access information, see Appendix A, "Resources.")*

Profile

Font Effects

Font Effects is a tool for under $100 that permits a LaserJet to print the sort of fonts you'd usually expect to see only from a PostScript printer. It can take any LaserJet-compatible font and add shadows, create outlines, stripe them, and fill them with gray or checkered patterns. With Font Effects, you can create unlimited special effects on fonts, and they all appear razor sharp.

Let's say you need a font with narrow characters — a "condensed" font. You don't have to buy another font. You simply use Font Effects to make the old font half as wide. Font Effects can enlarge or reduce fonts proportionally, so where you once only had a 30-point font, you can have a 60-point font. The jagged edges often associated with resizing bitmapped fonts are not a problem because of a remarkable "Fillet" function that fills in rough edges.

But we're not through yet. Font Effects gives you inverted or reverse fonts which print white on black. Although white type on a black background is harder to read than black on white, it can also attract attention and add visual interest to a page. Font Effects will reverse most type up to 24 points in size.

Want outline fonts? You got 'em. While outline fonts aren't best for general use, they can make good headlines, and are useful for creating "standing heads" — the ones above a regular column or editorial feature. These fonts can enhance the graphic appearance of a page, but I would not suggest having too many outline fonts on a page, because they can be hard to read.

Font Effects does another trick I like: it creates "gray" letters, with the gray ranging from a smooth medium tone to a very coarse checkerboard light gray. You can even combine any of these special effects, creating narrow, outline, shadow, slanted, 22-point fonts if you want. There's no limit to the number of times you can change a font. The process itself takes anywhere from about one minute, for smaller fonts, to as much as 10 minutes, for resizing and filleting large fonts. The fonts created by Font Effects work

Figure 22-5: With Font Effects, you can create your own special effects by specifying parameters for shading, obliquing, etc., or you can choose from this list of "precooked" effects.

```
                    Font Effects
                   Version 1.0B51
          Copyright (C) 1987 SoftCraft, Inc.
             Maximum square box =  552 x 552

  Input
  Output  thin outline
          thick outline
  Range   shadowed outline
          contour (or inline)
  Descri  checkered
          horizontal stripes with shadow
  Effect  striped drop shadow
          light drop shadow with separation
  Modify  diagonal striped 3D shadow
          reversed - white on black (adjust ABOVE and UNDER values - EBA »
  Adjust  initial caps - white on black (adjust ABOVE and UNDER values - »
          basketweave initial caps (adjust ABOVE and UNDER values - EBA a»
  Previe  filler for 2 color process to be used with 'thick outline'
  Genera  shadow_only for 2 color process
  Quit
```

```
The highlighted description will be deleted when the DEL key is pressed.
Press ENTER to save all remaining entries.   ESC restores the original list.
```

with any software that uses normal LaserJet Plus downloadable fonts. Ventura Publisher used almost all the new fonts flawlessly, although some fonts, notably the extremely slanted ones (90 degrees), didn't quite work right. Once again, Ventura doesn't have a specific font selection for outline or gray fonts, so you need to assign another name to them. I called the inverse fonts "bold-italic," or gave them entirely new names when creating the VFM files.

Font Effects provides fifteen different ways to modify type, all of which can be combined in endless variations. The effects include outlining, filling with patterns (stripes and checkerboard squares), contouring (also called "inline," where a white line is formed just inside the outside edge of characters), shades of gray, shadows, drop shadows, reverses, widening, narrowing, emboldening, slanting, and filleting.

While the sheer number of variables can be intimidating, fourteen standard effects are included, and even if you never create a custom effect, the standard ones are quite dazzling and more than adequate for most applications. I'd like to see more standard variations, but even with the few it has, Font Effects is admirable. LaserJet users will also appreciate the ability to create reverse fonts (white type on a black background), something LaserJet printers cannot do on their own.

If you do want to design your own effects, they can be saved and reused over and over again on different fonts. A preview feature allows you to see on-screen what your effects will look like. Currently the feature works with CGA, EGA, or Hercules graphics only.

Font Effects is a great way to enhance the type you already own and create distinctive fonts for logos, banners, advertisements, stationery, report covers — anything where big, flashy type is appropriate.

Like all SoftCraft manuals, this one is clear, well written, and created with SoftCraft's own products. A tutorial has step-by-step

Figure 22-6: *A sample of the special effects possible with the LaserMaster.*

examples, and the fourteen standard variations can also be used as starting points for new effects. The menu-driven program is logically designed and clear, making it easier to fathom the program's depths. To ease installation with Ventura, and to provide screen fonts complete with special effects, see WYSIfonts! (below).

Profile

LaserMaster Special Effects

LaserMaster printers and controllers offer high-speed, high-resolution output (this book was printed on a LaserMaster LM1000 Plain-Paper Typesetter). But above and beyond their speed and resolution, they also offer special effects.

With the LaserMaster's driver for Ventura Publisher, each of the seven colors listed in the font menu can invoke a different Laser-Master type effect. You can specify the effects you want for each color. Effects include outline; fill with a gray tone or pattern; print type at any angle including upside-down or backwards; or multiple effects combined. The Ventura driver also makes it possible to print text in unlimited point sizes, going above and beyond the normal 256-point ceiling.

You can also apply special fill patterns to frames, including any of the standard GEM patterns, or you can design a custom pattern. For more about the LaserMaster, see Chapter 4, "Printers."

Other Font Tools

The following programs provide a couple of additional functions to make your font life easier: installing fonts and compressing them on your hard disk.

Profile

WYSIfonts!

Installing fonts can be one of the most mystifying tasks a desktop publisher can face. Many people think you need only copy the fonts to the hard disk and Ventura will magically know they're there. In a perfect world, that's how it would be, but then again, in a perfect world we'd all be supplied free 386's with our nationalized health care cards. One utility that can help smooth the process is WYSIfonts!, which works with any HP-compatible downloadable font.

All too often what you get is not really what you see. What's a LaserJet owner to do? Fight back, with WYSIfonts! Not only does this program create width tables, it can also create on-screen fonts for any — yes, any — HP-compatible downloadable font. Screen fonts have long been the missing link in PC desktop publishing. Bitstream has solved that problem for Fontware users. But what if you have fonts from another manufacturer and want to see them on-screen? WYSIfonts! is the only way. The program also proves useful if you have purchased LaserJet soft fonts that don't have associated width tables. In that case, WYSIfonts! can generate the width tables and install the fonts for Ventura (as well as for Windows and PageMaker).

Figure 22-7: The main WYSIfonts! menu. Here you specify the location and names of the printer fonts for which you want to generate screen fonts. Alternatively, you can use the program to install fonts without generating screen fonts.

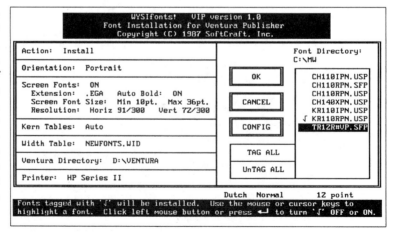

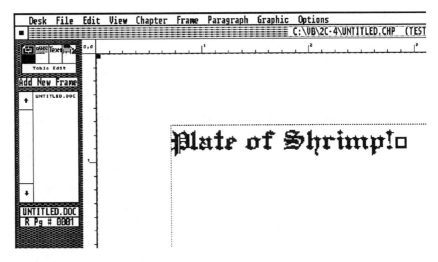

Figure 22-8: *It's not necessary to have a screen font to match every printer font you install in your system, but having screen fonts for unusual printer fonts such as this one make it easier to format text and perform kerning.*

The program is all menu-driven. You can even use a mouse if you're that keyboard-phobic. The program first creates screen fonts (which can take as long as 20 minutes for large sizes) and then creates width tables for Ventura. Once you're in Ventura, the fonts appear on-screen and you will be instantly spoiled. Fonts over 14 points look excellent on-screen, but smaller sizes can get mushy.

The only trick to installing fonts with WYSIfonts! is making sure they are named correctly. Some programs ask you lots of questions about each font to make sure they're installed correctly, but WYSIfonts! relies solely on the name of the font. The first two letters tell the name of the font, and let WYSIfonts! know the correct font number to use. Palatino, for example, is "PA." Next comes the font size. (Anything under 100 points must have a 0 on the end of it. For instance, 18 points is listed as 180). Then comes the weight of the font: R for regular (a throwback to HP's own strange way of naming fonts), B for bold, I for italics, and X or T for bold italics. Once the fonts are named correctly, WYSIfonts! can make a width table for 12 fonts in about two minutes. Even though the font naming can be tedious, it's easier than programs that require you to look up font names and numbers in the Ventura manual. WYSIfonts! worked with every HP-compatible soft font I tried, even PI fonts.

One warning about Ventura screen fonts: as explained in Chapter 21, "Adding New Fonts," Ventura can handle a lot, but only so many before it starts to complain. Make screen fonts only for the fonts you most need to see on-screen. Ventura will not use screen fonts smaller than 10 points or larger than 35K (about 72 points), and will scale existing fonts to fit these sizes. For the utmost speed and the best on-screen appearance, Ventura prefers to scale screen fonts in even increments. For example, an 18-point font can be quickly doubled to 36 points. When you go to Enlarged view, a 36-point screen font is used for 18-point type. In Reduced View, 36-point type is represented with 18-point screen fonts. If the exact sizes are not available, Ventura will scale screen fonts. If you've installed a 30-point screen font for a headline, and your 10-point body text is the same typestyle, Ventura will try to scale the body text, too. Ventura will reduce the 30-point screen font to 10-point for the body text, which takes a long time and doesn't look good. So if you're going to use a screen font for a typeface, make it in all the sizes you will use regularly, not just one.

Profile————————————————————————

FontSpace

LaserJet fonts take tons of disk space. It's not unusual to have 4 to 12 megabytes of fonts on your hard disk. But now there's an easy, efficient way to save 50 to 75 percent of the space you use for hard disks. It's called FontSpace, and in about 10 minutes your fonts will take less than half the space they did before.

FontSpace is a memory-resident program that automatically decompresses fonts *as* they are downloaded to the printer. It does this with such speed that you don't notice any performance loss, and it works with *all* programs — Ventura, WordPerfect, Windows. They (and you) don't even know it's there. Be assured that there is absolutely no loss of font quality.

For very large fonts the reduction may be as much as 98 percent; for fonts in the 8- to 12- point range, the reduction is about 55 percent. In one test, 12 megabytes of fonts became 4 megabytes. That means the program instantly freed 8 megabytes of hard disk space. The program is completely automatic. During the installation process, it searches your hard disk for fonts, and compresses them. If you use Fontware or other font generation programs, FontSpace will automatically compress these fonts *as they are being generated*. FontSpace even compresses automatically as you copy bitmapped fonts from a floppy to your hard disk.

If you have EMS, FontSpace takes a mere 3K of DOS memory, and 18K of EMS. If you don't, it takes 22K of DOS memory. The program is the personification of transparent and only takes 65K of disk space. If you use a LaserJet and have lots of fonts, *buy this program*. You'll wish you had it years ago.

Special Topics

23

Speed Tips

Although Ventura is a fast program to begin with, you may want
to make it even faster. This chapter is intended as a miscellany of
tips for getting better speed performance out of the program.

❖ Disk Caching

Try this experiment. Load Ventura with a blank chapter. Switch to
tagging mode. You'll notice that the hard disk light flashes. Switch
to a different mode and the light blinks again. What's happening
is that all the program information Ventura needs cannot fit in
RAM and still leave room for documents, so the program stores
some of that information on the hard disk and accesses it frequently. Disk reads are many times slower than accessing information from RAM. For this reason, a disk-caching utility is a perfect complement to Ventura. If you're using Windows Ventura,

then you automatically are using a disk-caching program, Microsoft's SmartDrive. If you're using the DOS/GEM version, Table 23-1 lists a number of the leading disk-caching programs.

Here's how disk caching works. The disk-caching program intercepts blocks of data that are frequently read from the hard disk or written to the hard disk and stores them in a RAM buffer. At the beginning of your computer session, there is no speedup since the first blocks of data must be accessed, as usual, from the hard disk. However, after your computer session has gone on for a while the improvement caused by the disk-caching program will become quite noticeable. The advantage of a disk-caching program over a RAM disk is that with the caching program you don't have to decide which files to store in RAM — the program does this automatically.

Table 23-1: Disk-Caching Utilities

Flash
Software Masters
6352 N. Guilford Ave.
Indianapolis, IN 46220
317/253-8088

Lightning
Personal Computer Support Group
4540 Beltway Dr.
Dallas, TX 75244
800/544-4699, 214/351-0564

Vcache
Golden Bow Systems
2870 5th Ave. #201
San Diego, CA 92103
800/284-3269, 619/298-9349

Super PC-Kwik
Multisoft Corporation
15100 S.W. Koll Parkway, Suite L
Beaverton, OR 97006
503/644-5644

PC Tools Deluxe
Central Point Software
15220 N.W. Greenbrier Pkwy.
Suite 200
Beaverton, OR 97006
503/690-8090

Since DOS/GEM Ventura needs nearly all 640K of a system's conventional memory to function effectively, you should configure the cache program to place the cache in extended or expanded memory, rather than in conventional memory. Extended memory refers to memory installed on your computer above and beyond the 640K recognized by DOS. Expanded memory, also called EMS (in reference to the Lotus-Intel-Microsoft Expanded Memory Standard) memory, must be installed on a memory add-in board that meets a particular standard formulated by Lotus, Intel, Microsoft, and others. Alternatively, on a 386 computer, utilities available from QuarterDeck and others can convert extended memory into EMS memory.

Even when a disk-caching program sets up its cache in extended or EMS memory, it still consumes some of the 640K of conventional memory. Obviously, it makes sense to use a disk-caching program that requires as little conventional memory overhead as possible. Table 26-1 in Chapter 26, "Memory Limitations and Solutions," shows how much conventional memory is used by various disk-caching programs.

Once you've set up a disk cache and loaded Ventura, you'll notice the difference almost immediately. The time needed for scrolling, moving between reduced and expanded mode, paging through a document, and other functions is cut by 50 percent or more. Loading Ventura (not the first time, but each subsequent time) is also speeded up.

As you might guess, an additional benefit of using a disk-caching utility is that it spares your hard disk from constant read/write operations and therefore probably increases the life of your hard disk.

Tip 23-1

Adjusting Buffers for Screen Fonts

This is a repeat from Chapter 21, but it's a useful one that is pertinent here as well. If you're using screen fonts, make sure that the buffers statement in your CONFIG.SYS file is set to 30. For optimum performance, you can even experiment with setting the buffers as high as 50. If you're using a disk-caching utility, however, you should always set the buffers to 3 or 4.

Tip 23-2

What's the Best Disk-Caching Utility?

In talking with other Ventura users, the disk cache most often mentioned as "the best" is Super PC-Kwik. That word-of-mouth recommendation was recently supported by tests in PC Magazine, which showed that Super PC-Kwik was the fastest disk cache in the group it surveyed, as well as the one offering the most features and the one capable of taking up the smallest amount of conventional memory overhead. Vcache rated a close second; Flash and PolyBoostII also earned high grades. Lowest on PC Magazine's report card were IBMCache, Mace Utilities, and SmartDrive.

Tip 23-3

Before You Run out and Buy a Disk-Caching Program...

You may already own a disk-caching program and not know it. For example, if you have Microsoft Windows, you've already got SmartDrive. IBM supplies IBM-Cache with all its Micro Channel PS/2 computers, and Compaq supplies Compaq Disk-Caching Utility with all its hard-disk computers. PC Tools also includes a disk cache, as does the Mace Utilities package, though the latter is reported to be fairly slow.

Tip 23-4

Optimizing Your Disk Cache and Your Spooler

If you have both extended and expanded memory, use the expanded memory for disk caching and the extended memory for print spooling (not the other way around). The reason is that disk-caching programs run about 20 to 30 percent faster in expanded memory, while print spoolers run about the same speed either way.

❖ PrintCache

Although PostScript printers make fantastic looking pages, they can waste an incredible amount of time by tying up your printer for 15 or 20 minutes while a chapter prints out. Fortunately, you don't have to put up with that kind of performance. The first way to speed up printing is to download your fonts at the beginning of each work session (see below). The second is to use Print-Cache (previously called LaserTORQ). PrintCache is a print spooler, i.e., a program that intercepts data on the way to the printer and then stores it in a memory reservoir, allowing you to immediately get back to work with Ventura while it feeds the print data to the printer. Documents don't get printed any faster with PrintCache, but at least the computer isn't tied up while the printer takes its time. Since PostScript printers are the slowest, they're the ones to benefit most from PrintCache, but in fact the program can be used with any laser printer. For more details on PrintCache, see Chapter 25, "Printing Tips."

Tip 23-5

Optimizing PrintCache

To get the best performance from PrintCache with a PostScript printer, it's important that you always download your fonts to the printer at the beginning of your work session. (Procedures for

downloading fonts are explained in Chapter 20, "Using Fonts.")
For some reason, this speeds up PrintCache considerably. See for
yourself!

❖ Downloading Fonts

If you're like most Ventura users, you probably print out part or all
of a document several times during a work session. Unfortunately,
every time the print command is issued, Ventura laboriously copies (or downloads) the same fonts to the laser printer's memory.
You can shortcut this redundancy by downloading all the fonts
you need for the day and then turning off Ventura's automatic
downloading. For details, see Chapter 20, "Using Fonts."

❖ Consolidating Your Hard Disk

DOS is something of a digital squirrel. If it can't store that latest
program or document in one neat continuous block, it breaks the
file up and stuffs pieces into any free space on the disk. Unfortunately, when you need the file — be it a Ventura overlay or a
frequently used chapter — the hard disk's read/write heads can't
suck it up in one sweep, but must poke around the disk. Disk
optimizers, which reunite scattered file fragments, can cut the
delays and minimize hard disk wear and tear.

One indication that disk optimizing is needed is if the hard disk
light flashes rapidly when you load a program; every blink means
that another portion of the disk is being searched. Diagnostic
routines typically found in disk optimizers can provide more detailed information, in the form of disk maps and statistical reports
showing the degree of fragmentation.

As with disk-caching utilities, there's a universe of disk optimizers
to choose from. Programs such as DS Optimize, Disk Optimizer
from Softlogic Solutions, Disk OrGanizer (DOG) in the public
domain, Speed Disk from the Norton Utilities Advanced Edition,
and Condense from the Mace Utilities can consolidate disk files in

a matter of minutes without disturbing copy-protected or hidden system files.

Running a disk optimizer like Speed Disk is simplicity itself. At the DOS prompt, type **SD n:**, where n: is the drive you want tidied up. Speed Disk takes about 20 minutes to rearrange the files on a nearly full 20MB disk, graphically illustrating its progress along the way.

To wrest the most from this speed tip, look for disk optimizers like DS Optimize that allow you to specify the order in which coalesced files should appear on the disk. For maximum performance, install DOS first, then Ventura.

❖ Avoiding Spill Files

When you are working with pictures or text files that exceed the RAM available to Ventura for holding such files, the program creates a "spill file" on the hard disk (also referred to as "swapping out"). When this happens, Ventura's performance slows

---

Table 23-2: Disk-Optimizing Utilities

DS Optimize
Design Software
1275 W. Roosevelt Rd.
West Chicago, IL 60185
301/231-4540

Mace Utilities
Paul Mace Software, Inc.
400 Williamson Way
Ashland, OR 97520
800/523-0258, 503/488-2322

The Norton Utilities
Peter Norton Computing, Inc.
2210 Wilshire Blvd.
Santa Monica, CA 90403
213/453-2361

Disk Optimizer
SoftLogic Solutions
520 Chestnut Street
Manchester, NH 03101
800/272-9900

down considerably, since the program must continually access the disk for information.

The simplest way to avoid spill files is to free up RAM. The first step is to eliminate any memory-resident utilities. Other steps are suggested in Chapter 26, "Memory Limitations and Solutions."

If you've freed up all the RAM you can, and still find yourself plagued by spill files, the next step is to install a RAM disk and direct Ventura to use it to catch the spill files that would otherwise be written to the hard disk. You can use any RAM disk program to set up the RAM disk. The best bargain is a utility called VDISK that is included on your DOS disk. To set up a 300K RAM disk in extended memory, simply place the statement

DEVICE = VDISK.SYS

in the system's CONFIG.SYS file. You'll also need to add **/O=D:** at the end of your VP.BAT file (assuming your RAM drive has been set up as drive D). For example,

DRVRMRGR VP %1
/S=SD_HERC5.EGA/M=11/O=D:

❖ Parallel Printer Interface

With many printers, including the HP LaserJet and most PostScript printers, you have the option of using a serial or a parallel interface. If you currently are making the connection with a serial interface, you'll find that performance improves greatly once you switch to a parallel interface. The difference in speed is especially noticeable for pages that include multiple fonts or graphics.

❖ Faster Screen Fonts

One of the biggest factors affecting Ventura's speed is the time it takes for the program to redraw the screen. If you're currently using VGA fonts, you can speed up redraw speed by switching to EGA fonts. The result is less readable text, but many people find that faster performance is worth it. To find out if you're currently using VGA fonts, select Set Printer Info from the Options menu. Check the extension listed next to the words Screen Fonts. If it says VGA, the next step is to quit Ventura and check your \VENTURA directory to see if EGA screen fonts are present. (If a large number of files with the EGA extension are present, those are the screen font files.) If EGA screen fonts are not in the \VENTURA directory, you'll need to do the following:

- Save your VP.BAT or VPPROF.BAT file under a new name (by renaming it to VP.BAK or VPPROF.BAK).

- Reinstall Ventura for an EGA monitor.

- Erase the new VP.BAT or VPPROF.BAT file created by the installation procedure.

- Restore your original batch file (by renaming VP.BAK or VP-PROF.BAK back to VP.BAT or VPPROF.BAT).

- Load Ventura, select Set Printer Info from the Options menu, and change the letters VGA to EGA.

❖ Speeding up the Display with the /F Switch

Unless you specify otherwise, Ventura sets up a buffer of 68K for holding the screen fonts used on the current page. If you have enough extra memory to do so, you can increase the speed of screen redraws by increasing the size of the screen font buffer. This is especially helpful if you are working with a display that has several fonts, such as the Ventura Scoop document located in the \TYPESET directory.

To check whether you have enough extra memory to enlarge your screen font buffer, open the diagnostics box in the desk menu (see Chapter 26, "Memory Limitations and Solutions," for a description of how to do that). Next to "External Memory in Use" you'll see two numbers. The number on the left shows how much is currently in use; the number on the right shows how much is available. The amount available (i.e., the number on the right) is the number to pay attention to. If it's slightly over 100K, you shouldn't change the screen font buffer, since Ventura will not load unless at least 100K of external memory is available. By increasing the screen font buffer, you'll be reducing the amount of available external memory.

Assuming at least 115K of external memory is available, you can use the /F switch to increase the size of the screen font buffer. Using a text editor or your word processor in unformatted mode, add /F=k at the end of your VP.BAT or VPPROF.BAT file, where k is the amount of memory you wish to allot to the screen buffer, expressed in kilobytes. Start with a fairly conservative setting, such as 88. This increases the screen font buffer from 68K to 88K. If you have enough extra memory, try experimenting with larger settings for the /F switch. Depending on your system, you may be able to go as high as 160K or so.

How much does a larger screen font buffer speed up Ventura? It depends on whether you are already using a disk cache, on the type of document your are creating, and on what view you are in. On a normal document with a disk cache being used, a higher /F setting does not make a discernable difference. On a system with no disk cache, a 128K setting reduced the redraw time of the Ventura Scoop page by 42 percent in Reduced View and by 15 percent in Normal View.

❖ Greeking Text

Greeking refers to the technique of representing areas of text on the screen with horizontal lines, a method that reduces the time it takes for the program to draw the screen. In Ventura, it applies only to Reduced and Facing Pages views. Under the Set Preferences selection of the Options menu, the settings for greeked text range from None to All. Note that the numbers 2, 4, 6, 8, 10 don't refer to the point sizes of the text that is to be greeked, but rather the pixel height of characters as shown on the screen. For example, if you select 10, then all characters 10 pixels in height or smaller are greeked. Usually, when you are working in Reduced or Facing Pages views, you're looking at the layout of the page and not at the text itself, so greeking your text makes a lot of sense.

❖ Selecting a Fast Double-Click Speed

Interestingly enough, increasing the double click speed not only makes mouse operations faster but also speeds up operations when you use keyboard alternatives to the mouse, such as pressing the Enter key instead of pressing OK. The reason is that even if you don't use the mouse itself, Ventura still waits the duration of the two clicks before it executes a command.

❖ Tagging in Text Editing Mode (Windows Version)

A surprising feature of the Windows version is that you can access all your tags without switching from text editing to tagging mode. Simply place the text cursor anywhere in a block of text, then click on the tag name in the list of tags. Naturally, it works even better if you drag the little window containing this list right on top of the document you are working on.

❖ Multiple-Paragraph Tagging

In tagging mode: Hold down the Shift key while clicking on all the paragraphs (they need not be adjacent). Then select the tag.

In text editing mode: Drag the mouse across all the paragraphs and pressing the desired function key.

❖ Move the Toolbox (Windows Version)

The toolbox is the window that shows the various mode icons and graphics tools. Since you often have to switch from one mode to another just before you pull down a menu option, the best place to locate this window is right under the middle of the menu line.

❖ Use the Alt Key Shortcuts (Windows Version)

The Windows version of Ventura is actual less dependent on the mouse than the DOS/GEM version. Every option of every menu can be accessed in a couple of keystrokes. Notice that one letter of every menu title is underlined. To open that menu, hold down the Alt key while you press that letter. Then press one of the letters underlined within that menu to open a dialog box. Even within dialog boxes, every option can be selected with a letter.

❖ Use the Macro Recorder (Windows Version)

To really make the keyboard options of the Windows version pay off, learn how to use the Windows 3 Macro Recorder. It looks like a movie camera and is located in the Accessories group. You may find the Macro Recorder hard to get used to at first, but keep trying — it's definitely worth the effort. One tip is to go into the Options menu of the Macro Recorder, select Preferences, and select the Ignore Mouse option. The point is that you're going to use the Macro Recorder to combine long strings of keystrokes into a smaller keystroke combination, so mouse movements are unnecessary and only get in the way.

An example of a useful macro is Alt-Shift-J, which changes a tag to justified alignment. Before creating the macro, switch to tagging mode and select a paragraph. Next, press Alt-Tab until you're back in the Program Manager. Open the Accessories group and click twice on the Macro Recorder icon. From the Options menu, select Preferences and turn on the Ignore Mouse option. Select OK. Now open the Macro menu and select Record. Fill in the description of the macro and set up the key combination, in this case Alt-Shift-J. Then select Start, which will put you back into Ventura.

You're now ready to record the keystrokes of the macro. The last key combination, Ctrl-Break, ends the macro:

Alt   P   A   Alt-A   L   Ctrl-Break

Likewise, you can set up related macros:

- Alt-Shift-C (changes a tag to centered)
- Alt-Shift-J (changes a tag to justified)

❖ Avoiding On-Screen Kerning

The effect of on-screen kerning is to give you some feedback on the appearance of lines of text when automatic kerning is in effect; however, performing the kerning slows Ventura down slightly. Even with a high-resolution monitor, on-screen kerning is not sufficiently precise to be worth much for regular text; it only makes sense for titles and headlines. Therefore, you're best off selecting only the largest point sizes for on-screen kerning, or simply specifying no on-screen kerning in the Set Preferences dialog box. Note that turning off automatic on-screen kerning does not affect your ability to use Ventura's manual kerning or to see the results of manual kerning onscreen.

❖ Keyboard Shortcuts

A table of keyboard shortcuts is provided in Chapter 8, "Preparing, Loading, and Editing Text." Some of the most useful of these are:

- Pressing Enter instead of selecting OK with the mouse.
- Saving with Ctrl-S.
- Pressing Esc to redraw the screen.
- Using Ins, Del, and Shift-Insert to insert, delete, and copy.

- Using Ctrl-F and Ctrl-L for fill and line attributes.
- Using Ctrl-Shift-[for left quotation marks and Ctrl-Shift-] for right quotation marks.
- Using Ctrl-Shift-M for Em spaces and Ctrl-Shift-N for En spaces.

❖ Ctrl-X

Everyone should paint the Ctrl key and the X key with Day-Glo paint so they can practice this maneuver during a power outage. Pressing Ctrl-X brings up the most recently accessed menu, a great shortcut when you're experimenting with different values for line spacing or In From Left. In the DOS/GEM version, Ctrl-X also acts as a keyboard shortcut for clicking on the Cancel button to get out of a dialog box. In the Windows version, pressing Esc jumps you out of the current dialog box.

Tip 23-6

Quicker Exits with Cancel

If you are in a dialog box and decide not to make any changes, you can either press OK or Cancel to get back to your page. Cancel is faster, because when you select OK the screen redraws itself completely, but when you press Cancel the screen does not redraw. Note: In the DOS/GEM version the shortcut for clicking on Cancel is Ctrl-X. In the Windows version the shortcut for clicking on Cancel is Esc. In both versions the shortcut for clicking OK is Enter.

❖ The Backup Box (DOS/GEM Version)

To change the filter on the Directory line, it's quicker and more accurate to use the Backup Box than to the erase the line and then type a new one. The use of the Backup Box is explained in Chapter 7, "Managing Files."

❖ Mouse Tips

When you select file names from lists, it's much quicker to double-click on a name than to click once to highlight the name and then select OK. For even faster mouse operations, get hold of Mickey, a utility that lets you use the right button of your mouse to select OK. It's profiled in Chapter 27, "Utilities."

❖ Pretagging Text

It's faster to tag your text files with a keyboard macro program such as SuperKey than to use Ventura's Tagging mode. The pretagging method is described in Chapter 8, "Preparing, Loading, and Editing Text."

❖ Using the Esc Key to Clear Lines (DOS/GEM Version)

In dialog boxes, rather than backspacing across a line you wish to erase, you can place the cursor anywhere on the line and press Esc. Unfortunately, this doesn't work in the Windows version.

❖ Hiding Pictures

Redrawing pictures when the page is scrolled or frames are moved is one of the biggest slowdowns in Ventura. To avoid this bottleneck, select Hide Pictures from the Options menu (DOS/ GEM version) or the Edit menu (Windows version). You have the option of either hiding a single picture or hiding all the pictures in your chapter. You can also tell Ventura to hide pictures when you print drafts of a document. That can save significant amounts of time, especially when you are printing large bitmapped graphics such as scanned images. Unfortunately, hidden pictures print as solid black boxes, a waste of toner.

❖ Using the Shift Key

When using a graphic tool several times, hold down the Shift key to avoid having to reselect the tool each time you use it. Holding down the Shift key while selecting paragraphs in Tagging mode also allows you to select multiple paragraphs to tag at once.

❖ Storing Graphic Defaults

Generally it is the case that when you are using the graphic tools you will be creating more than one object with the same characteristics. Rather than going through the process of selecting Line and Fill Attributes each time you create a graphic, use the Save To option to create default settings that you can use over and over.

❖ Faster Hyphenation

If you've been using the faster of the two hyphenation algorithms and then switch to the slower but more accurate one, you'll notice immediately how much longer it takes to load a chapter. For example, the following is a comparison of the time required to load a typical chapter:

No hyphenation: 18 seconds

USENGLSH algorithm: 22 seconds

USENGLS2 algorithm: 96 seconds

As you can see, USENGLS2 is over four times slower than USENGLSH, though also significantly better in finding hyphenation points and avoiding incorrect breaks.

I recommend that you keep both the USENGLSH and the US-ENGLS2 algorithm in your \VENTURA directory. To keep track of which is which, rename them both so that USENGLSH is called FAST and USENGLS2 is called SLOW. One of them should be given the extension HY1 and the other the extension BAK. This will cause Ventura to use the one with HY1 and ignore the other. Unless you're producing multilingual documents and really must have two hyphenation algorithms installed at the same time, it's never a good idea to keep two hyphenation algorithms active as HY1 and HY2, since Ventura will load them both into RAM and you will have less memory available for holding text and pictures.

Probably the best way to work is to have the FAST algorithm active as FAST.HY1 while you're first setting up a document, then rename it to FAST.BAK and rename SLOW.BAK to SLOW.HY1 when you get into the late stages with a document. Changing file names like this is better than trying to turn off hyphenation on a tag-by-tag basis.

❖ Math Coprocessor?

Since Ventura does not use floating-point arithmetic, it has no need for the 8087 or the 80287 math coprocessor. Having that chip installed in your computer will not enhance the program's performance.

❖ Loading a Chapter with the Program

With the DOS/GEM version, you can speed up the getting-started process by typing the path and name of the chapter you are working on at the command line, like this:

```
VP C:\BOOKDOCS\CHAPTER1.CHP
```

If you frequently work on the same document, you can even make the change in the batch file that you use to load Ventura.

With the Windows version, you can do same thing. With the Ventura icon highlighted, select Properties from the File menu. Then add the path and name of your file at the end of the existing startup information in the Command Line box. (Don't worry that the box won't fit everything you need to type. Once you start typing, the existing text in the Command Line box will automatically move over to make room for more text.

❖ Pre-loading the PostScript Prologu

DOS/GEM version: Each time it prints a file on a PostScript printer, DOS/GEM Ventura transmits a prologue, PS2.PRE, containing various PostScript definitions. Windows does the same thing, though it calls it the PostScript header. With the DOS/GEM version, you can save time by downloading the file PERMVP.PS each time you turn on the printer and deleting or renaming PS2.PRE from the \VENTURA directory. To download the file, use the DOS Copy command, naming your printer port as the destination. For example, if your printer is on LPT1, type

COPY PERMVP.PS LPT1:

The location of PERMVP.PS is on the \POSTSCPT directory of the Utility disk. Eliminating the need for Ventura to transmit the PS2.PRE prologue shaves about 10 seconds off the time required to print a chapter. Remember to restore PS2.PRE to the \VENTURA directory before you create print files for use on other printers or typesetters.

Windows version: With the Windows version, select Printer Setup from the File menu, then click on Options. Click on the Header box and select OK for Send Header to Printer. Having transmitted the header, you can now go back into the Options dialog box and click on Header Already Downloaded option.

24

Safety Tips

❖ Backing Up

Pull down the Options menu (DOS/GEM version) or the Edit menu (Windows version), select Preferences, and activate the Back Up Copy option. This way, if you accidentally save a file with changes you don't want, the previously saved version of that file original will still be intact, renamed with a "$" in the file name. This gives you one more chance to save a style sheet you might have changed by accident, and it can save the day should you encounter a computer error. You have to set this feature only one time, and Ventura will remember it.

❖ Renaming Style Sheets

The fastest way to get started using Ventura is to revise either the style sheets supplied with the program or those you buy from designers, rather than creating new ones from scratch. Unfortunately, the quickest way to wreck havoc is to alter the tags in a style sheet that is also used in a different chapter. You can avoid "Style Sheet Shock" by making the following procedure a habit.

Before revising an existing style sheet for use with a different chapter, rename the style sheet. This will keep you from changing a style sheet used in another chapter. Make it a practice to rename your style sheet as soon as you open the new chapter, using the Save as New Style option in the File menu. If you don't save your style sheet under a new name right away when you start working on a chapter, it's easy to forget and to save the chapter with the altered style sheet, which can radically change other chapters that go along with it.

❖ Renaming Text Files

This also applies to text files you might use in more than one Ventura chapter. Unless you specifically want the same file used in many chapters, use the File Type/Rename command under the Edit menu (DOS/GEM version) or the Frame menu (Windows version) to rename text files you use in more than one chapter. This will prevent accidental changes to your original files. In addition to renaming the text file, you can also use this command to change a text file from one word processor format to another and to move it into a new subdirectory.

❖ Saving

Save often. Ctrl-S is all you need to remember. My rule of thumb is to think about how much I could stand to lose should the power go off. My threshold for having to redo lost computer work is about ten minutes, so I save every ten minutes. It's saved me countless times.

Tip 24-1

Save Before Printing

One especially important time to save is right before printing a document. <u>Printing is the stage in creating a document where the program is most likely to freeze,</u> since it is easy to accidentally select the wrong printer or the wrong printer port, or to forget to turn on the printer. Theoretically, Ventura ought to be able to cope with any of these errors without freezing, but in practice this is where trouble most often occurs.

❖ Using Abandon

If you don't like what you've done, you can always use the Abandon option under the File menu to bail out. Ventura lacks an undo feature, but if you save often enough, you can use Abandon like undo. Abandoning a file doesn't mean you erase it from the disk — it means you ignore all the changes you've made since the last time you saved, restoring the file to its previous state. You can simply abandon any embarrassing, horrifying, or simply unwanted changes and get the original file back. The more often you save, the less you lose when you make a wrong move and then choose to abandon the file.

❖ Creating Separate Directories

If you are working with a long or complex publication, create a subdirectory just for that publication. This way you will have all the files important to that project in one place, making it more difficult to accidently delete, rename, move, or change them. With the DOS/GEM version, you can create a subdirectory from inside Ventura by using the DOS File Ops choice from the File menu. If you're using the Windows version, press Alt-Tab or Ctrl-Esc to cycle back to the Windows Program Manager, then use the File Manager to create a new subdirectory for your publication.

❖ Backing up to Floppies or Tape

Back up often onto floppies or onto a streaming tape drive. Use the Multi-Chapter feature, VPToolbox, Corel Vpcopy, or a good backup program to archive the Ventura files onto floppies or tape. Don't wait and learn the hard way, one day finding that the hard disk no longer works and all your valuable files are gone. Use Ventura's handy feature to copy all the files related to the chapter to a safe place. Follow the same guidelines you use for saving the chapters. If you can stand to redo a week's worth of work, back-up once a week.

❖ Limiting Chapter Size

Even though its feasible to have longer chapters, you should usually keep your chapters under 40 pages. Ventura can easily handle files larger than that, but when the chapters get too big, the program may begin swapping out to the hard disk, which slows things down considerably and makes Ventura more prone to crash. Because of Ventura's publication options, you can easily create tables of contents and indexes from many chapters, so it isn't necessary to cram everything into one file. Remember: shorter chapters are faster and safer.

❖ Saving Old Width Tables

When you buy new fonts, don't immediately merge your new width table in with your old. First save your current width table under a new name. Then merge your new width table with your newly renamed file. I've had some width tables from font manufacturers that didn't merge correctly, and they ended up ruining my main width table. Now I always save first under a new name.

Once I've tested the width table by printing out a page with some old fonts and some new fonts, I can save this new width table using my original width file name.

❖ Organizing Font Files

If you use many different fonts, be careful about how you keep track of them. This is easier said than done, as fonts (especially those from FontWare) tend to have cryptic names. If you're constantly adding and removing fonts from your ever-bulging hard disk, losing track of what files you currently have on the disk means wasted time printing out pages only to find Courier substituted for the font you wanted. Here's one way to keep track. First, print an inventory of your .SFP and .SFL files by pressing Ctrl-P at the DOS prompt and then typing **DIR *.SFP.** Next, press Ctrl-P again to turn off printing. Now type:

DIR *.SFP SFP.DOC

This creates a list of all your SFP files and puts it in a file called SFP.DOC.

If you have a hard disk management program such as XTREE or Window DOS, you can read your font files. Near the beginning of the file (surrounded by what will appear to be garbage) will often be the name of the font. Make a note of the fonts you aren't sure of. Use your word processing program to type the font name next to the file name in SFP.DOC. Print out this list, and update it whenever you add or remove fonts from your disk.

❖ Responding to the "Internal System Error!" Message

One of the most dreaded messages is "Internal System Error! *(number)* 1. Note what you just did & Error #. 2. Save your work. 3. Call & Report to Tech. Support." The reason this message appears is that RAM memory may have been corrupted. Your job is to get out of the situation as smoothly as possible without losing any of your current or previous work — in other words, you want to quit Ventura, but you also want to avoid damaging the chapter you've been working on. To have the best shot at accomplishing all these goals, here's the procedure to follow:

- From the Options menu, select Set Preferences and make sure that Keep Backup Files is set at Yes.

- From the File menu, select Save As and save your chapter under a new name.

- Quit Ventura.

- Reboot your computer.

- Load Ventura again.

- Load the version of the chapter you saved under a new name with Save As. If it's not damaged, you're OK and can continue working on it.

- If the chapter is damaged, quit Ventura again and locate the backup version of the chapter. It will have the original name and will use the extension $HP. Use the DOS Rename command to change the extension to CHP. Then load Ventura and open the chapter.

25

Printing Tips

One of the strengths of today's laser printers is that they are capable of serving three distinct purposes:

- For proofing a document before sending it for final output on a high-resolution PostScript imagesetter.
- For creating camera-ready masters, suitable for reproduction on a copying machine or with an offset printer.
- For creating final copies directly.

Whichever way you use your printer, the techniqes described in this chapter can speed up printing and improve the quality of your output. Some of these are also described in greater detail in other portions of this book, especially Chapter 4, "Laser Printers," and Chapter 23, "Speed Tips."

❖   Imagesetter Proofing

Since Ventura drives PostScript imagesetters, it is possible to use a laser printer for proofing a document before having it typeset. First, install Ventura for both your laser printer and for PostScript. For example, if you're using a LaserJet II, install for LaserJet II and PostScript. If you've already installed for the LaserJet but not for PostScript, simply insert Disk #1, type VPPREP, and when Ventura asks you if this is your first time installing the program, say No. When it asks you what printer you wish to use, say PostScript. When it asks if you want to use any other printers, say No. (Since you've already installed the program for the LaserJet II, the fonts and width table are already in place.)

Having installed Ventura for both LaserJet and PostScript, you proof documents for the Linotronic by printing to the LaserJet but selecting the PostScript width table. In the Options menu, select Set Printer Info. Click on the LaserJet Plus option, then click on Load Different Font Width and select PostScript. Ventura will now print on the LaserJet with regular LaserJet fonts, but the letter spacing will be governed by the PostScript width table. Word and letter spacing within each line won't look very good, because of differences between LaserJet and PostScript fonts, but line endings and word breaks will be the same as when you ultimately print on the Linotronic.

❖   Printer Intensity Control

It never fails. Improve something new and there are always those who say they liked the unimproved version better. That's the way it is with the Canon engines. While I find the newer SX engines better in every way, there are those who claim that text printed lighter and sharper on the old CX engines.

I have a feeling that these people don't know the secret of the little green knob. Sounds like a Nancy Drew story, doesn't it? But it's not the least bit mysterious, once you know it's there.

The old Canon engines had a light/dark control on the outside of the printer. The new SX engines have the light/dark control *inside* the printer, a place where many fear to tread.

But it's easy — so easy in fact that even an adult can do it. Press the big button on the top of the printer and the top will pop up. If you look straight down into the printer, the Light/Dark control (usually a green wheel) is located in the left front corner. This wheel will probably be set at 5, which is medium; 9 is very light, and 1 is very dark. While 5 may be too dark for detailed fonts, it's fine for many applications.

Most typesetting fonts look best at 8 or 9, because the lightness makes them look sharper. At 9, type will be as light and sharp as it ever was with a CX engine. But sometimes when the type is sharper, jagged edges are more obvious. Setting the printer on 3 or 1 causes extra toner to be used. This toner melts around the edges, filling in the jagged edges, but it also makes the type look heavier.

Generally, if you are going to use laser-printed pages as originals, you want to set your printer to medium. Setting the printer to light also has an additional plus, as it saves toner and makes your printer cartridge last longer. The only negative is that blacks will not be as dark and solid, and while this is fine for reproduction, it may not look the best on originals.

If you are going to use your pages "camera ready" for photocopying or offset printing, you want them to be light, probably 8 or 9. The fact that blacks aren't quite solid at this intensity doesn't matter, because the photocopying or offset printing process will render them as solid, dark black.

❖ The Collating Trap

One of the options in the Ventura print menu is "Collating Copies." If you're printing multiple copies of a document, it seems obvious that you'd want to turn this option on and avoid having to collate your document by hand. Note, however, that printing is significantly slower with collating turned on than with collating turned off. You may be better off simply printing the document with automatic collating turned off, and then collating the document yourself by hand.

❖ Crop Marks

Crop marks are the source of some confusion. When you print on a laser printer, which uses 8½- by 11-inch paper, you won't get any crop marks unless you change the size of the base page frame (using the Sizing & Scaling menu) to something smaller than 8½ by 11 inches. However, if you print on a Linotronic, you will get crop marks even if you've left your base page at 8½ by 11. The reason you get crop marks on the Linotronic is that its paper is wider than 8½ inches.

If you don't want to change the size of the base page but still want to have crop marks, you can draw them on the first page of your chapter using Ventura's drawing tools, then make them repeating graphics.

❖ Registration Marks

Since Ventura won't automatically put crop marks on regular letter-sized paper unless you reduce the size of the base page, how do you provide the print shop with the registration marks it needs?

As it turns out, if you're producing letter-sized documents, most printers don't need crop marks at all four corners. What they do need is a "registration mark," a mark that is located in the same position on every page of the document. This provides the person operating the camera at the print shop with a constant reference point.

Here's a simple way to make such a mark. Go into graphics mode and set the grid to ½ inch both vertically and horizontally. Now move your cursor to the upper left corner of the page, and draw a 1-inch square box. Make it a repeating box so that it appears on every page of your chapter in exactly the same position.

When you print out the document, most of the box will not appear, due to the unprintable zone of the laser printer. The only part of your box that will appear is the lower right corner, providing the camera operator with a registration mark. When the print shop strips your negatives (i.e., tapes them together onto multiple-page flats), they will hide the registration marks so that they won't actually print on the final document.

❖ Decreasing the Size of Print Files

If you've ever printed a document to disk (by selecting File as the destination in the Printer Preferences dialog box), you may have noticed that the resulting file is sometimes immense. For example, I've seen a two-page document result in a 1MB print file. Gigantic print files are undesirable for two reasons. First, they take a long time to run out on a Linotronic. Second, they may make the print file too large for even a 1.2MB floppy disk. The reason the print file is so large is that it includes all the fonts needed for the document.

The solution is to keep the fonts out of the print file. Using the Add/Remove Fonts option, designate the fonts as Resident. That tells Ventura that they're already in the printer and keeps Ventura from downloading them. Then, when you go to get the document typeset, tell the folks at the PostScript service bureau which fonts are needed for your document. They'll take care of downloading the fonts.

❖ A Penny Saved

If you use a PostScript printer, you can avoid wasting paper and toner on the startup test page that gets printed every time you turn on the machine. Simply pull out the paper tray before you start up the printer. The printer will warm up as usual, skipping the startup page. Then just push the paper tray back into the printer.

❖ Can You Trust Those Cheap Toner Refills?

You've no doubt seen the ads in the computer magazines for cheap toner refills. If you do a lot of printing, you can save a good deal of money using these services. The question is, are you jeopardizing the well-being of your expensive laser printer by using a refilled cartridge?

The answer is: probably not. For the past several years I've been asking people if they know of a printer that's been damaged by a toner refill. I've only heard of two instances. In one case, the refilled toner cartridge cracked open and spilled toner inside the printer. In another case, the toner itself was of poor quality and ended up getting into the moving parts of the printer and fusing.

The "wrong way" to refill a toner cartridge is to drill a hole, pour in more toner, and plug the hole. Don't use a refilled cartridge that has a plug. Reputable toner refill companies disassemble and clean the cartridge, add toner, and seal it up again. One thing you may notice with a refilled cartridge is that the print is slightly darker. The reason is that as the photosensitive drum inside the cartridge ages, it becomes more sensitive and tends to print a larger "spot."

Profile

PrintCache

If you've got a few extra bucks burning a hole in your pocket, the best print spooler I've seen for desktop publishing is PrintCache (formerly LaserTORQ). Not only is it fast, it doesn't take a lot of computer time and slow you down. Other spoolers (even the one in Windows) take so much computer time that even though you're back to work, everything's moving at a snail's pace, which kind of negates the whole purpose of a spooler.

PrintCache is specifically designed for PostScript or LaserJet (and compatible) printers. Because it can receive data as much as 20 times faster than the laser printer, your program can send the file to PrintCache as fast as it can, and PrintCache will dole it out to the printer in the background while you go back to work in Ventura.

While the subtitle of PrintCache is "The Printer Accelerator," it's important to remember that print spoolers don't make the printer print faster, they just let you get back to work faster. The actual print time will be about the same as it was without PrintCache. Even that is an accomplishment, however, as other printer spoolers can take twice as long to print a file. PrintCache takes only 19.4K of memory, an important consideration for most people using memory-hungry Ventura.

◆ Torqing PostScript

The largest speed improvement comes with PostScript printers. This is because PostScript printers can be slow in taking data — they're busy figuring things out and making the computer wait. PrintCache takes the data at top speed, and feeds it to the printer when it's ready. And you don't have to wait.

Here's an example. I used Ventura to print a one-page file with a 60K bitmapped graphic to a PostScript printer using a parallel interface. Ventura by itself took two and half minutes. Ventura with PrintCache took only one minute, which meant that I went back to work one and a half minutes sooner. That may not sound like much, but it's a 150 percent improvement. Multiply that number by the number of times you print each day, and you'll see how the time can add up. Print just ten times a day and you've gained 15 minutes.

These speed improvements are even more dramatic if you use a serial interface, because laser printers using a serial port can be so agonizingly slow. Using a serial connection, the same Ventura file tied up the computer for nine minutes without PrintCache, and only one minute with it.

The same file printed to a LaserJet tied up Ventura for four minutes without PrintCache. With PrintCache, I was back at work in two minutes, a 50 percent improvement.

PrintCache can create the buffer it needs in conventional memory (not recommended, since Ventura needs all the memory it can get), on a hard disk, in extended memory, or in expanded (EMS) memory.

I have only one complaint about the product. When you press ALT-T, a window pops up on the screen. It tells how large the buffer is, how much data is currently in the buffer, what percentage of the buffer is filled, as well as the status of the printer (Printing, Out-of-Paper, etc.) and, if you are printing to a LaserJet, controls for optimization. This useful feature works only in text mode, and won't pop up over graphics (except Hercules), which makes it less than useful when you are working in Ventura. (*For access information on PrintCache, see the Utilities section of Appendix A, "Resources."*)

❖ How to Print Full-Page Graphics on a 512K LaserJet

At 300-dpi, it takes about one megabyte of printer memory to print a full-page bitmapped graphic. That means on a standard

LaserJet Plus or LaserJet II with no additional memory, you're limited to less than a half-page graphic image. Here's where Print-Cache comes in handy again, with a feature called "Optimization," which can compress graphics so they take up to 60 percent less space in the printer's memory. In my test, a graphics file that overflowed the LaserJet's memory, printing on two pages instead of one, printed perfectly when optimized. Full optimization takes its toll in buffering speed, however, and even with spooling, the file tied up the computer for three and a half minutes, the same amount of time as unbuffered. Of course, it all printed out on one page though, so it was worth the wait.

Also, optimization works only on graphics, not downloadable fonts, so you will see less difference on desktop-published pages, unless lots of graphics are involved. PostScript printers do not require (and cannot use) optimization.

❖ Speeding up Printing By Hiding Graphics

Graphics print a good deal more slowly than text, so Ventura provides a new feature that lets you print quick drafts of a chapter minus all or some of the illustrations. To hide the pictures, select Hide Pictures from the Options menu (DOS/GEM version) or from the View menu (Windows version).

❖ What Kind of Paper to Use

You've no doubt seen the ads for the special laser printer papers, which supposedly provide superior quality when you are printing master copies for reproduction. Actually, as explained in a recent *Publish* magazine article, you'll do just as well if you simply use regular 20-lb xerox paper with a smooth (not a slick) finish.

❖ Speeding up Printing By Downloading the Postscript Prologue

Before it prints any PostScript file, DOS/GEM Ventura downloads a PostScript prologue file. Windows calls this a header file — same thing. You can speed up printing by downloading a permanent version of this file at the beginning of your work session. The procedure is explained in Chapter 23, "Speed Tips."

❖ Printing on Unsupported Printers

Publisher's Powerpak is a utility that lets you use printers with Ventura that aren't directly supported by the program. It combines a font generator and an array of drivers for over 200 dot-matrix, inkjet, bubblejet, and laser printers, most of which are not otherwise supported by Ventura. Its three typeface families match Helvetica, Times Roman, and Courier, and fonts can be any size from 6 to 250 points. (For access information on Publisher's Powerpak, see Appendix A, "Resources.")

❖ Saving Before Printing

Occasionally, when you tell Ventura to print your document, the program will freeze up. This can happen if you forget to turn on the printer or if you choose the wrong port. The solution is to get in the habit of saving your document just before issuing the print command. That way, even if Ventura crashes you won't lose any work.

❖ Wait for the Prompt

After you issue the print command, it's tempting to walk off and fill up your coffee cup while Ventura sends the chapter to the printer. However, if any of the pictures in your document are hidden, Ventura will first ask you whether or not you want the hidden pictures to print before it goes any further. If you wait too long to respond one way or another, the printer may "time out" and nothing will be printed. So make sure you wait for the "Print hidden pictures?" query before you take a break.

Tip 24-1

Press Enter An Extra Time

It's easy to tell Ventura to print and then to walk off for lunch, forgetting to wait for the "Print hidden pictures?" query. Here's a good trick to avoid this mistake. When you tell Ventura to print, make it a habit to press Enter an extra time before walking away. Ventura will remember the extra Enter, and if the "Print hidden pictures?" query comes up, Ventura will interpret the Enter as an OK.

❖ Printing Oversized Pages on a Standard Laser Printer

Many people are surprised to learn that Ventura can print pages larger than 8½ by 11. To do this, the program employs a technique called tiling, which means printing a page in overlapping sections. To use tiling, all you have to do is select the 11- by 17-inch page size in the Page Size and Layout dialog box, accessed from the Chapter menu.

If you've selected that size for your paper, a dialog box will appear at print time giving you three options: shrink, overlap, and nothing.

The shrink option only works with PostScript printers. It reduces the size of your document to fit on 8½- by 11-inch paper, and is useful for previewing pages and creating mockups.

The overlap option divides the page into overlapping "tiles." You then paste or tape these together.

❖ Printing Mirror-Image (Wrong-Reading) Pages

Even though Ventura doesn't have an option for printing mirror-image (wrong-reading) pages, you can do it with a PostScript printer. The trick is in modifying Ventura's PostScript header, or prologue, by adding a couple of lines of code.

If you just have one file to print wrong-reading, you can print the PostScript to disk (choose PostScript and filename from the Set Printer Info dialog box, print, and give Ventura a filename when it prompts you), then edit the resulting PostScript file with a text editor or word processor (as long as it will save straight text, sans formatting gibberish).

Find the section near the top of the file that looks like this:

/GEMMATINI{/landscape ed /p3 ed /p2 ed /p1 ed gr 72 300 div exch div dup scale clippath pathbox exch / prx ed exch dup /ply ed sub 1 add p3 sub 2 div ply add /ty ed dup prx exch sub 1 add p2 sub 2 div add landscape {p1 add} if ty translate landscape {90 rotate} if gs } bd

Add these two lines at the end, just before the "gs":

2550 0 translate

-1 1 scale

If you're printing landscape pages, use 3300 instead of 2550. When you're done it should look like this (the line breaks don't really matter):

/GEMMATINI{/landscape ed /p3 ed /p2 ed /p1 ed gr 72 300 div exch div dup scale clippath pathbox exch / prx ed exch dup /ply ed sub 1 add p3 sub 2 div ply add /ty ed dup prx exch sub 1 add p2 sub 2 div add landscape {p1 add} if ty translate landscape {90 rotate} if

2550 0 translate

-1 1 scale

gs } bd

You can set up an alternate PostScript header if you are planning on printing mirrored pages on a regular basis. Make a copy of PS2PRE (in the Ventura directory), name it something like PS2MIRR.PS, and modify it as described above. You might set up another copy for wrong-reading landscape printing. Make sure your copies do *not* have the filename extension .PRE.

Whenever you want wrong-reading printouts, type the following from the DOS prompt:

cd \ventura

rename PS2.PRE PS2.BAK

rename PS2MIRR.PS PS2.PRE

cd \

Or something to that effect. You get the idea — the header file you want to use should be named PS2.PRE.

Start Ventura and print as you normally would. When you want to go back to normal printing, rename the files to the way they were. If you get tired of all the DOS commands, write a little batch file that will do all the renaming with a single command.

❖ Printing Crop Marks on Standard-Sized Pages

As noted earlier in this chapter, Ventura doesn't normally print crop marks on 8½- by 11-inch pages, but there's a way to trick the program into doing so. First, select 11- by 17-inch paper as your page size, from the Page Size and Layout dialog box under the Chapter menu. Next, select the base page frame (by switching to frame mode and clicking on the underlying page) and change its dimensions to 8½ by 11, using the Sizing & Scaling menu under the Frame menu. Finally, select the overlap option when you print. The page will be printed in four sections, complete with crop marks.

26

Memory Limitations and Solutions

Because of the dynamic memory allocation capabilities of Windows 3.0, the Windows version of Ventura is much less prone to being afflicted by a shortage of memory than the DOS/GEM version. In the DOS/GEM version, memory is a scarce resource in Ventura, especially for those without an EMS (expanded memory) board. With the support of EMS in the Professional Extension, the memory shortage is much less severe. In fact, if you're using the Professional Extension with EMS, you can usually stop worrying about memory altogether.

The purpose of this chapter is to explain how Ventura allocates memory and set forth some options to give yourself a bit more working room and make the program run faster.

❖ Overview

The 640K of RAM that can be directly addressed by DOS is often referred to as "conventional memory." Ventura operates within this block of memory. In certain circumstances, the program can also make direct or indirect use of "expanded memory" and "extended memory." We'll discuss these in a little while, but let's start by looking at the 640K of conventional memory.

◆ Overhead

Even before you load Ventura, some of that 640K is spoken for:

- Some conventional memory is used by DOS's COMMAND.COM file. With DOS 3.3, this amounts to about 25K.

- Some conventional memory is used by device drivers (for the monitor, mouse, hard disk, etc.), which are automatically loaded into memory each time your computer starts up. To find out which device drivers are used by your system, type
  TYPE \CONFIG.SYS
  Drivers can be distinguished from other files because they end in the extension SYS. In some cases your mouse driver will be installed by your AUTOEXEC.BAT file rather than your CONFIG.SYS file. If that is the case, there will be a line in your AUTOEXEC.BAT file with the name MOUSE.COM (or something similar).

- Some memory may be taken up by memory-resident programs (also called TSRs, for "terminate and stay resident"). Such programs may include SideKick or similar accessory programs, screen-capture utilities like Hotshot, disk-caching utilities, and print spoolers. As a general rule, it's recommended that you minimize your use of memory-resident programs in order to leave an adequate amount of memory free for Ventura. Of course, under some circumstances you'll need to break that rule.

- Some memory may be taken up by your network-control software, if your computer is on a network.

Let's assume you've just booted up your computer and have loaded in all the memory-resident programs you normally use. To find out how much memory is now left over for Ventura, type **CHKDSK** from the DOS command line. DOS will respond with something like this:

```
19623936 bytes total disk space
     100 bytes in two hidden files
   81920 bytes in 34 directories
17653760 bytes in 624 user files
 1888256 bytes available on disk

  655360 bytes total memory
  589152 bytes free
```

The first five lines describe how storage is allocated on your hard disk; the last two lines report on memory. The final line, which in this example shows that 589K are free, is the most important one, since it shows how much room is actually available to run Ventura.

Tip 26-1

Using 16-Color VGA Monitors

Contrary to the warning that appears during the installation procedure for Ventura (base version), you can use a 16-color VGA monitor with the program. However, to do so, you'll have to remove all other drivers and memory-resident programs from your computer. Note that the drivers for VGA two-color monitors and EGA two-color monitors use approximately 10K less memory than the drivers for 16-color monitors, so memory isn't as tight with the two-color monitors.

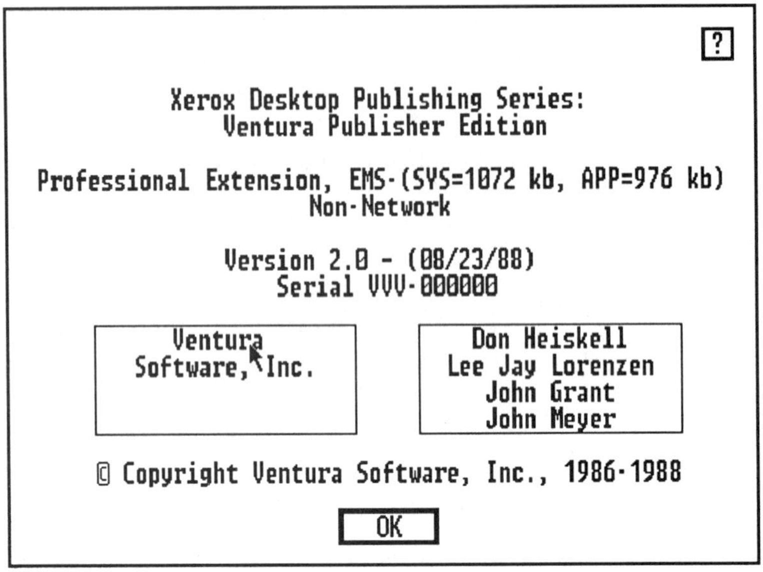

Figure 26-1: To access the diagnostics box, select Publisher Info from the Desk menu and click on the word Ventura as shown here.

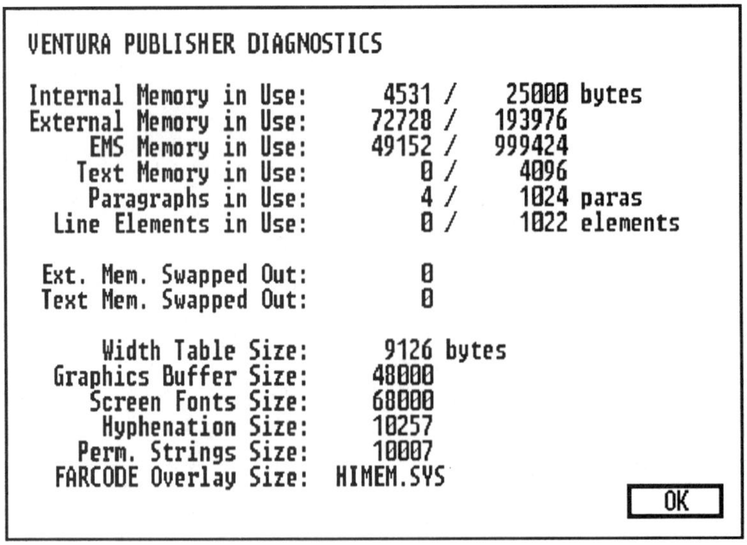

```
┌─────────────────────────────────────────────────┐ ┌─┐
│                                                  │?│
│         Xerox Desktop Publishing Series:         └─┘
│            Ventura Publisher Edition             │
│                                                  │
│  Professional Extension, EMS·(SYS=1072 kb, APP=976 kb)
│                    Non-Network                   │
│                                                  │
│            Version 2.0 - (08/23/88)              │
│                Serial VVV-000000                 │
│                                                  │
│     ┌──────────────────┐  ┌──────────────────┐  │
│     │     Ventura      │  │   Don Heiskell    │  │
│     │ Software, Inc.   │  │  Lee Jay Lorenzen │  │
│     │                  │  │    John Grant     │  │
│     │                  │  │    John Meyer     │  │
│     └──────────────────┘  └──────────────────┘  │
│                                                  │
│   © Copyright Ventura Software, Inc., 1986-1988  │
│                   ┌─────────┐                    │
│                   │   OK    │                    │
│                   └─────────┘                    │
└──────────────────────────────────────────────────┘
```

Figure 26-2: The diagnostics box. Where there are two numbers, the number on the right tells the maximum available, and the number on the left shows the amount currently in use. "HIMEM.SYS" shows that the FARCODE module has been loaded into high memory.

```
┌─────────────────────────────────────────────────┐
│ VENTURA PUBLISHER DIAGNOSTICS                    │
│                                                  │
│ Internal Memory in Use:      4531 /    25000 bytes
│ External Memory in Use:     72728 /   193976     │
│      EMS Memory in Use:     49152 /   999424     │
│    Text Memory in Use:          0 /     4096     │
│     Paragraphs in Use:          4 /     1024 paras
│  Line Elements in Use:          0 /     1022 elements
│                                                  │
│ Ext. Mem. Swapped Out:          0                │
│ Text Mem. Swapped Out:          0                │
│                                                  │
│       Width Table Size:      9126 bytes          │
│   Graphics Buffer Size:     48000                │
│      Screen Fonts Size:     68000                │
│       Hyphenation Size:     10257                │
│      Perm. Strings Size:    10007                │
│    FARCODE Overlay Size: HIMEM.SYS               │
│                                   ┌─────────┐    │
│                                   │   OK    │    │
│                                   └─────────┘    │
└─────────────────────────────────────────────────┘
```

◆ How Ventura Uses Memory

When Ventura is running, it uses memory for the following purposes:

- Storing the main Ventura program module, VP.APP (for the base version) or VPPROF.APP (for the Professional Extension). These modules require 451K and 499K respectively.
- About 64K is reserved in a buffer for screen fonts.
- About 48K is reserved in a buffer for graphics.

In addition to the parts of Ventura that are always loaded into memory, parts of the program — called overlays — are kept on the hard disk and loaded from the hard disk into memory as needed. Ventura also uses the hard disk for storing other data that is too large to be kept in RAM. Since retrieving or storing information on a hard disk is many times slower than retrieving information from RAM, the basic strategy for managing memory is to minimize the program's need to access the hard disk.

❖ The Diagnostics Box

An important tool for managing memory is Ventura's diagnostics box, which is not documented in the program manual. To see the diagnostics box, select Publisher Info in the Desk menu and then click directly on the word Ventura in the box. (See Figures 26-1 and 26-2.)

◆ "Internal Memory in Use"

The number on the right side of the slash is the amount of RAM reserved for internal program functions; the number on the left is the amount actually in use. You can't change these numbers.

◆ "External Memory in Use"

The number on the right side of the slash represents the amount of memory that is not in use for other purposes. For the base version of DOS/GEM Ventura, it defines the maximum size of a document that Ventura can work with in RAM. Exceeding this amount will not prevent you from loading or working with a document, but it will slow operations down considerably because Ventura will resort to swapping to the hard disk. In the Professional Extension, the amount of external memory available does not limit the size of documents, since documents are loaded into EMS.

◆ "EMS Memory in Use"

The number on the right side of the slash shows the amount of EMS memory available for Ventura to hold a document. The number on the left shows the amount currently being used. With the base version, both numbers will always be 0, despite the fact that the base version does load about 90K of system software into EMS if EMS memory is available.

◆ "Text Memory in Use"

The number on the right shows how much Ventura has allocated for holding the text portion of the current document; the number on the left shows how much of that allocation is currently being used.

◆ "Paragraphs in Use"

The number on the right shows the maximum number of paragraphs allowed in a document. The number on the left shows the current number. Note: a paragraph is any block of text that ends with an Enter.

◆ "Line Elements in Use"

The number to the right (normally 725) is the maximum number of line elements that are allowed in the current frame. The number on the left is the number currently in the frame. Every line of text counts as two line elements, and additional line elements are used up by changes in type, tabs, and especially leader tabs (a line containing a leader tab counts as six line elements). Note, however, that the number of paragraph breaks does not affect the number of line elements. If you have too many line elements in a frame, you'll get the error message "This frame is too complex to completely format." Steps that you can take to simplify a frame are described below.

◆ "Ext Memory Swapped Out"

This is the amount of document information that exceeds the available RAM and therefore has been written to the hard disk or to a RAM disk. Swapping out significantly reduces Ventura's performance. If you are using the Professional Extension with EMS memory, you rarely have to worry about swapping out, since the entire document is automatically placed in EMS.

◆ "Text Memory Swapped Out"

This is the portion of the current document that is swapped out.

◆ "Width Table Size"

This is the amount of RAM taken up by the portion of the font width table used by the screen display. It can be as little as 1K and as much as 35K, depending on how many fonts are installed.

◆ "Graphics Buffer Size"

This is the size of the picture file that Ventura can handle without swapping out to the hard disk. The limitation applies most frequently to images, i.e., bitmapped graphics such as files with the IMG extension. Cropping and moving bitmapped pictures will go much faster if you keep the size of files smaller than the graphics buffer. You can adjust the size of this buffer using the /A switch. For more information, see the discussion below.

◆ **"Screen Fonts Size"**

This is the amount of RAM reserved for storing the bitmaps used by Ventura to display fonts on screen. If a screen font file exceeds the size of this buffer, it can't be displayed on the screen. You can adjust the size of this buffer using the /F or /A switch. For more details, see the discussion below.

◆ **"Hyphenation Size"**

This is the amount of conventional memory that must be reserved for applying hyphenation, generally about 10K. The actual hyphenation dictionaries are much larger, but don't reside in RAM at all times.

◆ **"Perm. Strings Size"**

This is amount of RAM that must remain allocated at all times to hold certain essential information such as error messages.

◆ **"FARCODE Overlay Size"**

The C compiler used in the development of Ventura allows program segments of up to 64K. FARCODE is program information outside that limit, to which Ventura needs speedy access and therefore keeps in RAM. This shows the size of the programs stored as FARCODE. If you are using a memory manager such as HIMEM.SYS or 386^{MAX}, the FARCODE modules will be loaded in high memory, as discussed below. In that case, the diagnostics box will list HIMEM.SYS here instead of the amount of memory used by the FARCODE module.

❖ **Memory Management Options**

There are at least eight specific measures that you can take to enhance Ventura's use of memory. They are as follows:

• Install expanded memory.

- Use a RAM disk for spill files.

- Use disk caching, and select a disk cache that requires a minimal amount of overhead in conventional memory.

- Adjust the BUFFERS= lines in your CONFIG.SYS file.

- Adjust the size of the screen fonts buffer. In many cases, allocating more memory for screen fonts produces a noticeable improvement in performance.

- Adjust the size of the graphics buffer. Generally, this means reducing the size of the buffer in order to provide more memory for other purposes.

- Install HIMEM.SYS, a driver that is included with Microsoft Windows. This frees up conventional memory for other purposes; however, it does not apply to computers with the 8086 chip.

- Install 386^{MAX}, a utility program that makes more memory available to Ventura by moving drivers and memory-resident programs outside conventional memory.

◆ Extended and Expanded Memory

Memory in a computer beyond the 640K recognized by DOS is of two types, extended and expanded. Expanded memory refers to memory above 640K that is configured in accordance with the Lotus-Intel-Microsoft Expanded Memory Specification, or LIM EMS.

You can use any version of EMS numbered 3.0 or above. EMS boards are made by a variety of vendors. You should look for one that is expandable, so that you can increase its capacity by adding more RAM chips when the current memory shortage slacks off and prices come down. If you have a 386 computer, you won't need to buy an EMS board, since most 386 computers provide a utility that can convert any memory installed on the system above 640K into EMS. If for some reason you have a 386 computer that lacks such a utility, get hold of 386^{MAX}.

If you don't install the Professional Extension, EMS benefits you in two ways:

- If EMS is present, Ventura moves up to 108K of system software into EMS, freeing up an equivalent amount of conventional memory.
- EMS can be used to for disk caches and print buffers.

If you do install the Professional Extension, EMS becomes even more useful:

- First, Ventura moves up to 108K of system software into EMS, freeing up an equivalent amount of conventional memory.
- Second, Ventura uses EMS to handle documents too large or complex to fit in conventional memory.
- Third, you can speed up Ventura by setting up a disk cache and/or a print buffer in EMS.
- Fourth, Ventura uses EMS memory to hold the EDCO hyphenation dictionary that is provided with the program. The dictionary takes up 1.2MB of EMS.

How much EMS do you need? If you are using the Professional Extension, Xerox recommends that you have a minimum of 256K of EMS in your system. If you don't plan on using the EDCO hyphenation dictionary, a 1MB or 2MB cache should suffice. If you plan on using the EDCO hyphenation dictionary, I recommend that you have at least 2.5MB of EMS memory in your computer. That breaks down to 1.2MB for the dictionary, 90K for system software, 512K for a disk cache, and 512K for your document.

Extended memory can't serve as many purposes as EMS. It cannot be used directly by either the base version or the Professional Extension. However, it can be used for disk caches, RAM disks, and print buffers. Most 386 computers come with software utilities that let you configure extended memory as EMS memory. In addition, there are utilities such as 386^{MAX} that can convert extended memory to EMS memory.

If you have both EMS and extended memory in your computer, use both. For example, you might use the extended memory for a print buffer and use the EMS for Ventura, for a disk cache, and for the EDCO hyphenation dictionary.

◆ Using a RAM Disk

If you have memory beyond 640K, you have the option of using it for a RAM disk or for disk caching. Generally, it's preferable to use disk caching, since this speeds up Ventura operations virtually across the board. In contrast, a RAM disk only makes a difference if you have documents that are too large to fit in memory. When a document is too large to fit completely in memory, Ventura creates an overflow file on the hard disk. By directing this overflow file to the RAM disk, you can speed up operations considerably. The procedure for using a RAM disk for spill files is described in Chapter 23, "Speed Tips."

Note that if you are using the Professional Extension and have EMS memory on your computer, you don't have to worry about overflow files, since Ventura automatically uses the EMS memory to hold the document.

◆ Disk Caching

As explained in Chapter 23, "Speed Tips," using a disk cache is probably the most important step you can take to make Ventura run faster. Disk caches work by storing information in RAM that otherwise would be accessed from the hard disk. Since RAM access is many times faster than hard disk access, the disk cache speeds up the program. Disk caches can help almost any program, but they're especially useful with Ventura because the program is too large to fit into RAM all at once and therefore loads pieces of itself — called "overlays" — as needed from the hard disk.

Most disk caching utilities allow you to set up the cache in either extended memory or EMS memory, and to specify the size of the cache. If you have extended memory or EMS memory to spare, it's desirable to set up a fairly large cache, say 512K to 1MB. To manage the cache, the caching program does take up some conventional memory. Interestingly enough, caching programs vary significantly in the amount of conventional memory overhead they require, as shown in Table 26-1.

Conventional Memory Overhead for Disk Caching Utilities (Kb)

CACHE PROGRAM	EXTENDED MEMORY		EXPANDED MEMORY	
	512K Cache	1,024K Cache	512K Cache	1,024K Cache
Flash 5.33	49	61	49	61
Lightning 4.80	N/A	N/A	37	54
Super PC-Kwik 2.19	45	65	17	17
Vcache 3.1	21	29	20	28

Table 26-1: *The numbers in this table were derived by comparing the amount of memory reported by CHKDSK before and after loading a disk caching program. It should be noted that the numbers above are based on the default configuration for the cache. For some caches, it is possible to decrease the amount of conventional memory overhead by changing the parameters, though this will generally lead to reduced effectiveness of the cache in speeding up Ventura. In PC Magazine's roundup of disk-caching programs (February 14, 1989), the minimum conventional memory overheads for a 512K cache in extended memory were reported as follows: Flash 25K, Super PC-Kwik 16K, Vcache 20K, PC Tools Deluxe 20K, Mace Utilities 10K, SMARTDrive 14K, IBM-Cache 19K, and Compaq Disk Caching Utility 16K. For a 512K cache in expanded memory, PC Magazine reported the following minimum conventional memory overheads: Flash 25K, Super PC-Kwik 7K, Vcache 19K, PC Tools Deluxe 16K, Mace Utilities 9K, SMARTDrive 14K, and Compaq Disk Caching Utility 8K.*

◆ Adjusting Buffers in CONFIG.SYS

If you are using a disk-caching utility, you can reduce the amount of RAM allocated for buffers in your CONFIG.SYS file. In the absence of a disk-caching utility, Xerox recommends that you set buffers equal to 20. However, when you are using a disk cache, most of those buffers are redundant and the buffers line in CON-FIG.SYS can be reduced to 3 or 4. Since each DOS buffer takes up 512 bytes of RAM, you'll save about 8K.

◆ Disabling FASTOPEN

FASTOPEN is a program provided with DOS 3.3 and later versions. It speeds up file access by creating a small cache where it stores the location of each file that you open. If you use a disk cache, FASTOPEN won't speed anything up but will use up some memory, so you're better off removing the FASTOPEN line from your CONFIG.SYS file.

◆ Adjusting the Screen Fonts Buffer

By default, Ventura sets up a 68K buffer for screen fonts. Usually, this should be sufficient, but there are certain situations in which you should increase the buffer:

- If you are using a large number of different fonts on a page.
- If you are using VGA rather than EGA screen fonts. In general, VGA screen fonts take up about twice as much memory as EGA fonts.
- If you are using large fonts, for which the screen font files are larger than 68K. If a screen font is too large for the buffer, Ventura will not be able to display it.

As described in Chapter 23, "Speed Tips," increasing the size of the screen fonts buffer can reduce the time needed to refresh the screen by 40 percent or more.

Although it's more likely that you'll need to increase the size of the screen font buffer, there are some situations where you might want to reduce it. For example, if Ventura refused to load because not enough memory was free, setting the /F switch to 32 might help.

To change the screen font buffer, use a text editor or a word processor in plain ASCII mode to add /F=k at the end of VP.BAT or VPPROF.BAT, where k is the number of bytes you wish to allocate for the screen font buffer. For example, if you wanted to change the size of the screen font buffer to 90K, and your VP.BAT file is

```
CD C:\VENTURA
DRVRMRGR VP%1/S=SD_WY705.EGA/M=11
```

then you should add /F=90 to change it to

```
CD C:\VENTURA
DRVRMRGR VP%1/S=SD_WY705.EGA/M=11/F=90
```

Of course, when you increase the size of the screen font buffer, you have to give up memory somewhere else. If you set the /F switch above 68K, Ventura reduces the amount of memory available for the document. That means you won't be able to work with as large a document as otherwise. If you have the Professional Extension, increasing the screen font buffer should have no ill effects as long as the amount of external memory available is well above 100K. To find out the amount of available external memory, check the right-hand figure next to External Memory in Use in the diagnostics box.

Even changing the buffer slightly, such as from 68K to 80K, can make a difference in speed. According to Ventura Software, the maximum is in the range of 128K to 192K. (Note: don't use the /F switch if you are also using the /A switch.)

◆ Adjusting the Graphics Buffer

The default for the graphics buffer is 48K. That sets the upper limit for the size of a graphic that can be included on a page without the need to spill some of the data for that graphic onto the hard disk. Whenever Ventura has to use a spill file, performance is seriously diminished because the program has to do time-consuming reads from the hard disk every time it refreshes the screen (such as when you move from one page to the next, or when you press the Esc button).

If memory is tight on your computer — for example, if you're having trouble getting Ventura to load — you can decrease the graphics buffer to free up memory for other purposes. Note: you can only reduce the graphics buffer, not increase it.

To reduce the size of the graphics buffer, add the following at the end of the VP.BAT or VPPROF.BAT file:

/A=k

where k is an integer between 0 and 32 that specifies how much memory to take away from the graphics and screen font buffers (half is taken away from the graphics buffer and half from the screen fonts buffer). Unfortunately, you can't reduce the size of the graphics buffer without decreasing the size of the screen fonts buffer by the same amount.

If you use 0 as the value for k, the screen fonts buffer will be reduced by 16K but the graphics buffer won't be affected. Generally, however, if you want to adjust the size of the screen fonts buffer, you should use the /F switch.

Here are a few final caveats about the /A switch:

- Don't use the /A switch if you're using the /F switch.
- Some printers and graphics converters (such as JLaser) may not work properly if you reduce the graphics buffer.

◆ Memory Magic with HIMEM.SYS (286 and 386 Computers Only)

Most AT and 386 computers come with at least 1MB of memory; however, 360K of that is worthless because only 640K can be addressed by DOS. Here's a nifty piece of software that, as if by magic, adds as much as 64K to the 640K of conventional memory available to your system. It was created by Microsoft, which unfortunately doesn't sell it separately.

To get HIMEM.SYS, you have to purchase Windows. Why Microsoft doesn't sell HIMEM.SYS as a stand-alone product is somewhat of a mystery. If they did, they could call it Magic, charge $25, and sell thousands of copies.

During the installation procedure for Windows, HIMEM.SYS is automatically copied onto your hard disk and the following line is added to your CONFIG.SYS file:
DEVICE = HIMEM.SYS.

If you don't plan to install Windows, you can install HIMEM.SYS yourself simply by copying the file into your root directory, adding the DEVICE = HIMEM.SYS line to your CONFIG.SYS file, and rebooting your computer.

Now load Ventura and check the diagnostics box. Next to FAR-CODE Overlay Size, you'll see the word HIMEM.SYS. This means that the 47K (base version) or 60K (Professional Extension) normally taken up by FARCODE (a program module used by Ventura) is now taken care of by HIMEM.SYS and no longer takes up any conventional memory. You can verify that by comparing the amount of external memory available with and without HIMEM.SYS. The difference is 2K less than the size of FARCODE (the reason for the 2K discrepancy is that HIMEM.SYS itself requires about 2K of conventional memory).

Here's how HIMEM.SYS works (in layman's terms). DOS locates blocks of data by specifying an address within the 640K of conventional memory plus an offset. For example, if the address is 512 and the offset is 30, DOS will look for the data at position 542. In theory, an address of 620 with an offset of 40 should wrap around to the bottom of conventional memory and result in position 20. However, due to a bug in the 80286 chip, it is possible to fool DOS into not wrapping the address around to the bottom of conventional memory, and as a result up to 64K of additional "conventional" memory is opened up above 640K. HIMEM.SYS works by loading whatever program modules it can find into that 64K area.

Note: you can use HIMEM.SYS with any 80286-based or 80386-based computer. You can't use it with a PC or XT (8088 or 8086 chip).

Tip 26-2

Conflicts between HIMEM.SYS and Other Programs That Use Extended Memory

Since HIMEM.SYS was created by programmers at Microsoft, you'd expect it to conform to all the relevant rules, regulations, and specifications pertaining to extended memory. Apparently, it does not. Don't use HIMEM.SYS in conjunction with other programs that make use of extended memory, such as disk caches and print spoolers. My own tests have shown that neither the leading caching program (Super PC-Kwik) nor the leading print spooler (LaserTORQ) coexist satisfactorily with HIMEM.SYS when they're using extended memory. Unless a vendor specifically tells you that it has adjusted its program to coexist with HIMEM.SYS in extended memory, you can assume that the two won't get along.

◆ More Memory Magic: 386^{MAX}

As the name suggests, 386^{MAX} (or "386 to the Max") is a memory management program specifically for 80386-based computers. Like HIMEM.SYS, the main purpose of 386^{MAX} is to increase the amount of memory available to DOS by allowing DOS to use extended memory between 640K and 1MB (we'll refer to this memory as "high memory" and refer to conventional memory as "low memory").

With Ventura, you can use 386^{MAX} to do two things:

• Move your drivers and memory-resident utilities into high memory, thus freeing up conventional memory.

• Install portions of Ventura's system software into high memory, again freeing up conventional memory.

To use 386^{MAX}, copy the files 386MAX.SYS and 386MAX.COM into your root directory and add the following line to your CONFIG.SYS file:

DEVICE = \path\386MAX.SYS

If you have extended memory in your computer, 386^{MAX} can configure it as expanded memory. If you already have an expanded memory board, you can either reconfigure the board as extended memory or else add the command EMS=0. If you have a high-resolution monitor, you may also have to add a command that prevents 386^{MAX} from attempting to use the address space in high memory used by the monitor. For example, if you are using a Wyse 700 monitor, you need to add the command VIDMEM = A000-B3FF. If you are using 386^{MAX} in conjunction with an EMS board and a Wyse 700 monitor, the line in your CONFIG.SYS file will look like this:

DEVICE = \path\386MAX.SYS EMS=0 VIDMEM=A000-B3FF

Having placed the device line in your CONFIG.SYS file, you must indicate to 386^{MAX} which of your drivers and memory-resident utilities are to be moved into high memory. This is done using the commands "386MAX LOADHIGH" and "386MAX LOADLOW." For example, a modified AUTOEXEC.BAT file might look like this:

prompt pg
PATH=C:\QMSJS
386MAX LOADHIGH
JETSTART
\MOUSE1\mouse
path=c:\bat;c:\dos;c:\mw;C:\QMSJS
utility\kwik\superpck /a+/s:1024
386MAX LOADLOW

The final step is to modify VP.BAT or VPPROF.BAT so that as many system files as possible are loaded into high memory. To do this, use the OPENHIGH and CLOSEHIGH commands. For example:

C:386MAX OPENHIGH
C: CD \VENTURA

```
DRVRMRGR   VPPROF   %1   /S=SD_WY700.VGA/M=32/F=128
C:386MAX CLOSEHIGH
```

❖ What Are the Limits?

Since the initial release of Ventura in 1986, the size of allowable text files, style sheets, chapters, and publications have all increased steadily. The following are the limits currently imposed by Ventura:

- **Size of text files:** Without expanded memory, the maximum amount of text per chapter is 2MB, less 16K for every 1,000 paragraphs. Of course, that's the absolute limit, which can only be approached if Ventura resorts to a good deal of swapping out to the hard disk, a slow, error-prone process. With the Professional Extension and expanded memory, the maximum amount of text per chapter is 4MB or the total amount of EMS in your computer, less 16K per 1,000 paragraphs. The main advantage of the Professional Extension is that its use of EMS means that there is never any need to create overflow files on the hard disk.

- Maximum number of tags in a style sheet: 128 (including tags generated by Ventura itself).

- Number of chapters per publication: 128.

- Number of paragraphs per chapter: 1,000 per 16K of memory up to 64,000.

- Number of line elements per frame: 725 in the base version of Ventura; up to 16,000 in the Professional Extension if EMS is available. This means that in the Professional Extension, the "Frame Too Complex" error message need no longer cramp your style — you're unlikely to ever encounter it, no matter what sort of page you create.

- Maximum size of a paragraph: 7,990 bytes.

Tip 26-3

Overcoming Line Element Limits

The limit of 725 line elements per frame is most likely to cause problems if you are creating a multi-column document in a small point size such as a phone directory. Let's assume you are creating a three-column directory. To place more than 725 line elements on a page, draw two frames over the second and third columns. Load the document into the base page as usual, then select the first frame and click on the name of the text file in the sidebar. Text will now flow into the second column. Repeat the procedure to flow text into the second frame. Now mark the two frames as repeating frames. Ventura will automatically repeat the format for as many pages as necessary to contain the whole document.

Tip 26-4

Minimizing the Size of Database Output

Every paragraph, no matter how long, consumes at least 64 bytes of RAM. So a one-word paragraph will take up 64 bytes, the same as a paragraph with nine words. You can reduce the amount of RAM consumed by a document by setting up your database program to generate two consecutive line breaks rather than paragraph breaks to start each new line. (You need two consecutive line breaks because Ventura will ignore single-line breaks.) To generate a line break, set up your database program to emit an R surrounded by angle brackets (<R>). Of course, you still have to insert a paragraph mark occasionally, to avoid violating the 7,990-byte limit for individual paragraphs.

27

Utilities

Recent medical studies have shown that it's the little things in life which can kill you. So it's not surprising that it's also the little things in life which can save you. Utility programs help you overcome limitations and can make the difference between your computer-life being frustrating or fruitful.

In addition to the utilities discussed in this chapter, a number of other utilities are covered elsewhere in this book:

- Chapter 5, "Monitors": Soft Kicker

- Chapter 9, "Working with Style Sheets": Pub*Star, VPTool-box

- Chapter 19, "Screen Snapshots": Frieze, Hotshot Graphics

- Chapter 22, "Font Tools": FaceLift, ATM for Windows, Bitstream Fontware, SuperPrint, Publisher's PowerPak, MoreFonts, SoftCraft's Fontware, Type Director, Font Effects,

Publisher's Type Foundry, SoftType, fontART, Font Effects, and WYSIfonts!

- Chapter 23, "Speed Tips": Various disk caching and disk optimizing programs

- Chapter 25, "Printing Tips": PrintCache

- Chapter 26, "Memory Limitations and Solutions": HIMEM.SYS, 386[MAX]

Profile

XVP/Tabs

One of the high points of the Professional Extension is the table generator. While this feature is exceptional, its ability to read 1-2-3 print files is somewhat limited, especially with financial information. If you often rely on information from worksheets, XVP/Tabs automates many worksheet-related features that are still manual in the Professional Extension.

While the Professional Extension requires that you print your 1-2-3 worksheet to a file before loading it into Ventura, XVP/Tabs can import Lotus worksheet (WKS) files directly. This means two things: first, you don't have to format your spreadsheet carefully (with at least two spaces between each column), as you do with the Professional Extension, and you don't have to print the worksheet to an ASCII file.

More importantly, XVP/Tabs automatically calculates all tab stops and sets them in the Ventura style sheet. It then tags the worksheet so that it works with the style sheet. It also sets up single and double ruling lines for the rows in the worksheet which used dashes or equal signs as separator rows.

XVP/Tabs automates the following features which are necessities for properly formatting financial data: aligns dollar signs in columns, works with mixed number formats, allows you to use bold for any range, moves dollar signs outside parenthesis of negative numbers, maintains indenting of row labels, understands

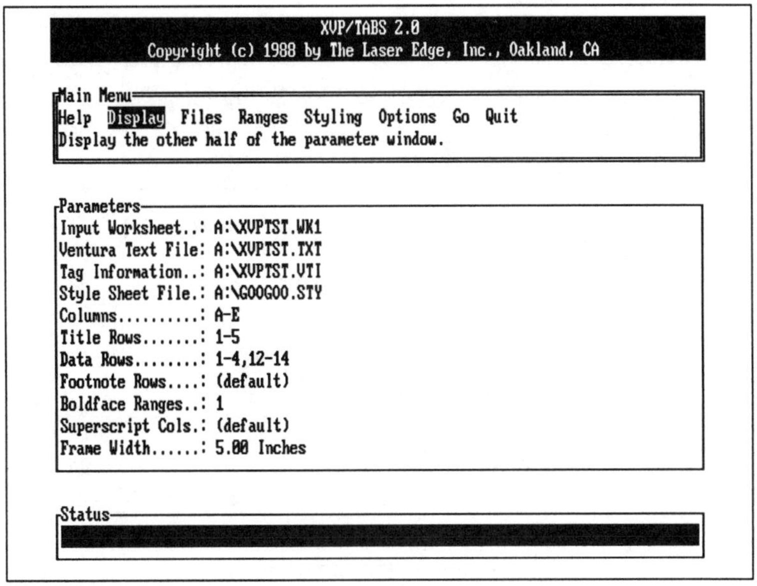

Figure 27-1: In the Main Menu for XVP/Tabs, you define the portions of your spreadsheet that you want to import into Ventura.

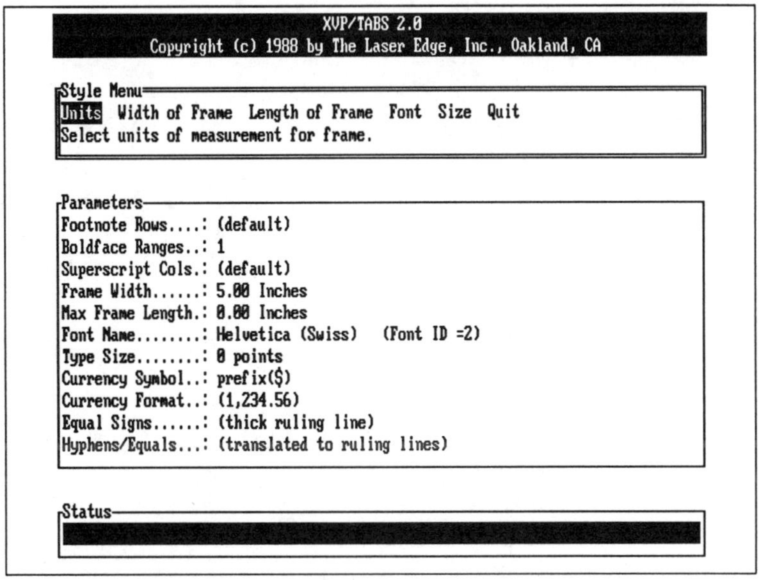

```
                        XVP/TABS 2.0
            Copyright (c) 1988 by The Laser Edge, Inc., Oakland, CA

Main Menu
Help  Display  Files  Ranges  Styling  Options  Go  Quit
Display the other half of the parameter window.


Parameters
Input Worksheet..: A:\XVPTST.WK1
Ventura Text File: A:\XVPTST.TXT
Tag Information..: A:\XVPTST.VTI
Style Sheet File.: A:\GOOGOO.STY
Columns..........: A-E
Title Rows.......: 1-5
Data Rows........: 1-4,12-14
Footnote Rows....: (default)
Boldface Ranges..: 1
Superscript Cols.: (default)
Frame Width......: 5.00 Inches


Status
```

Figure 27-2: More formatting information is supplied in the Style Menu, including currency units, width and length of frame, font, and type size. XVP/Tabs then creates your Ventura tags.

```
                        XVP/TABS 2.0
            Copyright (c) 1988 by The Laser Edge, Inc., Oakland, CA

Style Menu
Units  Width of Frame  Length of Frame  Font  Size  Quit
Select units of measurement for frame.


Parameters
Footnote Rows....: (default)
Boldface Ranges..: 1
Superscript Cols.: (default)
Frame Width......: 5.00 Inches
Max Frame Length.: 0.00 Inches
Font Name........: Helvetica (Swiss)    (Font ID =2)
Type Size........: 0 points
Currency Symbol..: prefix($)
Currency Format..: (1,234.56)
Equal Signs......: (thick ruling line)
Hyphens/Equals...: (translated to ruling lines)


Status
```

and preserves titles centered over two columns, and keeps footnote references formatted properly. The program understands foreign currency punctuation as well.

Profile

DataTAG

Ventura is a natural for typesetting all types of databases and directories. It even has features designed especially for this, such as automatic headers and footers — but it's not all that easy. Because directories often have columns just like spreadsheets, you might be tempted to use a tab conversion program with a database file, and while this would work, it's not the most practical way to go. DataTAG is the best idea for printing files from any database program with Ventura. It's one of those simple programs that does its job, sometimes without much grace, but always with speed, accuracy, and efficiency.

DataTAG works especially well with Ventura, where you can automatically add ruling lines, gray screens, and keep groups of lines together. DataTAG uses standard comma-delimited files, which almost every database in creation can generate. Even many spreadsheets use this format, and DataTAG could be used with spreadsheets as well, though a program such as Tabin would be more suitable. DataTAG looks at a file and sees how many fields are in each record. It then asks you what you want to tag each of the fields. DataTAG then creates a separate line for each field, preceded with whatever tag name you specify. The documentation that comes with the program consists of a few pieces of paper, but it's enough.

All is not perfect, however. My biggest complaint is that if you want to publish the same database over and over, you still must manually type the tag names for each field, and this is both tedious and an obvious place for good old human error to creep in. If you enter a tag name even slightly different from what's in your Ventura style sheet, you won't get the results you expected.

The program's author has said this will be corrected in a future version. Still, DataTAG is the easiest way to import database files and reports into Ventura. It's one of those programs that is so simple, someone should have invented it sooner, and it's something you quickly come to depend on.

Profile

XVP/Base

XVP/Base, from the makers of XVP/Tabs, is specifically designed to import dBase files into Ventura. Unlike DataTAG, which works with any program that creates comma-delimited files, XVP/Base works with dBase only.

If you use dBase, you know how difficult it can be to program a special report. But now, lo and behold, XVP/Base can do the programming for you. You start by creating a sample page in Ventura, with sample data formatted the way you will want the final data to look. VP/Base enables you to insert Ventura formatting codes into your sample page, so you can format different fields in different ways: some bold, some italic, and some in different fonts entirely. VP/Base then checks the Ventura file, and creates a dBase program. When you run the dBase program, your data is specifically formatted for Ventura. It's a slick system, and because you can run the dBase program VP/Base creates over and over, you can update your dBase repeatedly as it changes.

Profile

WP2VP

WP2VP is designed to fine-tune formatted WordPerfect documents prior to importing into Ventura. One pass through WP2VP converts a standard WordPerfect file to one that follows strict typesetting conventions. It converts underlines to italics, corrects the kerning around em dashes and between the period marks in an ellipsis, and replaces double spaces after periods with typographically correct single spaces. It also converts WordPerfect's own footnote commands to Ventura format. WP2VP is fast and safe, as it creates a new file and leaves your old one unchanged. It's also easy to configure. A file in regular WordPerfect format has a list of conversion features; you simply choose the ones you want.

The companion program to WP2VP is VP2WP, which does just the opposite: it strips Ventura codes from your file, leaving straight WordPerfect text. Once again, you can configure the program to leave in tag names, or any other Ventura codes, so your file is exactly the way you want it. You can even configure VP2WP to insert specific WordPerfect functions such as centering, bold, indent, shift indent (left and right margins), and tabs, to replace specific Ventura tags. The config file lets you specify what Word-Perfect functions to substitute for Ventura tags. Just being able to automatically convert underlines to italics is worth the price of WP2VP. Just being able to remove some of Ventura's more verbose codes without endless, confusing search and replace is worth the price of VP2WP.

Figure 27-3: This is the configuration file for WP2VP, showing the typographical adjustments that will automatically be made.

```
CONFIGURATION FILE FOR wp2vp«
«
Switches moved to the left margin in this file will be OFF (they must«
immediately follow a [HRt]).  Switches can be toggled ON or OFF from their«
configuration file settings by including them on the command line.«
«
OFF  ON «
«
-f         = when ON, converts footnotes to Ventura format.«
«
-h         = when ON, converts 2 hyphens to a Ventura dash.«
«
-i         = when ON, converts underline to italics.«
«
-k         = when ON, kerns certain triplets.«
«
-p         = when ON, substitutes 1 space for 2 spaces.«
«
-q         = when ON, converts double-quotes (") to Ventura«
                     left- and right-hand quotes (<169> and <170>).«

                                                              «
    ↓ on conventional screens, Press  PgDn  for 3 more switches below  ↓«

A:\WP2VP.CFG                                    Doc 1 Pg 1 Ln 1" Pos 0.25"
```

TAGteam

TAGteam takes WordPerfect file conversion one step farther than mere conversion — it actually does the tagging for you. For example, instead of entering "@HEADLINE" in your WordPerfect file, you can instruct TAGteam to give this tag to any line that was centered and bold. This feature is especially useful when you are creating paragraphs for which Ventura requires more than one tag. The most frequent case in which this is necessary is when a paragraph is justified, but needs a tab, such as when you have a paragraph number, a tab, then the rest of the paragraph. Ventura can't use regular tabs in justified paragraphs, but you can achieve the same effect using the Breaks feature, so that the second paragraph will start where the first leaves off. When TAGteam sees a paragraph with a tab in the middle, it breaks the paragraph into several separate paragraphs, each with its own tag. Then all you have to do to achieve the right formatting is adjust the Breaks.

TAGteam does not automatically turn underlines into italics, but it does allow you to insert less conspicuous codes, which it will translate into Ventura's. ALT 174 and ALT 175 take a lot less space than <MI> and <D> and are ignored by style and grammar checking programs (one warning: many European countries use these symbols instead of quotation marks). TAGteam will also translate other ALT commands in the file into full Ventura tag names.

If you often work with symbols, TAGteam will automatically translate the symbols of the IBM-PC symbol set into the Ventura symbol set. Because Ventura's symbols aren't in the same order as the PC's, this is no small task, since it means changing fonts and selecting different characters in Ventura's font set.

TAGteam also works the other way around, taking fully-tagged Ventura files and stripping the codes or converting them to its own less obtrusive format. One drawback is that unlike WP2VP, you can't control what codes are not converted — it's all or nothing. TAGteam has an easy-to-use menu-driven interface and comprehensive documentation. It does more than WP2VP, but allows you less control over what features you want to use or avoid.

❖ Additional PostScript Support

Profile
VP/Saddle

Remember those leather wallet kits you got as a kid? I bet you didn't know that Ventura could sew through leather, did you? Well, it can't. And if you fell for that one, you don't know what a saddle stitch is. If you take apart a booklet or magazine, you'll notice that page 2 and 3 are on two different pieces of paper. In a sixteen page booklet, page 2 and page 15 are on the same piece of paper, page 3 and page 14 on another, and so on. When you duplicate these pages back to back, and staple them in the middle, you get a finished publication.

But Ventura normally doesn't work this way. It normally puts one page on one piece of paper, or at most, two smaller pages on a single sheet. Since Ventura won't flow text backwards, there's no way to put page 2 where page 16 should be, then flow the text back to page 3 at the front.

So until VP/Saddle, you had to print the pages, paste them together in the proper order, and take them some place to be produced in mass quantities.

Now Ventura can work this minor miracle, if you have a PostScript printer and VP/Saddle. VP/Saddle is a fiendishly clever piece of work. You create your file as usual, using half size pages (5½ by 8½ inches) in the page layout menu. You print the file to disk, then run VP/Saddle. The disk file is actually a PostScript program that Ventura has written. VP/Saddle goes through and rearranges this file, so that pages print out in the correct saddle-stitched order. VP/Saddle takes only a few seconds and requires no special formatting.

◆ Two-Up

That would be enough for one program, but VP/Saddle does more. The Two-Up option allows you to make two copies of half size pages on the same piece of paper. When you do go to the dreaded photocopy machine, your money goes twice as far — each single copy making two copies of your page.

◆ Enlarged Format

VP/Saddle's Enlarged Format is a way to improve the apparent print quality from a laser printer. If you are working with half size, or trade paperback-size pages (6 by 9 inches), this feature will enlarge your page to fill an entire 8½- by 11-inch piece of paper. When you go to have your publication mass-produced, the printer can set his camera to shrinking the pages to the size you wanted originally, thus improving the visible resolution of your type. You could do this without VP/Saddle, but you would have to calculate everything manually, and select type sizes larger than you really wanted. VP/Saddle allows you to create pages the size you are going to actually use, which saves a lot of confusion.

Overall, VP/Saddle is a clever, inexpensive, and useful program for owners of PostScript printers. You may not appreciate how useful these features are until you actually try them, but believe me, they can make a big difference.

❖ File/Style Management

Profile

VP Manager

You've heard the annoying old adage: "Too many cooks spoil the broth," and there are times when this is all too true. If you've got a big group working with one Ventura chapter or publication, you can run into questions like these: What's this chapter about? What do all the tags in this style sheet do? What files are in this chapter?

Who's working on this chapter? Who worked on it last? How far along is it? What draft is it? Where's that chapter we did that touted mayonnaise as the cure-all for the next century?

VP Manager is designed specifically for work groups using Ventura. Work Group Computing is the latest buzzword in the techno biz, and you work groups out there (you know who you are) will be pleased to know you don't have to wait for software aimed straight between your eyes. The best part is that VP Manager runs right inside of Ventura. This means that the interface is consistent with Ventura: there aren't new commands to learn, and you don't have to leave Ventura and run a separate program or try to scratch out illegible notes which look like a chicken wrote them.

VP Manager starts with a Mac-like desktop that can display all your files, or just Ventura chapters and style sheets. The desktop provides file management, and besides letting you copy, rename, or move chapters, it makes Ventura's Multi-Chaptering functions as easy as dragging a little chapter icon from one window to another.

◆ Chapter Description and History

VP Manager allows you to keep track of who did what, and when. You can enter a 144-character description of each chapter and give each chapter a category as well as assign keywords that you can search for later. The program displays the name, location, and date of all associated files, text, graphics, styles, and width tables. You can print a quick rundown on all your tags and their basic features, such as typeface, size, weight, tabs, and special effects. The report generator gives you printed reports on any chapter or publication. You can search for chapters using the keywords or categories you entered.

◆ Do you need it?

The trick with any program like this is that you do have to go out of your way and enter all the information, otherwise the program

Figure 27-4:
The Chapter
Info menu of VP
Manager lets
you attach a
144-character
description of a
chapter, along
with keywords
and other
descriptive
information.

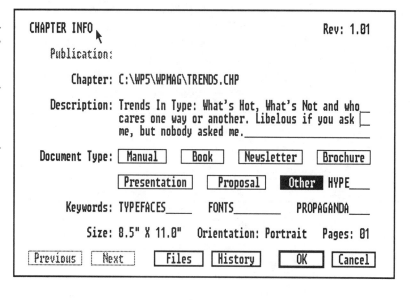

Figure 27-5:
With the Job
Tracking menu of
VP Manager, you
can identify the
status of a docu-
ment as it moves
through the
various stages of
editing and
production.

is useless. If you're not willing (or won't remember) to enter the information necessary to properly catalog your chapters, then most of VP Manager's features won't do you much good. But if you are diligent about such details, VP Manager will help you keep track of your Ventura files. And if you have a number of people doing work on the same files, VP Manager can take the mystery and confusion out of the who's, what's, and when's of our Ventura publications.

Profile

VPMover

Problem: you want to archive complete Ventura Publisher chapters onto floppies, but either they don't fit or they take so much space that you end up with stacks and stacks of floppies.

Solution: VPMover. VPMover is an inexpensive and thoughtfully designed utility that allows you to "multi-chapter" Ventura chapters and save tons of disk space by putting them into ARC (or ZIP or LZH) files—simultaneously.

First, let me explain "multi-chaptering" and "ZIP" programs. Because a single Ventura chapter can contain files spread over countless directories or even hard disks, you can't just copy the file individually. If you did, Ventura would no longer know where to look for the files. Ventura's own multi-chaptering function copies all the files associated with the chapter, and then edits the new chapter file so it knows the location of all the newly copied files.

"ARC" is a program which does two basic things: the program uses sophisticated algorithms to compresses files so they end up being only 30 to 80 percent of their original size (the average is about 50 percent), and a single ARC file can contain many other files. The only way to use or view these files once they've been "arced" is to "unarc" them, using an unarcing program. Currently there are three standards, the ARC format, the newer ZIP format, and the LZH format out of Japan. All three save about the same amount of space and take about the same amount of time. These programs can take from a few seconds to a few minutes to archive files, depending on their size. VPMover can use any ARC, ZIP, or LZH program, and it comes with a copy of LZH because that program is in the public domain.

I know, you're thinking, "Why can't I just use any old ARC program and do it myself?" but it's not that simple. It would be difficult to use just an arcing program because first you'd have to locate all the necessary files. Even then, it wouldn't be true "multi-chaptering," because it wouldn't update the chapter file so that Ventura would know where all the files are now located.

But VPMover does it all in one easy step. VPMover looks at your Ventura chapters, finds all the files no matter where they are, and adds them to a single ARC file. Besides arcing your original chapter file, VPMover creates a new one that contains the arced location of your files. If you need to use them again, you can either unarc them in the same directory where you arced them, or use the "replace" batch file VPMover creates to copy them all back to their original locations. If you wish, VPMover will also do a standard multi-chapter copy, without compressing the files.

VPMover is the kind of software that has been so refined there are no rough edges. It's a simple utility and what it does it does well. It even permits you to choose whether or not you want to move or arc your Ventura width table. This is an important feature because PostScript and LaserMaster width tables can take from 150K to 400K, depending on how many fonts they contain. Ventura always copies the width table, and this can be frustrating when the width table nearly fills a standard disk, or won't even fit on one. This feature alone makes VPMover's multi-chaptering more convenient than Ventura's own.

In most cases, after you've Arced a chapter, you want to delete the original files, and once again VPMover automates the process. You can set it to delete the files automatically or to ask you before it deletes each file. To make sure you don't delete a file which might be used in another Ventura chapter, VPMover comes with an additional utility that searches throughout your hard disk (or disks), reads all your Ventura chapters, and searches to see if any files are shared by more than one chapter. If it finds any shared files, it creates a list of those files — an invaluable feature.

VPMover's interface is menu/mouse driven. The manual is concise but clear, and the publisher provides good technical support. Most importantly, the program is completely reliable. The more you use Ventura, the more you need this gem of a utility.

Profile

MouseWare

This program, formerly "Mickey," allows you to control the speed of your mouse when you're inside Ventura (or any other mouse-driven program). There's not much to it: press ALT-F, the computer beeps, the mouse moves faster. Press ALT-F again, the beep gets higher, the mouse moves faster. ALT-S makes it goes slower, and ALT-R resets the mouse to its standard speed. It works.

◆ The Other Button

MouseWare's other big feature is that it allows you to use the second mouse button, the one on the right. Ventura can only use one button, the left one, but MouseWare turns the right button into the Enter key. The real advantage is that instead of having to move the mouse to press OK in menus, you just press the right button. It's a handy little feature.

MouseWare is clever and useful, but it does have a few drawbacks. First is that it takes about 22K of memory. Ventura needs every byte of memory it can get, so 22K is mucho memory for these few, albeit useful, features. If you have EMS this isn't a problem, but if you don't, Ventura will probably run slower and have to write to disk more often.

Second, MouseWare works best with the Microsoft Bus or InPort mouse. If you use it with a serial mouse (such as the PC Mouse or

Logitech) you have to load the mouse driver as well, and that takes another 10K of memory. MouseWare worked fine with EGA, VGA, Hercules, and the full-page Genius monitor. It may not perform perfectly on all full page monitors, so try to check it out first.

Profile

VP to the Max

If you're disappointed that Ventura 3 doesn't have any new features, you're not alone. Luckily, *VP to the Max* has come to the rescue. It's a new "desk accessory" for Ventura which gives both Ventura 2 and 3 (under GEM) important new features—*without taking any memory away from Ventura.*

VP to the Max adds four new items to the Ventura Desk menu: Spell Checker, Thesaurus, Style Sheet View, and Search & Replace. Spell Check is the most important. It's all too easy to make text errors while working on page layout, and it's always a good idea to spell check one last time before your final printout.

Because of the way Ventura can integrate so many different files, it used to be a pain to manually spell check all your files. Now you just pull down the menu and VP to the Max automatically spell checks *all* the files associated with a Ventura chapter, including the captions. The program uses the 116,000-word Merriam-Webster dictionary.

You may spend hours (or days) making everything look perfect in Ventura, but the better a page looks the more typos and spelling erros [sic] jump right off the page. VP to the Max helps you look your best. And if you're the kind of person who likes to use Ventura as a word processing program, then this is what you've been waiting for.

The search and replace feature is a real boon. It means you don't have to go back into your word processing program to make repetitive changes. You can even search and replace style sheet tags or "set font" changes, a real time saver.

The Style Sheet Viewer displays an overview of all your tags, including the name, font size, typeface, weight, alignment, number of tabs, and special effects.

There are two small drawbacks. First, VP to the Max can only spell check ASCII files. This means that once you load your normal word processor files into a Ventura chapter, you must click on "File type/rename," and change the text file to ASCII. Because you can change back to your own word processing format at any time, this is only a minor inconvenience. The second drawback has to do with the way the thesaurus works. It doesn't automatically search on the word under the cursor—you have to type the word manually.

But it's hard to complain about a program which does so much so well. Considering the features VP to the Max adds, it's the best way to upgrade Ventura. In fact, if you're planning on staying with Ventura under GEM (and you don't need all the bug fixes of 3.0), you might think about adding VP to the Max rather than shelling out for the not-all-that-different Ventura 3. VP to the Max is one of the most useful utility programs you can add to Ventura.

28

Label Sheets

In this chapter, I'll explain a simple, straightforward way to print your label sheets with Ventura. Let's assume you're using the standard 1- by 2¾-inch (or 1- by 2⅝-inch) labels sold by Avery and others, and that you're using a laser printer. One option is to print a set of masters on plain paper, then xerox these onto actual label sheets whenever you do a mailing. Another option is to feed the label sheets themselves through the printer. If you do the latter, you'll need to pay attention to a few cautions. First, don't use any label sheet with spaces between labels or with missing labels, since that may cause labels to come loose and get stuck inside the printer. Second, open the rear output tray so that the labels can be ejected flat without having to negotiate the hairpin turn into the paper tray.

In buying labels, it's a good idea to hunt down one of the new types that Avery or James River Corporation make specifically for laser printers. For the 1- by 2⅝-inch size, the Avery labels are part numbers 5260 and 5160, and the James River Corporation labels can be located under the "Pro-Tech Laser Specialties" name.

❖ **Overview**

It's possible to print labels directly from your database program or by using the mail-merge capabilities of your word processing program, but the job is far easier with Ventura. Although most database programs do have a label-printing module, these don't necessarily work well with laser printers. Likewise, the word processor mail-merge approach has problems of its own. For one thing, since not every address has the same number of lines, you have to do a lot of if/then programming to avoid skipped lines in addresses. In addition, it can be confusing to correctly align text in three columns even with the best word processing software.

With Ventura, labels are easy. In a nutshell, the strategy is to set up your database as a text file and then load it into Ventura. In the text file, each address is a single paragraph, within which the lines that make up the address are separated by line breaks. Between each pair of addresses is a blank paragraph that acts as a space filler exactly one inch tall. The space filler measures its height from the top line of one address to the top line of the next address, making it possible to have two, three, four, or five-line addresses without disrupting the placement of addresses in a regular grid on the page.

The space-filler paragraph is the secret ingredient that makes labels easy to print with Ventura. With this approach, your style sheet will need only two tags, one containing the formatting information for the address itself, the other containing the formatting information for the space-filler paragraph.

❖ Preparing the Text File

Now let's get more specific. Before doing anything with Ventura, you need to convert your database into a text file. Let's say you're using dBASE and your database has this structure:

Name
Address1
Address2
City

In my case, it happens to be a dBASE file called IL-LUSTRATORS.DBF. To convert the database to a text file, I type these commands:

Use ILLUSTRATORS
Copy fields Name,Address1,Address2,City to LABELS
sdf delimited with "

In response to these commands, dBASE creates a file called LABELS.TXT. Next, I quit dBASE and from the DOS command line type the following:

Type LABELS.TXT

My data appears in the format shown in Figure 28-1.

Let's give this format the name Format A. As you can see, some labels in my database need three lines and some need four, but as we noted above, dealing with this won't be any problem.

Before you import your own database into Ventura, you'll need to load the text into your word processor and use search-and-replace operations to change it into a new format, which we'll call Format B. It is shown in Figure 28-2.

There are several differences between Format A and Format B. In Format A, each field is separated by a quotation mark followed by a comma followed by a quotation mark. In Format B, each field is separated by the expression <R>, which is Ventura's way of

```
"Computer Support Corporation","15926 Midway
Rd.","Dallas, TX 75244"¶
"Artware Systems, Inc.","3741 Benson Dr.","Raleigh, NC
27609"¶
"T/Maker Co.Maker Co.","1973 Landings Dr.","Mountain
View, CA 94043"¶
"Micrografx, Inc.","1303 Arapaho","Richardson, TX 75081"
"Dynamic Graphics","6000 N. Forest Park Dr.","Peoria, IL
61616"¶
"Image Club","#206 - 2915 - 19th St. NE","Calgary,
Alberta","Canada T2E 7A2"¶
"Desktop Graphics","400 Country Dr.","Suite H","Dover,
DE 19901"¶
"Hewlett-Packard Personal Software Division","3410
Central Expressway","Santa Clara, CA 95051"¶
"Network Technology Corp.","6825 Lamp Post
Lane","Alexandria, VA 22306"¶
"Software Complement","8 Pennsylvania Ave.","Matamoras,
PA 18336"¶
"ImageWorld","P.O. Box 10415","Eugene, OR 97440"¶
"CompuCraft","P.O. Box 3155","Englewood, CO 80155"¶
"GoldMind Publishing","12155 Magnolia Ave. ","Suite
3B","Riverside, CA 92503"¶
"Metro ImageBase, Inc.","18623 Ventura Blvd. ","Suite
210","Tarzana, CA 91356"¶
"PC QUIK, Inc.","394 S. Milledge Ave. ","Suite
200","Athens, GA 30606"¶
```

Figure 28-1: *This is how your data appears when first converted by dBASE into a text file (Format A).*

```
Computer Support Corporation<R>15926 Midway
Rd.<R>Dallas, TX 75244¶
@FILLER = ¶
Artware Systems, Inc.<R>3741 Benson Dr.<R>Raleigh, NC
27609¶
@FILLER = ¶
T/Maker Co.Maker Co.<R>1973 Landings Dr.<R>Mountain
View, CA 94043¶
@FILLER = ¶
Micrografx, Inc.<R>1303 Arapaho<R>Richardson, TX 75081¶
@FILLER = ¶
Dynamic Graphics<R>6000 N. Forest Park Dr.<R>Peoria, IL
61616¶
@FILLER = ¶
Image Club<R>#206 - 2915 - 19th St. NE<R>Calgary,
Alberta<R>Canada T2E 7A2¶
@FILLER = ¶
Desktop Graphics<R>400 Country Dr.<R>Suite H<R>Dover, DE
19901¶
@FILLER = ¶
Hewlett-Packard Personal Software Division<R>3410
Central Expressway<R>Santa Clara, CA 95051¶
@FILLER = ¶
Network Technology Corp.<R>6825 Lamp Post
Lane<R>Alexandria, VA 22306¶
@FILLER =
```

Figure 28-2: *After being converted into this form (Format B), the data is ready for importing into Ventura.*

denoting a line break (i.e., a command to start a new line without starting a new paragraph).

Another difference between the two formats is that in Format A, the records are separated by a quotation mark followed by a paragraph break followed by another quotation mark. In Format B, the records are separated by two paragraph breaks followed by the expression "@FILLER = " followed by two paragraph breaks. Note that the = sign must be preceded and followed by a space.

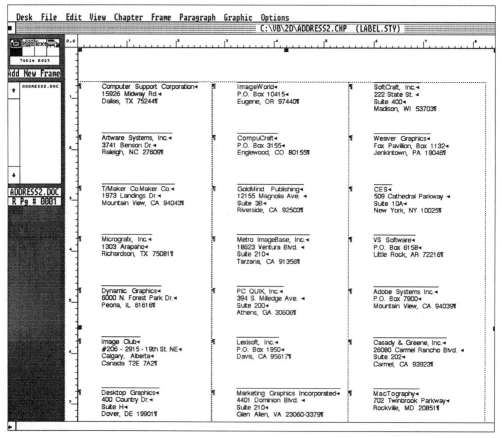

Figure 28-3: *As shown here, the filler tag keeps all the labels aligned in a regular grid, no matter whether they have two-line or three-line addresses. The Ruling Line Above (text-wide) feature has been used to add the short horizontal line above each address.*

This expression tells Ventura that the blank paragraph between two records is to be formatted with a tag called FILLER.

When you're finished converting the file to Format B, save it as an unformatted or ASCII file and give it the extension TXT.

In converting from Format A to Format B, you'll need to find out how your word processor searches and replaces paragraph breaks. In Microsoft Word, you can search for paragraph breaks by using the expression ^p (caret p) in the search-and-replace dialog box. In WordPerfect, you can just press the Enter key when you need to indicate a paragraph break.

❖ Formatting in Ventura

Once you have your database in Format B, you can load Ventura. From the File menu, select Load Different Style and load the DEFAULT.STY style sheet from the \TYPESET subdirectory. Then from the File menu, select Save As New Style and name the new style LABEL.STY.

Now you can load the database. Switch to frame mode and from the File menu select Load Text/Picture. Select the ASCII format and indicate the correct subdirectory and filename. Your unformatted database should appear on the screen. If it does not, select the frame icon, click on the page, then click on the file name in the Assignment List on the left side of the screen.

Note that the expression "@FILLER = " is no longer visible. Ventura has converted it into a tag for the blank paragraph that separates each pair of records.

To set the margins for your page, select Margins & Columns from the Frame Menu. Select 3 for number of columns, enter 1" for the top and bottom margins, and enter 0 for the left and right margins. If you have laser printer label paper, the kind with half of a label at the top and bottom, you can use ½" for the top and bottom margins.

Now it's time to specify the settings for the tags. Switch to tagging mode and click on one of the records in your database. The word Body Text should appear in the Selection Box at the lower left of the screen. This is the default tag that Ventura assigns to any untagged text.

From the Paragraph menu, select Font. You can choose any font available for your printer as long as the size is 10 to 12 points. Again from the Paragraph menu, select Spacing. Enter 0 for Above and Below and 2 picas for In From Left.

Now click on one of the paragraph marks that separates your records. If you can't see a paragraph mark, press Ctrl-T. Once you have selected one of these in-between paragraph marks, you'll see the word FILLER in the Selection box at the lower left of the screen. This is the name of the tag that controls the formatting of the space between each pair of records.

From the Paragraph menu, select Spacing. Make all settings 0 except Below. Set Below to one inch.

Highlight one of the records again. From the Paragraph menu, select Breaks. Set Line Break to None. This forces Ventura to consider only the amount of vertical space taken up by the paragraphs marked FILLER (one inch) and to ignore the vertical space taken up by the addresses themselves. After you press OK, you'll see all the records align themselves so that the top line of each address is exactly one inch from the top line of the next address.

You may be wondering why it was necessary to use two different styles for the label sheet. Wouldn't it have been sufficient merely to have set the Space Below for Body Text such that each pair of records would have been separated by a specified distance? That would work, but only if every address in your database had the same number of lines. Usually, however, that's not the case. Some addresses need only three lines, others need four or five. By using a separate tag for the space between records, you can vary the number of lines in your addresses without affecting the placement of addresses on subsequent labels.

Now you can save your document and print it on any laser printer. You can experiment with fonts and add ruling lines and other enhancements. Next time you have to format a set of label sheets, you'll be able to use the same style sheet and have the same formatting automatically applied.

29

Printing Envelopes

Despite the fact that desktop publishing programs like Ventura have greatly simplified the production of long, complex documents, it still can be surprisingly frustrating to accomplish a simple task like printing out an envelope on your laser printer.

The purpose of this chapter is to lay out a simple, yet powerful, strategy for printing envelopes. Whether you address your envelopes one at a time or print batches of envelopes using addresses generated from a database, this procedure will make things easier.

Let's assume that you're using Commercial #10 envelopes, also known as legal envelopes. The dimensions of this type of envelope are 4⅛ by 9½ inches. Here is the general strategy:

- For the destination address, you'll reduce the size of the base page frame so that it forms a "window" in which you

The return address is a repeating frame, with Upper Left X at 2.00 inches, Upper Left Y at 2.50 inches, Frame Width 3.50 inches, and Frame Height 1.50 inches. (To show the boundaries of the frame, I've surrounded it with a box. Normally, there won't be any box.)

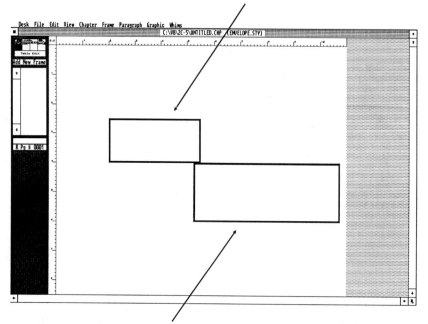

The base page is used to hold the destination address. Using the Sizing & Scaling menu, it is shrunk down so that its Upper Left X is at 5.25 inches and Upper Left Y is at 4.00 inches. The Frame Width is 5.50 inches and the Frame Height is 2.00 inches. (To show the boundaries of the base page frame, I've surrounded it with a box. Normally, there won't be any box.)

Figure 29-1: *The two frames used for the envelope are shown here. A repeating frame is used for the return address and the base page (reduced in size) is used for the destination address.*

can either type addresses directly or load addresses from a file.

- For the return address, which is optional, you'll use a separate frame, type the text once in the frame, and make it a repeating frame so that it automatically is placed on every envelope when you create a batch of envelopes.

- Your style sheet will have two tags, one for the return address and one for the destination address. The destination address tag will use a "Page Break: After" setting so that at the end of each address, Ventura will jump to the next page. To avoid having each line of your address end up on a different page, you'll end each line with a line break (Ctrl-Enter) and only use a paragraph break (Enter) at the end of the whole address.

Now let's look at the procedure in detail.

❖ Procedure

Load Ventura and load the DEFAULT style sheet from the \TYPESET directory. From the Chapter menu, select Page Size & Layout. Lay out the page for landscape orientation, letter-sized paper, and single sides.

◆ The Destination Address Window

Change the dimensions of the base page frame to match the size of your "address window," the area where you will be placing the destination address. To change the size of the base page, select frame mode and click on the base page. From the Frame menu, select Sizing & Scaling. For Upper Left X enter 5.25 inches, for Upper Left Y enter 4.00 inches, for Frame Width Enter 5.50 inches, and for Frame Height enter 2.00 inches.

◆ The Return Address Window

If you want to have Ventura print a return address on each envelope, draw another frame above and to the left of the destination frame. To position the frame correctly, click on the frame and select Sizing & Scaling again. For Upper Left X enter 2.00 inches, for Upper Left Y enter 2.50 inches, for Frame Width enter 3.50 inches, and for Frame Height enter 1.50 inches.

◆ Testing Positions

To test the position of the destination and return address frames on the envelopes, switch to frame mode and click on the destination frame. From the Frame menu, select Ruling Box Around. For Width, enter Frame; for Height of Rule 1, enter .003 inches. Repeat this procedure to set up a ruling box around the return address frame.

Now you can print out a sample envelope. First, open the rear output tray of your laser printer. This will eliminate most paper jams and keep the envelopes from curling too much. To feed envelopes into the printer, it is not necessary to buy a special envelope feeder. On the printers that use the Canon SX engine, such as the LaserJet II, LaserJet IID, Apple LaserWriter IINT, and QMS PS 810, all you have to do is adjust the guides on the manual feed guide (the plastic hood that fits over the paper tray) so that they fit your envelope. Insert an envelope in the guide, face up and stamp end first. When you direct Ventura to print your page, the LaserJet will feed the envelope instead of a sheet of paper.

Having printed an envelope, check on the position of the destination and return address frames and if necessary adjust the settings under Sizing & Scaling in the Frame menu. Next, select Margins & Columns in the Frame menu and make sure all margins for both the destination and return address frames are set to 0.

When you have finished adjusting the sizes of the two frames, get rid of the ruling boxes and try entering an actual address in each frame. Start with the return address. End each line by pressing

Ctrl-Enter, which has the effect of starting a new line without starting a new paragraph. When you're done entering the return address, create a new tag and name it "Return." For Alignment, select Left. For Spacing, enter 0 for Space Above and 0 for In From Left.

◆ **Making the Return Address Repeat**

To make the return address repeat on every envelope, select frame mode, select the return address frame, and select Repeating Frame from the Frame menu.

◆ **Formatting the Destination Address**

Now enter a sample destination address. Again, end each line by pressing Ctrl-Enter, and this time create a new tag called "Destination." Give this tag the same Alignment and Spacing as the Return tag.

If you are printing multiple envelopes, you want each destination address to print on a new page. *Don't try to do this using repeating frames.* Instead, select Breaks from the Paragraph menu and select Page Break: After. By using Ventura's page break feature, you'll be able to create an envelope with a blank destination address simply by pressing Enter.

◆ **Saving the Style Sheet and the Chapter**

Now you're done formatting the frames and tags that you'll need to print envelopes either one at a time or in batches. Save the style sheet and chapter you've created using the Save As New Style and the Save As options from the File menu. For simplicity's sake, call them ENVELOPE.STY and ENVELOPE.CHP.

Let's say you just want to print a single envelope. The procedure is simple: load ENVELOPE.CHP and place the cursor in the destination frame at the beginning of whatever address happens to be in that frame. Either delete the current address or else, as described in the following tip, press Enter to send that address to the next frame. Now enter the address you want, ending each line with Ctrl-Enter rather than Enter so that all the lines of the address remain on the same page. When you're done, select Print from the File menu, and for Which Pages select Current.

Tip 29-1

Building a Personal Mailing List

If you're like most people, you have a certain number of addresses to which you frequently send letters. If so, here's a way to build up a collection of preaddressed envelopes. Use Save As to create a new version of your Envelope chapter as ENVLIST.CHP. Whenever you address an envelope, place the cursor at the beginning and press Enter to "bump" the last address to the next page. Now enter the new destination address and print the current page. If you make a habit of always bumping the last address you entered before addressing a new envelope, after awhile all the addresses you repeatedly need will be in your "stack," and to print an envelope you'll merely have to page through the stack (using PgDn) until you get to the envelope you want to print.

❖ Printing Multiple Envelopes

So far, we've assumed that you're entering one address at a time directly in Ventura; however, the method described in this chapter works just as well for a list of addresses created with a word processor or database program.

If you create addresses with your word processor, make sure to separate each line of the address with a line break or with <R> rather than with a paragraph break. To enter a line break in Microsoft Word, press Shift-Enter. To enter a line break in Word-Perfect, type <R>.

With dBASE, you can use the label generator and print to file, or else use a program such as the one shown in Figure 29-2. This program prints the addresses in California, from the file

```
* DSKPRT.PRG   Print California Addresses
USE NYW INDEX NYWNAME
SET TALK OFF
SET ALTERNATE TO Envelope
SET ALTERNATE ON
CLEAR
TEST = 0
DO WHILE .NOT. EOF()
   IF STATE = 'CA'
      IF CNAME  ' '
         TEST = 1
      ENDIF
      IF TEST = 0
         ? TRIM(FNAME),TRIM(MNAME),TRIM(LNAME)+
         CHR(60)+'R'+CHR(62)
         ? TRIM(ADDRESS)+CHR(60)+'R'+CHR(62)
         ? TRIM(CITY)+',  '+TRIM(STATE),TRIM(ZIP)+CHR(13)+
         CHR(10)
      ELSE
         ? TRIM(FNAME),TRIM(MNAME),TRIM(LNAME)+CHR(60)+'R'+
         CHR(62)
         ? TRIM(CNAME)+CHR(60)+'R'+CHR(62)
         ? TRIM(ADDRESS)+CHR(60)+'R'+CHR(62)
         ? TRIM(CITY)+',  '+TRIM(STATE),TRIM(ZIP)+CHR(13)+
         CHR(10)
      ENDIF
   ENDIF
   SKIP
   TEST = 0
ENDDO
SET ALTERNATE OFF
CLOSE ALTERNATE
RETURN
```

Figure 29-2: A dBASE program to prepare addresses for loading into the envelope destination frame.

NYW.DBF, indexed on NYWNAME to an ASCII disk file. Naturally you will substitute your own DBF and NDX files. You must also substitute your own filename choice for "Envelope." When the file is printed to disk it will have the name ENVELOPE.TXT.

Your selection criteria should be substituted for IF STATE = 'CA'. Notice that this program, in a simple manner, takes care of addresses that have a company name or any type of optional address line, such as c/o (in care of). The CHR(60)+'R'+CHR(62) places a new line character string (<R>) at the end of all lines except the last line. After the ZIP field, an extra carriage return and line feed are printed to give Ventura a paragraph break.

Tip 29-2

About Envelopes

Avoid feeding the following kinds of envelopes into a laser printer:

- *damaged envelopes or those already run through the printer*
- *those with unusual construction or texture, or bulky side seams*
- *those with metal clasps, strings, transparent windows*
- *those with peel-off or pressure-sensitive adhesives*
- *those with ink or dyes that can't stand 200 degrees C*
- *those made of synthetic materials*

Make sure your envelopes have a sharp, thin crease on the leading edge. Diagonal or center-seam envelopes work the best.

30

Voodoo Tricks

Like any other big, powerful computer application, Ventura has some rough edges, some mysteries. This chapter is devoted to explaining how to fix some of the things that inexplicably go wrong from time to time (or all the time, depending on your particular karma).

❖ Crashing

There are two ways to crash. One is for Ventura to simply dump you unceremoniously back at the DOS prompt. I call this "being deported." The other way is for the system to simply freeze up. I call this "being jailed." Call them what you like, these dismissals from the good graces of the program are no fun. Fortunately, there are some things you can do to avoid crashing.

Probably the most frequent cause of crashes is a document that is too large to hold in conventional memory. When a document is too large, Ventura "swaps out" the excess portion of the document to a "spill file" on your hard disk. Spill files aren't supposed to cause crashes, but sometimes they do. Perhaps the simplest solution, at least with the base version (with the Professional Extension and EMS, it doesn't really matter), is to limit the size of your chapters to about 20 pages. Another solution is to free up conventional memory so that there's more available for your document. A variety of measures such as adding EMS to your system (yes, it does help to have EMS even when you're using the base version) are outlined in Chapter 26, "Memory Limitations and Solutions."

If a chapter you are trying to work on is frequently crashing, the first thing you should try is to delete the VP.INF (or VPPROF.INF, in the case of the Professional Extension) from your \VENTURA directory. This file becomes corrupted when Ventura crashes, and once it is corrupted, it can lead to more crashes. After you delete VP.INF, you'll notice that all your defaults (like whether column guides are hidden or shown, whether the ruler is hidden or shown, etc.) have been lost. But it's easy enough to reset them. In

Figure 30-1: If you click repeatedly on the Quit button, you have a good chance of being returned to your document unscathed.

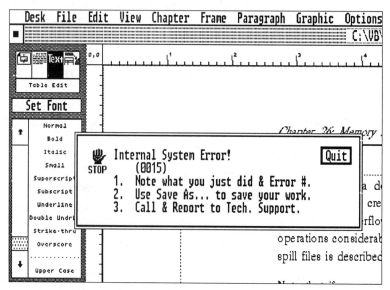

any case, the next time you save your chapter, you'll notice that Ventura has created a new VP.INF.

❖ Some Appeals are Granted

Sometimes when Ventura decides to crash, the screen simply freezes. Other times it shows you a dialog box such as the one shown in Figure 30-1. This dialog box may seem like a sort of rude joke, since when you click on the Quit button you generally get no response. But surprisingly enough, if you obsessively click on the Quit button (20 or 30 clicks), you sometimes are mysteriously granted clemency: the dialog box disappears, and you're free to resume working on your document. Don't assume that everything's OK! Those error messages meant that your computer's memory got corrupted somehow, so what you need to do is make a clean getaway and return when the coast is clear. First, go into the Set Preference dialog box in the Options menu and turn the "Keep Backup Files" option on. Save under a new name. Exit Ventura, reboot, load Ventura again, and open the chapter you just saved with Save As. It should be OK, but if it's not you can rename the backup chapter file by changing the $HP extension of the file to CHP using the DOS Rename command, and load the chapter.

❖ Watch Out for the Pause Button

Pressing the Pause button on some keyboards can cause the screen to freeze up. If this happens, pressing either Delete key will release you from bondage.

❖ Post-Crash Hard Disk Cleanup

When Ventura freezes up, you usually have to press Ctrl-Alt-Del or even turn off the computer to resume work. Either way, you often end up with lost clusters on your hard disk, which are the remnants of temporary files created by the program. To get rid of these lost clusters type **CHKDSK /F**. This will convert the lost clusters into files, which you can then delete.

❖ Those Disappearing Screen Fonts (DOS/GEM Version)

One of the nice new features of Ventura is that it can display large screen fonts (72 points or more) at their actual size. Sometimes, however, the program suddenly loses the ability to display these large screen fonts (usually due to a lack of sufficient memory for the screen buffer to hold the fonts). When this happens, the first thing to do is to delete the VGAFSTR.INF or EGAFSTR.INF file from your \VENTURA directory. Usually that will solve the problem. To make sure it doesn't happen again, you might experiment with increasing the size of your screen font buffer using the /F switch in the VP.BAT file, as explained in Chapter 23, "Speed Tips."

❖ Backup Files

If you've had the Back Up Copy option on (did you read the "Safety Tips" chapter?), then you have an extra level of insurance in case a chapter refuses to load or continually crashes. Find the file with the same name as your chapter (CHP) file but with the extension $HP. This is the previous version of your chapter file. Delete the CHP file and rename the $HP file so that it has the extension CHP. Now reload.

❖ Redrawing the Screen with Esc

Sometimes "junk" such as stray characters or ruling lines accumulates on the screen. Or when you highlight a passage of text and then attempt to highlight a different passage, the first passage stays highlighted. In any such case where the screen display becomes degraded, pressing Esc will cause it to redraw. There are other ways to redraw the screen, such as pressing PgDn and then PgUp, or clicking on the scroll bar, but press Esc is the quickest.

❖ A Totally Scrambled Screen

If you've installed Hotshot's screen capture utility (GRAB) with a Wyse WY-700, you're in for a rude surprise the first time you press the hot key (Alt-H). The screen suddenly turns into complete chaos. To eliminate the chaos, press F2 and proceed as usual.

❖ Delete Key Won't Work

On some keyboards, one of the delete keys won't work. If this happens to you, try using the delete key on the numeric keypad.

❖ Shift-Ctrl

Sometimes the text cursor refuses to respond when you press the arrow keys, making it hard to edit your document. The reason this is happening is that you accidentally pressed the Shift-Ctrl combination, putting Ventura into its "no mouse" mode where the arrow keys substitute for the movement of the mouse. To get back into Ventura's regular mode, press Shift-Ctrl again, using the Shift and the Ctrl keys on the right side of the keyboard.

❖ Disappearing Formats

Sometimes when you load Ventura, you'll find that words or phrases that were formatted to be italic or bold have mysteriously lost their formatting. The most common reason is that you have placed an index mark or an anchor mark within the word, causing everything after the mark to lose its formatting. The only solution is to avoid placing such marks within formatted text.

❖ Fixing an Isolated Paragraph Mark

After you load text into Ventura, you'll sometimes notice a blank line with nothing on it but the paragraph sign (¶). This happens if there is a space after the period in the last sentence of a paragraph. To get rid of the unwanted blank line, select text mode, place the cursor in front of the paragraph mark, and press Backspace.

❖ Things that Go Beep in the Night

When you're loading text, you may hear a beep. This occurs if there are more than 128 text files in the directory from which you are loading text. The purpose of the beep is to notify you that only the first 128 files in the directory are being listed.

❖ Problems Changing Text Attributes

Sometimes when you try to apply text attributes to a word or phrase, using the list of attributes in the text mode sidebar, you'll find that the attributes won't take effect. The first thing to do is to press Esc, which will cause the screen to redraw. The next thing you should do is highlight the passage, select Normal from the list of attributes, and then select your attributes again. If this does not work, the problem is that hidden attribute settings are preempting the attributes you wish to apply to the text. For example, when you highlight a passage and select Bold, the text will remain in italics. In that case, position the cursor just in front of the material you are attempting to reformat and press Del. You'll know you're in the right location when you see the words "Attr. Setting" in the lower left corner of the screen.

❖ Create a Null Paragraph Before Inserting Text

Sometimes when you try to paste a block of text from the clipboard into a new location, the text inexplicably takes on the attributes of the paragraph immediately above it or — equally annoying — applies its attributes to the preceding paragraph. The solution is to create a null paragraph at the insertion spot (by pressing Enter once) and format this paragraph as Body Text (usually pressing F10 in text mode will work), then press Ins to paste the text from the clipboard.

❖ Moving Large Blocks of Text Within a Chapter

If you want to move a small passage of text from one place to another, you simply highlight the text by holding down the mouse button while you drag the cursor across the passage, press Del, move the cursor to the new insertion point, and press Ins. If the passage spans more than one page, however, you have a problem, since it's not possible to highlight more than one page of text at a time. The solution is to temporarily change the Body Text tag to a very small point size, such as two or three points. You can then highlight the entire passage, press Del, move to the insertion point, press Ins, then change the tag back to the normal font size.

❖ Amaze Your Friends by Customizing Ventura's Menus! (DOS/GEM Version)

Did you buy the English-language version of Ventura because there's no version for your language? Do you want to have a special version of Ventura that contains obscene, insulting error messages? Do you feel like changing the Desk menu so that Walter J. Fudd is listed as one of the members of the Ventura programming team? It's all up to you, since the text strings used for the titles and contents of Ventura's menus are all located in two easily edited text files called VP.RSC and VP.RS1 (or

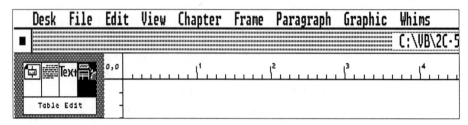

Figure 30-2: *As shown here ("Whims" substituted for "Options" on the menu line) you can change the titles of Ventura's menus by editing the VP.RSC and VP.RS1 files. Will this make you more productive? Definitely not. Will playing with your VP.RSC and VP.RS1 files cause Ventura to crash? Quite possibly. Is it something you should waste your time doing just so your friends and associates will call you a nerd? Of course.*

VPPROF.RSC and VPPROF.RS1 for the Professional Extension). ***Be forewarned, however: messing around with these files can easily cause Ventura to crash the next time you load it!*** Still, if you back up any altered files you change before proceeding, you should be able to recover in case you make a mistake.

To change one of the files (after backing it up), load the file into your text processor and substitute any characters for the text strings in the file, but *keep the length of any character strings you change exactly the same.* For example, as shown in Figure 30-2, I've changed the name of my Options menu to "Whims," by editing VPPROF.RS1. Since the word *Whims* has only five letters, while *Options* has seven, I added two blank spaces after *Whims* so that the new text string kept the same number of characters as the old text string.

When you're done making your replacements, save the file (unformatted, of course), then reload Ventura.

31

Using Ventura
Without a Mouse

The premise of this chapter — that anyone would even consider using Ventura without a mouse — may strike you as silly. Frequently, however, people want to start using the program before they have had time to purchase a mouse, or they're having some difficulty configuring Ventura for use with a particular mouse and want to get started anyway. This chapter is intended for those who find themselves sans mouse, for whatever reason.

❖ Windows Version

In the Windows version, there's no way to cursor around the screen without having a mouse installed. The only thing you can do is press Alt F X, which takes you into the File menu and then selects the Exit command. Because you can't move around the screen in the Windows version, it really isn't practical to use this

Table 31-1: Keyboard Equivalents
for Mouse Operations (DOS/GEM version)

Assign function keys (from any mode) . . . . .Ctrl-K
Call up most recent menu . . . . .Ctrl-X
Cancel a menu . . . . .Ctrl-X
Click the mouse button . . . . Home
Copy text, graphics, or frames to the clipboard . . . . Shift-Del
Cut text, graphics, or frames to the clipboard . . . . Del
Edit special item . . . . Ctrl-D
Fill Attributes . . . . .Ctrl-F
Go to page . . . . Ctrl-G
Hide sidebar . . . . Ctrl-W
Hide tabs and returns . . . . .Ctrl-T
Insert text, graphics, or frames from the clipboard . . . . Ins
Insert special item . . . . Ctrl-C
Line attributes . . . . .Ctrl-L
Move the cursor in finer increments . . . . Shift-Cursor
Press and hold the mouse button . . . . End
Release the mouse button . . . . Home
Renumber chapter . . . . .Ctrl-B
Save chapter . . . . .Ctrl-S
Select "Add New Frame" Ctrl-2
Select "Add New Tag" Ctrl-2
Select Enlarged view . . . . .Ctrl-E
Select frame mode . . . . Ctrl-U
Select graphics mode . . . . .Ctrl-P
Select tagging mode . . . . Ctrl-I
Select text editing mode . . . . Ctrl-O
Select Reduced view . . . . .Ctrl-R
Select Normal view . . . . Ctrl-N
Select OK in a menu . . . . Enter
Select "Set Font" Ctrl-2
Select "Ins New Table" Ctrl-2
Send graphic to back . . . . .Ctrl-Z
Send graphic to front . . . . Ctrl-A
Select all graphics in the frame . . . . Ctrl-Q

version without a mouse. It's a different story in the DOS/GEM version, however.

❖ General Operations (DOS/GEM version)

- To get around the screen without a mouse, use the up and down cursor keys. The cursor will move in discrete jumps. To get more precise positioning, hold down the Shift key while you move the cursor keys. The cursor will move much more slowly and in smaller increments.

- In situations where you'd need to click the button on the mouse, press the Home key.

- In situations where you'd need to hold down the button on the mouse, such as dragging a frame or a graphic, press End. Then to "release" the button on the mouse, press Home.

- Use the keyboard shortcuts shown in Table 31-1 to avoid continually traveling to the menu line.

❖ Special Techniques (DOS/GEM version)

- When you first boot up the program, you should be able to move the cursor around the screen using the cursor keys instead of the mouse. If not, hold down the Shift key on the right side of the keyboard while pressing Ctrl.

- To create a new tag, press Ctrl-I to select tagging mode. Place the cursor within a paragraph and press Home to select the paragraph. Then press Ctrl-2 to select Add New Tag.

- To get rid of a menu you have pulled down, move the cursor outside the menu and press Home.

- To draw a frame, select frame mode with Ctrl-U, press Ctrl-2 to select Add New Frame, move the cursor to the upper left corner of the new frame, press End, cursor to the lower right corner, and press Home.

- To move a frame, place the cursor inside it and press End, then move the cursor to the new location and press Home.

- To stretch a frame, place the cursor over one of the small black squares that function as grabber marks. Press End — the cursor should change to a pointing finger, allowing you to stretch the edge of the frame by moving the cursor keys. If the cursor does not change to a pointing hand, hold down the Shift key while you move the cursor more carefully on top of the grabber mark. Incidentally, it is easier to select the corner grabber marks than the side marks. When you've finished stretching the frame, press Home.

- In text editing mode, you need to use the cursor keys to move the special text editing cursor, which is different from the normal cursor. The text editing cursor holds your place in the text while the other cursor selects operations from menus. To change the cursor keys so that they move the text editing cursor rather than the regular cursor, hold down Shift on the right side of the keyboard while pressing Ctrl.

- To activate Set Font in text editing mode, press Ctrl-2.

❖ Editing VP.BAT (DOS/GEM version)

If your mouse doesn't work, it may be that you selected the wrong kind of mouse during Ventura's installation procedure. Rather than go through the whole procedure again, you can install a different mouse by editing the VP.BAT or the VPPROF.BAT. Load VP.BAT or VPPROF.BAT into your word processor and look at the part that says "M=XX," where XX is a two-digit number such as 01, 21, etc. The first digit stands for the port used by the mouse: 0 for COM1, 1 for COM2, and 2 or 3 for ports other than the COM ports. The second digit stands for the type of mouse: 1 for a Mouse Systems or PC Mouse, 2 for any other type of mouse that uses MOUSE.COM or MOUSE.SYS, 3 for the Microsoft Serial mouse, and a colon (:) instead of a number for an IBM PS/2 mouse. Change the two-digit number, save the file (unformatted), and type VP or VPPROF to load Ventura again.

Appendices

Appendix A

Resources

Ventura wasn't designed to serve as a stand-alone, all-in-one solution. To really get the most out of the program, you'll need other software and hardware tools. Fortunately, Ventura's popularity has made it the focal point of a mini-industry of printers, high-resolution monitors, scanners, graphics programs, fonts, font-editing tools, clip art libraries, special-purpose utilities, user groups, magazines, video training tapes, and much more. This appendix is intended to serve as a sort of traveler's guide to that industry. In some cases our notes are extensive; in other cases we provide no more than an address. Be aware that the information was assembled during Summer and Fall, 1990, and that most products in the computer industry are updated every year or two. As Stewart Brand, publisher of the *Whole Earth Software Catalog*, so aptly put it, trying to keep up with the computer industry is like "trying to count the fragments of an exploding hand grenade." So, happy shopping, and don't forget to keep your flak jacket on!

Clip Art

Adonis Corporation
12310 NE 8th St.
Bellevue, WA 98005
206/747-8186
The company runs a service that provides you with a Windows program for quickly browsing through over 20,000 images of clip art. You can then receive individual images via modem for $4 to $20 each. The catalog includes libraries from numerous companies. In addition to the downloading fee, there is a $35 annual membership fee.

ArtDisks 1–7
DV Franks
3721 Sue Ellen Dr.
Raleigh, NC 27604
919/872-5379
919/878-6123 fax
The topics of ArtDisks 1–7 are buildings, landscapes, and decor; people, animals, and birds; humor and wit; aquatic life; works of art; and Christian images. They appear to be scanned from old books, and all are in MacPaint format except Works of Art (PICT II format) and Christian Images (EPS format). Available on IBM disks.

ArtRight Images
ArtRight Software Corporation
1130 Morrison Drive
Ottawa, Ontario
Canada K2H 9N6
613/820-1000
613/820-2651 fax
These collections are available in Corel Draw (CDR) and EPS formats.

Atech Clip-Art
Atech Software
5962 La Place Court
Carlsbad, CA 92008
800/748-5657
619/438-6883
There are three PCX collections of 50 images each: Business Fun, People, and Holidays.

AtlasPC
MicroMaps
P.O. Box 757
Lambertville, NJ 08530
609/397-1611
800/334-4291
There aren't a lot of maps in these collections, but the quality is excellent. You'll find maps of U.S. states showing county boundaries and major cities, and maps of each continent showing country borders. The formats are EPS and PCX, and all the collections are available on IBM disks.

Canned Art: Clip Art for the Macintosh

Peachpit Press
1085 Keith Ave.
Berkeley, CA 94708
415/527-8555
800/283-9444
415/524-9775 fax

This is not a collection of clip art. Rather, it's a 900-page book (published by yours truly) that shows the contents of approximately 800 clip art collections from over 35 clip art vendors—approximately 15,000 images in all. The size and format of each disk are listed, as well as whether the disk is available in Mac and/or IBM format. The book includes a large topic index, to help you locate the particular piece of clip art you need.

The Church Art Works

875 High Street NE
Salem, OR 97301
503/370-9377
503/362-5231 fax

Five volumes of images in TIFF format are available on IBM disks: Youth Art, Church Life, Sports, Holidays & Seasons, and Books of the Bible.

ClickArt Collections

T/Maker Co.
1390 Villa Street
Mountain View, CA 94041
415/962-0195
415/962-0201 fax

Some of these clip art collections are in EPS format, others in Mac-Paint format. The quality of the EPS Business Art collection (pictures of objects like scissors, staplers, phones, computers, etc.) is superb. The other collections are so-so. All are available on IBM disks. For samples, see Chapter 17, "Clip Art."

Cliptures

Dream Maker Software
7217 Foothill Blvd.
Tujunga, CA 91042

Two volumes of business-related images in EPS format on IBM disks.

Designer ClipArt

Micrografx, Inc.
1303 Arapaho
Richardson, TX 75081
214/234-1769

This collection includes 30 clip art packages from business images and borders to holidays, maps, and religious icons for use with Micrografx Draw, Graph, or Designer.

DeskTop Art/EPS

Dynamic Graphics
6000 N. Forest Park Dr.
Peoria, IL 61614
309/688-8800
800/255-8800
309/688-3075 fax

This is themed clip art in Encapsulated PostScript (EPS) format on IBM disks. For samples, see Chapter 17, "Clip Art." Dynamic Graphics also puts out a bit-mapped collection.

---

clip art

LaserJet fonts

PostScript fonts

font tools

graphics software

monitors

LaserJet-compatible printers

PostScript printers (300 dpi)

PostScript printers and typesetters (above 300 dpi)

other printers

printer controllers

scanners

utilities

user groups

bulletin boards

newsletters and magazines

style sheets

training

PostScript service bureaus

other resources

Digit-Art LaserGraphics

Image Club Graphics
#5, 1902 – 11th Street SE
Calgary, Alberta
Canada T2G 3G2
403/262-8008
800/661-9410
403/261-7013 fax

Currently, Volumes 1–15 of the Digit-Art collection of clip art are available in EPS format on IBM disks. In contrast to some clip art collections, which seem dated, the Image Club illustrations are innovative and contemporary. Since the volumes are not rigidly organized by category, you'll need to write for the Image Club catalog before selecting. For samples, see Chapter 17, "Clip Art."

Dimensions, Natural Images

Artbeats
P.O. Box 20083
San Bernardino, CA 92406
714/881-1200

The Dimension package contains high-tech images and Natural Images represent wood grain, stars, flowers, and water drops. These are all-over designs, intended for use as backgrounds. Each EPS design comes in a high and a low contrast version for IBM or Mac.

GEM Draw Business Library

Digital Research, Inc.
60 Garden Court, Box DRI
Monterey, CA 93942
800/443-4200

Drawn with GEM Draw, these images are not as good as those in most other collections, but the borders are very useful. For a sample, see Chapter 17, "Clip Art."

Graphics Gallery 2.0

Hewlett-Packard Personal
Software Division
3410 Central Expressway
Santa Clara, CA 95051
408/749-9500

This program comes with 300 images, which range from simple shapes to an elegant, classical set of "initial caps" (fancy capital letters). Thousands of additional clip art images are available for $95 per set. These work only with HP Graphics Gallery software.

High Resolution Image Libraries

Network Technology Corp.
6825 Lamp Post Lane
Alexandria, VA 22306
703/765-4506

Images with Impact!

3G Graphics
11410 N.E. 124th Street
Suite 6155
Kirkland, WA 98034
206/367-9321
800/456-0234

Over 500 high-resolution, EPS images (on IBM disks) are grouped into Graphics & Symbols, Business, and Accents & Borders series. The quality is acceptable, but not great.

Mac-Art Library

Kentary, Inc.
P.O. Box 3155
Englewood, CO 80155
303/791-2077
This is a 12-disk library of Mac-Paint clip art on Macintosh disks. Topics include animals, farm life, geography, kitchen, sports, tools, buildings, flowers, trees, plants, greeting cards, people, transportation, signs, symbols, and borders. Check with the manufacturer to see whether it is available on IBM disks.

Mac the Knife

Miles Computing
5115 Douglas Fir Road
Suite I
Calabash, CA 91302
818/340-6300
Although Miles Computing offers a variety of disks, the only one available on IBM disks is Mac the Knife 6: Taking Care of Business. The images appear to be scanned from old books and are in Mac-Paint format.

Metro ImageBase Electronic Art

Metro ImageBase, Inc.
18623 Ventura Blvd. #210
Tarzana, CA 91356
818/881-1997
800/525-1552
This is a superb and very large collection of clip art in TIFF, IMG, and PCX formats, all available on IBM disks. It is derived from the collection of Metro Creative Graphics, a long-time clip art supplier that boasts a library of over a million images. Packages include seasons and holidays, exercise and fitness, weekend sports, team sports, business graphics, computers and technology, art deco, borders and boxes, food, people, and travel. A utility for conversion between formats comes with each package. For examples, see Chapter 17, "Clip Art."

Migraph, Inc.

200 South 333rd St. #200
Federal Way, WA 98003
206/838-4677
206/838-4702 fax
This company has two collections. ScanArt is in IMG format, and DrawArt Professional is in GEM format. Of the two, the DrawArt images are of somewhat higher quality.

Moonlight ArtWorks

Hired Hand Design
3608 Faust Ave.
Long Beach, CA 90808
213/429-2936
This company offers three excellent collections of simple logos and symbols, all in EPS format on IBM disks.

ProArt Professional Art Library

Multi-Ad Services
1720 W. Detweiller Drive
Peoria, IL 61615
309/692-1530
800/447-1950
309/692-8378 fax
These collections, all in EPS format on IBM disks, cover business, holidays, sports, bor-

---

clip art

LaserJet fonts

PostScript fonts

font tools

graphics software

monitors

LaserJet-compatible printers

PostScript printers (300 dpi)

PostScript printers and typesetters (above 300 dpi)

other printers

printer controllers

scanners

utilities

user groups

bulletin boards

newsletters and magazines

style sheets

training

PostScript service bureaus

other resources

ders/headings, food, and people. In general, they're among the most professionally rendered clip art available. If you need a a consistently "commercial" look, this is a great collection.

PS Portfolio

Ltek, Inc.
4546 B10 El Camino Real
Los Altos, CA 94022
415/361-0652

Publisher's PicturePak

Marketing Graphics
Incorporated
4401 Dominion Blvd. #210
Glen Allen, VA 23060-3379
804/747-6991
The clip art in this collection is in PCX and CGM format. Five editions are available: Executive and Management, Finance and Administration, Sales and Marketing, and Federal and State Government. Each contains approximately 200 pictures. For examples, see Chapter 17, "Clip Art."

Spectrum Clip Art

The Dover Clip Art Collection
6520 Edenvale Blvd., Suite 118
Glen Lake, MN 55346
800/727-9724
6500 images in PCX, EPS, and AI format on CDROM.

Stephen & Associates Clip Art Collection

Stephen & Associates
5205 Kearny Villa Way
Suite 104
San Diego, CA 92123
619/571-5624
Thirty collections of clip art in PCX format: semiconductor images, architectural and hydraulic-pneumatic symbols, music, wild animals, sports, religion, etc. Available on IBM disks.

Studio Advertising Art

4305 East Sahara Avenue #1
Las Vegas, NV 89104
702/641-7041
800/453-1860 ext. R-641
These images are all in EPS format on IBM disks. The quality is good and the themes are varied. Of particular note is the Road & Warning Signs collection. Note that Studio also has a quarterly subscription service, with 50 images in each release for $40.

The Underground Grammarian

P.O. Box 203
Glassboro, NJ 08028
609/589-6477
The ten volumes of Typographers' Ornaments sold by this company (all in EPS format) are without a doubt the finest computer clip art available. The remaining collections, all in TIFF format, are not particularly exciting except the Will Bradley disk. All the collections offered by this company are available on IBM disks.

Visatex

1745 Dell Ave.
Campbell, CA 95008
408/866-6562
800/722-3729
Visatex has two collections, one of U.S. presidents and the other of Hollywood greats. They're both in MacPaint format on IBM disks.

Vivid Impressions

Casady & Greene, Inc.
P.O. Box 223779
Carmel, CA 93923
408/624-8716
800/359-4920
408/624-7865 fax
The Vivid Impressions Volume 1 is a collection of 130 EPS clip art images on IBM disks. The theme of the collection is holidays and festive events.

Works of Art

Springboard Software
7808 Creekridge Circle
Minneapolis, MN 55435
612/944-3915
800/445-4780
Although the quality of these MacPaint images (all available on IBM disks) is not that great, the price ($40–$50 per disk) and the diversity and sheer quantity of images make up for it. Includes everything from skaters to skeletons, with lots in between. Some terrific scary monsters on the Holiday disk.

LaserJet Fonts

Acorn Plus Inc.

4219 West Olive #2011
Burbank, CA 91505
213/879-5237
This company sells a number of bitmapped fonts, the most notable of which is its Computer Keys, Reversed font.

Adobe Type Library

Adobe Systems Inc.
1585 Charleston Rd.
P.O. Box 7900
Mountain View, CA 94039-7900
800/833-6687
The newest version of the Adobe Type Library includes a utility called Font Foundry that will convert any of 153 different Adobe PostScript typeface packages into LaserJet format. It will also install the fonts into Ventura and create matching screen fonts.

Agfa Compugraphic

90 Industrial Way
Wilmington, MA 01887
800/873-3668
Compugraphic's fonts are in outline format compatible with the Type Director font generator or with the HP LaserJet III printer. Generally not as good as Bitstream's fonts.

clip art

LaserJet fonts

PostScript fonts

font tools

graphics software

monitors

LaserJet-compatible printers

PostScript printers (300 dpi)

PostScript printers and typesetters (above 300 dpi)

other printers

printer controllers

scanners

utilities

user groups

bulletin boards

newsletters and magazines

style sheets

training

PostScript service bureaus

other resources

Bitstream, Inc.

215 First St.
Cambridge, MA 02142
617/497-7514
800/522-3668
617/868-4732 fax

This is the company that created the Swiss and Dutch faces provided with Ventura, along with the Fontware font generation kit (see "font tools" below). Bitstream dominates the LaserJet font market, for good reason: the quality is unsurpassed, the selection currently includes 207 faces and continues to grow, and prices are falling! For full-page samples of the 50 leading Bitstream fonts, check out Peachpit's book *TypeStyle*.

Digi-Fonts, Inc.

3000 Youngfield St. #285
Lakewood, CO 80215
800/242-5665

This company offers a font generation kit and 272 font outlines for the LaserJet II and scalable font outlines for the LaserJet III. The installation program for Ventura costs an additional $40. The quality is very good, though not as good as Bitstream or Font Factory fonts. Prices are very low.

FontCenter Fonts

Jim Boemler
509 Marin St. #227
Thousand Oaks, CA 91360
805/373-1919

The quality of these inexpensive fonts is superb, though you'll have to generate your own width tables. A font downloading utility

is provided with the fonts. Over 16 typeface families available.

Font Factory Fonts

The Font Factory
P.O. Box 5429
Kingwood, TX 77339
713/358-6954

This company's fonts come with width tables and an installation utility for Ventura. They work in conjunction with the FontMaker font generating program, which produces bitmapped fonts for screen and printer, and scalable fonts for the LaserJet III. The Plus series is especially useful because it matches the standard typefaces found in PostScript printers.

Hewlett-Packard Fonts

Boise Division
P.O. Box 15
Boise, ID 83707
208/323-6000
800/538-8787

Hewlett-Packard's Intellifont outline fonts work with the Type Director font generator, described in "Font Tools" below. Several dozen typefaces are available, and type director lets you make fonts for the Ventura International and other character sets.

The LaserJet Font Book

Peachpit Press
1085 Keith Ave.
Berkeley, CA 94708
415/527-8555
800/283-9444
415/524-9775 fax

This is the only full-fledged type specimen book for LaserJet fonts. It shows samples of hundreds of LaserJet fonts, provides advice on selecting and using fonts, and rates the comparative quality of the various font vendors.

LJ Fonts

Weaver Graphics
5165 South Highway A1A
Melbourne Beach, FL 32951
407/728-4000
407/728-5978 fax
Weaver's high-quality bitmapped fonts include sizes from 6 to 72 points. They come with Ventura width tables (WID files), matching screen fonts, kerning information, and a portrait-to-landscape conversion program.

Mephistopheles Systems Design

3629 Lankershim Blvd.
Hollywood, CA 90068
818/762-8150
Unlike most LaserJet fonts, these fonts are actually licensed from the original developer, Linotype. (So they can really call them by their true names, such as Times Roman and Helvetica, instead of using substitute names such as Dutch and Swiss.) The quality is good, and each set comes with an installation utility that automatically installs the fonts in Ventura, Windows, WordPerfect, and other programs.

Metro Software

2509 N. Campbell #214
Tucson, AZ 85719
602/299-7313
800/621-1137
Metro Software's fonts work with its FontPack font generating program. Each disk comes with one master font, which you can scale, slant, shadow, and otherwise manipulate.

MicroLogic Software, Inc.

6400 Hollis Street, Suite 9
Emeryville, CA 94608
800/888-9078
415/652-7079 fax
These fonts work with the More-Fonts font generator, described in "Font Tools" below. They can be used with either the LaserJet II or the LaserJet III.

SWFTE

P.O. Box 5773
Wilmington, DE 19808
302/658-1123
800/237-9383
SWFTE's fonts can be generated with its Glyphix font generator but the company has not yet released an expected on-the-fly font generator for the DOS/GEM version of Ventura. Look for a an on-the-fly font generator for Windows. The quality has improved significantly since earlier versions of the program, though it is still not as good as Bitstream and Font Factory fonts.

clip art

LaserJet fonts

PostScript fonts

font tools

graphics software

monitors

LaserJet-compatible printers

PostScript printers (300 dpi)

PostScript printers and typesetters (above 300 dpi)

other printers

printer controllers

scanners

utilities

user groups

bulletin boards

newsletters and magazines

style sheets

training

PostScript service bureaus

other resources

Typefoundry Series
Standard Series
Leonard Storch Series
SoftCraft, Inc.
16 North Carroll Street
Suite 500
Madison, WI 53703
800/257-2300

SoftCraft sells scalable fonts in Bitstream's Fontware format and also has a large library of bit-mapped fonts in LaserJet format. Among the scalable fonts are the most commonly used serif and sans serif faces as well as some decorative ones. The bitmapped fonts include a number of un-usual typefaces: Olde English, Formal, Script, Computer, Callig-rapher, Chess, Twist, Shadow, Accents and Ligatures, Copyright and Symbols, Math Symbols, Cyrillic, French Classic, Spanish Classic, International Phonetic, German, Greek, Indic, Nouveau, Hebrew, Proto-IndoEuropean, Classic Shadow, Modern, Vertical Borders, LCD, Outline, Carib-bean, Code/OCR, Orbit, Elegant Script, Optical, Hershey Oriental, Japanese, Manual Alphabet, and Music. In the less common typefaces, point sizes are quite limited.

A new series of high-quality bitmap fonts from Storch Enterprises in addition to Times Roman and Helvetica has Futura, Old Anglo, Dunhigh, and decora-tive and special effects like out-line, 3-D, patterned, and reverse type. Point sizes are limited, however.

VN Labs
4320 Campus Dr. #114
Newport Beach, CA 92660
714/474-6968

This company offers a Ventura Package for $225 per langauge that includes screen drivers and characters as well as fonts in 10-, 12-, and 18-point sizes for a par-ticular. Languages include Arabic, Cyrillic, Farsi, French, German, Greek, Hebrew, Italian, Polish, Portuguese, Russian, Spanish, Turkish, and Vietnamese.

VS Library of Fonts
Compugraphic/ITC
Library
VS Software
P.O. Box 165920
Little Rock, AR 72216
501/376-2083
501/372-7075 fax

These fonts are considered among the easiest to install of any LaserJet fonts. The quality of the Compugraphic/ITC Library is first-rate; the VS Library is not as good. The company provides, to anyone who requests it, the most complete and useful font catalog of any developer. Fonts are pack-aged in Libraries, Families and FontPaks including Designer Col-lection, Executive Type Classics, Times/Triumvirate Combo, Ex-ecutive Headlines, and Ventura Supplemental FontPak. The Ven-tura Supplemental FontPak is especially useful because it provides the missing medium, italic, bold, and bold italic fonts in Dutch and Swiss for 6-, 8-, 10-, 12-, 14-, 18-, 20,- 24-, and 30-point sizes. All VS fonts include

width tables (WID files) and screen fonts for Ventura. The Laser Word Processor Tool Kit installs the fonts and allows drivers to be generated for popular word processors.

PostScript Fonts

Adobe Type Library
Adobe Systems Inc.
P.O. Box 7900
Mountain View, CA 94039
415/962-2000
The Adobe Type Library comprises a large selection of fonts (currently over 600 typefaces), most of which are classic designs licensed from the Allied and ITC collections. It includes ITC American Typewriter, ITC Avant Garde, ITC Benguiat, ITC Bookman, Courier, ITC Fritz Quadrata, ITC Galliard, ITC Garamond, Glypha, Goudy Old Style, Helvetica, Helvetica Black, Helvetica Condensed, Helvetica Light, Helvetica Narrow, ITC Korinna, ITC Lubalin Graph, ITC Machine, Melior, ITC New Baskerville, New Century Schoolbook, Optima, Palatino, Sonata, ITC Souvenir, Symbol, Times, Trump Medieval, ITC Zapf Chancery, and ITC Zapf Dingbats. A complete catalog is free from Adobe.

Bitstream, Inc.
215 First St.
Cambridge, MA 02142
617/497-7514
800/522-3668
617/868-4732 fax
While Adobe is definitely the dominant player in the PostScript font world, Bitstream could be described as the company that tries harder. Bitstream's collection of PostScript fonts is equally vast and equally superb. The only problem is that service bureaus tend to stock Adobe fonts only, so getting your documents typeset on a Lino can be a real problem if you don't bring your own fonts to the typesetter.

Fluent Laser Fonts
Casady & Greene, Inc.
26080 Carmel Rancho Blvd.
#202
Carmel, CA 93923
800/359-4920 (orders only)
408/624-8716 (information)
The Casady & Greene collection includes original decorative faces such as Gazelle, Kells, Abilene, and Collegiate. More than 140 PostScript typefaces are available in all, including six packages such as Headlines, Classic, Modern, and new Glasnost (Cyrillic) fonts.

Hewlett-Packard PostScript Fonts
Hewlett-Packard
19310 Pruneridge Avenue
Cupertino, CA 95014
800/5752-0900
HP now offers true PostScript fonts for its LaserJet IID, IIP, III,

clip art

LaserJet fonts

PostScript fonts

font tools

graphics software

monitors

LaserJet-compatible printers

PostScript printers (300 dpi)

PostScript printers and typesetters (above 300 dpi)

other printers

printer controllers

scanners

utilities

user groups

bulletin boards

newsletters and magazines

style sheets

training

PostScript service bureaus

other resources

and IIID printers. These are cartridge-based and include 35 typefaces in Avant Garde, ITC Bookman, Helvetica, New Century Schoolbook, Palatino, Symbol, Times Roman, Zapf Chancery, and Zapf Dingbats, among others.

Hot Type

Image Club Graphics Inc.
#5, 1902 – 11th Street SE
Calgary, Alberta
Canada T2G 3G2
403/262-8008
800/661-9410
403/261-7013 fax
Image Club sells four sets of PostScript fonts on PC disks. Most are decorative typefaces such as Brass, Surfstyle, Compacto, Sofa, Scoreboard, and Rubber Stamp.

MacTography PostScript Type Sampler

MacTography
702 Twinbrook Parkway
Rockville, MD 20851
301/424-1357
This is a catalog showing of type specimens for over 17 different PostScript font vendors. It includes over 800 fonts, which can be purchased either from the vendor of the fonts or through MacTography. The catalog indicates which fonts are available in IBM format.

Font Tools

Adobe Type Manager for Windows

Adobe Systems Inc.
P.O. Box 7900
Mountain View, CA 94039
415/962-2000
This program works with Windows programs, creating scalable fonts onscreen from PostScript printer fonts.

BackLoader

LaserTools Corporation
1250 45th St. #100
Emeryville, CA 94608
415/420-8777
415/420-1150 fax
Formerly sold by Roxxolid, this utility downloads LaserJet and DeskJet fonts in the background while you continue working.

Bitstream Fontware Installation Kit

Bitstream, Inc.
215 First St.
Cambridge, MA 02142
800/522-3668
617/497-6222
Bitstream's Fontware Installation Kit, which can generate either LaserJet or PostScript fonts, as well as corresponding screen fonts, is provided free with Ventura Publisher. The program creates fonts that are optimized for professional quality at all sizes and resolutions, so that what is seen on the screen

matches printed output. Once created, the fonts are stored on hard disk and are accessible from the Xerox Ventura Publisher screen menu.

The Fontware Library features over 200 professional quality typefaces in a variety of weights and styles. Each Fontware typeface package contains four individual typefaces: some have four weights of one typeface family (roman, italic, bold, and bold italic), others have a combination of two or more faces in one or more weights.

For more information on Fontware, see Chapter 22, "Font Tools."

FaceLift for Windows

Bitstream, Inc.
215 First St.
Cambridge, MA 02142
800/522-3668
617/497-6222
This program creates scalable screen fonts on the fly for printer fonts in Bitstream's Speedo format. It also replaces the functions of Fontware by creating fonts from master outlines and downloading them to the printer.

fontART

Creative Software & Systems
7127 Laurel Canyon Blvd
North Hollywood, CA 91605
818/764-3414
800/937-2387
The special effects font program is described in Chapter 22, "Font Tools."

FontGen V

VS Software
P.O. Box 165920
Little Rock, AR 72216
501/376-2083
This is a font editing program that can be used to create, merge, and scale fonts in LaserJet format from any bitmap font. It provides a window in which editing is done one character at a time. Alternatively, the entire font can be viewed and edited at once, using various editing tools to generate and manipulate character bit maps—down to the level of a single pixel. A handbook on typefaces, fonts, and "how-to" for creating and changing fonts comes with the package. FG V also accepts graphics in PCX, IMG, and TIFF formats.

Font Library Manager

VS Software
P.O. Box 165920
Little Rock, AR 72216
501/376-2083
This utility compresses fonts and stores them in a special file. You can then download them as needed to the printer by making selections from a menu.

FontMaker

The Font Factory
13601 Preston Road
Suite 500 West
Dallas, TX 75240
800/272-4663
FontMaker is a font generator, similar to Bitstream's Fontware. It is based on the GEM interface, so typefaces and font generating options are selected from a set of

clip art

LaserJet fonts

PostScript fonts

font tools

graphics software

monitors

LaserJet-compatible printers

PostScript printers (300 dpi)

PostScript printers and typesetters (above 300 dpi)

other printers

printer controllers

scanners

utilities

user groups

bulletin boards

newsletters and magazines

style sheets

training

PostScript service bureaus

other resources

clip art

LaserJet fonts

PostScript fonts

font tools

graphics software

monitors

LaserJet-compatible printers

PostScript printers (300 dpi)

PostScript printers and typesetters (above 300 dpi)

other printers

printer controllers

scanners

utilities

user groups

bulletin boards

newsletters and magazines

style sheets

training

PostScript service bureaus

other resources

menus that look much like Ventura's own dialog boxes. You can generate both screen and printer fonts in sizes from 6 to 128 points in roman, bold, italic, and bold italic styles. The master typeface outlines used by the program are licensed from ITC and Compugraphic. Currently, approximately 20 typefaces are available. In addition to the HP LaserJet family, the program supports the NEC Pinwriter and Toshiba 24-wire dot matrix printers. According the The Font Factory, Font-Maker is "an order of magnitude" faster than Bitstream's Fontware.

Font Solution Pack
SoftCraft, Inc.
16 N. Carroll St., Suite 500
Madison, WI 53703
800/351-0500
608/257-3300
For $495 you can get all the features of over a dozen other SoftCraft font utilities. These include Font Special Effects, Laser Fonts, Spinfont, and WYSIfonts!, enabling you to generate, install, edit, pattern, and customize fonts for any HP compatible printer. All options are menu-driven.

FontSpace
Isogon Corp.
330 Seventh Ave.
New York, NY 10001
212/967-2424
212/967-3198 fax
This utility automatically compresses and decompresses LaserJet bitmapped soft fonts. Working in a completely transparent fashion, it reduces the amount of

disk space needed to store a font by at least 50 percent and for large fonts as much as 97 percent.

Font Special Effects Pack
SoftCraft, Inc.
16 N. Carroll St., Suite 500
Madison, WI 53703
800/351-0500
608/257-3300
Font Special Effects lets you take any Bitstream font and apply special effects to it such as shadows, outlining, and patterns. It also lets you scale fonts and install and manage fonts for Word-Perfect, Word, and OfficeWrite. The results can be previewed on the screen. The program is profiled in Chapter 22, "Font Tools."

Glyphix
SWFTE International
P.O. Box 219
Rockland, DE 19732
800/237-9383, 302/658-1123
This font-generating program, is similar to Bitstream's Fontware.

HP w/ESP
Esper Systems
P.O. Box 18470
Knoxville, TN 37928-2470
615/687-8016
This program saves room on your hard disk by rotating LaserJet portrait fonts to landscape orientation on the fly. It also lets you print fonts larger than 36 points.

Laser Fonts

SoftCraft, Inc.
16 N. Carroll St., Suite 500
Madison, WI 53703
608/257-3300
800/351-0500
Laser Fonts lets you use the Bitstream fonts provided with Ventura with WordPerfect, Microsoft Word, or OfficeWriter. It creates the necessary drivers for the fonts, takes care of downloading them to the printer, and can even create outline and shadow fonts.

MoreFonts

MicroLogic Software
6400 Hollis St. #9
Emeryville, CA 94608
800/888-9078
415/652-5464
415/652-7079 fax
This is a LaserJet font generating program that not only generates standard fonts of various sizes, but also allows you to create special effects such as wood grain, stripes, and shadows. Supports both the LaserJet II and the LaserJet III.

Publisher's PowerPak

Atech Software
5964 La Place Court, #125
Carlsbad, CA 92008
619/438-6883
800/748-5657
This utility combines a font generator and an array of drivers for over 300 dot-matrix, inkjet, and laser printers, most of which are not otherwise supported by Ventura. Its three typeface families match Helvetica, Times Roman, and Courier, and fonts can be created on-the-fly in any size from 6 to 250 points. Over 800 fonts are available. Also scales fonts on-the-fly for the screen. For more details, see Chapter 22, "Font Tools"

Publisher's Type Foundry

ZSoft Corporation
450 Franklin Rd. #100
Marietta, GA 30067
404/428-0008
This font-editing program is profiled in Chapter 22, "Font Tools."

SoftCraft Font Editor

SoftCraft, Inc.
16 N. Carroll St., Suite 500
Madison, WI 53703
608/257-3300
800/351-0500
This program can be used to edit any fonts in HP LaserJet format. It provides two windows, one showing the font at actual size and the other zoomed in for editing individual pixels. The program can draw lines, curves, circles, and rectangles, and can also automatically slant, enlarge, reduce, rotate, and embolden a character.

SoftCraft Fontware Program

SoftCraft, Inc.
16 N. Carroll St., Suite 500
Madison, WI 53703
608/257-3300
800/351-0500
SoftCraft's version of Bitstream Fontware has certain differences from the version being distributed free with Ventura Pub-

---

clip art

LaserJet fonts

PostScript fonts

font tools

graphics software

monitors

LaserJet-compatible printers

PostScript printers (300 dpi)

PostScript printers and typesetters (above 300 dpi)

other printers

printer controllers

scanners

utilities

user groups

bulletin boards

newsletters and magazines

style sheets

training

PostScript service bureaus

other resources

lisher. First, it can generate larger fonts—up to 240 points. Second, it can create condensed, expanded, or oblique fonts. Third, it provides greater flexibility in deciding what characters you want to include in your font. The program is profiled in Chapter 22, "Font Tools."

Spinfont

SoftCraft, Inc.
16 N. Carroll St., Suite 500
Madison, WI 53703
608/257-3300
800/351-0500

Spinfont lets you create circular, slanted, rotated, and white-on-black text images from Bitstream typeface outlines. The results can be saved in PCX or TIFF formats for loading into Ventura as a graphic.

SuperPrint

Zenographics
4 Executive Circle
Irvine, CA 92714
714/851-6352

This is a printer and screen driver that replaces the regular Windows print driver and offers scalable type and fast printing speed. For details, see Chapter 22, "Font Tools."

Type Director

Hewlett-Packard Company
3000 Hanover St.
Palo Alto, CA 94303-0890
415/857-1501

This font generator is profiled in Chapter 22, "Font Tools."

Type Studio

Adisys
25 Alexander Street #200
Vancouver, B.C. V6A 1B2
Canada
604/685-8168

With this package you can expand, condense, outline, shade, fill rotate, tilt, and skew, as well as generate screen fonts and new typefaces. For use on PostScript printers.

WYSIfonts!

SoftCraft, Inc.
16 N. Carroll St., Suite 500
Madison, WI 53703
608/257-3300
800/351-0500

WYSIfonts! installs any LaserJet soft font for Ventura or Microsoft Windows and also generates matching screen fonts. It is profiled in Chapter 22, "Font Tools."

Graphics Software

1-2-3, Freelance, Symphony, Graphwriter

Lotus Development Corporation
55 Cambridge Parkway
Cambridge, MA 02142
617/577-8500

There are various ways to import graphics generated by these programs into Ventura. From 1-2-3, you can save graphics with the PIC extension and then load them into Ventura as line art (i.e., object graphics). Freelance and Graphwriter also produce files in VideoShow format, and Freelance also can produce files in CGM format. Both VideoShow and CGM are line art formats that can be imported into Ventura.

Arts & Letters

Computer Support Corporation
15926 Midway Rd.
Dallas, TX 75244
214/661-8960

This drawing program runs under Windows. It is profiled in Chapter 16, "Graphics Tools." It comes with over 2,200 professionally drawn pieces of clip art. It allows you to manipulate the images by sizing, slanting, flipping, rotating, etc. Images can be converted into EPS (with a bitmap for the screen) or CGM, either of which can be loaded into Ventura. A more sophisticated and powerful version of the program that allows you to create clip art is called the "Arts & Letters Graphic Editor."

AutoCAD, AutoSketch

Autodesk, Inc.
2320 Marinship Way
Sausalito, CA 94965
415/332-2344

There are several ways to import AutoCAD files into Ventura. One is to create them in SLD (slide) format using the ADE-2 Package and the AutoCAD MSLIDE command. In this form they can be imported directly into Ventura. A

second method is to save them in AutoCAD in DXF format and then use Ventura's DXFTOGEM utility, located on the Utilities disk, to convert them to GEM format. They can then be imported into Ventura, but will not include a number of attributes including shape entity, text mirroring, curve fitting, 3D rendering, and tapering widths in polylines. A third avenue is via HPGL format. If you have created a picture in AutoCAD in landscape mode, make sure that you rotate it before importing it into Ventura.

Corel Draw

Corel Systems Corporation
Corel Bldg., 1600 Carling Ave.
Ottawa, Ontario K1Z 8R7
613/728-8200
613/728-9790 fax

This object-oriented graphics program, which runs under Microsoft Windows, is one of the handful of graphics programs on the PC—others include Illustrator, Micrografx Designer and Artline—that let you draw curves. Other features include the ability to distort letter shapes, draw with calligraphic pen shapes, and fit text to a curve. Corel Trace, a tracing utility bundled with Corel Draw, can trace any sort of artwork from logos and letterforms to architectural drawings. It accepts TIFF and PCX formats and exports EPS files for import into Corel Draw. Fonts can be imported from Altsys Fontographer and ZSoft Type Foundry, and exported to Type Foundry for modification. GEM, AutoCAD DXF, and HPGL

clip art

LaserJet fonts

PostScript fonts

font tools

graphics software

monitors

LaserJet-compatible printers

PostScript printers (300 dpi)

PostScript printers and typesetters (above 300 dpi)

other printers

printer controllers

scanners

utilities

user groups

bulletin boards

newsletters and magazines

style sheets

training

PostScript service bureaus

other resources

files are supported. A detailed description is provided in Chapter 16, "Graphics Tools."

Designer

Micrografx, Inc.
1303 Arapaho
Richardson, TX 75081
214/234-1769
800/272-3729
214/234-2410 fax

Designer is not the slug that many Windows programs are. Like Illustrator and Corel Draw, the program lets you trace over scanned bitmapped images, creating high-resolution object graphics. You can rotate PostScript fonts to any angle, but you have slightly less control over type than you have with Artline and Corel Draw. Designer uses many of the same commands as its less talented sibling, Windows Draw, but it adds curves, the ability to mix object-oriented and bitmapped graphics (though you can't edit the bitmapped graphics), rotations, and color mixing. Scanned images are imported to the program through the Windows Clipboard. Objects can be snapped together for a perfect fit. You can connect irregularly-shaped objects and fill them with any of the standard patterns or a pattern of your own design. You can give each object a name, creating an inventory of stock parts that you can call up at will.

Curve drawing in Designer is more intuitive than in Illustrator. You can select a single curve or all the curves in an object, add new edit points, or delete them.

Other features include: spline and parabolic curves, freehand lines, squares, circles, and rectangles. You can't enter text directly into the page, but have to do so through a small text-editing window. With PostScript, you have access to 43 built-in fonts. The program includes a clip-art library of over 400 symbols. For more details on this clip art collection, see Chapter 17, "Clip Art."

Draw Plus

Micrografx, Inc.
1820 N. Greenville Ave.
Richardson, TX 75081
212/234-1769
800/272-3729
214/234-2410 fax

Windows Draw (now Draw Plus) was the precursor to Micrografx Designer. While Draw is a good general-purpose program, it pales in comparison with Designer.

GEM Draw Plus

Digital Research Inc.
75 Garden Court, Box DRI
Monterey, CA 93940
408/649-3896
800/443-4200

This first-generation drawing program has been surpassed by the likes of Corel Draw and Micrografx Designer. One plus for graphics generated with GEM Draw Plus is that they have the GEM extension and can be imported into Ventura as line art (i.e., object graphics). For that reason they do not degrade when you scale or stretch them. The program provides tools for creating geometric shapes such as rectangles and circles; it also includes an extensive library of images that can be cropped and adapted. A panning feature lets you define a portion of the screen to work with at various levels of magnification. Among the features of the program are several fonts for incorporating text into graphics.

GEM Paint

Digital Research Inc.
70 Garden Court, Box DRI
Monterey, CA 93942
408/649-3896
800/443-4200

Not as powerful as PC Paintbrush Plus, GEM Paint offers a similar set of drawing tools and saves its files with the IMG extension in image (i.e., bit-mapped) format. It allows pixel editing, but at the resolution of the screen rather than at the 300-dpi resolution allowed by Paintbrush.

GEM Artline

Digital Research Inc.
75 Garden Court, Box DRI
Monterey, CA 93940
408/649-3896
800/443-4200

Developed in Germany, GEM Artline is specifically designed to work hand-in-hand with Ventura and other desktop publishing applications. The program is similar to Adobe Illustrator, Corel Draw, and Micrografx Designer in that it allows you to create draw art, which does not degrade when scaled or when printed at different resolutions. One of the

strong points of the program is that its sophisticated drawing tools can be used not only for freehand drawing, but to manipulate text characters. Thus, you can create logos by applying special effects such as rotations and obliquing to text. Tools include scaling, coloring, rotating, mirroring, and merging one image element with another. GEM Artline also has a clip art library, provides eight typestyles and includes the Bitstream Installation Kit for additional typefaces. All the special effects can be printed on LaserJet as well as PostScript printers. For more details on Artline, see Chapter 16, "Graphics Tools."

Generic CADD

Generic Software, Inc.
11911 North Creek Pkwy. South
Bothell, WA 98011
206/487-2233

Using the DeskConvert utility from Generic Software, you can convert Generic CADD drawings into Encapsulated PostScript, PCX, or TIFF format, suitable for loading into Ventura.

Gray F/X

Xerox Imaging Systems, Inc.
535 Oakmead Pkwy.
Sunnyvale, CA 94086
408/245-7900

This is a grayscale editing program that lets you enhance and manipulate images digitized by a grayscale scanner. To use the program you need a VGA board or a more expensive graphics board. You also need lots of hard

clip art

LaserJet fonts

PostScript fonts

font tools

graphics software

monitors

LaserJet-compatible printers

PostScript printers (300 dpi)

PostScript printers and typesetters (above 300 dpi)

other printers

printer controllers

scanners

utilities

user groups

bulletin boards

newsletters and magazines

style sheets

training

PostScript service bureaus

other resources

disk space, since grayscale image files are typically at least several hundred kilobytes in size. Once you have manipulated an image, you can store in in TIFF, compressed TIFF, PCX, IMG, EPS, or Halo CUT format. TIFF files should work fine with Ventura, but you may have trouble importing and printing EPS, IMG, and PCX files.

Halo DPE
Media Cybernetics, Inc.
8484 Georgia Avenue
Silver Spring, MD 20910
301/495-3305
301/495-5964 fax
This scanner-oriented program is useful for creating line art logos or letterhead files in IMG, TIFF, and CUT formats, which can be imported into Ventura as images (i.e., bitmapped graphics). You can operate many scanners directly from within Halo DPE. In addition to normal painting features such as circles and shading, the program works with extended memory, provides image rotation, and has a zoom feature for pixel editing. HALO's built-in GRAB program can capture screens as HALO, GEM, or Windows files for editing.

Illustrator for Windows
Adobe Systems Inc.
1585 Charleston Rd.
Mountain View, CA 94039
415/961-4400
800/344-8335
Originally introduced for the Macintosh, Illustrator has now been adapted for the IBM PC. Re-

nowned for its sluggishness under Windows, Illustrator probably will continue to fare poorly against Corel and Designer until it receives a major upgrade. Like Artline, Corel Draw, and Micrografx Designer, Illustrator lets you draw true curves. It saves its images as object graphics; once transferred to a PC, they can be imported into Ventura as Encapsulated PostScript files.

PC Paintbrush family
ZSoft Corporation
450 Franklin Road #100
Marietta, GA 30067
404/428-0008
PC Paintbrush IV Plus and Publisher's Paintbrush are close relatives of PC Paintbrush, the all-time most popular graphics program for the PC (over a million copies sold to date). All three programs create files with the PCX or PCC extension, which can be imported into Ventura as images (i.e., bitmapped graphics). For drawing, PC Paintbrush IV Plus provides tools such as a paintbrush, a paint roller, boxes, circles, pattern fills, cutting and pasting, and an eraser. It provide controls for operating a variety of scanners from within the program, allowing you to store scanned images in PCX format. Among the scanners supported are Dest PC Scan Plus, the Shape-Scan, the Datacopy 730, the Canon IX-12, and the HP ScanJet. Once you've saved a scanned image in PCX format, you can edit it or clean it up using PC Paintbrush IV Plus's editing tools. The PC Paintbrush IV Plus pack-

age also includes the Frieze screen-capture utility. Scanning and editing of grayscale images are among the new features of both products.

Publisher's Paintbrush starts with the features of PC Paintbrush IV Plus and adds a few more. Tools can be used in any of four zoom-out modes. Another addition is a set of text features that allow characters to be slanted and the baseline to be placed at an angle. The program supports both extended and expanded (EMS) memory, making it possible to create large bitmapped images. Like PC Paintbrush IV Plus, Publisher's Paintbrush includes the Frieze screen capture utility and also provides controls for a variety of scanners.

Perspective Junior
Three D Software Inc.
860 Via de la Paz
Pacific Palisades, CA 90272
213/459-8525
As its name implies, this increasingly popular program is used for creating three-dimensional charts. It lets you import WKS files from 1-2-3, convert them into three-dimensional format, and apply functions such as tilting, rotating, stretching, and compressing along any of the axes. You can import them into Ventura as image (i.e., bit-mapped) files in IMG format.

SLEd
VS Software
P.O. Box 165920
Little Rock, AR 72216
501/376-2083
SLEd provides a variety of graphics functions, including Bezier curves, airbrush shading, scaling, rotation, mirroring, and variable pen width. Fonts can be loaded into the program and combined with graphics to create logos. Images can be saved in IMG or PCX format, suitable for loading into Ventura.

Touch-Up
Migraph
200 South 333rd Street
Suite 220
Federal Way, WA 98003
206/838-4677
800/223-3729
This GEM-based design tool lets you edit and enhance scanned, imported, or original images and export them to Ventura.

Monitors

DPS1 Controller
LaserMaster Corp.
7156 Shady Oak Rd.
Eden Prairie, MN 55344
612/944-6069
The DPS1 Controller works in conjunction with EGA and Multisync monitors. It provides true on-the-fly scaling of screen fonts

clip art

LaserJet fonts

PostScript fonts

font tools

graphics software

monitors

LaserJet-compatible printers

PostScript printers (300 dpi)

PostScript printers and typesetters (above 300 dpi)

other printers

printer controllers

scanners

utilities

user groups

bulletin boards

newsletters and magazines

style sheets

training

PostScript service bureaus

other resources

and comes with 35 Bitstream fonts which are width-compatible with PostScript fonts. The controller raises the resolution of the display to 1,024 by 1,024 pixels, automatically moves the viewing window without scroll bars when you move the cursor near the edge of the page, and provides a number of special effects such as squeezing and rotating screen fonts.

DualPage Monitor, SinglePage XL Monitor

Cornerstone Technology, Inc.
1990 Concourse Drive
San Jose, CA 95131
408/435-8900
800/562-2552

The DualPage is a 19-inch monochrome monitor with up to 16 levels of gray and a resolution of 1,600 by 1,280 pixels, or 109 by 121 pixels per inch. For Ventura Publisher, Cornerstone provides Bitstream fonts that are enhanced with gray-scale pixels around the edges. The SinglePage XL is a 15-inch monochrome monitor with vertical orientation, four levels of gray, and 768 by 1008 resolution. Cornerstone also manufactures a 15-inch SinglePage XL Controller and Monitor for PC and PS/2 compatible systems.

Genius Series

Micro Display Systems, Inc.
1310 Vermillion Street
P.O. Box 455
Hastings, MN 55033
612/437-2233
800/328-9524

There are a variety of monitors in this series, ranging in price from $995 to $8,650. The most notable feature of the Genius Plus Full Page Display System, the one we have used, is that as well as being an excellent graphics monitor, it lets you use WordPerfect, Microsoft Word, WordStar and many other popular text-based programs in full screen mode. That means you can see 66 lines of text (over a full page) on-screen. This portrait monitor is taller than it is wide, with a screen size of 8 by 10.5 inches. Resolution is 736 by 1,008 pixels (100 pixels per inch). Pixels are square, which makes the aspect ratio of the image the same as that of the printed page. This monitor is profiled in Chapter 5, "Monitors."

GlassPage 1280 Monitor, GS 1280 Outline Font Monitor

LaserMaster Corp.
7156 Shady Oak Rd.
Eden Prairie, MN 55344
612/944-6069

The GlassPage monitor is profiled in Chapter 5, "Monitors." Its board piggybacks onto a LaserMaster 1000 or LX6 controller board. The GlassPage has two notable features. The first is that it uses the same outline fonts as the LaserMaster controller, so you get a true WYSIWYG display in which the typefaces and sizes on the screen really match those on your printed page. The second is a two page "hot view" that automatically scrolls you horizontally when your mouse approaches the edge of the screen. The GS 1280 Outline Font monitor is similar to the GlassPage except that it has the ability to show 16 levels of gray. It also uses a technique called anti-aliasing, which sharpens the appearance of type on the screen.

L-View, PageView, SilverView
Sigma Designs
46501 Landing Parkway
Fremont, CA 94538
415/770-0100
The L-View (previously Laser-View), the largest and most expensive member of this trio, has gone through considerable changes. It can now be used as the primary display, since it provides a Hercules emulation. Resolution has been increased to 120 dpi. In addition to Ventura, drivers are available for Windows, GEM, GEM/3, AutoCAD, 1-2-3, Symphony, Dr. Halo, and PC Paintbrush Plus. The PageView display uses a 15-inch monochrome monitor with vertical orientation and a resolution of 96 dpi. The SilverView uses a 21-inch monochrome monitor with horizontal orientation and a resolution of 72 dpi. It can emulate VGA.

NEC Monograph System
NEC Home Electronics
1414 Massachusetts Ave.
Boxborough, MA 01719
508/264-8000
The Monograph System is square in shape and measures 14 inches

diagonally. Resolution is 1024 by 1024 with square pixels.

Page Manager 100
Vermont Microsystems
11 Tigan Street
Winooski, VT 05404
800/354-0055
800/655-2860
This is a full-page display that features a 16-inch square screen and 100-dpi resolution. It includes an Intel 82786 graphics coprocessor chip and 384K of font memory for faster screen redraw. Since the only graphics board emulation is the low-resolution CGA mode, you may find this monitor uncomfortable to use with your word processing program.

Radius Two-Page Display
Radius, Inc.
1710 Fortune Dr.
San Jose, CA 95131
408/434-1010
This display comes in two sizes, 21-inch and 24-inch. The price is quite a bit lower than prices of other comparable large-screen monitors, such as the L-View Display System and the Viking 2. The Radius Two-Page Display is profiled in Chapter 5, "Monitors."

clip art

LaserJet fonts

PostScript fonts

font tools

graphics software

monitors

LaserJet-compatible printers

PostScript printers (300 dpi)

PostScript printers and typesetters (above 300 dpi)

other printers

printer controllers

scanners

utilities

user groups

bulletin boards

newsletters and magazines

style sheets

training

PostScript service bureaus

other resources

Viking 2/72, Viking 2/91, Viking 2/115, Viking 21, Viking 21/91, Viking Trinitron, Viking 2 G/S, Viking Portrait, Viking 2400

*Moniterm Corporation
5740 Green Circle Drive
Minnetonka, MN 55343-9990
612/935-4151*

The Viking 2/72 is a 19-inch monochrome monitor with a horizontal orientation and 72-dpi resolution. The Viking 2/91 is the same, except that the resolution is 91 dpi. The Viking 2/115 is the same except that resolution is 115 dpi. The Viking 21 is a 21-inch color monitor with 72-dpi resolution and a horizontal orientation. The Viking 21/91 is a 21-inch color monitor with 91-dpi resolution and a horizontal orientation. The Viking Trinitron is a 19-inch color monitor with 75-dpi resolution and a horizontal orientation. The Viking 2 G/S is a 19-inch grayscale monitor with a horizontal orientation. The Viking Portrait is a 19-inch monochrome monitor with 91-dpi resolution and a vertical orientation. The Viking 2400 is a 24-inch portrait monitor with a horizontal orientation. The Viking monitors use a Hitachi graphics coprocessor chip, which enhances the speed of the display considerably.

WY-700

*Wyse Technology
3471 North First St.
San Jose, CA 95134
800/433-1000*

The WY-700, which is identical to the Amdek 1280, is extremely popular due to its affordability (under $1,000) and its extensive software support. It is profiled in Chapter 5, "Monitors."

LaserJet-Compatible Printers

LaserJet, LaserJet Plus

*Hewlett-Packard Co.
19310 Pruneridge Ave.
Cupertino, CA 95014
800/752-0900*

The original LaserJet and the LaserJet Plus are no longer on the market, but hundreds of thousands are still in use. The LaserJet can only use font cartridges, not downloadable fonts on floppy disks. The LaserJet Plus has 512K of memory, of which approximately 290K can be used for downloaded fonts. Both use the Canon LBP-CX engine, which has excellent print quality. Although more than a score of font cartridges are available, with Ventura you can only use the F cartridge, which provides one display font (14.4-point Helv), three text fonts (10-point TMS RMN in regular, italic, and bold) and one footnote font (8-point TMS RMN). Though limited, this range of sizes is suitable for letters, memoranda, simple business reports, and some technical documentation.

With the LaserJet, you cannot print text in landscape mode, and graphics are severely limited by the 59K of printer memory available for storing graphics. If you select other fonts and try to print them on the LaserJet, Ventura will render them at a crude 75-dpi resolution. Despite its drawbacks, you can use the LaserJet as a draft printer in conjunction with a PostScript phototypesetter. This is done by selecting the LaserJet as the printer and then specifying a PostScript width table. A number of upgrade options are available for the LaserJet and the LaserJet Plus (see "Printer Controllers" below).

LaserJet Series II, IID, IIP, and III

Hewlett-Packard Co.
19310 Pruneridge Ave.
Cupertino, CA 95014
800/752-0900
These printers differ from the original LaserJet in that they use newer engines and include more memory (512K, upgradeable to 4.5MB). The LaserJet III has additional graphics capabilities, scalable fonts, and features Resolution Enhancement Technology, which improves the appearance of type at small sizes. All LaserJet printers can be upgraded easily to PostScript with an add-on cartridge (see "Printer Controllers" below). These printers are profiled in Chapter 4, "Laser Printers."

MicroLaser

Texas Instruments
P.O. Box 202230
Austin, TX 78720
800/527-3500
This printer has several nice features, the most important of which is that you can buy a basic LaserJet-compatible model and then upgrade later to PostScript simply by inserting a new circuit board. The drawback is that the engine in this printer isn't as nicely engineered as the Canon engine used in the LaserJet family. The hardware is a bit clunky and the print quality isn't up to LaserJet level.

Personal Page Printer II Model 31

IBM Corp.
101 Paragon Dr.
Montvale, NJ 07645
800/426-7257
This six-page-per-minute printer emulates a LaserJet II. Though slow, it has good print quality.

Qume CrystalPrint Series II

Qume Corporation
500 Yosemite Dr.
Milpitas, CA 95035
408/942-4000
800/223-2479
This printer is one of the most inexpensive alternatives to the HP LaserJet II. The CrystalPrint Series II emulates the LaserJet II, but is more compact at 35 pounds, compared with about 50 pounds for the LaserJet II. Drawbacks are a less heavy-duty engine, a paper tray that only holds 100 sheets,

clip art

LaserJet fonts

PostScript fonts

font tools

graphics software

monitors

LaserJet-compatible printers

PostScript printers (300 dpi)

PostScript printers and typesetters (above 300 dpi)

other printers

printer controllers

scanners

utilities

user groups

bulletin boards

newsletters and magazines

style sheets

training

PostScript service bureaus

other resources

and a maximum speed of six pages per minute.

PostScript Printers (300 dpi)

Business LaserPrinter, Business LaserPrinter II, Business LaserPrinter IIS

GCC Technologies, Inc.
580 Winter St.
Waltham, MA 02154
617/890-0880

Although these printers are being sold primarily to the Macintosh market, their Centronics interface makes them well-suited for use with a PC. Less expensive than most other PostScript printers, they use a compact Ricoh engine and come with a full complement of 35 resident Adobe fonts. A notable feature of the BLP II is that it is perhaps the only Post-Script printer that can print all the way to any edge of a page.

ColorScript 100, Models 10, 20, and 30

QMS, Inc.
Product Inquiries
P.O. Box 81250
Mobile, AL 36689-1250
800/631-2692, ext. 424

The ColorScript was the the first color PostScript printer to hit the market, and the price has now dropped below $10,000. All models use a thermal transfer process to apply color. Model 10 can print up to legal-size paper; Models 20 and 30 can handle pages of up to 11 by 17 inches.

LaserWriter IINT and IINTX

Apple Computer Inc.
20525 Mariani Ave.
Cupertino, CA 95014
408/996-1010

The Apple LaserWriter was the first PostScript printer, and the Apple family continues to be the most popular. These latest models both use the Canon LBP-SX engine (same as HP's and QMS's printers), which is reliable and has excellent type quality as well as solid blacks. Both models come with the standard set of PostScript fonts: Courier, Helvetica, Times Roman, Palatino, Bookman, Avant Garde, New Century Schoolbook, Symbol, ITC Zapf Chancery, and ITC Zapf Dingbats. The NT uses a Motorola 68000 microprocessor and has 2MB of RAM (nonexpandable). The NTX uses a faster 68020 microprocessor and has 2 megabytes of RAM, expandable to 12 megabytes. Unfortunately, both printers provide a serial port rather than a faster parallel port. Until Apple adds a parallel port, you're better off with a PS 810.

LZR 1260

Dataproducts Corp.
6200 Canoga Ave.
Woodland Hills, CA 91367-2499
818/887-8000

This is a first-rate printer — the top of the line among PostScript printers under $10,000. It prints twelve pages per minute and has excellent print quality. The printer is 85 pounds (a LaserJet II weighs 50) and the list price is correspondingly hefty.

OmniLaser 2000 Series

Texas Instruments
P.O. Box 202230
Austin, TX 78720
800/527-3500

There are three laser printers in this series. The 2106, 2108, and 2115 include the PostScript page description language. HP LaserJet emulation is also available. The OmniLaser 2108 and 2115 use the massive Ricoh 4080 engine, while the OmniLaser 2106 uses the compact Ricoh 1060 engine. Neither of the Ricoh engines is as good as the Canon engines used in the LaserJet series.

QMS PS-410, QMS-PS 810, QMS-PS 810 Turbo, QMS-PS 820, QMS-PS 820 Turbo, QMS-PS 1500

QMS, Inc.
Product Inquiries
P.O. Box 81250
Mobile, AL 36689-1250
800/631-2692, ext. 424

The QMS-PS 810 is one of the most popular PostScript printers available. It uses the excellent Canon LBP-SX engine, which gives it good paper handling, crisp print quality, solid blacks, and long-lasting toner cartridges. The 810 Turbo is faster because it uses a 20-MHz 68020 chip rather than a 16-MHz 68000 chip. The 820 printers are the same, except that they provide dual bins. The 1500 is also a dual-bin printer, but it is built with a heavier-duty engine. The 410 is the newest: a 4-page-per-minute printer with a fast 68020 processor. It won a *Personal Publishing* magazine 1990 Product of the Year award, mainly because of its ability to sense whether an application wants to print in LaserJet emulation mode or in PostScript mode and to automatically adjust accordingly.

QMS-PS 2210 and 2200

QMS, Inc.
Product Inquiries
P.O. Box 81250
Mobile, AL 36689-1250
800/631-2692, ext. 424

The QMS-PS 2210 and 2200 are 22-page-per-minute PostScript printers that can print on 11- by 17–inch paper. They include the standard set of 35 Adobe fonts and have Centronics, RS232, RS422, and AppleTalk interfaces.

QuadLaser PS

Q/Cor
One Quad Way
Norcross, GA 30093
404/923-6666
800/548-3420

The QuadLaser PS has 3MB of memory and comes with the standard set of 35 Adobe type-

clip art

LaserJet fonts

PostScript fonts

font tools

graphics software

monitors

LaserJet-compatible printers

PostScript printers (300 dpi)

PostScript printers and typesetters (above 300 dpi)

other printers

printer controllers

scanners

utilities

user groups

bulletin boards

newsletters and magazines

style sheets

training

PostScript service bureaus

other resources

faces. It has AppleTalk, RS232, and Centronics interfaces, and includes LaserJet Plus emulation.

ScripTEN
Qume Corporation
500 Yosemite Dr.
Milpitas, CA 95035
408/942-4000
This is a ten-page-per-minute PostScript printer that uses the Hitachi "write-white" engine. Although bulky at 90 pounds, the printer produces good print quality, with crisp type and solid blacks. It comes with 3MB of RAM and includes both serial and parallel ports.

PostScript Printers & Typesetters (Above 300 dpi)

CG 400-PS
Compugraphic Corp.
200 Ballardvale St.
Wilmington, MA 01887
800/822-5524
617/658-5600
This is a 400-dpi Postscript printer capable of printing up to 18 original pages per minute. The

additional 100 dots per horizontal and vertical inch actually increase the quality of output considerably (160,000 dots per square inch, in contrast to the 90,000 dots per square inch produced by most laser printers). The printer uses Adobe's Atlas controller, which is based on the Motorola 68020 chip and is faster than the controllers used in most standard PostScript printers. One reason for the increased speed of the Atlas controller is that while one page is being printed, the next page is being prepared. The printer includes a 20MB hard disk and 6MB of internal RAM for storing fonts, font cache, and bitmap memory. The CG 400-PS comes with 73 built-in typefaces. The combination of 400-dpi resolution, 18-ppm speed, and 100,000-page-per-month duty cycle, makes the CG 400-PS an ideal choice for high-quality, high-volume demand printing.

Lasersmith PS-415, PS-415 GT, PS-830+, PS-830 GT
Lasersmith
430 Martin Ave.
Santa Clara, CA 95050
408/727-7700
The PS-415 is a PostScript-compatible printer that uses a Canon CX engine (the one used by the original LaserJet) but prints at 415-by-415 dots per inch. It includes 3MB of RAM and 35 resident fonts. The PS-415 GT uses a RISC processor. According to Lasersmith it is 11 times as fast as an Apple LaserWriter IINT. The

PS-830+ doubles the resolution of the 415 in the horizontal direction. The PS-830 GT also doubles the resolution and also features a fast RISC processor. All these printers are astonishingly low priced. For example, the PS-415 is only $2,495 and the PS-830 GT is only $4,695.

Linotronic Series

Linotype Co.
425 Oser Ave.
Hauppauge, NY 11788
800/645-5278
516/434-2000

The resolution of the Linotronic 200 is 1,690 dpi, that of the Linotronic 300 is 2,540 dpi. Both print on paper or film up to 12 inches wide. With bitmapped and object graphics, the 300 is one and one-half times faster than the 200; with halftones the two are roughly comparable in speed. Both can be used with the full library of PostScript fonts. Typically, service bureaus provide access to Linotronic printers on a per-hour and per-page fee basis. Because of its higher resolution and faster speed, the 300 is preferable for printing halftones.

Printware 720 IQ

Printware
1385 Mendota Heights Rd.
St. Paul, MN 55120
612/456-1400

The Printware 720 IQ is a 1,200-dpi (horizontal) by 600-dpi (vertical) laser printer that uses Printstyle, a PostScript-compatible page description lan-

guage. The printer is rated at a maximum of eight pages per minute and accepts plain paper stock up to 8.5 by 14 inches. The 720 IQ allows on-line selection of black and one other color, such as red, brown, or blue.

VT600P

Varityper
11 Mount Pleasant Ave.
East Hanover, NJ 07936
201/887-8000
800/631-8134

This is a 600-dpi PostScript printer, rated at a maximum of ten pages per minute. Like the Agfa P400PS, it uses the fast Atlas controller. Built into the printer is a 20MB hard disk for storing typefaces. The VT600P uses plain paper (up to 8.5 by 14 inches) and provides serial and parallel ports. Resident fonts include the Adobe 35 LaserWriter-Plus set; more fonts can be loaded onto the printer's 20MB hard disk. Varityper also offers a version of the VT600P which prints on 11-by-17–inch paper.

clip art

LaserJet fonts

PostScript fonts

font tools

graphics software

monitors

LaserJet-compatible printers

PostScript printers (300 dpi)

PostScript printers and typesetters (above 300 dpi)

other printers

printer controllers

scanners

utilities

user groups

bulletin boards

newsletters and magazines

style sheets

training

PostScript service bureaus

other resources

Other Printers

DeskJet, DeskJet Plus, DeskJet 500
Hewlett-Packard
Customer Information Center
Inquiry Fulfillment Dept.
19310 Pruneridge Ave.
Cupertino, CA 95014
800/752-0900
408/738-4133
With prices continually dropping, the DeskJet printers provide remarkable 300-dpi near-laser output. They're even quieter than a laser printer, though nowhere near as fast. Although Ventura doesn't have a DeskJet driver, you can print on any DeskJet model by installing Ventura for a PostScript printer and then using a software-based PostScript interpreter such as Freedom of the Press (see below under "Utilities"). Output will be quite slow, but you'll be getting PostScript pages at a bargain. Another way to print on the DeskJet is with the Publisher's PowerPak driver (see "Utilities").

LaserMaster 1000 Plain-Paper Typesetter
7156 Shady Oak Road
Eden Prairie, MN 55344
612/944-9330 phone
612/944-0522 fax
The LaserMaster 1000 is based on a 400-dpi Canon engine, but the resolution is increased to 1000 dpi in the horizontal direction. In the vertical direction, resolution is also enhanced through a proprietary technology that smooths out the rough spots on fonts. The printer is profiled in Chapter 4, "Laser Printers."

Xerox 4020 Color Inkjet
Xerox Corporation
P.O. Box 24
Rochester, NY 14692
800/832-6979
Although this printer cannot rival laser printers in speed, its color capabilities are excellent. With Ventura, you can assign color attributes to type, frame backgrounds, ruling lines, and graphic fills. Imported graphics, such as Lotus charts, are also automatically assigned colors. With the 4020, both text and pictures print at 240 by 120 dots per inch, and eight colors are available. Swiss (Helvetica) and Dutch (Times Roman) are available in sizes from 8 to 36 points; there is no Symbol font.

Xerox 4045 Laser CP
Xerox Corporation
P.O. Box 24
Rochester, NY 14692
800/832-6979
This is a ten-page-per-minute printer with 300-dpi output. It also includes an optional copier. It is rated for print volumes of 2,000 to 10,000 pages per month. Basic memory is 128K, but can be expanded to 512K to allow more typefaces per page and larger graphics. Ventura provides two drivers for the 4045, one for

300-dpi graphics and the other for 150-dpi graphics. The latter can be used to print a page that exceeds the memory of the 4045 if printed at 300 dpi. The 4045 cannot print white text on a black background. It is compatible with the Diablo 630 and the Xerox 2700 II laser printer. Fonts can be converted from LaserJet format using Ventura's font conversion utilities; however, since the 4045 uses write-white technology rather than the write-black technology used by the LaserJet, converted fonts may suffer in quality.

Printer Controllers

Adobe Systems PostScript Cartridge

Adobe Systems, Inc.
1585 Charleston Rd.
P.O. Box 7900
Mountain View, CA 94039
415/961-4400
This is the fastest PostScript cartridge for the LaserJet II printer.

Gradco's TurboPrint

General Peripherals, Inc.
7 Morgan
Irvine, CA 92718
800/447-2326
Developed by Conographic Corporation and formerly named the ConoDesk 6000, this is a Post-Script-compatible upgrade card for the LaserJet II or any other printer with a Canon engine. It comes with 35 scalable fonts. Its main advantage is high speed, which it accomplishes by means of specialized coprocessor chips.

HP LaserJet PostScript Cartridge

Hewlett-Packard Co.
19310 Pruneridge Ave.
Cupertino, CA 95014
800/752-0900
This PostScript cartridge plugs into a LaserJet IIP, IID, or III. It will not work with a LaserJet II. It is the fastest PostScript cartridge for the LaserJet family, using the latest version of PostScript with improved font rendering. When you use this cartridge with the LaserJet III, you also get the benefit of that printer's resolution enhancement technology.

ImageScript

PCPI
10865 Rancho Bernardo Rd.
San Diego, CA 92127
619/485-8411
800/225-4098
This PostScript-emulation cartridge for LaserJet Series II, IID, IIP, and III has forty-seven resident fonts. Previously the output quality was not as good as Adobe's and HP's cartridges. Recently, however, the Image-Script cartridge has been upgraded and the price has been slashed. With a suggested list price of $299, this cartridge is a real bargain.

clip art

LaserJet fonts

PostScript fonts

font tools

graphics software

monitors

LaserJet-compatible printers

PostScript printers (300 dpi)

PostScript printers and typesetters (above 300 dpi)

other printers

printer controllers

scanners

utilities

user groups

bulletin boards

newsletters and magazines

style sheets

training

PostScript service bureaus

other resources

JetScript

The Laser Connection, Inc.
7852 Schillinger Park West
Mobile, AL 36608
800/523-2696
205/633-7223

This is a PostScript add-on board that converts an HP LaserJet II into a PostScript printer. Less convenient that a PostScript cartridge, it also has another drawback—you can's share the JetScript between two computers.

JLaser controllers

Tall Tree Systems
2585 E. Bayshore Road
Palo Alto, CA 94303
415/964-1980

There are a number of versions of the JLaser controller. The newest one, the JLaser 5, is capable of printing up to 256 shades of gray with Ventura. The JLaser board installed in the computer and connected via a special high-speed cable to the printer. Most models currently require a Canon CX or SX engine. With these boards, you can continue to operate your printer as usual through its normal cable. But with Ventura and other software programs that have JLaser drivers, the JLaser controller will automatically take control of the printer.

LaserMaster Series III Controllers

LaserMaster Corp.
7156 Shady Oak Rd.
Eden Prairie, MN 55344
612/944-6069

LaserMaster originally made a name for itself providing fast output for AutoCAD users, and now provides a set of extremely fast controller boards for laser printers. Like the JLaser board, the LaserMaster Series III controllers are installed in the computer and connected to most types of laser printers. They are profiled in Chapter 4, "Laser Printers."

PacificPage

Pacific Data Products
9125 Rehco Road
San Diego, CA 92121
619/552-0880

This plug-in PostScript-clone cartridge comes in various versions for the LaserJet II, IIP, or III printer. It includes the standard 35 scalable fonts that are resident in most PostScript printers.

PS Jet and PS Jet Plus

The Laser Connection, Inc.
7852 Schillinger Park West
Mobile, AL 36608
800/523-2696
205/633-7223

PS Jet and PS Jet Plus are kits that convert an HP LaserJet or other printer using the Canon LBP-CX engine into a PostScript printer. The kits also provide an HP LaserJet emulation, allowing you to continue using software packages that lack PostScript drivers.

PC Publisher Kit
QMS/Laser Connection
One Magnum Pass
Mobile, AL 36618
800/523-2696
205/633-7223
The PC Publisher Kit is an add-on board that adds DDL and Post-Script compatibility to a LaserJet II printer.

TIGer-CUB
Advanced Vision Research
2201 Qume Drive
San Jose, CA 95131-9801
408/434-1115
408/434-0968 fax
An add-in card that speeds up printing of complex pages at 300 dpi. It works with the HP LaserJet II and most Canon-engine printers.

TurboPrint
Gradco Printer Systems
7 Morgan
Irvine, CA 92718
714/454-0108
800/628-1538
This controller comes with 35 scalable, rotatable fonts and supports the Bitstream type library. Add-on memory board is for HP LaserJet Series II and III. The system uses Conographic technology, which is fully compatible with the PostScript language.

Scanners

Abaton Scan 300
Abaton, A Division of Everex
48431 Milmont Dr.
Fremont, CA 94538
415/683-2226
800/444-5321
This scanner is the same as the MicroTek.

Dest PC Scan 2000 and 3000 Series
Dest Corporation
1015 East Brokaw Road
San Jose, CA 95131
408/436-2700
408/436-2750 fax
These are flatbed grayscale that come with Publish Pac and PC Paintbrush software.

Handy Scanner 3000 Plus
DFI, Inc.
2544 Port Street
West Sacramento, CA 95691
916/373-1234
916/373-0221 fax
The Handy Scanner is the highest resolution hand-held scanner available. It will scan an image four inches wide and 20 inches long at up to 400 dpi. The $359 scanner comes with the excellent Halo DPE graphics software and has the ability to recognize up to 32 levels of gray. It saves to PCX, TIFF, MSP, CUT (HALO DPE), or IMG formats. An optional OCR (Optical Character Recognition) software is available for an un-

clip art

LaserJet fonts

PostScript fonts

font tools

graphics software

monitors

LaserJet-compatible printers

PostScript printers (300 dpi)

PostScript printers and typesetters (above 300 dpi)

other printers

printer controllers

scanners

utilities

user groups

bulletin boards

newsletters and magazines

style sheets

training

PostScript service bureaus

other resources

believably low $99 (or $249 for the advanced "trainable" version of the software). Once you've mastered the hand-eye coordination necessary, the image quality is surprisingly good for such an inexpensive scanner. DFI also offers a system which turns any home video camera into a video scanner.

Logitech ScanMan Plus
Logitech
6505 Kaiser Drive
Fremont, CA 94555
415/795-8500
415/792-8901 fax
The ScanMan is one of the new breed of hand-held image scanners. It will scan an image up to four inches wide by fourteen inches long at up to 400 dpi in 32 shades of gray. It saves files in TIFF, PCX, or MSP format.

ScanJet Plus
Hewlett-Packard
1820 Embarcadero Rd.
Palo Alto, CA 94303
800/367-4772
This scanner is profiled in Chapter 6, "Scanners."

SX-1000 Scanning System
Desktop Technology
986 Mangrove, Suite B
Sunnyvale, CA 94086
408/738-4001
800/759-4001
This innovative device converts any Epson model FX, MX, RX, and LQ printers into an inexpensive ($250) scanner. The material to be scanned is placed between

the rollers of the Epson printer and is then digitized by the scanner device, which replaces the printhead of the Epson. The scanner can record eight levels of gray. Images are saved in TIFF or PCX format.

Utilities

2-UP Publisher
Laser Age Software Company
3231 Ocean Park Blvd. #104
Santa Monica, CA 90405
213/470-1397
Creates 2-up and saddle-stiched layout on HP LaserJet printers.

386-to-the-Max
Qualitas, Inc.
8314 Thoreau Dr.
Bethesda, MD 20817-3164
This utility allows you to free up conventional memory by loading drivers and other programs into extended memory on an 80386-based computer. It is discussed in Chapter 26, "Memory Limitations and Solutions."

AdVentura
The Golem Press
Box 1342
Boulder, CO 80306
303/590-1367
This utility converts text from Ventura to Editwriter format.

Arabic Adaption of Ventura Publisher

Glyph Systems, Inc.
P.O. Box 134
Andover, MA 01810
508/470-1317

BackLoader

See "Font Tools"

Code to Code

Alphabytes, Inc.
111 Eighth St. SE
Washington, DC 20003
202/546-4119
This shareware utility removes Ventura formatting codes from a document so that you can edit it more easily. When you're finished, it replaces the codes again.

Collage Plus

Inner Media, Inc.
60 Plain Rd.
Hollis, NH 03049
603/465-3216
Collage Plus is a set of screen-capture utilities: SNAP captures an image and lets you view it; SAVE is the same as SNAP except that it doesn't allow viewing; VIEW makes it easy to look at images. Using the SHOW utility, you can quickly display, rename, or delete any graphic images. SHOW may also be used from a batch file to produce a custom video slide show. Collage works only on PCX and TIFF graphics. It supports VGA, EGA, HGC, CGA, and MDA monitors. One of the strong points of this program

is its ability to convert colors to shades of gray.

ColorSep/PC

Ozette Technologies
P.O. Box 208
Morrisville, PA 19067-0208
215/493-2720
The program creates color separations from Ventura print files.

DataPub

HB Type and Graphics
1615 Alabama St.
Huntington Beach, CA 92648
714/536-3939
This menu-driven utility processes and tags your database files prior to importing into Ventura.

DataTAG

Publishing Solutions
205 E. 78th St. #17T
New York, NY 10021
212/288-2470
A utility for loading database files into Ventura, DataTAG is profiled in Chapter 27, "Utilities."

dbPublisher for Ventura

Digital Composition Systems
1715 W. Northern Ave. #201
Phoenix, AZ 85021
602/870-7667
800/527-2506
This program reads dBASE DBF files directly and lets you sort and tag the fields you want to import into Ventura. It also works with other database programs, including R:BASE and Paradox. You work within dbPublisher to create a tagged text file. The pro-

clip art

LaserJet fonts

PostScript fonts

font tools

graphics software

monitors

LaserJet-compatible printers

PostScript printers (300 dpi)

PostScript printers and typesetters (above 300 dpi)

other printers

printer controllers

scanners

utilities

user groups

bulletin boards

newsletters and magazines

style sheets

training

PostScript service bureaus

other resources

gram then automatically runs Ventura and loads your chapter. The program comes with predefined style sheets for catalogs, newsletters, form letters, labels, directories, and price lists.

The DeskTop

Logical Solutions
11524 SW 56th Place
Portland, OR 97219
503/452-1029
This utility, which works only with the GEM version, provides a variety of document management functions. It lets you move, copy, and delete files; keep track of chapters by revision number; and view the contents of a style sheet.

DESQview

Quarterdeck Office Systems
150 Pico Blvd.
Santa Monica, CA 90405
213/392-9851
213/399-3802 fax
This multitasking windows program for the PC is compatible with most popular software, and it works with a mouse.

Editor's Desk Set

Metroplex Digital Corp.
P.O. Box 815729
Dallas, TX 75381-5729
214/231-8944
This is a combination package that includes CodeCard, Mouse-Ware, PubStar, TagCommand, and VPMover.

Flash

Software Masters
6352 N. Guilford Ave.
Indianapolis, IN 46220
317/253-8088
This is a disk caching utility. For details, see Chapter 23, "Speed Tips," and Chapter 26, "Memory Limitations and Solutions."

Font Library Manager

See "Font Tools"

Font Maker

See "Font Tools"

FontSpace

See "Font Tools"

Freedom of Press

Computer Applications Inc.
5 Middlesex Technology Center
900 Middlesex Turnpike
Billerica, MA 01821
800/873-4367
Like GoScript, Freedom of Press lets you print PostScript files on a non-PostScript printer. The program comes with drivers for a number of printers, as well as 35 PostScript fonts. It's especially good in combination with the HP DeskJet. The main drawbacks of the program is its slow speed.

GoScript

LaserGo, Inc.
9369 Carroll Park Drive, Suite A
San Diego, CA 92121
619/450-4600
619/450-9334 fax
This utility translates PostScript commands into bitmapped im-

ages, allowing you to proof Post-Script output on your IBM PC/XT/AT, PS/2, or compatible screen and print on dot-matrix, ink-jet, and laser printers. You can also save your print files in TIFF or PCX format. GoScript includes 13 scalable fonts; GoScript Plus includes 35 scalable fonts.

The Graphics Link Plus

TerraVision, Inc.
2351 College Station Road #563
Athens, GA 30605
404/769-5641
404/769-8013 fax

This is a graphics conversion utility that converts graphics files among a variety of formats, including PCC, PCX, IMG, TIF, WPG, CompuServe GIF, Windows Paint MSP, Dr. Halo CUT, and Show Partner/FX GX1. It also converts up to 256 color values into grayscale equivalents.

GrafPlus

Jewell Technologies, Inc.
4740 44th Ave. SW #203
Seattle, WA 98116
206/937-1081

This is a screen snapshot utility.

Hebrew Adaptation of Ventura Publisher

Glyph Systems, Inc.
P.O. Box 134
Andover, MA 01810
508/470-1317

HiJaak

Inset Systems, Inc.
71 Commerce Drive
Brookfield, CT 06804
203/740-2400
800/828-8088

This is a utility for capturing files or screens and converting pictures from one graphics format to another. For details, see Chapter 19, "Screen Snapshots."

HotShot Grab, HotShot Graphics

Symsoft
924 Incline Way, Box 5
Incline Village, NV 89450
800/344-0160

HotShot Grab is a simple screen snapshot utility. HotShot Graphics adds a painting program for enhancing captured screens. The two are profiled in Chapter 19, "Screen Snapshots."

HP w/ESP

See "Font Tools"

Index!

Trinity Software
P.O. Box 3610
9380 C-1 Forestwood Lane
Manassas, VA 22110
703/369-2429
800/247-9079
703/369-4386 fax

This utility speeds up the process of inserting index references into a Ventura chapter. Instead of entering a separate index code for each occurrence of a term, you enter the term and the code just once in Index!'s database.

clip art

LaserJet fonts

PostScript fonts

font tools

graphics software

monitors

LaserJet-compatible printers

PostScript printers (300 dpi)

PostScript printers and typesetters (above 300 dpi)

other printers

printer controllers

scanners

utilities

user groups

bulletin boards

newsletters and magazines

style sheets

training

PostScript service bureaus

other resources

clip art

LaserJet fonts

PostScript fonts

font tools

graphics software

monitors

LaserJet-compatible
printers

PostScript printers
(300 dpi)

PostScript printers
and typesetters
(above 300 dpi)

other printers

printer controllers

scanners

utilities

user groups

bulletin boards

newsletters and
magazines

style sheets

training

PostScript service
bureaus

other resources

Intelligent HP Driver for Ventura
Esper
P.O. Box 18470
Knoxville, TN 37928
615/687-8016

JetPropulsion
Digital Products, Inc.
108 Water Street
Watertown, MA 02172
617/924-1680
Speed up your LaserJet III or IIP by 200 percent to 500 percent by compressing graphics data! Also compatible with DeskJet and DeskJet Plus if they use the PCL5 control language.

KeyCap
Information Conversion Services
1625 South Fairview
Park Ridge, IL 60068
312/266-8378
The utility translates documents from Xerox Memorywriter format into Ventura.

LaserJet III Ventura driver
VPUG, Inc.
7502 Aaron Place
San Jose, CA 95139
408/227-5030
Ventura Professional! magazine and Softare Systems Consulting developed this driver to connect Ventura to the new LaserJet III. You can also add any LJ III-compatible soft font to the width table included in the package.

LetrTuck+
EDCO Services, Inc.
12410 N. Dale Mabry Hwy.
Tampa, FL 33618
800/523-8973
813/962-7800
This is a program that lets you modify kerning tables for higher-quality typography.

Link
Computer Solutions for Publishing
21171 Banff Lane
Huntington Beach, CA 92646
714/536-7008
This is a utility for printing Ventura files on a Compugraphic typesetter.

MouseWare
Metroplex Digital Corporation
P.O. Box 815729
Dallas, TX 75381-5729
214/231-8944
This memory-resident utility lets you use the righ button of your mouse to select OK within dialog boxes or to change viewing modes. It also lets you speed up or slow down your mouse.

PC Tools Deluxe
Central Point Software
15220 N.W. Greenbrier Pkwy.
Suite 200
Beaverton, OR 97006
503/690-8090
503/690-8083 fax
The file management tools of PC Tools are useful for finding Ventura files and backing up chapters. Also, PC Tools includes an excellent disk caching program.

Pizazz Plus

Application Techniques, Inc.
10 Lomar Park Dr.
Pepperell, MA 01463
508/433-5201
A screen snapshot utility.

PrintCache

LaserTools Corporation
1250 - 45th Street #100
Emeryville, CA 94608
415/420-8777
415/420-1150 fax
An intelligent spooler, PrintCache can use extended memory, expanded (EMS) memory, or the hard disk to buffer data on the way to the printer. The program makes it possible to full-page, 300-dpi graphics to be printed on a 512K LaserJet Plus or LaserJet II. It works with Windows 3.0.

PRN2TBL

Advanced Systems Ltd.
803 W. Main St. #112
League City, TX 77573
713/333-9717
This utility converts Lotus 1-2-3 files into Ventura tables.

Publisher's Powerpak

See "Font Tools"

Pub*Star

Metroplex Digital Corporation
P.O. Box 815729
Dallas, TX 75381-5729
214/231-8944
This utility pops up within your word processor (WordPerfect, WordStar, WordStar 2000, or Microsoft Word) and lets you insert Ventura codes for index

marks, trademark symbols, hidden text, etc. For more details, see Chapter 9, "Working with Style Sheets."

SoftKicker 2.0, SoftKicker Plus

Aristocad, Inc.
1650 Centre Pointe Dr.
Milpitas, CA 95035
408/946-2747
800/338-2629
800/426-8288 (CA)
SoftKicker, a utility that works with EGA and VGA monitors, allows you to move around your page without using the scroll bars. It is profiled in Chapter 5, "Monitors." SoftKicker Plus is similar to SoftKicker, but works within Windows.

Sundial

Metroplex Digital Corp.
P.O. Box 815729
Dallas, TX 75381-5729
214/231-8944
This program functions as an address manager and label maker.

Super PC-Kwik

Multisoft Corp.
15100 SW Koll Parkway
Suite L
Beaverton, OR 97007
503/644-5644
503/646-8267 fax
This is one of the most highly-rated disk caching utilities on the market. For details, see Chapter 23, "Speed Tips," and Chapter 26, "Memory Limitations and Solutions."

clip art

LaserJet fonts

PostScript fonts

font tools

graphics software

monitors

LaserJet-compatible printers

PostScript printers (300 dpi)

PostScript printers and typesetters (above 300 dpi)

other printers

printer controllers

scanners

utilities

user groups

bulletin boards

newsletters and magazines

style sheets

training

PostScript service bureaus

other resources

Table Manners

Desktop Publishing Group
978 Douglas Ave. #104
Altamonte Springs, FL 32714
407/862-7755
800/257-8087
This utility processes Lotus 1-2-3 files for loading into Ventura.

Tag!

Trinity Software
P.O. Box 3610
9380 C1 Forestwood Lane
Manassas, VA 22110
703/369-2429
This utility lets you see your text in one window and your tags in another, assisting the process of assigning tags before you load your text file into Ventura.

TagCommand

Metroplex Digital Corporation
P.O. Box 815729
Dallas, TX 75381-5729
214/231-8944
This utility provides several style sheet and tag management features. It lets you view the attributes of a tag, change every tag in a style sheet to a single type style, and find tags that aren't being used in a chapter.

TagMaster

Committed To Results, Inc.
P.O. Box 468024
Cincinnati, OH 45246
513/860-4402
This utility assists in pre-tagging database and spreadsheet files.

Tagteam

Sage Productions
5677 Oberlin Dr.
San Diego, CA 92121
619/455-7513
This is a utility that smooths the connection between WordPerfect and Ventura. When you're going from WordPerfect, it speeds up tagging by automatically converting WordPerfect formats into Ventura tags. When you're using WordPerfect to re-edit a text file that has already been tagged in Ventura, it strips away those bothersome "@TAGNAME =" codes and converts other embedded codes into a less conspicuous form.

TagWrite

Zandar Corp.
P.O. Box 480
Newfane, VT 05345
800/662-9667
802/254-3399 fax
This is an automatic tagging utility that works with Word-Perfect (4.2 through 5.1), Microsoft Word (4.0 through 5.0), OfficeWriter 6.1, Word for Windows/RTF, and ASCII text files.

Tiffany Plus

Anderson Consulting & Software
P.O. Box 40
North Bonneville, WA 98639
800/733-9633
This is a heavy-duty screen capture utility for Windows 3.0. It offers numerous options for saving your screen shots, including three kinds of TIFF formats and two kinds of PCX files. You can capture either the entire screen,

the currently active window, or the current menu or dialog box.

Typesetter's Connection
The Computer Group
14 Ellis Potter Court
Madison, WI 53711
608-273-1803
A utility for printing Ventura files on a Compugraphic typesetter.

Type Studio
Publisher's Shareware
P.O. Box 72
Rockwall, TX 75087
This is a shareware utility for creating special effects with PostScript fonts. Effects include rotating, condensing, expanding, drop shadows, tilting, and outlining, alone or in combination. To get a disk, send $9 to the above address. If you continue to use the program, Publisher's Shareware requests a $39 licensing fee.

Vcache & Vopt
Golden Bow System
P.O. Box 3039
San Diego, CA 92103
800/284-3269
619/483-0901
619/483-1924 fax
Vcache is an excellent set of disk caching programs. The package includes versions for regular, extended, or expanded memory, as well as speed-up for diskettes, screens, and keyboards. Vopt is a "disk-optimizing" program which keeps the files on your hard disk contiguous.

VenEdit
QPlus Inc.
2020 Beechwood Blvd.
Pittsburgh, PA 15217
412/521-9525
This is a text editor designed specifically for use with Ventura. It lets you do spell checking on text files that have been indexed, a problem with regular word processors.

Ventura Publisher Fax Card Driver
Software Systems Consulting
735 Tarento Dr.
San Diego, CA 92106
619/226-4112

VP2WP
See WP2VP

VP/Base
See XVP/Base

vpEMCEE
Four Seasons Publishing Co.
246 East 46th St.
New York, NY 10017
212/599-2141
This utility keeps track of graphics and text file locations associated with Ventura chapters. It can also compress files and copy them to a different location.

VP-Fax
Software Systems Consulting
735 Tarento Dr.
San Diego, CA 92106
619/226-4112
This utility works from within Ventura, letting you print Ventura

clip art

LaserJet fonts

PostScript fonts

font tools

graphics software

monitors

LaserJet-compatible printers

PostScript printers (300 dpi)

PostScript printers and typesetters (above 300 dpi)

other printers

printer controllers

scanners

utilities

user groups

bulletin boards

newsletters and magazines

style sheets

training

PostScript service bureaus

other resources

documents to a PCX file which
you can then transmit using a PC
fax board.

VP Manager 1.02
Aristocad, Inc.
1650 Centre Pointe Dr.
Milpitas, CA 95035
408/946-2747
800/338-2629
800/426-8288 (CA)
This utility, which is profiled in
Chapter 27, "Utilities," provides
Ventura with additional file
management and document
management capabilities, as well
as automatic timed backup.

VPMover
Metroplex Digital Corporation
P.O. Box 815729
Dallas, TX 75381-5729
214/231-8944
This utility will move all the files
associated with a chapter into a
single compressed archive file.

VP/Saddle
See XVP/Base

VPToolbox, VPToolbox Advanced Edition
SNA, Inc.
P.O. Box 3662
Princeton, NJ 08543
609/799-9605
609/799-9639 fax
An extremely useful file and style
sheet management utility. It is
profiled in Chapter 9, "Working
with Style Sheets."

VP/Tabs
See XVP/Base

VP to the Max
Aristocad, Inc.
1650 Centre Poine Dr.
Milpitas, CA 95035
408/946-2747
800/338-2629
800/426-8288 (CA)
This utility provides you with
search and replace, spell checking, a thesaurus, and ability to
see style sheet attributes—all
without leaving Ventura. The one
big drawback is that the spell
checker only works with text that
was generated in ASCII, not in
word processor format.

VTune
Eti Software
2930 Prospect Avenue
2nd Floor
Cleveland, OH 44115
216/241-1140
800/336-2014
216/241-2319 fax
This utility pops up from within
Ventura when you load a text file.
It gives you a variety of options
for "conditioning" the text file by
converting multiple spaces to
tabs, removing extraneous carriage returns, creating automatic
fractions, etc.

VP Utility Pak I
Digital Presentation Services
220 West 24th St.
New York, NY 10011
212/924-7661
This set of utilities contains three
programs. The first processes

spreadsheets that have been printed to disk, replacing spaces between columns with tabs. The second removes extra carriage returns and spaces in a document, and globally adds Ventura character attributes such as bold and italic to words and phrases throughout a document. The third utility automatically places the correct Ventura indexing codes to mark every occurrence of the same word in a document.

WithStyle

Pecan Software Systems, Inc.
1410 39th St.
Brooklyn, NY 11218
718/851-3100
A style sheet management and editing utility. It lets you examine, print, and edit tag attributes, and transplant tags from one style sheet to another.

WP2VP, VP2WP

R. Abrams
816 Rome
Los Angeles, CA 90065
(no phone number available)
These utilities take care of a number of housekeeping details necessary for importing Word-Perfect files into Ventura and converting text files from other formats to WordPerfect 5.0 format. The price is $35 for either utility or $65 for both. For more details, see Chapter 27, "Utilities."

WVBridge

Eti Software
2930 Prospect Avenue
2nd Floor
Cleveland, OH 44115
216/241-1140
800/336-2014
216/241-2319 fax
This utility translates Wang and other word processing files into Ventura format.

XIP

Xitron, Inc.
1428 East Ellsworth
Ann Arbor, MI 48108
313/971-8530
A utility that translates Ventura files for outputting on a Linotronic 202 typesetter.

XPort

Micrografx, Inc.
1303 Arapaho
Richardson, TX 75081
214/234-1769
800/272-3729
214/234-2410 fax
This utility coverts graphics files among CGM, MacDraw PICT, AutoCAD DXF, Micrografx DRW, and GEM formats.

XVP/Base, XVP/Tabs, VP/Saddle

The Laser Edge
4432 Pampas Ave.
Oakland, CA 94619
800/777-1581
These utilities are profiled in Chapter 27, "Utilities." XVP/Base imports dBASE data into Ventura Publisher. XVP/Tabs imports spreadsheet data into Ventura,

clip art

LaserJet fonts

PostScript fonts

font tools

graphics software

monitors

LaserJet-compatible printers

PostScript printers (300 dpi)

PostScript printers and typesetters (above 300 dpi)

other printers

printer controllers

scanners

utilities

user groups

bulletin boards

newsletters and magazines

style sheets

training

PostScript service bureaus

other resources

converting the spaces between columns into tabs. VP/Saddle lets you print two-up and saddle-stitch documents, as well as facing pages and enlarged pages, on PostScript printers.

User Groups

National Association of Desktop Publishers (NADTP)

1260 Boylston Street
Boston, MA 02215
617/426-2885
800/874-4113
NADTP is an independent, non-profit trade association devoted to desktop publishing in general (Mac and PC), not just Ventura. Membership benefits include a bimonthly 64-page journal and substantial discounts on hardware, software, training, and books.

VPUG Central

Bob Moody and Lynn Walterick
7502 Aaron Place
San Jose, CA 95131
408/227-5030
408/224-9086 fax
This is the headquarters of the Ventura Publishers Users Group. It is an incorporated entity that publishes the monthly magazine *Ventura Professional!* (see "Newsletters and Magazines" be-

low) as well as the Ventura Professional Forum, an electronic bulletin board (see "Bulletin Boards" below). For those living in the San Francisco Bay Area, the group holds a meeting every first Monday at 6:00 p.m.

Arizona

Arizona VPUG

John Mosier
Laserworks
2101 North 24th St.
Phoenix, AZ 85008
602/230-1752
This group is still listed in Ventura Professional's list of user groups, which says that it meets on the fourth Tuesday of the month. However, when we attempted to contact Arizona VPUG at this address, our letter was returned.

California

Arcadia SGV-VPUG

Mel Minami or Tatjana Standish
The Computer Lab
Arcadia, CA
818/445-1626
Meets on the fourth Tuesday of the month.

East Bay Ventura Users

Evonne Hopkins or Shirley
Schlueter
415/460-8462

Fresno VPUG

Dennis Patrick
Brandon and Tibbs
5085 East McKinley Ave.
Fresno, CA 93727
209/453-0336

Irvine VPUG

Marcia Couey or Laura Kilby
Techwriter's Ink
Marcia: 714/552-7272
Laura: 714/966-1180
Meets on the second Wednesday
of the month.

PC Publishers of Northern California

Eric Leong
San Francisco, CA 94110
415/635-0159
Meets on the third Thursday of
the month.

San Bernardino VPUG

Ramona Hagar
The Earth Technology Corp.
San Bernardino, CA
714/381-3356 ext. 352
714/883-5573

San Diego VPUG

Terry Gilman or Jim Mack
619/2725-9292
Meets on the third Tuesday of the
month.

San Mateo VPUG

Eleanor L. Church
United States Postal Service
280 Medio Ave.
Half Moon Bay, CA 94019
415/726-3181
This group meets on the second
Monday of every month and publishes an informative monthly
newsletter.

Santa Barbara VPUG

Dana Trout
P.O. Box 2450
Goleta, CA 93118
805/685-7937
Meetings are at 7 p.m. on the first
Friday of every month at the
Goleta Main Library. The group
also publishes a newsletter, "The
Goleta Publisher," and lends
books, training videos, and peri-
odicals.

Southern California VPUG (SC-VPUG)

Randy Tobin
1309 Riverside Drive
Burbank, CA 91506
818/955-5830
This group meets on the fourth
Wednesday of the month and
produces a newsletter.

Upland VPUG

Anthony Beyenhos, Jr.
714/981-0814
Meets the third Tuesday of the
month.

Ventura County VPUG

Bob Tracy
1873 Dewayne Ave.
Camarillo, CA 93010
805/482-7092
Meets on the third Tuesday of the
month (none in December).

---

clip art

LaserJet fonts

PostScript fonts

font tools

graphics software

monitors

LaserJet-compatible printers

PostScript printers (300 dpi)

PostScript printers and typesetters (above 300 dpi)

other printers

printer controllers

scanners

utilities

user groups

bulletin boards

newsletters and magazines

style sheets

training

PostScript service bureaus

other resources

clip art

LaserJet fonts

PostScript fonts

font tools

graphics software

monitors

LaserJet-compatible printers

PostScript printers (300 dpi)

PostScript printers and typesetters (above 300 dpi)

other printers

printer controllers

scanners

utilities

user groups

bulletin boards

newsletters and magazines

style sheets

training

PostScript service bureaus

other resources

Colorado

Denver Ventura Publishers
Marsha Casey or Gene McCray
303/889-4421 or 303/288-1077
Meets on the first Wednesday of the month.

Front Range VPUG (FRVPUG)
Pat Hake or Jeannine Parker
Northglenn, CO
Pat: 303/457-0123
Jeannine: 303/694-2993

Florida

Florida VP
John Glenn
813/538-2832
This group publishes a newsletter but does not have meetings.

NF VPUG
William R. Ploss
904/376-2843
Meets third Thursday of the month.

VPUG of Tampa
Mike Meccia
3812 Hollister Place
Brandon, FL 33511
813/978-4604
Meets on the third Tuesday of the month.

Georgia

Ventura Users of Atlanta
Carol Lovelady
Lovelady Consulting
1100 Martin Ridge Road
Roswell, GA 30076
404/992-1545 (Voice)
404/423-4469 (BBS)
This group publishes the monthly newsletter *InPrint*. Other activities have included a design contest, a bulletin board, and a services directory. Meetings are on the second Tuesday of the month.

Illinois

Chicago VPUG
Paul Hanover
Alternative Type & Graphics
Chicago, IL
708/981-1973
One group meets on the last Thursday of the month in Des Plaines, the other in downtown Chicago on the first Thursday.

Chicago Electronic VPUG
George Weinert, Sysop
312/342-7652 (BBS)

Indiana

Central Indiana VPUG
Jerilyn Sander
317/257-1121
Meets on the third Wednesday of the month at 11:45 a.m.

Kentucky

Louisville VPUG
Ginny Smith or David Brooks
Louisville, KY
Ginny: 502/581-7117
David: 502/560-2562
This group meets at 11:30 a.m.,
one Thursday a month.

Maryland

Baltimore VPUG
Rick Vaughn or Jackie Watts
301/327-0069
This group meets the fourth
Thursday of the month.

Rockville VPUG
Donald Price
301/251-0971
Meets on the second Tuesday of
the month.

Massachusetts

Boston VPUG
Kathleen McGrath
617/329-4500, ext. 479 or
617/641-2864

Woods Hole VPUG
Dick Campbell 508/540-1309
or Dave Shephard 508/548-9600
This group meets the first Thursday of the month at 4:30 p.m.

Michigan

Detroit VPUG
Eileen Brundage
Governor Information Products
Detroit, MI
313/554-2200

Mid-Michigan VPUG
Cheryl Gierman
Michigan State University
162 Student Services Bldg.
East Lansing, MI 48824-1113
517/353-6650
Meets third Tuesday of the
month.

Minnesota

Twin Cities VPUG
Cheryl Edwards
Laser Images Publishing and
Graphics
5900 Baker Rd.
Minnetonka, MN 55345
612/829-7483
Though I haven't seen any issues
lately, in the past this group published an amusing and informative newsletter called *Hitchhiker's
Guide to Ventura*, which rose
above the dull plains of desktop
publishing with inspired passages like this one from the 12/88
issue: "There is nothing quite so
exasperating as placing an
original on the glass and letting
your scanner rip, only to have
something resembling a sixties
op-art poster slide out of your
laser printer." Meets fourth Tuesday of the month.

---

clip art

LaserJet fonts

PostScript fonts

font tools

graphics software

monitors

LaserJet-compatible
printers

PostScript printers
(300 dpi)

PostScript printers
and typesetters
(above 300 dpi)

other printers

printer controllers

scanners

utilities

user groups

bulletin boards

newsletters and
magazines

style sheets

training

PostScript service
bureaus

other resources

clip art
LaserJet fonts
PostScript fonts
font tools
graphics software
monitors
LaserJet-compatible printers
PostScript printers (300 dpi)
PostScript printers and typesetters (above 300 dpi)
other printers
printer controllers
scanners
utilities

user groups
bulletin boards
newsletters and magazines
style sheets
training
PostScript service bureaus
other resources

New Jersey

New Jersey VPUG
Barry Heil
201/351-6860
Meets the third Wednesday of the month.

New Mexico

Ventura Publishers of Albuquerque
Tara Kenny 505/842-9532 or Harold Washington 505/848-1771
Meets the second Wednesday of the month.

New York

Greater Buffalo VPUG
Paul Haumesser
PCI
704 Washington St.
Buffalo, NY 14203-1416
716/865-7181

Long Island VPUG
Ken Rubman
516/333-4488
Meets on the first Tuesday of the month.

NYXVP Users Group
Steve Terry
Electronic Directions
23 East 4th St.
New York, NY 10003
212/533-9651
212/677-1686

Meets on the second Monday of the month.

Rochester Area VPUG
Elecia Almekinder
716/454-2770

North Carolina

Charlotte VPUG
Ms. Perry Primm
704/846-6016

Ohio

Adventuras
Terri Halpin
513/860-4402
This group meets the second Thursday of the month and draws folks from the Cincinnati, Dayton and North Kentucky areas.

Oklahoma

Tulsa VPUG
Rob Amagna
8011D South Wheeling Ave.
Tulsa, OK 74136
918/492-3862

Oregon

Portland VPUG
Joe and Debbie Engel
503/281-3291

This group meets the third Monday of the month.

Pennsylvania

Pittsburgh VPUG
Tom Bates
La Roche College
Pittsburgh, PA
412/367-9300, ext. 180
Meets on the second Wednesday of the month.

Texas

Austin VPUG
Mary Rio
512/282-6699
Meets the last Tuesday of the month.

Dallas/Association of Desktop Publishers
Debbie Dickson
Responsive Computer Systems
Plano, TX
214/423-5944
Meets on the second Tuesday of the month.

San Antonio VPUG
Dean Kennedy
512/684-4567
Meets the first Saturday of the month at 9:30 a.m.

PUG Houston (VPUGH)
Derrick Booth
P.O. Box 270897
Houston, TX 77277
713/840-8098

Meets on the third Monday of the month.

Virginia

Nova-VPUG
Sally Smith
703/237-3755
Meets on the third Tuesday of the month.

Washington

Northwest VPUG (NWVPUG)
Chad Canty
Seattle Micro Publishing
c/o Banc Press
2001 Sixth Ave. #1703
Seattle, WA 98121
206/328-4144
206/322-8655

Wisconsin

Madison VPUG
Art Saffran
State Bar of Wisconsin
P.O. Box 7158
Madison, WI 53707
608/257-3838

Milwaukee VPUG
Gordon Kraemer
Laser Images Again & Again
5429 Montgomery Dr.
Greendale, WI 53129
414/421-0179
414/421-8824

clip art

LaserJet fonts

PostScript fonts

font tools

graphics software

monitors

LaserJet-compatible printers

PostScript printers (300 dpi)

PostScript printers and typesetters (above 300 dpi)

other printers

printer controllers

scanners

utilities

user groups

bulletin boards

newsletters and magazines

style sheets

training

PostScript service bureaus

other resources

Australia

VPUG Australia
Cynthia Kuiper
Future Technologies, Ltd.
433 Kent St., 5th Floor
Sydney NSW 2000
(02) 261-4211

Canada

Ottawa Carleton VPUG
Terry Taller
613/829-5320

**Vancouver Electronic
Publishing Association/
Ventura Special Interest
Group**
Lance Bracken
Vancouver, B.C. V5T 4E9
604/682-8372

Bulletin Boards

**Adobe Conference on
CompuServe**
*Dial your local CompuServe
access number. For information
on CompuServe, call
800/848-8199. In Ohio call
614/457-0802.*
To access the Adobe Conference,
type GO ADOBE from the
CompuServe prompt. The bul-

letin board has a special section
on Adobe's PC fonts, including
screen fonts for the 35 resident
typefaces and a downloading
utility.

Chicago Electronic VPUG
c/o George Weinert
312/342-7652

Columbus VPUG BBS
Shawn Ingram
Information Exchange BBS
Enhanced Data Systems
Columbus, OH
614/863-9064 (voice)
614/863-9065 (BBS)

**Eastern Publisher's
Exchange**
713/781-2432

**Ventura Conference on
CompuServe**
*Dial your local CompuServe
access number. For information on CompuServe, call
800/848-8199. In Ohio call
614/457-0802.*
To access the Ventura Conference, type GO XEROX from
the CompuServe prompt.

**Ventura Professonal
Forum**
408/227-4818
408/227-0223
This bulletin board is open to
anyone, though some special
files are open only to subscribers
to *Ventura Professional* magazine. The parameters for this for-

um are 2400/1200/300 baud, 8 bits, no parity, 1 stop bit.

Western Publisher's Exchange
714/739-5150

Newsletters and Magazines

PC Publishing
Hunter Publishing Company
950 Lee Street
Des Plaines, IL 60016
Since being acquired by Hunter Publishing, *PC Publishing* has greatly improved the quality of its coverage of Ventura-related topics. The magazine includes regular columns on Ventura and PostScript, and has feature articles on fonts.

Personal Publishing
Hitchcock Publishing Company
25W550 Geneva Rd.
Wheaton, IL 60188-2292
312/665-1000
Published monthly, this is the oldest desktop publishing magazine, covering both hardware and software for both the Macintosh and the PC.

Publish!
501 Second St. #600
San Francisco, CA 94107
415/546-7722
A sister publication of *PC World* and *Macworld*, this magazine covers a wide range of desktop publishing topics, both Macintosh and PC. It is the best source of guidance on design.

Seybold Report on Desktop Publishing
Seybold Publications, Inc.
Box 644
Media, PA 19063
215/565-2480
It doesn't come cheap ($192 for 12 monthly issues in the U.S., $198 in Canada, and $210 overseas), but if you really want to know what's what in the desktop publishing industry, this is the newsletter to read. If you're interested in topics like PostScript clones, color desktop publishing, or the latest on the font wars, the in-depth feature articles in Seybold are better than anything you'll find in regular computer or desktop publishing magazines.

Step-by-Step Electronic Design
Dynamic Graphics, Inc.
6000 North Forest Park Dr.
Peoria, IL 61614-3592
This monthly color newsletter offers valuable and timely information on new design techniques, typography, graphics, and software and hardware. Special features include the how-to of complex design production and a question-and-answer section.

clip art

LaserJet fonts

PostScript fonts

font tools

graphics software

monitors

LaserJet-compatible printers

PostScript printers (300 dpi)

PostScript printers and typesetters (above 300 dpi)

other printers

printer controllers

scanners

utilities

user groups

bulletin boards

newsletters and magazines

style sheets

training

PostScript service bureaus

other resources

Ventura Professional!

Ventura Publisher Users Group (VPUG)
7502 Aaron Place
San Jose, CA 95139
408/227-5030
408/224-9086 fax
Bulletin Board: 408/227-4818
(2400/1200/300 baud, no parity, 8 bits, 1 stop bit)
Ventura Professional is the magazine of VPUG, which also operates the Ventura Professional Forum. Each issue of *Ventura Professional* is devoted to a special topic, such as fonts, databases, or newsletters. Among the regular departments is Xerox Pipeline, in which professional Ventura support personnel answer tough technical questions.

Style Sheets

Document Gallery Style Sheets

MicroPublishing
21150 Hawthorne Blvd. #104
Torrance, CA 90503
213/371-5787
For details on this collection, see Table 9-2 in Chapter 9, "Working with Style Sheets."

Style Sheets for Business Documents, Style Sheets for Newsletters, Style Sheets for Technical Documentation

New Riders Publishing
P.O. Box 4846
Thousand Oaks, CA 91360
818/991-5392
For details on this collection, see Table 9-2 in Chapter 9, "Working with Style Sheets."

Ventura Designer Style Sheets

BCA/Desktop Designs
P.O. Box 2191
Walnut Creek, CA 94595
800/727-8953
415/946-1716
For details on this collection, see Table 9-2 in Chapter 9, "Working with Style Sheets."

VPDesigner Style Sheets

HyperFormance, Inc.
4906 Fitzhugh Avenue
Suite 107
Richmond, VA 23230
804/355-0083
This set includes over 40 style sheets. Sample chapters are illustrated in the manual, which also details the production process.

Will-Harris Designer Disks

Designer Disks, Dept. V
P.O. Box 1235
Point Reyes, CA 94956
For details on this collection, see Table 9-2 in Chapter 9, "Working with Style Sheets."

Training

Desktop Publishing Solutions
ABC Information Systems
P.O. Box 1228
Royal Oak, MI 48068-1228
This is a video training course for Ventura. It includes two videocassettes, a workbook, and exercises on a floppy disk.

Video*Tutor* training videos
VideoTutor
110 Wild Basin Road #280
Austin, TX 78746
This series of video training tapes includes a basic package and an advanced package.

PostScript Service Bureaus

This list of PostScript service bureaus was originally downloaded from the Adobe Forum on CompuServe and then pared down considerably by a sending a letter to each service bureau. Those that did not respond were eliminated from the list. Adobe updates the list quarterly. To access the Forum, type GO ADOBE from the CompuServe prompt. For information about CompuServe, call 800/848-8199. In Ohio call 614/457-0802.

Another source of information on service bureaus is the Association of Imaging Service Bureaus, 5700 L.W. Market St., Greensboro, NC 27409; phone 800/962-9480 or 919/855-0400; fax 919/292-9203.

Nearly all of the service bureaus listed here have either a Linotronic 100 (1,270 dpi) or Linotronic 300 (2,540 dpi) typesetter. Some have a Varityper VT600, a plain-paper typesetter with 600-dpi resolution. Typically, Linotronic output runs $4 to $8 per page, while Varityper output may be as cheap as $1 per page. Many service bureaus provide other services, including scanning and porting files from Mac disks to PC disks.

Alabama

Bransby Productions
2124 Metro Circle
Huntsville, AL 35801
205/880-0452

Computer Publisher
400 River Hills Business Park
Suite 405
Birmingham, AL 35242
205/991-0032

clip art

LaserJet fonts

PostScript fonts

font tools

graphics software

monitors

LaserJet-compatible printers

PostScript printers (300 dpi)

PostScript printers and typesetters (above 300 dpi)

other printers

printer controllers

scanners

utilities

user groups

bulletin boards

newsletters and magazines

style sheets

training

PostScript service bureaus

other resources

Comp-U-Type
1920 10th Avenue South
Birmingham, AL 35205
205/323-8898
205/323-8830 modem

Arizona

Alphagraphics
3760 N. Commerce Dr.
Tucson, AZ 85705
602/293-9200
800/332-1616

Arkansas

Royal Graphics
523 West 7th St.
Little Rock, AR 72201
501/375-8255

California

5th Street Computer
1794 Fifth St.
Berkeley, CA 94710
415/843-8973

Advanced Electronics
329 Howard Drive
Santa Clara, CA 95051
408/984-3689

Applied Graphics Technologies (was Computer Typesetting)
601 Rodier Drive
Glendale, CA 91201
213/245-4111

Aptos Post Typography
101 Madeline Drive
Suite 202
Aptos, CA 95003
408/688-7474

Cal Sierra Lt.
737 Arnold Dr.
Martinez, CA 94553
415/372-4200

Design & Type, Inc.
739 Bryant St.
San Francisco, CA 94107
415/495-6280

DynaType Graphics Center
501 East Harvard St.
Glendale, CA 91205
818/243-1114
818/243-0734 fax
818/243-2502 modem

Gary Walton Graphics, Inc.
229 Polaris Ave., #8
Mountain View, CA 94043
415/961-0778

Graphics Plus
3760 South Robertson Blvd.
Suite 202
Culver City, CA 90232
213/559-3732

Krishna Copy Center
66 Kearny St.
San Francisco, CA 94108
415/986-6161

Krishna Copy Center
543 Mission St.
San Francisco, CA 94105
415/543-3688

Krishna Copy Center
2111 University Ave.
Berkeley, CA 94704
415/540-5959

Matrix Communications
229 Pajaro
Salinas, CA 93901
408/757-4164

One-Stop Desktop
2054 University Ave.
Berkeley, CA 94704
415/843-4960

Personal Publishing Service Bureau
1317 East Edinger
Santa Ana, CA 92705
714/558-0323
714/558-0324

Pinnacle Publishing Services
55 Osgood Place
San Francisco, CA 94133
415/989-8973

Southern California PrintCorp.
1010 East Union St. #205
Pasadena, CA 91107
818/795-7795

Synergistic Data Systems, Inc.
P.O. Box 127
Sierra Madre, CA 91025
818/351-7717 voice mail
818/351-8622 office

TechArt
400 Pacific Ane.
San Francisco, CA 94133
415/362-1110
415/362-2811 fax

Trunk Line
8800 Venice Blvd.
Los Angeles, CA 90034
213/204-2777
213/204-0270 BBS

The Typesetting Shop, Inc.
5236 Claremont Avenue
Oakland, CA 94618
415/654-5404
415/256-6300

Colorado

Mel Typesetting
1519 South Pearl Street
Denver, CO 80210
303/777-5571

clip art

LaserJet fonts

PostScript fonts

font tools

graphics software

monitors

LaserJet-compatible printers

PostScript printers (300 dpi)

PostScript printers and typesetters (above 300 dpi)

other printers

printer controllers

scanners

utilities

user groups

bulletin boards

newsletters and magazines

style sheets

training

PostScript service bureaus

other resources

PS: Computer Graphics, Inc.
4730 Walnut Street, #101
Boulder, CO 80301
303/939-9881

Connecticut

Atlantic Group
10 Fairfield Ave.
Stamford, CT 06902
203/359-4228

District of Columbia

Electric Logic
2025 Eye St. NW
Suite 220
Washington, DC 20006
202/223-9115

Florida

Comp-U-Type
1523 San Marco Blvd.
Jacksonville, FL 32207
904/346-0853
904/346-0856

George Hall Typography, Inc.
3417 W. Lemon
Tampa, FL 33609
813/870-1862

Georgia

Comp-U-Type
3019 Peachtree Street, NE
Atlanta, GA 30305
404/364-9272
404/364-9263 modem

Comp-U-Type
229 Mitchell Street, SW
Atlanta, GA 30303
404/ 659-3696
404/659-8392 modem

Comp-U-Type
3700 Holcombe Bridge Road
Suite 1
Norcross, GA 30092
404/263-7364
404/263-0126 modem

Comp-U-Type
3204 Northlake Pkwy.
Atlanta, GA 30345
404/934-5220
404/934-5571 modem

Comp-U-Type
2250 Cobb Parkway #42
Marietta, GA 30080
404/952-6294
404/952-6324 modem

Comp-U-Type
1182 Grimes Bridge Rd. #400
Roswell, GA 30075
404/587-3100
404/587-4512 modem

Comp-U-Type
5975 Roswell Road, #125
Atlanta, GA 30328
404/843-2050
404/843-3047 modem

Hawaii

Creative Resources
839 Queen St.
Honolulu, HI 96813
808/533-1715

Illinois

Alternative Type & Graphics
9700 W. Foster Ave.
Chicago, IL 60656
312/992-2050

Electronic Imaging Inc.
515 North Neil Street
Champaign, IL 61820
217/351-1550
217/351-1558 fax

Holland Printing
1007 E. 162nd St.
South Holland, IL 60473
708/596-9000

Lasercom, Inc.
1701 E. Lake Ave.
Glenview, IL 60025
312/724-2490

Xpress Graphics
137 N. Oak Park Ave. #200
Oak Park, IL 60301
312/848-8651

Indiana

David G. Dull & Associates
25762 Minor Rd.
Elkhart, IN 46514
219/262-8611

Iowa

Computer Graphic Center
605 12th St.
Des Moines, IA 50309
515/282-0000

Kansas

Commercial Art Service
9112 Constance St.
Lenexa, KS 66215
913/894-9391

Kentucky

Cobb Typesetting
901 Monmouth St.
Newport, KY 41071
606/291-1146

clip art

LaserJet fonts

PostScript fonts

font tools

graphics software

monitors

LaserJet-compatible printers

PostScript printers (300 dpi)

PostScript printers and typesetters (above 300 dpi)

other printers

printer controllers

scanners

utilities

user groups

bulletin boards

newsletters and magazines

style sheets

training

PostScript service bureaus

other resources

Louisiana

Professional Publications
1646 Belmont Ave.
Baton Rouge, LA 70808
504/346-0707

Maine

G & G Laser Typesetting
1030 Congress St.
Portland, ME 04102
207/774-7338

Maryland

F.E.A. Laser Service
2404 Ravenview Rd.
Timonium, MD 21093
301/252-8910

Spectrum Arts Ltd.
1823 Eutaw Pl.
Baltimore, MD 21217
301/462-6900

Massachusetts

TeleTypesetting
474 Commonwealth Ave.
Boston, MA 02215
617/266-6792

TeleTypesetting
311 Harvard Street
Brookline, MA 02146
617/734-9700

Wordwrap, Inc.
10 Church Street
North Attleboro, MA 02760
508/695-8066
508/695-8096 fax

Michigan

Mac Typenet
P.O. Box 3009
37911 West Twelve Mile Rd.
Entrance B
Farmington Hills, MI 48333
313/553-0880

Minnesota

NWprintcrafters, Inc.
287 East Sixth St.
St. Paul, MN 55101
612/227-7721

TypeMasters
4246 Park Glen Road
Minneapolis, MN 55426
612/927-9260
612/927-0589 fax

Nevada

Laser Graphix
3250 B Polluc
Las Vegas, NV 89102
702/871-5511

New Hampshire

Amanuensis
300E Bedford St.
Manchester, NH 03101
603/624-2704

New Jersey

Graphic Connexions, Inc.
10 Abeel Rd.
Cranbury, NJ 08512
609/655-8970

Harmony Press
1 Harmony Brass Castle Rd.
Phillipsburg, NJ 08865
201/454-1544

New York

Associated Graphic Services, Ltd.
13 Northern Blvd.
Albany, NY 12210
518/465-1497
518/426-3437 fax

Axiom Design Systems
6 West 18th St.
New York, NY 10011
212/989-1100

Graphique Advertising Group
306 Warren Street
North Babylon, NY 11703
516/321-4907

Micropage
900 Broadway
New York, NY 10003
212/533-9180

Ohio

Jala Advertising Inc.
640 Northland Blvd.
Cincinnati, OH 45240
513/742-4102

Oregon

Dynagraphics, Inc.
300 N.W. 14th Street
Portland, OR 97209
503/228-9453

Pennsylvania

Centre Grafik
950 West Valley Rd. #3004
Wayne, PA 19087
215/688-2949

CR Express
841 Chestnut St.
Philadelphia, PA 19107
215/829-9611

General Press Corporation
P.O. Box 316, Allegheny Dr.
Natrona Heights, PA 15065
412/224-3500

clip art

LaserJet fonts

PostScript fonts

font tools

graphics software

monitors

LaserJet-compatible printers

PostScript printers (300 dpi)

PostScript printers and typesetters (above 300 dpi)

other printers

printer controllers

scanners

utilities

user groups

bulletin boards

newsletters and magazines

style sheets

training

PostScript service bureaus

other resources

Rhode Island

Aquidneck Graphics & Publishing Services
Aquidneck Industrial Park
Middletown, RI 02840
401/849-9930

South Carolina

Patrick Graphics
1500 Highway 501
Myrtle Beach, SC 29577
803/448-7777

Tennessee

Macfactory
120 20th Ave. S.
Nashville, TN 37203
615/327-3437
615/327-1758

Texas

Ink Spot Printing Services, Corp.
1346 Lee Trevino
El Paso, TX 79936
915/598-1138

The Lazer's Edge, Inc.
4001 Broadway
San Antonio, TX 78209
512/494-9586

Lisat Systems
4204 Woodcock Drive
Suite 201
San Antonio, TX 78228
512/736-6400

Type Case, Inc.
611 Alston Ave.
Fort Worth, TX 76104
817/332-7563
817/336-1381 fax

Virginia

Tamarac Press
220 Industrial Dr.
Fredericksburg, VA 22401
703/898-7600

Washington

Seattle Imagesetting, Inc.
Bldg. Q, Suite 111
19428 66th Ave. S.
Kent, WA 98032
206/251-5856
206/251-5965 fax

Seattle Imagesetting, Inc.
3940 150th Ave. S.
Redmond, WA 98052
206/881-1866
206/883-8305 fax

Seattle Imagesetting, Inc.
1415 First Ave. S.
Seattle, WA 98104
206/382-1633

Wisconsin

Desktop Publishing Centers
300 North Van Buren St.
Milwaukee, WI 53202
414/223-4333

Granite Finance Corp. Computer Services Group
2885 South Moorland Rd.
New Berlin, WI 53151
414/797-7411

Canada

Ampersand Typographers
57 Research Rd.
Toronto, Ontario M4G 2G8
416/422-1444

Boldface Technologies Inc.
6046 A 97th St.
Edmonton, Alberta T6E 3J4
403/437-0632

Management Graphics, Inc.
1450 Lodestar Rd., Unit 1
Downsview, Ontario M3J 3C1
416/638-8877

Other Resources

CGMpix
41 Sutter St. #1850
San Francisco, CA 94101
800/452-4445 ext. 1130
800/626-9541 ext. 1130 (CA)
This company converts company logos and other graphics into CGM files, which can be imported into Ventura, scaled to any size, and printed on any kind of laser printer.

LaserColor
Imagineering
3875 Nautical Dr.
Carlsbad, CA 92008
619/434-7718
If you're tired of always printing monotonous black with your laser printer, you'll love this low-tech solution. It's an assortment of colored film that lets you apply color to any text or graphics on a page. The procedure is simple. You cut out a piece of the film, attach it to the area to which you want to transfer color, and run the page through the laser printer as though you were printing a blank page. The heat of the laser printer rollers seals the color onto the black toner, and the results are fantastic!

clip art

LaserJet fonts

PostScript fonts

font tools

graphics software

monitors

LaserJet-compatible printers

PostScript printers (300 dpi)

PostScript printers and typesetters (above 300 dpi)

other printers

printer controllers

scanners

utilities

user groups

bulletin boards

newsletters and magazines

style sheets

training

PostScript service bureaus

other resources

other resources

Logos On-Line
Software Complement
8 Pennsylvania Ave.
Matamoras, PA 18336
717/491-2492, 717/491-2495
This custom service renders a company's logo or signature in PostScript, EPS format.

Wordscapes
4546 B10
El Camino Real #177
Los Altos, CA 94022
415/968-8737
This service converts company logos and other graphics into Encapsulated PostScript files, which can be imported into Ventura, scaled to any size, and printed on PostScript (not LaserJet) printers. They can also format custom graphics into PostScript fonts that are Ventura compatible.

Appendix B
Graphics Program Compatibility

Ventura's ability to import text in Computer Graphics Metafile (CGM), Document Exchange Format (DXF), Hewlett-Packard Graphics Language (HPGL), and VideoShow (NAPLPS) formats gives you access to a large number of drawing, business graphics, scientific graphics, and CAD packages. The lists provided here were compiled by third-party vendors of products that support each format. However, the fact that a product appears on one of the lists does not mean that it has been tested for actual compatibility with Ventura. CGM files in particular have an erratic track record: some import into Ventura, others do not.

CGM

20/20 - Access Technology
A/GRAPH - Donovan Data Systems
Allspice - Acotech
Apollo - ABA Groups
ARC+ - Architecture and Computer Aids
Artline - Digital Research
Arts & Letters - Computer Support Corporation
ASI Font System - Analytical Software
Business Strategist and Business Simulator - Reality Development Corporation
CADTEC - Itautec Information S/A
Cadwrite - IBM
CASE Manager - Computer Aided Structural Engineering
COGO Pac - Maptech
Concept 100 - Concept Technologies
Corel Draw - Corel Systems Corporation
Custom/QC - Stochos
DaVinci Business Graphics Package - Professional Research Consultants
Designer - Micrografx
Display - ISSCO
ESTIMATION/Automatics - Tipnis
Excalibur - Communication Dynamics
Fortgraph APA - Digital Communications Associates
Freelance - Lotus
GAF - Simulation Software Systems
GPOS-7 - Planmetrics
GRAFTIME - Genigraphics Corporation
Graph 6 Application Development Facility - Honeywell Corporation
Graphics Operating System - University of Texas
Harvard Presentation Graphics - Software Publishing
Hornet 5000 - Claremont Controls
IRMAGRAF - Eastman Kodak

Labtech Notebook - Laboratory Technology Corporation
LARSA - Innovative Analysis
LLCOGO - Lewis and Lewis
MathPlan 3.0 - Wordperfect Corporation
Matrix-X - Integrated Systems
Mavis - Robinson Associates
Metal Building Program - International Structural Engineers
Micro Cadam - CADAM
MicroCAD - Imagimedia Technologies
MicroCUBE - McDonnell Douglas
MicroTrak - SofTrak Systems
OPTEC - Sciopt Enterprises
Opus - Optim Electronics
PC Link A Graph - ISSCO
PC-DOE - CA Systems International
pcEXPRESS - Information Resources
Personal Engineer - Computervision Corporation
PlotTrack - SofTrak Systems
PMS80 - Pinnell Engineering
PROCAD 4.02 - Interactive CAD Systems
Q.E.D. DAC - Hart Scientific
R:BASE Graphics - Microrim
Redliner - Auto-Trol Technology
Route Assist - Logistics Resource
Sigma-Plot and Sigma-Scan - Jandel Scientific
Simscript II.5 - CACI
SIPSURF - Delfts Spline Systems
Sound Presentations - Communication Dynamics
SPC-PC - Quality America
SPD - Tektronix
ST-PC Translator - Sangamo Weston
Super Sceptre - Austria Microsystems
Surface Display System - Design Professionals Management Systems
Technology Futures Software Library - Technology Futures
TextCharts - Hewlett-Packard
Timepiece - Communications Dynamics
VIA - Tektronix
Viewpoint Graphics - Computer Aided Management

VSA Software - Applied Computer Solutions
XICAMM - Xiris Corporation.

DXF

ACAM Standalone - Leonard Systems, Inc.
ANSSYS/PC Products - Swanson Analysis Systems, Inc.
Autoyacht/Autoship - Coastdesign, inc.
Bartsch NC/Step - Bartsch Corp.
CAMEAZE - P-CAN CAD-CAM Inc.
CAMplot - Tipnis Software Systems, Inc.
Contour - Civilsoft, Inc.
COSMO/M - Structural Research and Analysis Corp.
Details Library - Laticrete International, Inc.
Electronic Symbols Library - GT Systems
Equalizer - Microdata Technology, Inc.
Formats - CAD Technology Corp.
GeoCAD/CAM - Anderson-O'Brien, Inc.
GEOCAM - Com Technology, Inc.
GEOCAM - Solutionware Corp.
GEOLINK - Solutionware Corp.
GEOPATH IV - CIM Technology, Inc.
Geopoint IV - Anderson-O'Brien
GEOTEK1 - Datamat Programming Systems, Inc.
GEOTEK2 - Datamat Programming Systems, Inc.
GEOTEK3 - Datamat Programming Systems, Inc.
GRAFX+ - Datacut Inc.
Hand-Drafted Drawing Capture - FSA, Inc.
Highway Design Program-HDP - Civilsoft, Inc.
Image - Burghof Engineering Co.
Inertia/Inerbeam - Modern Computer Aided Engineering, Inc.

Inertia/Inerfram - Modern Computer Aided Engineering, Inc.
Inertia/Inerprop - Modern Computer Aided Enginerring, Inc.
Inertia/Inertruss - Modern Computer Aided Engineering, Inc.
INTEGRATOR-X - Autographic Digitrol, Inc.
MECH-LIB2 - CAD Technology
MSL/pal 2 - MacNeal-Schwendler Corp.
NC Wire EDM - Tipnis Software Systems, Inc.
Power Writer - Compucor
Pro-Vision - Caetec Systems, Inc.
Process Planning Automatics - Tipnis Software Systems, Inc.
Tubecad - Cone & Cone

HPGL

3-D GRAPHIXX - Universal Integraphix Corp.
4-Point Graphics - International Microcomputer Software
ACSL - Mitchell, Gauthier & Associates
ACX VM Printer Manager - ACX Software
ADC 400 - Holguin Corp.
Advanced Graphics Software - Auto-Trol Technology Corp.
AMS Time Machine - Diversified Information Services
ANALECT DSS Graphics - Dialogue, Inc.
ANVIL-1000 MD - Manufacturing and Consulting Services
ANVIL-4000 - Manufacturing and Consulting Services
AQUABASE - Tecsoft Inc.
ARMCHEM - H & H Molecular Graphics

ASYST Scientific Software - Hewlett-Packard Company

ATLAS - Strategic Locations Planning

ATLAS AMP - Strtegic Locations Planning

AURA - BPI

AutoCAD - Autodesk, Inc.

AutoCAD AEC - Autodesk, Inc.

Automated Drafting System - Holguin Corp.

AutoSketch - Autodesk, Inc.

Autmn - Zenographics, Inc,

Azimuth 87 - Azimuth

Banyan Network Server - Banyan Systems, Inc.

Boardroom Graphics - Analytical Software, Inc.

BPS Business Graphics - Business & Professional Software

CAD-1+ - Robo Systems Corp.

CAD-2 - Robo Systems Corp.

CADAPPLE - T & W Systems

CADD200-300 - Tensegrity, Inc.

CADKEY - Micro Control Systems, Inc.

CAD Master 2000 - Datagraphics Business Systems

CAE-1 - Personal CAD Systems, Inc.

CAE-2 - Personal CAD Systems, Inc.

Cascade X - Cascade Graphics Systems

CEADS-MACRO - Holguin Corp.

CGX/3 - Jared Graphics, Inc.

ChartBuster - Interchart Software, Inc.

Chart-Master - Decision Resources, Inc.

COGO-80-86 - Civilsoft

COGO-PC PLUS - Civilsoft

Context MBA - Hewlett-Packard Company

CONTOUR - Civilsoft

Conturing System - Precision Visuals, Inc.

Contour Plotting System - Holguin Corp.

Control Charts - Software Consulting Group

Coordinate Geometry Plus - The Lietz Company

CPERT - Collins & Associates

CPS/PC - Radian Corp.

Cricket Graph - Cricket Software

CURVE DIGITIZER - West Coast Consultants

DASH-PLOT-HP - Futurenet

Data Evaluation Program - R & L Software

Data Evaluation System - R & L Software

Data Grapher - Hewlett-Packard Company

Data CAD - Microtecture Corp.

Design Board Professional - Mega CADD, Inc.

DGI ORGANIZATION - Decision Graphics, Inc.

DGI SIGNMAKER - Decision Graphics, Inc.

DGI TYPE SHOP - Decision Graphics, Inc.

DGS-2000 - Data Automation

DI-3000 - Precision visuals, Inc.

DI-TEXTPRO - Precision Visuals,

DiagramMaster - Decision Resources, Inc.

Diagraph - Computer Support Corp.

DISSPLA - ISSCO

DRAFIX I - Foresight Resources Corp.

Drawit - Graphicus

DV-Tools - V.I. Corp.

EARTHWK - Civilsoft

Earthwork (SURVOL) - Holguin Corp.

EasyCAD - Evolution Computing

EMU-TEK - FTG Data Systems

ENABLE - The Software Group

ENCORE! - Ferox Microsystems, Inc.

EnerCharts - Enertronics Research, Inc.

EnerConnect-Program 1 - Enertronic Research, Inc.

EnerConnect-Program 2 - Enertronic Research, Inc.

EnerGraphics - Enertronics Research, Inc.

ESP-200 Volume 1: COGO-200 - Pacsoft, Inc.

ESP-200 Volume 2: PacDraft-200 - Pacsoft, Inc.

ESP-200 Volume 3: Roads-200 - Pacsoft, Inc.

Excelerator - Index Technology Corp.

Executive Picture Show - PC Software

Facilities Design & Management - Design Futures, Inc.

FIGARO - TEMPLATE Software

FINGRAPH II - Graphic M*I*S, Inc.

Framework III - Ashton-Tate

Freelance - Graphic Communications, Inc.

GEM Draw - Digital Research, Inc.

GEM Wordchart - Digital Research, Inc.
Generic CADD - Generic Software, Inc.
GEOCONTOUR - GEOCOMP Corp.
GEOPLOT - Geoglobal Systems, Inc.
Giraph Business Graphics - Compuvision International
GK-2000 - Precision Visuals, Inc.
GKSGRAL - TEMPLATE Software
GRAF - Computer Resources, Inc.
Grafit - Graphicus
GRAFKIT - GEOCOMP Corp.
GRAFMAKER - Precision Visuals, Inc.
GRAFPAK-GKS - Advanced Technology Center
GRAPHER - Golden Software, Inc.
GraphiC - Scientific Endeavors Corp.
Graphic-11 - Data Processing Design, Inc.
Graphics/1000-II - Hewlett-Packard Company
Graphics/9000 - Hewlett-Packard Company
Graphics Connection - California Computer Applications
Graphics Editor - Hewlett-Packard Company
Graphics Instruction Device (GRID) - Responsive Logic
Graph-in-the-Box - New England Software, Inc.
GraphPlan - Chang Laboratories, Inc.
GraphStation - Software Clearing House, Inc.
GraphTalk - Software Solutions
Graphwriter - Graphic Communications, Inc.
GRFX1-The Font System - RDS Systems, Inc.
GSS0-Chart - GSS
GSS-Drivers - GSS
HALO - Media Cybernetics, Inc.
Harvard Graphics - Software Publishing Corp.
High Tech Business Graphics - Lati-Corp, Inc.
HiWIRE - Wintek Corp.
HOLGUIN-CAD - Holguin Corp.
HP Draw - Hewlett-Packard Company

HP Easychart - Hewlett-Packard Company
HP EGS - Hewlett-Packard Company
HP-GKS - Hewlett-Packard Company
HP Graphics Presentations - Hewlett-Packard Company
HP Logic DesignStation Software - Hewlett-Packard Company
HP Map - Hewlett-Packard Company
HP META-Modal - Hewlett-Packard Company
HP Printed Circuit Design System - Hewlett-Packard Company
HP Project Management - Hewlett-Packard Company
HP Vista - Hewlett-Packard Company
HP's Charting Gallery - Hewlett-Packard Company
HP's Drawing Gallery - Hewlett-Packard Company
HP's DSG/3000 - Hewlett-Packard Company
HP's Gallery Collection - Hewlett-Packard Company
HP's TextCharts/PC - Hewlett Packard
IB Graph - Data Processing Design, Inc.
IDRAW - Design Futures, Inc.
IN-A-VISION - Micrografx, Inc.
InterDRAW - Interchart Software, Inc.
InterORG - Interchart Software, Inc.
Javelin - Javelin Software Corp.
Jet-Plot - Responsive Logic
Jet-Sketch - Responsive Logic
KeyChart - Softkey/Software Products Inc.
Kinetic Graphics System - Kinetic Presentations, Inc.
Kinetic Graphs - Kinetic Presentations, Inc.
Kinetic Layout - Kinetic Presentaitons, Inc.
Kinetic Words - Kinetic Presentations, Inc.
LC DATA - Collins & Associates
Mac3D - Challenger Software
MacPlot Professional - Microspot/Compservco
MacPlots II - Computer Shoppe
MacPlot Standard - Microspot/Compservco
Map Builder - Geosoft Corp.
Map-Master - Decision Resources, Inc.
Master Diagram System - Holguin Corp.

MAXpc Mapping Software - National Planning Data Corp.
McCAD EDSC - VAMP, Inc.
McCAD PCB - VAMP, Inc.
MD-PLOT - Maersk Data, Inc.
ME Series 5, 10, and 30 - Hewlett-Packard Company
Metafile - Precision Visuals, Inc.
MiCAD - Eesof, Inc.
Microsoft Chart, Version 2.0 - Microsoft Corp.
Microsoft Windows - Microsoft Corp.
MicroStation - Bentley Systems, Inc.
microwave SPICE - Eesof, Inc.
Mirage - Zenographics, Inc.
MODLER - Alphametrics Corp.
Molkey - H & H Molecular Graphics
MSYS I: Scientific Data Plotting - Marcus Systems
MSYS III; Business Charts - Marcus Systems
MultiMap - Planning Data Systems
Nimbus - Media Cybernetics, Inc.
NOVA*GKS - Nova Graphics International
OMNIPLOT - Microcompatibles
Open Access - Software Products International
Open Access II - Software Products International
Org Plus - Banner Blue
OSLO, Super-Oslo - Sinclair Optics, Inc.
Palette - Palette Systems Inc.
PCB-1 - Personal CAD systems, Inc.
PCB-2 - Personal CAD systems, Inc.
PCB-3 - Personal CAD systems, Inc.
OCB-THERMAL - Pacific Numerix
PCchart/PCartist - Aztek
PC-DRAW - Micrografx, Inc.
PC/FOCUS - Information Builders, Inc.
PC-Slide - Management Graphics, Inc.
Personal Architect System - Computervision Corp.
Personal Designer System - Comptervision Corp.
Personal Machinist System - Compervision Corp.
PERT+ - Professional Applications

PertPlotter - Westiminster Software
PFS: Graph - Software Publishing Corp.
PFS: Professional Planner - Software Publishing Corp.
PicSure - Precision Visuals, Inc.
Picture Perfect - Computer Support Corp.
PLANTRAC - Computerline, Inc.
Plot88 - Plotworks, Inc.
PLOTCHEM - Tecsoft Inc.
PLOT IT - Collins & Associates
Plot-It - Mesa Graphics Inc.
Plots II - Computer Shoppe
Plotstart - SoftStyle, Inc.
Plotter Driver Program - BV Engineering
PlotTrak - Softrak Systems
POINTE - Neotek Software, Inc.
Polymaps - Chautauguasoft Division of CRIS
PRESENTATION GRAPHICS - Arens Applied Electomagnetics, Inc.
Primavision/Primavera Project - Primavera Systems, Inc.
Prime Plotter HP Plotter Interface - Primesoft Corp.
Print Server - Nestar Systems
Project Scheduler 5000 Plus Graphics - Scitor Corp.
Project Scheduler Network - Scitor Corp.
Project Workbench - Applied Business Technology
PseudoPlot - Bentley Systems, Inc.
QMS ConceptDesigner - QMS Concept Technolgies
Quik Circuit - Bishop Graphics CAD Systems
RANDMAP - Rand McNally
RENDER - Multiware, Inc.
Robo CAD-PC - Robo Systems Corp.
SAMNA Decision Graphics - SAMNA Corp.
SAS/Graph Software - SAS Institute, Inc.
SAS/RTERM - SAS Institute, Inc.
Schedule Grafix - Digital Engineering
Scientific Plotter, Version II - Interactive Microware, Inc.
Scientific Plotter-PC+ - Interactive Microware, Inc.

Series 80 Graphics Presentations Pac - Hewlett-Packard Company
SIGMA-PLOT - Jandel Scientific
Sign-Master - Decision Resources, Inc.
Site Comp II V.5 - Land Innovation, Inc.
SlideWrite - Advanced Graphics Software, Inc.
SlideWrite Plus - Advanced Graphics Software, Inc.
Smart Software System - Innovative Software Inc.
smARTWORK - Wintek Corp.
Sound Presentations - Communication Dynamics, Inc.
Space Tracker - Facilities Management Dynamics, Inc.
SPSS Graphics - SPSS, Inc.
Starbase Graphics Library - Hewlett-Packard Company
STORMWATER HYDROLOGY - Pacsoft, Inc.
"super" MicroCAD - Imagimedia Technologies, Inc.
SuperCalc3 - Computer Associates International
SuperCalc4 - Computer Associates International
SuperProject Plus - Computer Associates International
Symphony, Release 1.0 - Lotus Development Corp.
Symphony, Release 1.1. - Lotus Development Corp.
TalkShow/PC - Interchart Software Inc.
Tekalike - Mesa Graphics Inc.
TELLAGRAF - ISSCO
TEMPLATE - TEMPLATE Software
The "WHAT IF..?" System - H.E.A.D. Consulting, Inc.
TMODEL: UTILITY-HPPLOTU - Professional Solutions, Inc.
TOPOGRAPHY - Pacsoft, Inc.
Touchstone - Eesof Inc.
TRANSLATE - Tecsoft Inc.
TYP-SET ENTER Computer, Inc.
Vanguard CAE Design System - Case Technology

VersaCAD Advanced - T & W Systems, Inc.
VeryGraphic - Optima, Inc.
ViewPoint w/Graphics - Compter Aided Management, Inc.
VTEK - Scientific Endeavors Corp.
VUE - National Information Systems, Inc.
Wescom Engineering Software - Wescom Software, Inc.
Wescom Surveying Software - Wescom Software, Inc.
Windows Draw - Micrografx
Words & Figures - Lifetree Software Inc.
Workview Series - Viewlogic Systems, Inc.
XL/NC II - PMX, Inc.
XT.CAD Professional - Microdex

VideoShow

Autumn - Zenographics
Microsoft Chart - Microsoft
ChartMaster - Decision Resources
Ego - Zenographics
EnerGraphics - Enertronics
FlexDraw - TNET
Freelance - Lotus
Graphwriter - Lotus
Graphic Decision Support System - Data Business Vision
Hot Shots - New Vision Technologies
Image Management System - Electronic Cottage
Impressionist - ExecuComp
Mirage - Zenographics
orgCHART - TNET
PC Presents! - Imedia
PC Slide Showmaker - Management Graphics
PictureIt - General Parametrics

PicturePak Eye Openers - Marketing
    Graphics
PicturePak Business World - Marketing
    Graphics
PicturePak Maps - Marketing Graphics
SignMaster - Decision Resources
Speaker Support Plus - Meta-4
VideoShow - General Parametrics
VIP - Matrices
Visual Express - Visual Media

Appendix C

Glossary

alley The space between columns in a multi-column document. Ventura refers to this as the gutter.

ascender The part of a lowercase letter that extends above the body of the letter (as in b or d).

ASCII American Standard Code for Information Interchange. It refers to a type of file that contains only the characters of a standard computer keyboard.

Assignment List The bar on the left side of the screen in Ventura. Used in tag mode for listing available tags, in text mode for listing text attributes, in table mode for listing table attributes, and in frame mode for listing files contained in a chapter. In graphics mode the assignment list is replaced by the graphic tools.

attribute Variations applied to plain type, such as boldface, underlining, or strikethrough.

AUTOEXEC.BAT A file in the root directory of a PC containing commands that are automatically executed when the computer is started up.

autoflow A feature of Ventura that causes text loaded into a chapter to automatically flow from column to column and from page to page.

autotrace A feature in drawing programs such as Corel Draw that automatically converts a bitmapped graphic into an object graphic

background printing This feature, provided by print spoolers and by Microsoft Windows, lets you resume working on a document while your document prints.

backup button A small black box contained in dialog boxes. Selecting it moves you one step up in the hierarchy of directories.

baseline The invisible line on which type rests and below which descenders hang.

batch pagination An approach toward computer typesetting in which formatting commands are embedded in text and then executed as the document is printed.

Bézier curve A curve used in drawing programs, defined by two end points and two intermediate control points.

bitmap A representation of a character or a graphic image in which each printed dot is stored as a digital bit.

bleed A graphic that extends off the edge of the page (also can be used as a verb).

body text The name of the default style applied to plain text in a document.

booting To start or restart a computer.

box text A tool available in Graphics mode that allows you to draw a box on the screen and then type text into that box. Unlike text contained in frames, box text can be moved anywhere on the page without disturbing the underlying text or graphics. It is useful for labelling graphics and for creating tables.

break A point at which a new line, column, or page begins.

byte A unit of digital information that stores one character.

chapter A document, consisting of text and/or pictures, formatted by means of a style sheet. Also refers to the file that contains pointers to text, graphic, style sheet, and other files generated by Ventura.

characters set The set of characters that makes up a font. Usually it includes the keyboard characters plus a variety of special symbols. Same as symbol set.

clip art Collections of commercial illustrations, either in hard-copy form or on disk.

clipboard A buffer that stores the most recently deleted material. There are actually three separate clipboards, the first for holding the most recently deleted frame, the second for the most recently deleted picture, and the third for the most recently deleted text passage.

CONFIG.SYS A file stored in the root directory of a PC hard disk, containing instructions on system configuration.

controller The software and hardware that directs the functioning of a laser printer.

CPU Central processing unit. The brain of a computer or laser printer.

crop To cut off an unwanted portion of a picture.

crop mark A small mark that indicates a corner of the final document.

current selection box A small box at the lower left corner of the screen that displays the current file (in Frame mode), tag (in Tagging mode), and location of text attributes (in Text mode).

descender The part of a lowercase letter that extends below the baseline (as in p and q). The size of a font is measured from ascenders to descenders.

dialog box A box that appears on the screen when you select an item from a menu, allowing you to enter settings.

dingbats Special characters such as ballot boxes, pointing hands, scissors, and fancy stars. The Zapf Dingbats font, a font designed by Hermann Zapf and comprised entirely of dingbats, is resident in most PostScript printers.

discretionary hyphen A hyphen that is embedded in a text file and is only displayed if it coincides with a line break. If a discretionary hyphen is contained in a word, Ventura's hyphenation algorithm will not perform any additional hyphenation on that word.

dithering In computer graphics, using dot patterns to simulate gradations of gray.

download To transfer files from an electronic bulletin board to the computer, or to transfer font files from the computer into the memory of a laser printer.

dpi Dots per inch. The standard way of measuring the resolution of monitors and printers. Resolution of monitors ranges from about 70 to 115 dpi; resolution of printers ranges from 300 dpi for a standard laser printer to 1200 or 2400 dpi for an imagesetter.

driver A software module that translates the output of an application into a format required by a particular printer, monitor, or other device.

drop cap The first letter of a paragraph, set in a much larger point size than the rest of the paragraph and set lower than the initial baseline of the paragraph.

dummy A mockup of publication.

em A unit of measurement equal to the number of points of the type being set. For example, in 12-point type, the length of an em is 12 points.

EMS Expanded Memory Specification. A standard for formatting memory beyond the 640K recognized by DOS.

en A unit of measurement equal to half an em.

EPS Encapsulated PostScript. A file format used by Ventura and other programs to exchange PostScript graphic files.

expanded memory Memory above the 640K recognized by DOS, formatted according to the Expanded Memory Specification.

extended memory Memory above the 640K recognized by DOS, but not formatted according to any specification.

extension The three letters to the right of the period in a DOS file name. Indicates the type of file.

feathering The addition of small amounts of leading to make a column justify vertically.

filter A file designation containing the characters * and ?. The * holds the place of any number of characters, while the ? holds the place of a single character. For example, when Ventura encounters the filter P?C.*, it will produce the following matching files, among others: PIC.TXT, POC.TXT, PAC.DOC, PXC.ASC, PIC.GEN.

flush left or flush right Text that is aligned with the left (or right) margin.

folio The sequential page numbers appearing at the top or bottom of pages throughout a document.

font The complete set of characters, including punctuation symbols, for a typeface. In traditional typography this meant the actual metal type. With the advent of computer "fonts" it refers to files stored on disks or on ROM cartridges.

font editor A program used to create fonts from scratch or to alter the appearance of an existing font.

font generator A program that creates soft fonts at particular sizes from master font outlines.

font ID A number used to access a font.

footer A design element repeated at the bottom of each page of straight text, often incorporating the page number.

frame A container drawn on the page in order to load a text or graphic file. In addition, Ventura automatically creates an underlying frame for each page.

frame handles The eight small black boxes located at the corners and on the sides of a frame. By placing the cursor on one of these and holding down the mouse button while dragging the mouse, you can stretch a frame.

galley A laser-printed or typeset draft of a document.

global Referring to any operation that applies to the entire document.

Greeking The technique of speeding up the display by representing small text on the screen with dummy type or straight lines.

grid The design "skeleton" on which a document is built; includes design standards for columns and frames, margins, leading and tracking, justification, headers and footers, and graphics.

gutter In traditional typography, the space on the page between the inside edge of the type and the spine of a bound book. As used in Ventura's Margins and Columns dialog box, gutter refers to the alley between two columns of text.

header A design element repeated at the top of each page of straight text; can include chapter titles, book titles, and/or page numbers.

icon A small symbol used by a computer program. In Ventura, icons are used to represent the various program modes and to represent drawing functions. In Microsoft Windows, icons represent programs and windows.

images In Ventura, images refer to pictures stored as bits (0's and 1's). Such pictures cannot be enlarged without a reduction in quality.

indent The horizontal offset of the first line (or designated number of lines) of text.

interline spacing The amount of vertical space between lines of text, measured from baseline to baseline. The default is 1.2 times the point size of the current font.

italic Slanted style of a given typeface, used for emphasis, for instance to offset book titles from the main text.

item selector The name for a type of dialog box used to load text, picture, or chapter files.

jaggie Jagged edges on printed type.

justified text A line of type that is precisely spaced so that it rests flush against both margins of the column.

kerning Moving two letters closer together to give them a better fit.

landscape Refers to printing a page so that, when positioned for reading, the page is wider than it is long.

leader characters Characters (usually periods) used to fill up the space between tabs. Frequently used in tables of contents.

leading The space, in points, between lines of type and measured from baseline to baseline. For example, a 10/12 specification for type means 10-point type on 12 points of leading (6 lines to the inch).

letter spacing Adjusting the space within words to assist line justification.

line art In traditional graphic arts, line art refers to pictures that use no shading. In Ventura, line art refers to graphics that are stored as mathematic descriptions and hence can be scaled without any reduction in quality.

memory-resident program A program that is loaded into memory and remains there even when you stop using it and switch to another program, such as Ventura. A "hot key" reactivates the memory-resident program at any time.

mode One of the four ways of working in Ventura (five in the Professional Extension), selected by means of the icons in the upper left corner of the screen. The four modes are Framing, Tagging, Text Editing, and Graphics. The Professional Extension adds Table Generation.

moiré Patterns produced when images are improperly scaled.

object graphics Graphics that are stored as geometrical descriptions. Referred to as "line art" in Ventura Publisher.

obliquing A method of simulating italic type by tilting roman characters.

orphan The last line of a paragraph appearing by itself at the top of a column. Traditional page layout calls for avoiding orphans.

outline font A type of font in which the shape of each character is stored as a geometrical description rather than as a bitmap.

paragraph In Ventura, paragraph has a special meaning, referring to any block of text ended by a hard carriage return (pressing Enter).

parallel communications A method of data communications in which a group of digital bits is transmitted simultaneously. Faster than serial communications.

PCC The bitmapped graphics file format used by the PC Paintbrush family of programs and by other paint and screen capture. Similar to PCX.

PCL Printer Command Language. The set of commands that direct the operations of LaserJet and LaserJet-compatible printers, controlling the appearance of text and graphics on the page.

PCX The bitmapped graphics file format used by the PC Paintbrush family of programs and by other paint and screen capture programs. Similar to PCC.

PDL Page description language. A computer language designed for controlling the appearance of pages on a monitor or printer.

permanent font A LaserJet soft font that is not erased unless the LaserJet is turned off.

pica Typographic unit of measurement equal to 12 points or 1/6 inch.

PICT   The object graphics file format used by MacDraw and other drawing programs.

pixel   The smallest unit of a digitized picture, either on the screen or printed.

point   Typographic unit of measurement equal to 1/12 pica or 1/72 inch. The "point size" of a font is measured from the bottom of the descenders to the top of the ascenders.

portrait   Refers to printing a page so that, when positioned for reading, it is taller than it is wide.

PostScript   A computer programming language created by Adobe Systems specifically for controlling laser printers.

proportional spacing   The method of setting type in which wide letters, such as W, receive more space and thin letters, such as i, receive less space.

publication   A file containing information about a sequential group of chapter files.

ragged justification   Unjustified type, that is, centered or flush to one side but not to the other.

RAM   Dynamic memory in a computer or printer. Information stored in RAM is lost when the power is turned off.

resident font   A font that is permanently stored in the laser printer.

roman typeface   The regular, upright, unslanted version of a typeface.

rule   A line used as a design element on the page.

sans serif   A typeface designed without serifs, such as Helvetica.

scaling   Enlarging or reducing a picture.

screen snapshot A printed picture of the contents of the computer display. Also called a screen dump.

selection The term for choosing a menu option, a command, or an element on the page by moving the cursor on top of it and then clicking with the mouse.

serifs Small counter strokes that "finish off" the ends of the body strokes of a letter. In theory, serifs help the eye to recognize the shapes of different letters, thus aiding readability.

soft font A font stored on a floppy disk or on a PC's hard disk.

spaceband The spacing between words in a passage of text. In Ventura you can enter a minimum, a maximum, and an optimum setting.

spine The back of a bound book.

style sheet A collection of tags contained in a computer file.

symbol set See "character set."

tag A set of formatting instructions for a type of paragraph. Up to 128 different tags may be stored in a style sheet.

thin space A space the width of a period.

TIFF Tagged Image File Format. A graphics format for storing scanned images.

toner Fine plastic particles that act as the "ink" for a laser printer.

tracking The spacing of the letters throughout a passage of text. Typically loosened or made tighter to accommodate justification or enhance readability, while still maintaining an overall effect of uniformity.

typeface A particular type design, such as Palatino or Goudy.

underlying page The frame that Ventura automatically generates for each page in a chapter.

utility A small program designed for a specific, narrowly defined purpose.

Ventura International The main character set used by Ventura Publisher. It includes the standard keyboard characters plus a variety of typographic symbols and accented foreign characters.

vertical justification Adjustment of the line spacing within a block of text so that it fills a certain vertical distance.

VP US A smaller character set generated by Fontware. It includes the standard keyboard characters plus the most important typographic symbols.

widow The first line of a paragraph appearing alone on the bottom of a column, or the last word (or part of a word) in a paragraph appearing alone at the bottom of a paragraph. In traditional page layout, widows were avoided.

wildcard Characters such as * and ? which take the place of any other characters in specifying a DOS file.

WYSIWYG "What You See Is What You Get"; a description of programs, such as Ventura, in which the picture on the screen is an accurate representation of the page that is ultimately printed.

Index

B

D

E

I

N

S

W

Y

Z

X

More from Peachpit Press...

THE EASY VENTURA BOOK
(includes tutorial disk)
▲ *Rick Altman*
An ultra-simple tutorial for first-time users of
Ventura Publisher 3 Gold Series (DOS/GEM version).
Developed by Ventura author and
trainer Rick Altman and tested during a 2-year
period by over 1,500 students. *(318 pages)*

HELP! THE ART OF COMPUTER TECHNICAL
SUPPORT
▲ *Ralph Wilson*
The first practical guide for hundreds of
thousands of technical support workers and
managers. *(210 pages)*

THE LASERJET FONT BOOK
▲ *Katherine Pfeiffer*
Doubles as a buyer's guide to LaserJet fonts
and a tutorial on using type effectively in
your documents. Shows hundreds of LaserJet
fonts from over a dozen vendors. Includes
LaserJet III scalable fonts. *(320 pages)*

LASERJET IIP ESSENTIALS
▲ *Cummings, Handa, and Whitmore*
An introductory guide to fonts, graphics and
upgrades for HP's low-cost laser. *(320 pages)*

LEARNING POSTSCRIPT: A VISUAL
APPROACH
▲ *Ross Smith*
An easy "show-and-tell" teaching guide to
the PostScript page description language.
(426 pages)

THE LITTLE WINDOWS BOOK
▲ *Kay Nelson*
A quick and accessible guide to Windows 3.
Includes numerous tips, tricks, and charts of
keyboard shortcuts. *(144 pages)*

MASTERING COREL DRAW
▲ *Dickman and Altman*
Provides beginning lessons and advanced
tips and tricks on using this remarkable new
drawing program for Windows 3.0. *(240 pages)*

TYPESTYLE: HOW TO CHOOSE AND USE
TYPE ON A PERSONAL COMPUTER
▲ *Daniel Will-Harris*
How to choose the right laser printer fonts,
which fonts mix well together, etc. Covers
not only the mechanics, but also the psychology
of type. *(368 pages)*

VENTURA BY EXAMPLE, MAC EDITION
▲ *Webster & Associates*
A self-teaching guide to Windows Ventura
with 20 step-by-step modules based on the
sample files provided with Ventura. *(650 pages—available March 1991)*

VENTURA BY EXAMPLE, WINDOWS EDITION
▲ *Webster & Associates*
A self-teaching guide to the Macintosh version
of Ventura with 20 step-by-step
modules based on the sample files provided
with Ventura. *(650 pages)*

Order Form: 800/283-9444

Call, fax, or mail to Peachpit Press

Quantity	Title	Price	Total
	The Easy Ventura Book (with disk)	$ 29.95	
	HELP! The Art of Computer Technical Support	19.95	
	LaserJet IIP Essentials	21.95	
	The LaserJet Font Book	24.95	
	The Little Windows Book	12.95	
	Learning PostScript: A Visual Approach	22.95	
	Mastering Corel Draw	21.95	
	TypeStyle: How to Choose and Use Type	24.95	
	Ventura By Example: Macintosh Edition	24.95	
	Ventura By Example: Windows Edition	24.95	
	Ventura Tips & Tricks, 3rd Edition	27.95	

Tax of 6.75% applies to California residents only. UPS ground shipping: $3 for first item, $1 each additional. UPS 2nd day air: $6 for first item, $2 each additional. Air mail to Canada: $5 first item, $3 each additional. Air mail overseas: $14 each item.	Subtotal	
	6.75% Tax	
	Shipping	
	TOTAL	

Name	
Company	
Address	
City	
State	Zip
Phone	

☐ Check enclosed   ☐ Visa   ☐ MasterCard

☐ Company Purchase Order #

Credit Card Number

Card Holder Name

Expiration Date

Peachpit Press ▲ 1085 Keith Ave. ▲ Berkeley, CA 94708
Phone: 800/283-9444 or 415/527-8555 ▲ Fax: 415/524-9775
Satisfaction guaranteed or your money refunded